EARLY WOMEN WRITERS

LONGMAN CRITICAL READERS

General Editor

STAN SMITH, Professor of English, University of Dundee

Published Titles

K.M. NEWTON, *George Eliot*
MARY EAGLETON, *Feminist Literary Criticism*
GARY WALLER, *Shakespeare's Comedies*
JOHN DRAKAKIS, *Shakespearean Tragedy*
RICHARD WILSON AND RICHARD DUTTON, *New Historicism and Renaissance Drama*
PETER WIDDOWSON, *D.H. Lawrence*
PETER BROOKER, *Modernism/Postmodernism*
RACHEL BOWLBY, *Virginia Woolf*
FRANCIS MULHERN, *Contemporary Marxist Literary Criticism*
ANNABEL PATTERSON, *John Milton*
CYNTHIA CHASE, *Romanticism*
MICHAEL O'NEILL, *Shelley*
STEPHANIE TRIGG, *Medieval English Poetry*
ANTONY EASTHOPE, *Contemporary Film Theory*
TERRY EAGLETON, *Ideology*
MAUD ELLMANN, *Psychoanalytic Literary Criticism*
ANDREW BENNETT, *Readers and Reading*
MARK CURRIE, *Metafiction*
BREAN HAMMOND, *Pope*
GRAHAM HOLDERNESS, BRYAN LOUGHREY AND ANDREW MURPHY, *Shakespeare's Roman Plays*
STEVEN CONNOR, *Charles Dickens*
REBECCA STOTT, *Tennyson*
ANDREW HADFIELD, *Spenser*
SUSANA ONEGA AND JOSE ANGEL GARCIA LANDA, *Narratology*
TESS COSSLETT, *Victorian Women Poets*
BART MOORE-GILBERT, GARETH STANTON AND WILLIAM MALEY, *Postcolonial Criticism*
JOHN DRAKAKIS, *Tragedy*
ANITA PACHECO, *Early Women Writers*

EARLY WOMEN WRITERS:
1600–1720

Edited and Introduced by

ANITA PACHECO

LONGMAN
LONDON AND NEW YORK

Addison Wesley Longman
Edinburgh Gate
Harlow
Essex CM20 2JE
England
and Associated Companies throughout the world.

*Published in the United States of America
by Addison Wesley Longman Inc., New York.*

First published 1998

ISBN 0 582 30462 8 CSD
ISBN 0 582 30463 6 PPR

British Library Cataloguing-in-Publication Data

A catalogue record of this book is available
from the British Library

Library of Congress Cataloging-in-Publication Data

Early women writers : 1600–1720 / edited by Anita Pacheco.
    p.   cm. — (Longman critical readers)
    Includes bibliographical references (p.   ) and index.
    ISBN 0–582–30463–6 (ppr). — ISBN 0–582–30462–8 (csd)
    1. English literature—Early modern, 1500–1700—History and
criticism.   2. Women and literature—Great Britain—History—17th
century.   3. Women and literature—Great Britain—History—18th
century.   4. English literature—Women authors—History and
criticism.   5. English literature—18th century—History and
criticism.   I. Pacheco, Anita.   II. Series.
PR113.E27   1998
820.9'9287—dc21   97–12383
                                                         CIP

Set by 35 in 9/11½ pt Palatino
Produced by Longman Singapore Publishers (Pte) Ltd.
Printed in Singapore

Contents

General Editors' Preface

The outlines of contemporary critical theory are now often taught as a standard feature of a degree in literary studies. The development of particular theories has seen a thorough transformation of literary criticism. For example, Marxist and Foucauldian theories have revolutionised Shakespeare studies, and 'deconstruction' has led to a complete reassessment of Romantic poetry. Feminist criticism has left scarcely any period of literature unaffected by its searching critiques. Teachers of literary studies can no longer fall back on a standardised, received, methodology.

Lecturers and teachers are now urgently looking for guidance in a rapidly changing critical environment. They need help in understanding the latest revisions in literary theory, and especially in grasping the practical effects of the new theories in the form of theoretically sensitised new readings. A number of volumes in the series anthologise important essays on particular theories. However, in order to grasp the full implications and possible uses of particular theories it is essential to see them put to work. This series provides substantial volumes of new readings, presented in an accessible form and with a significant amount of editorial guidance.

Each volume includes a substantial introduction which explores the theoretical issues and conflicts embodied in the essays selected and locates the areas of disagreement between positions. The pluralism of theories has to be put on the agenda of literary studies. We can no longer pretend that we all tacitly accept the same practices in literary studies. Neither is a *laissez-faire* attitude any longer tenable. Literature departments need to go beyond the mere toleration of theoretical differences: it is not enough merely to agree to differ; they need actually to 'stage' the differences openly. The volumes in this series all attempt to dramatise the differences, not necessarily with a view to resolving them but in order to foreground the choices presented by different theories or to argue for a particular route through the impasses the differences present.

The theory 'revolution' has had real effects. It has loosened the grip of traditional empiricist and romantic assumptions about language and literature. It is not always clear what is being proposed as the new agenda for literary studies, and indeed the very notion of 'literature' is questioned by the post-structuralist strain in theory. However, the uncertainties and obscurities of contemporary theories appear much less worrying when we see what the best critics have been able to do with them in practice. This series aims to disseminate the best of recent criticism and to show that it is possible to re-read the canonical texts of literature in new and challenging ways.

RAMAN SELDEN AND STAN SMITH

The Publishers and fellow Series Editor regret to record that Raman Selden died after a short illness in May 1991 at the age of fifty-three. Ray Selden was a fine scholar and a lovely man. All those he has worked with will remember him with much affection and respect.

Acknowledgements

I would like to give my special thanks to Jean Gregorek of Antioch College for her invaluable assistance with the Introduction and Glossary. I am grateful to my Commissioning Editor, Liz Mann, of Addison Wesley Longman, for her support and encouragement. I would also like to thank my mother, Prof. Josephine F. Pacheco, and Elizabeth Harrison for their careful editing of the manuscript.

The Publishers are grateful to the following for permission to reproduce copyright material:

Blackwell Publishers for the essay 'Aphra Behn and Women's Literary Authority' by Jane Spencer in *RISE OF THE WOMAN NOVELIST: FROM APHRA BEHN TO JANE AUSTEN* – 1986 Basil Blackwell; The Johns Hopkins University Press for the essay 'Gestus and Signature in Aphra Behn's *THE ROVER*' by Elin Diamond in *ENGLISH LITERARY HISTORY (ELH) Journal* – vol 56, 1989; Indiana University Press for the essays 'The Ragged Rout of Self: Margaret Cavendish's *TRUE RELATION* & the Heroics of Self-Disclosure' by Sidonie Smith in *POETICS OF WOMEN'S AUTOBIOGRAPHY* (1987) and 'Anne Finch, Countess of Winchelsea: an Augustan Woman Poet' by Katherine Rogers in *SHAKESPEARES SISTERS: FEMINIST ESSAYS ON WOMEN POETS* ed. S.M. Gilbert & S. Gubar – 1979; Tennessee Technological University for the essays 'Excusing the Breach of Nature's Laws: the Discourse of Denial and Disguise in Katherine Philips' *'Friendship Poetry'* by Celia A. Easton in Journal *RESTORATION: STUDIES IN ENGLISH LITERARY CULTURE 1660–1700* vol 14 1990 and 'Once a Whore and Ever? Whore and Virgin in *THE ROVER* and its Antecedents' by Nancy Copeland in Journal – *RESTORATION: STUDIES IN ENGLISH LITERARY CULTURE 1660–1700* vol 16 1991 pp. 20–7; Routledge and the author for the essay '"Yet Tell Me Such Fiction": Lady Mary Wroth's *URANIA* and the Femininity of Romance' by Helen Hackett in *WOMEN, TEXTS AND HISTORIES 1575–1760* ed. Clare Brant and Diane

In memoriam
John Stachniewski
1953–1996

Introduction

This collection of critical essays on five women writers of the early
modern period testifies to the at least moderate success of one of
academic feminism's principal projects: to rectify the historical
invisibility of women by rescuing female-authored texts from the
oblivion to which they have all too often been consigned by a largely
male canon of great literature. The goal of incorporating early women's
writing into the academic curriculum thus entails more than a claim for
the literary and historical importance of these texts. It also challenges
the humanist discourse which has traditionally validated the literary
canon as above politics, as the product of timeless and universal
aesthetic criteria. Many feminist and oppositional critics would argue
that, far from springing spontaneously into existence, the canon is a
cultural construct which has tended to reproduce and reinforce the
marginalization of women and other social groups.

Early women's writing: Anglo-American *v* French feminism

From its inception, then, feminist criticism has sought to uncover the
political meaning and the cultural foundations of what has long passed
for objectivity, universality and nature: history, the canon and, of
course, gender identity. Not all feminist critics, however, would
agree that this political agenda is best served by the study and
institutionalization of previously neglected women writers. Indeed, the
two main strands of feminist criticism – the Anglo-American and the
French[1] – have disagreed over just how important the reading of female
authors is to the struggle against patriarchy. The study of women's
writing is associated most closely with the Anglo-American school,
which since the mid-1970s has given a central place to the study of
women's culture, to the recovery of a tradition of women's writing, and
to the exploration of the distinctive qualities of female-authored texts.

In her 1979 essay 'Towards a Feminist Poetics', Elaine Showalter dubbed this empirical, woman-centred, socio-historical approach 'gynocritics'.[2] Of course, any attempt to define the specificity of women's writing immediately appears to run the risk of collapsing into the same biological essentialism through which patriarchy has traditionally sought to naturalize gender inequalities. For Anglo-American critics like Showalter, however, it is not principally women's biology but their position within patriarchy which makes their writing different from men's; as Showalter observes, 'the female literary tradition comes from the still-evolving relationships between women writers and their society'.[3]

It seems reasonable enough to assume that a woman's experience of oppression will somehow be inscribed in her writing, and certainly the recovery of that experience is vital to the feminist enterprise. Nevertheless, gynocriticism's prioritizing of female experience as the object of critical scrutiny is not necessarily as straightforward as it might appear. It may, for example, foster a view of women as a homogeneous subculture and so come perilously close to suggesting that there is after all an essential female nature, even if it is historically and socially rather than biologically produced.[4] Such an essentialist view of female experience can have the effect of uniting women writers into a kind of feminist sisterhood, conveniently overlooking women's long history of collusion in the ideology which oppresses them and the important differences of class and race that have historically divided women from each other. If female experience is culturally produced, as the gynocritical focus on patriarchal oppression strongly suggests, then we cannot detach women from that culture or erase the social and economic conditions which colour their experience of subordination. This is especially true when we are dealing with 'a sex-gender system as highly controlled and class-differentiated' as that of seventeenth-century England.[5]

Gynocriticism's empirical approach raises related questions about the nature of literary texts, for to read women's writing in order to gain knowledge about what women in the past have felt and experienced is implicitly to claim that a work of literature is a mirror on the author's life, giving the reader unmediated access to the world in which she lived and wrote. In this, it has been argued, gynocriticism concurs with humanist ideology in seeing language as expressive of an external, knowable reality and the author as the sole origin of textual meaning.[6] Gynocriticism, then, invests the woman writer with the autonomy and unity of the humanist subject – the very aesthetic category which has underpinned the formation of a male canon of great writers. This conception of the author has also been called seriously into question by numerous theoretical approaches, feminist included, all of which endorse the structuralist and poststructuralist premise that language and culture precede and shape the human subject and her experiences, and not the other way around.

The central tenets of French feminist theory, radically different from those of early Anglo-American feminism, derive from its appropriation of poststructuralism and Lacanian psychoanalysis.[7] The poststructuralist axiom that language is not merely expressive of social reality but productive of it means that it is only through language (conceived of in its broadest sense), rather than, say, political reform, that real social and political change can be brought about. Moreover, because the symbolic structures of the West – the world as it is represented in language – are irrevocably patriarchal, we cannot take it for granted that a female author will write outside of its representational schemes. French feminist theory, then, prioritizes textuality over author-centred empiricism: *écriture féminine* refers not to the biological sex of the author but to a certain kind of writing – poetic, playful, non-rational – which challenges and disrupts the male symbolic order.

It is often said that French feminist theorists are interested not in 'women' but in 'woman'. This focus springs logically from the view that sexual difference, the dichotomy masculine/feminine, is also linguistically constructed. French feminist psychoanalytic theory explains this perspective, for it holds that in the pre-Oedipal phase of childhood – what Julia Kristeva calls the 'semiotic' – there is no gender. This comes only with the Oedipal crisis and the acquisition of language, when the child enters the symbolic order, ruled by 'the Law of the Father', with its closed, rational, authoritarian discourses and its governing concept of sexual difference. Woman, then, is a product of male discourse, and in the patriarchal order, the feminine, or woman's essence, is constituted of all those concepts and values which are repressed and marginalized. Figured as negativity, absence, irrationality, disorder and darkness, woman is the Other displaced from the ordered, rational systems of men. Hélène Cixous, for example, following the philosopher Jacques Derrida, points out the way Western thought has for centuries conceptualized the world through hierarchical binary oppositions, such as culture/nature, activity/passivity, each of which reinforces the fundamental opposition between male and female, privileging the masculine principle and relegating the feminine to a secondary, inferior status.

The force which is theoretically capable of breaking this discursive stranglehold resides in the repressed primary processes of pre-Oedipal experience, centred on the mother's body and lodged within the unconscious. For Kristeva, writing which recaptures the tones and rhythms of the semiotic has the revolutionary potential to unsettle oppressive male discourses. Drawing on Derrida's theory of the differential play of language, Cixous posits a feminine writing whose celebration of linguistic indeterminacy and open-endedness undermines the rigidly fixed meanings of patriarchal binary logic. Because this subversive writing originates in a genderless or bisexual libido, it cannot be available solely to women, though French feminist theorists tend to accord women a special kinship with feminine writing, either because of its strong links with the maternal body, or because men in general are more deeply implicated in the phallocentric order.

Despite this systematic deconstruction of the dichotomy masculine/ feminine, there remains a strong urge in some French feminist writing to oppose patriarchy's negative definitions of woman with positive ones, or to define the femininity which patriarchy excludes and silences. Cixous and Luce Irigaray in particular have been accused of succumbing to this urge, collapsing feminine writing into female writing, the subversive power of which issues from a specifically female body.[8] Consequently, French feminist theory would appear as vulnerable as its Anglo-American counterpart to charges of collusion in patriarchal ideology: its celebration of the female body as a revolutionary force smacks of biological essentialism, while its philosophical, linguistic orientation minimizes the importance of women's historical struggle and, by sidelining the study of female-authored texts, may simply, in Nancy K. Miller's words, 'reauthorize our oblivion'.[9]

The two essays on Anne Finch in this collection illustrate the different critical practices of Anglo-American gynocriticism and French theory. Finch is the latest of the writers considered in these pages, normally classed, alongside Swift and Pope, as an Augustan. Her biography is in two respects typical of early modern women writers: her literary vocation was enabled by the privileges of upper-class status, and her political allegiances were royalist. The latter is an important consideration in an historical period characterized by a massive shift in the structures of power, as the steady expansion of commercial and bourgeois culture and the rise of Whig principles of government by consent led to the gradual erosion and eventual collapse of Stuart absolutism during the Civil Wars of the 1640s and the Glorious Revolution of 1688.

Katharine Rogers's essay undertakes the gynocritical project of identifying the distinctively female qualities of Finch's writing. Her central claim is that although Finch was in many ways a typical Augustan poet, who employed the poetic genres and verse forms associated with that literary period and shared many of its characteristic values, her experience of marginality affected the content of her poems, making them 'subtly different from those of her male contemporaries'. According to Rogers, it is Finch's inability to assume the public role of the male Augustan poet that gives her nature poetry its distinctively personal tone; her alienation from typically masculine views of love and marriage that makes emotional sincerity rather than cynicism the essential feature of her love poetry; and her perspective as a woman and a poet which prompts her to critique reductive and trivializing constructions of femininity.

Rogers's focus on gender as a formative influence on Finch's poetry was long overdue. Previous critical studies, concerned primarily to identify Finch as a proto-Romantic nature poet, had largely ignored this unquestionably crucial feature of her work. Moreover, although Rogers argues that Finch necessarily wrote from a different space than her male contemporaries, her essay also touches on the ways in which this 'typical Augustan', who on occasion viewed her own poetic ability as sceptically as any man, was a product of the male-dominated culture she inhabited. In general, though, Rogers's central distinction between male form and female content diminishes ideological pressures and appears to attribute to Finch a unified and coherent female identity. Rogers's gynocritical belief in female experience as the basis of difference in writing thus tends to suppress the multiple determinants of human experience – material, political, ideological – and so seems at times to represent the woman writer, in humanist fashion, as the autonomous source of textual meaning.

Ruth Salvaggio's essay on Finch sets itself the ambitious task of reconciling Anglo-American and French perspectives. For Finch to write 'as a woman', Salvaggio argues, meant simultaneously to write 'in the historical predicament of an actual woman', and to give poetic expression to 'those processes that disrupt the structures of male discourse and systems'. Salvaggio's title alludes to her claim that to 'place' Finch historically is to discover in her poetry traces of 'her displacement, as a woman, in and from the Enlightenment world of men', whose rigid hierarchical systems of thought were predicated on the exclusion of cultural elements represented as 'feminine'. Yet in celebrating that displacement, in giving voice to the suppressed Other, Finch's poetry can be seen as a form of feminine writing which subverts the opposition between masculine and feminine principles which is the underlying paradigm of Enlightenment discourse.

Salvaggio's essay represents a bold attempt to integrate the reading of women's texts into a French theoretical framework. However, in seeking to yoke the woman writer to the poet who wrote 'woman', she runs the risk of the slippage from feminine to female writing we noted earlier in some French feminist thinking. Indeed, although Salvaggio's claim that Finch's poetry deconstructs dualistic oppositions presupposes the constructed nature of gender identity, it is not always entirely clear whether the 'femininity' she analyses is textual or sexual, a property of the poems or of the woman writer by virtue of her femaleness. This may, of course, be Salvaggio's intention, for her essay gestures towards women's creative transformation of the marginal role assigned to them in the symbolic order as a means of installing themselves as its subjects rather than its objects; hence, Finch the female author becomes in Salvaggio's reading the agent of 'the indeterminate and subversive processes that have long been associated with woman'.

Early women's writing: materialist feminism and the new literary history

There is another strand of feminism which shares the Anglo-American concern to recover women's history but which, by anchoring its analysis of that history in the material conditions of women's oppression, is arguably better equipped to give a nuanced account of female experience and the relationship between women's writing and the wider culture in which it is produced. Ideology is a central concept in this materialist–feminist analysis. While Marx defined ideology as a 'false consciousness' produced by the economic structure and its attendant class-relations, materialist feminism has on the whole adopted Althusser's view of ideology as simultaneously unconscious and omnipresent – as the complex system of representations through which individuals imagine their relationship to their real conditions of existence.[10] This belief that ideology pervades our perception of reality, that it is located in material practices with material effects, is clearly incompatible with humanist views of human nature: far from possessing a transhistorical essence, human beings are produced within a historically specific ideological formation which pre-exists and therefore shapes their experiences.

The anti-humanist perspective of materialist feminism gained wider currency with the emergence in the 1980s of American new historicism and its British counterpart, cultural materialism, the new theories and practices of literary history which have had such a marked impact on the study of Renaissance literary texts, including female-authored ones.[11] In addition to Althusser's definition of ideology, new historical critics find support for the view that there is no nature outside culture in Michel Foucault's theory of discourse: the privileged languages of social institutions which sustain unequal power relations in a given historical period by defining cultural norms and excluding whatever deviates from them.[12]

When it comes to literature, new historical critics would agree with materialist feminists that the cultural power of discursive formations precludes seeing the author as a sovereign individual subject, the sole origin of her/his own meaning. Nor can we see the literary text either as a transcendent entity floating above history, politics and ideology, or as little more than the passive reflection of its historical 'background'. Instead, literature must be understood as ideologically inscribed, as itself 'an agent in constructing a culture's sense of reality'.[13]

Yet how does this view of the power of cultural representations account for social struggle and historical change? This is a vital question in any discussion of early women's writing, for the presence of female authors during the sixteenth and seventeenth centuries means that contemporary ideologies of gender were not simply uncontestable. Dominant discourses of gender produced in religious, legal and medical writings prescribed a model of the ideal woman as obedient, private, silent and chaste – a construction of femininity which made writing and especially publishing one's work deeply transgressive acts for a woman. Moreover, as several of the essays in this collection make clear, the attributes of the normative 'Woman' tended to be collapsed into one another, so that a woman's public speech (or writing) became symptomatic of sexual promiscuity, while both in turn signified a violation of her proper place: enclosed within the domestic sphere.[14] Hence the popular correspondence throughout this period between the 'poetess' and the 'punk', or prostitute.

It is evident, then, both that patriarchal ideology wielded considerable coercive power during the early modern period, and that certain women did effectively manage to resist the meanings it assigned to female authorship. This situation would not appear to be fully accounted for by the new historicist 'containment theory', which claims that because established authority legitimates itself in relation to that which threatens it, subversive elements in Renaissance literary texts are necessarily contained, ultimately appropriated by the ruling culture for its own hegemonic ends.[15] Materialist feminists and cultural materialists would argue that cultures are nowhere near as monolithic as this theory suggests; that they are, on the contrary, complex and unstable structures composed of competing discourses and multiple, overlapping determinations. We have already mentioned the way that the educational and economic privileges of upper-class status facilitated the literary productions of a few fortunate seventeenth-century women. This suggests that contemporary discourses of gender were not static, seamless wholes but that they changed shape as they interacted with other determinants of identity, like class, religion and politics. Within such a complex cultural matrix, meaning was not so much imposed as produced, creating a space for resistance to as well as internalization of dominant cultural codes. This allows for the possibility that the process of appropriation through which ruling culture seeks to sustain itself might work both ways: 'subordinate, marginal or dissident elements could appropriate dominant discourses and likewise transform them in the process'.[16] Patriarchal domination, by this account, is not an immutable condition but a process, 'one always being contested, always having to be renewed'.[17] History, as a consequence, becomes the dialectic between culture and human interventions in culture, or social agency, which is assumed in Marx's statement that men and women 'make their own history' though not 'under circumstances chosen by themselves'.[18]

Most of the critics in this volume are concerned to explore the relationship between early women's writing and the period's powerful discourses of femininity in a manner which avoids humanist notions of unfettered subjectivity without replacing them with views of patriarchal ideology as monolithic and unalterable. They chart both the 'mixed process of acceptance and resistance'[19] with which early women writers responded to gender ideologies and the different ways in which seventeenth-century English culture created the conditions in which they could become agents – not free, but capable of manoeuvring within their unchosen circumstances, of appropriating patriarchal discourses in their own interests. It is this process of negotiating ideological constraints which Elaine Hobby calls 'making a virtue of necessity': 'Women's legal and economic position, and the ideological statements made justifying their subjection are the "necessity" they lived under. In different ways, their own writings show us, they were able to "make a virtue" of this: to turn constraints into permissions, into little pockets of liberty or autonomy.'[20]

Self-representations

Seventeenth-century women writers frequently turned 'constraints' into 'permissions' by producing an early modern version of feminine writing, which strained to conform to rather than flout the feminine ideal. They might, for example, project an image of feminine modesty by disparaging their own literary efforts or by eschewing topics considered to lie outside of the woman's sphere. This process of self-representation, whether conscious or not, is explored in several of the essays in this collection. Elaine Hobby's study of the mid-seventeenth-century poet Katherine Philips argues that her favourable public image as 'the Matchless Orinda', 'the archetypal blushing poetess, who shied away from any public recognition of her works', represents not a reflection of 'the real Katherine Philips' but a self-construction designed to reconcile her writing and her literary ambitions with contemporary ideologies of femininity. Hobby's essay usefully problematizes this particular mode of appropriation of patriarchal discourse. For while Philips's strategic self-representation successfully expanded the definition of femininity to include the woman writer, thereby enabling other women to follow her example, it simultaneously established a highly restrictive model of female authorship which disadvantaged a less orthodox successor like Aphra Behn.

Philips was a married woman as well as a poet, and the essays in this volume make it abundantly clear that women's position within the institution of marriage was a central concern for seventeenth-century women writers. Their historical period marked a transition from the absolutist concept of marriage, in which women functioned as commodities, as 'objects of exchange and the guarantee of dynastic continuity', to the liberal concept, which envisaged marriage as an affective union based on mutual consent.[21] Yet the companionate ideal appears to have granted women only a limited right to choose their partners,[22] and to have offered no serious challenge to the legal view of marriage as the absorption of the wife's identity into that of her husband:

> It is true, that Man and Wife are one person, but understand in what manner.
>
> When a small brooke or little river incorporateth with Rhodanus, Humber, or the Thames, the poore Rivulet loseth her name, it is carried and recarried with the new associate, it beareth no sway, it possesseth nothing during coverture. A woman as soone as she is married is called covert, in Latine nupta, that is, vailed, as it were, clouded and over-shadowed ... she hath lost her streame.... I may more truely farre away say to a married woman, her new selfe is her superior, her companion, her master....[23]

For Philips, who lived and wrote during the Civil Wars and Commonwealth, the coercion and subordination of wedlock was inseparable from political defeat and isolation: a royalist and High Church Anglican, she was married at sixteen to James Philips, a prominent parliamentarian 38 years her senior.

In accordance with her theory of Philips's strategic self-construction, Hobby reads her friendship poetry as an attempt to secure a measure of political fellowship and personal autonomy without overtly violating the demands of her conjugal role. Addressed to women who shared Philips's royalist allegiances, these poems, under cover of an acceptably private and feminine subject matter, privilege friendship between women as an area of life 'characterised by choice and freedom'. Yet Hobby's analysis also points to the way the political and religious conflicts of the seventeenth century lent patriarchal license to such critical perspectives on the marital relationship by providing women with male authority figures – king and/or God – whose claim on their loyalty and obedience could take precedence over that of their husbands.

Celia A. Easton's study of Katherine Philips is also interested in the process of the poet's self-representation. She suggests that Philips's poetry earned the (condescending) praise of her male contemporaries in part because its neo-platonic spirituality apparently dissociated it from the 'unfeminine' realm of public life, politics and physicality. Easton interprets the 'urging for transcendence' evident in Philips's poems as the voice of the woman, who, in seeking to obey 'Nature's laws', 'the rules of decorum and propriety' governing women's lives, attempts to suppress any traces of a 'political, public, or physically affectionate life'. Thus, in her friendship poems, Philips consistently defines female friendship in transcendent terms, as a marriage of souls. Easton, however, deconstructs this privileging of soul over body, uncovering the classic Freudian scenario of the return of the repressed: the woman's denial of the political and corporeal world is resisted by the poet, Orinda, whose political and military metaphors, reworked from courtly love conventions, reintroduce repressed energies in disguised form. This reading prompts consideration of the claims which have been made for Philips as an early feminist and lesbian poet. Although Easton considers both labels to be anachronistic, she discovers in Orinda's adaptation of the courtly love tradition a female discourse that is separatist, anti-phallocentric and homoerotic.

Although Hobby and Easton come to similar conclusions about the woman-centred vision of Philips's friendship poetry, their essays take rather different views of the relationship between those poems and patriarchal ideology. Hobby tends to interpret discourses of femininity as an external impediment – a view which allows her to draw a fairly clear distinction between the gynocentric meaning of Philips's poems and their conventionally 'feminine' subject matter. According to Easton, ideological imperatives are internalized, and therefore inscribed in the poetry itself, where they exist in a state of irreducible tension with dissenting impulses. In place of organic unity, Easton finds underlying strains and conflicts, poetic texts which are neither simply what they profess to be nor simply susceptible to twentieth-century feminist readings.

In her study of the autobiography of Margaret Cavendish, the Duchess of Newcastle, Sidonie Smith also discovers two competing textual voices which point to the complexity of her relationship to her culture's normative model of womanhood. As a married woman who had forfeited all claim to an identity separate from her husband's,

Cavendish doubly defied patriarchal dictates, and reinforced her reputation for eccentricity, by writing about her own life for publication.[24] Moreover, in her autobiography, she asserts, with astonishing audacity, the independent identity and historical significance which entitle her to public recognition and posthumous fame. However, as Smith points out, this self-representation repeatedly collides with Cavendish's rival claim to be a paragon of feminine virtue – silent and self-effacing. Smith argues persuasively that Cavendish invokes this conflicting persona not merely in a strategic effort to defuse public censure of her 'unwomanly' activities, but also because she is in part a product of this discourse, and so identifies deeply with it. Yet even in Cavendish's most fulsome endorsements of the ideal, Smith detects traces of disenchantment with its oppressive demand for something akin to self-annihilation. Smith's account of 'the mixed process of acceptance and resistance' evident in Cavendish's autobiography, as in Philips's poetry, indicates the way in which a construction of femininity predicated on rigorous self-suppression can generate resentment and resistance as well as anxious impersonations of the ideal self.

Proto-feminism and the female subject

The essays we have considered thus far make strong cases for reading the work of Anne Finch, Katherine Philips and Margaret Cavendish as forms of resistance to patriarchal ideology, however muted or self-contradictory. Yet we must immediately acknowledge that whatever woman-centred or proto-feminist attitudes these writers exhibit co-existed with deeply conservative political allegiances. All three women loyally supported the Stuart monarchy and its absolutist claims: Philips and Cavendish during the Civil Wars and Commonwealth, Finch during and after the Glorious Revolution of 1688, when the Catholic James II was deposed in a bloodless coup which signalled the demise of divine-right Toryism and the triumph of Parliamentary rule. During the seventeenth century, this concurrence of political conservatism with a consciousness of gender inequality was in fact the rule rather than the exception. As Catherine Gallagher points out in her essay on Cavendish: 'It is an odd but indisputable fact that the seventeenth-century women whom we think of as the forerunners and founders of feminism were, almost without exception, Tories.'

Margaret Cavendish has by now been firmly integrated into the history of feminist thought. In her book *Reason's Disciples: Seventeenth-Century English Feminists*, Hilda Smith claims that she 'understood, better than any of her sisters, the multifaceted nature of women's oppression'.[25] Yet Smith concedes that Cavendish frequently contradicted her own critique of patriarchy with assertions that women were, in fact, less able than men; that it was nature rather than culture which rendered them inferior. Sidonie Smith interprets this inconsistency as another expression of the divided ideological loyalties which fracture Cavendish's autobiography and which the political upheavals of the Civil Wars in all likelihood exacerbated. A member of a landed royalist family whose estate and assets were seized after the victory of the Parliamentary forces, Cavendish also lost two brothers in the conflict and spent fifteen years in exile with her husband. As Smith notes, these circumstances may well have intensified Cavendish's attachment to traditional patriarchal concepts of order which, drawing an analogy between the family and the state, validated the authority of the king as father of his people and of the *pater familias* as king of his household.[26]

Catherine Gallagher, by contrast, sees the relationship between Toryism and feminism in terms not of logical inconsistency but of 'deep affinity', arguing that 'the ideology of absolute monarchy provides, in particular historical situations, a transition to an ideology of the absolute self'. Identifying Cavendish's feminism with her assertions of her own singularity, Gallagher shows that she repeatedly anchors these claims to self-sufficiency in the figure of the absolute monarch, who serves as an 'authoritative metaphor' for Cavendish's self-construction as a sovereign female subject. Here, too, Gallagher differs from Sidonie Smith, whose reading of Cavendish's autobiography stresses instead the difficulty of figuring an autonomous female self within a culture which treated women as extensions of their male relations. As Smith observes of the autobiography's poignant final passage, Cavendish 'can rely only on her ascriptive status as wife and daughter to place her historically'.

The construction of subjectivity which Gallagher and Smith examine has been a central concern of new historical critics, whose repudiation of humanist ideas of the self has provoked interest in the way different subject positions are produced within particular social formations. The early modern period has proved fruitful ground for this historical enquiry, for the question of human identity looms large in an age poised between a moribund medieval world, which defined the self in relation to God and a divinely ordained social hierarchy, and the gradual emergence in its stead of what has remained the conceptual orthodoxy of the West: the self-creating, autonomous subject of bourgeois liberal humanism. In *The Subject of Tragedy*, Catherine Belsey argues that this supposedly free, rational individual was male; women, by contrast, were largely excluded from the order of subjectivity. We have already seen that the liberal concept of marriage ostensibly invested women with the autonomous subject's right to choose, in contrast to their reduction to commodity status within the absolutist model. Belsey shows, however, that women found at best an unstable and contradictory position within a liberal humanist discourse committed at once to the ideal of human freedom and to the wife's submission to the authority of her husband.[27] Yet it is precisely such flagrant internal contradictions which have made dominant ideologies unexpectedly productive for oppressed groups – in the present case by allowing women to question how they could simultaneously be subjects on the grounds of their common humanity and non-subjects on the grounds of their gender.

The aristocratic Cavendish, consumed with dreams of sovereignty, may seem an unlikely candidate for an early form of bourgeois subjectivity. Yet her absolutist model of the self, in Gallagher's reading, bears some similarity to a recognizably modern mode of subjectivity insofar as it is defined not 'by incorporation in the body politic' but by 'an interiorized self-recognition'.[28] Unable to realize her ambition for power, Cavendish strives to create an empire of the mind where, as she puts it in her book *The Blazing World*, she 'will endeavour to be, Margaret the First'.

However, if Cavendish's gender dictates a private, interiorized identity, this does not explain why she figured that identity in absolutist terms. Was she simply an ambitious woman whose public aspirations were frustrated by her gender? Gallagher argues instead for the social production of Cavendish's sovereign self: the exclusion of women from true political subjecthood, from any public role but that of monarch, would have deprived Cavendish of any model for female political life other than a monarchical one. Gallagher, then, like Belsey, provides an example of how the contradictions surrounding 'woman' – the political non-person who, through the accident of royal birth, could become a monarch – opened a discursive space in which a woman might install herself as a sovereign subject. In Gallagher's view, this process was further encouraged by the king's own reduction to a sovereign private figure during the Interregnum.

The liberal humanist subject emerged fully only in the latter half of the seventeenth century. Consequently, Jeff Masten finds in Mary Wroth's sonnet sequence *Pamphilia to Amphilanthus*, written before 1621, no more than traces of a distinctively female version of a modern subjectivity. As far as we know, Wroth's sonnet sequence and her prose romance, *The Countess of Montgomery's Urania*, were the first to be written by an Englishwoman, and her intervention in these two male-created genres was no doubt facilitated by her class position and more especially by her literary pedigree: Wroth was the niece of Sir Philip Sidney and Mary Herbert, the Countess of Pembroke. Masten reads *Pamphilia to Amphilanthus* as a woman's appropriation of the male, public discourse of Petrarchism to carve out a private, interior discursive space. Relating the sonnets' 'privatizing poetics' to their manuscript history and to the *Urania*, Masten argues that they gesture towards a female subjectivity predicated on the withdrawal from circulation between men. For Wroth the early seventeenth-century woman, then, personhood resided, as we might expect, in the refusal to participate in the patriarchal traffic in women on the marriage market. For Wroth the female author, it resided equally, if paradoxically, in resisting the public circulation of her words, their translation into the sexually transgressive meanings which male culture attached to a woman's public voice.

Both Gallagher and Masten warn against the temptation to attach a twentieth-century feminist meaning to these emergent female subjects. In Gallagher's view, Cavendish's microcosmic self ends up generating 'an infinite, unfathomable regression of interiority' which precludes any real political engagement with the world. Criticizing the tendency in some feminist criticism 'to read gender at the expense of history' – that is, to turn our literary foremothers into our contemporaries – Masten insists on the historical prematurity of Wroth's nascent female subject, which can be figured in her poems only in terms of 'emptiness, lack, loss, and absence'.

Gender/genre/representation

As Janet Todd has pointed out, attention to genre can prove a useful means of historicizing women's texts, for it allows us to grasp the extent to which female authors satisfied or frustrated the expectations created by particular generic conventions.[29] Most of the essays in this volume address at some level the question of what happens when a woman tackles a genre or poetic tradition whose conventions have been shaped by men, and a consensus clearly emerges that early women writers did, to varying degrees, appropriate literary conventions for their own ends. It is in large part the awareness of genre which allows that claim to be made in a nuanced fashion, without isolating women writers from their historical moment.

In her study of Mary Wroth's negotiations of the conventions of the prose romance, a genre created by men even if it was widely gendered as feminine, Helen Hackett carefully avoids simple and anachronistic 'feminist' readings of the *Urania*, insisting that we 'acknowledge the ideological and generic constraints upon Wroth's discourse, some of which she strains against, others of which she reproduces'. Thus, Hackett would agree with Masten that in the *Urania* Wroth figures her heroine's constancy as 'a new, though limited, form of female autonomy', and uses her female characters' reading and writing as a means of privileging a 'private female space'. At the same time, however, she draws attention to the way Wroth's text remains deeply implicated in patriarchal definitions of appropriate masculine and feminine roles.

Hackett also introduces us to Laura Mulvey's psychoanalytic theory of the operation of the male gaze in traditional narrative cinema. Derived from the theories of the French psychoanalyst Jacques Lacan, Mulvey's theory has had a significant impact on feminist literary criticism because it provides a model of the way representations of women, literary as well as cinematic, have been structured by 'the unconscious of patriarchal society'.[30] In Mulvey's view, the first stage of this process – the affirmation of male power through the reduction of the woman to a passive, eroticized object – stimulates as much anxiety as visual pleasure, for as the embodiment of sexual difference, the objectified woman carries with her the threat of castration, which the male unconscious can defuse in two ways: by fetishizing the female figure, turning its physical beauty into an obsessional object as a means of disavowing its threatening aspect; or by reasserting mastery by subjecting it to sadistic voyeurism. Patricia Parker and Nancy Vickers have applied Mulvey's theory to Renaissance literature, particularly to the Petrarchan blazon – the itemizing of a woman's charms which turns her not only into an object but also into a commodity exchanged between male speaker and male audience. Hackett employs these theories to expose moments in the *Urania* when Wroth clearly writes as a man, reproducing male ways of looking at and representing the female body. Yet Hackett also discovers episodes in which the gaze, exchanged between female characters, 'marks an epiphanic moment of revelation and mutual affirmation'.

The two essays on Aphra Behn's *The Rover* also examine the connection between gender and genre in a manner which foregrounds the play's representations of women. Of the five authors considered in this volume, Behn has come closest to achieving canonical status, and the extra coverage she receives here is a recognition of her special prominence in early modern literary studies. Behn was also one of the earliest professional women writers; unlike the other female authors considered in this book, she wrote for a living. Indeed, the notoriety she attracted during and after her lifetime stemmed in part from her position as a professional dramatist in the Restoration theatre. Part of the problem was subject matter: far from seeking to defend her sexual reputation by shying away from risqué topics, Behn wrote comedies which were as bawdy as those of her male contemporaries. Yet, as we have seen, any woman who published her writing risked being likened to a prostitute, due to the perceived correspondence between linguistic and sexual violations of the enclosed woman's sphere. As a professional who sold her wares in the literary market-place, Behn was doubly vulnerable to this analogy.

If Behn was criticized during her own period for writing like a man, feminist critics have on occasion followed suit. Katharine Rogers, for example, has claimed that her literary works 'show values and perceptions hardly distinguishable from those of the male writers with whom she competed'.[31] Nancy Copeland's essay on *The Rover*, much like Helen Hackett's on the *Urania*, argues for a more ambivalent engagement with the male-dominated genre of Restoration comedy. Behn inherited from her source play, Thomas Killigrew's *Thomaso*, the comic *topos* of the hero's choice between virgin and whore. In Copeland's view, the two dramatists treat this theme quite differently. While Killigrew's play reinforces the two principal patriarchal definitions of women, Behn's works to blur the distinction between them. This amounts to a radical questioning of a patriarchal order for which chastity constituted the single most precious commodity – the prerequisite for profitable marriage alliances and the continuity of the male line of inheritance. Such a social order, founded on the control of female sexuality, inevitably mystified the virgin and demonized the prostitute. Behn's unsettling of these fixed meanings was facilitated, in Copeland's view, by the emergence of the companionate ideal of marriage, which gave greater legitimacy to the female sexual subject. It also, of course, lent its cultural clout to Behn's favourite and related dramatic theme: the exploitation of women on the marriage market.

However, while Copeland attributes to Behn a radical reworking of her source material, she also insists on the conservatism of her comic genre. The obligatory happy ending, which joins virgin and hero in marriage, necessitates the drawing of the traditional boundary lines between women. Copeland's account of the play's competing ideological impulses, however, privileges subversion over discursive power: Behn's interrogation of patriarchal constructions of female sexuality, far from being ultimately contained, disrupts comic closure, producing a gap in the text through which we can glimpse the arbitrariness of the code of female honour even as that code is being re-affirmed in the play's closing moments.

These essays, by focusing not only on representations of women but also on the exchange mechanisms of the seventeenth-century marriage market, help us to see the similar function performed by each: the way the female body was stripped of subjectivity and circulated as a sexual commodity. According to Elin Diamond, this similarity is central to *The Rover*, which she reads as a complex 'metonymic chain' which links the portrait of the courtesan Angellica Bianca to the Restoration actress and to the traffic in women from which Behn's virgins are attempting to break free. Employing Brecht's concept of the *gestus*, Diamond reads Willmore's theft of Angellica's portrait as a 'gestic' moment, when 'contradictory social attitudes in both text and society are made heuristically visible to spectators'. Behn's adaptation of her source play is again a crucial issue; reworking Killigrew so that Willmore's act of appropriation takes place before he has actually seen Angellica, Behn turns the portraits into fetishes, into 'substitute objects for the female body'. Thus Willmore, the play's representative of royal power and authority, enacts the operations of a theatre apparatus whose reduction of the Restoration actress to an eroticized object for male consumption replicated the male ownership and exchange of female bodies in the patriarchal social order.

In Diamond's view, Angellica's portrait also contains the authorial signature of the female dramatist who inhabited a culture of gender which equated her professional status with prostitution. Diamond's claim for the importance of gendered signature in the study of women's texts, while it clearly refuses the poststructuralist reduction of 'woman' to a discursive category, does not revert to a humanist view of the female author. Behn in her reading is not a transhistorical being expressing herself but a subject in culture and history, ideologically constrained but not determined, whose works 'encode the conditions of her literary and theatrical production'.

Gender and race

With Jane Spencer's and Laura Brown's influential essays on Behn's novel *Oroonoko, or the Royal Slave*, we turn to an issue central to materialist–feminist criticism: the relationship between gender and racial oppression. Both critics argue that it is the position of the woman in Behn's novel which opens a space for sympathetic identification with the plight of a comparably marginalized and oppressed figure – the African slave. Spencer and Brown, then, intervene in the longstanding debate over Behn's attitude towards slavery and race in this early colonial narrative. How, for instance, are we to read her portrait of the African prince as, in Laura Brown's words, 'a European aristocrat in blackface'? In Spencer's view, it works to identify the African hero as 'the truly civilized man' in contrast to the duplicitous European characters, who largely fail to embody their own civilized values.[32] Spencer alludes to the political allegiances which fuelled this critique of English society: Behn, like so many seventeenth-century women writers, was a royalist, for whom the Civil Wars and Monmouth's rebellion (and, one might add, the Glorious Revolution of 1688, the year in which Behn wrote and published *Oroonoko*) spelled nothing less than a collapse into barbarism.

Gender enters the picture through Behn's female narrator – a fictionalized self-portrait. Spencer argues persuasively that it is the narrator's marginal position in colonial culture which enables her to sympathize with the royal slave and which also serves to uncover 'similarities in the positions of the European woman and the enslaved African man': although both Oroonoko and the narrator have exalted class status, both are ultimately powerless within a white male colonial culture which defines them, at bottom, in terms of kindred forms of innate inferiority: his race and her gender.

Spencer sees *Oroonoko* as marking 'an important stage in the history of women's quest for literary authority', a view which necessarily situates the text in relation to contemporary ideologies of gender. Yet it also locates Behn's novel within a diachronic history of the woman's novel, which seeks to map out the development over time, however erratic, of a tradition of women's writing. On this level, her reading of *Oroonoko* adopts the feminist historicist methodology forged in the 1970s by Showalter and Gilbert and Gubar, which has been accused of merely applying to women's literature the same progressive, continuist view of history – 'the almost providential retelling of the past to capture a predetermined progress'[33] – which has characterized the formation of the male literary tradition. Laura Brown, by contrast, anchors her feminist account of *Oroonoko* in the synchronic analysis favoured by new historicism; that is, she positions the novel within its own discursive formation, examining it in relation to discourses of gender and colonialism prevalent in late seventeenth-century England.

Given this theoretical grounding, it is not surprising that Aphra Behn figures less prominently in Brown's essay than in Spencer's; according to Brown, it is the discursive instability of Behn's text which serves to reveal the mutuality of racial and gender oppression. Thus, she acknowledges much more fully than Spencer that Behn's portrait of her African hero lends support to the dualistic accounts of alterity (or 'otherness') with which critics like Tzvetan Todorov and Abdul JanMohamed have characterized the relationship between colonizer and racial Other: Behn's naturalization of the royal slave as a European aristocrat suggests that she could imagine the African only 'as absolutely different and hence inferior, or as identical and hence equal'.

In a reading that is both feminist and Marxist, Brown seeks to uncover the dialectical process in the novel which takes us beyond the static oppositions of alterity. This she finds in the two conflicting discourses of a text which is at once an aristocratic romance and a 'bourgeois' colonial history. In Brown's view, these two incompatible narrative strands are yoked through the figure of the woman, whose mediatory role reveals the similarities between racial and gender oppression and makes possible the central ideological contradiction – the superimposition within the text of aristocratic and bourgeois systems – which opens up 'a site beyond alterity', a genuinely critical sympathy with the condition of slavery. Thus, the political volatility with which Behn characterizes the British colonial enterprise in Surinam links the story of the royal slave to the political struggles of the Civil Wars, and makes the novel's climactic moment simultaneously a re-enactment of the heroic martyrdom of Charles I and a 'brutally visceral' revelation of the historical experience of slavery. It should by now be clear that although Brown adopts new historicist methods, her dialectical reading, which finds in a colonial narrative the history of the colonial Other, challenges the new historicist view of 'the pervasive, preemptive nature of power'.

It is possible to interpret the relationship between gender and race in *Oroonoko* less optimistically. One could argue, for instance, that the text's royalist ideology, rooted in hierarchical principles, precludes a genuinely critical perspective on slavery;[34] or that study of Behn's treatment of her heroine Imoinda reveals that her own literary self-fashioning was complicit in racist misogyny.[35] These points bring us back to the question of female experience with which this introduction began. This question remains a hotly contested issue in feminist theory and criticism, especially for feminists of colour, who argue that any attempt to construct a common history of marginalization obscures the ways in which European women benefited from and, at times, actively participated in the colonial enterprise, while simultaneously ignoring or misrepresenting the very different histories of oppression and struggle of men and women of colour. It is of course easy to understand why white European and North American feminist critics, aspiring to radical social change, should seek textual evidence of the commonalities of oppressed groups. But one could also argue, with bell hooks, that genuine social transformation can occur only if 'we confront the realities of sex, race, and class, the ways they divide us, make us different, stand us in opposition, and work to reconcile and resolve these issues'.[36]

Notes

1. As Toril Moi has pointed out, the terms 'Anglo-American' and 'French' refer not to the critics' national origins, but to 'the intellectual tradition within which they work'. See Toril Moi, *Sexual/Textual Politics: Feminist Literary Theory* (London: Methuen, 1985), p. xiv.

2. ELAINE SHOWALTER, 'Towards a Feminist Poetics', in *Women Writing and Writing about Women*, ed. Mary Jacobus (London and Sydney: Croom Helm, 1979), pp. 22–41.

3. ELAINE SHOWALTER, *A Literature of Their Own: British Women Novelists from Brontë to Lessing* (Princeton: Princeton University Press, 1977), p. 12.

4. See TORIL MOI, 'Feminist Literary Criticism', in *Modern Literary Theory: A Comparative Introduction*, ed. Ann Jefferson and David Robey, 2nd edn (London: B.T. Batsford Ltd., 1986), p. 209.

5. ANN ROSALIND JONES, *The Currency of Eros: Women's Love Lyric in Europe, 1540–1620* (Bloomington and Indianapolis: Indiana University Press, 1990), p. 6.

6. For critiques of the humanist assumptions of gynocriticism, see Toril Moi, *Sexual/Textual Politics: Feminist Literary Theory*, pp. 6–8, 66–9, 76–9; and Mary Jacobus, 'Is There a Woman in This Text?' *New Literary History*, 14, no. 4 (Autumn, 1982), pp. 137–9. See also Mary Eagleton, ed. *Feminist Literary Criticism. Longman Critical Readers* (London and New York: Longman, 1991), pp. 5–20.

7. Any summary of French feminisms inevitably elides important differences between the theories of its main proponents. Titles in the Further Reading section can provide closer acquaintance with the work of specific theorists.

8. See TORIL MOI, *Sexual/Textual Politics: Feminist Literary Theory*, pp. 110–26, 143–9; Monique Plaza, '"Phallomorphic Power" and the Psychology of "Woman"', *Ideology and Consciousness*, 4 (1978), pp. 31–2; and Janet Todd, *Feminist Literary History: A Defence* (Cambridge: Polity Press, 1988), pp. 55–60.

9. NANCY K. MILLER, 'The Text's Heroine: A Feminist Critic and Her Fictions', *Diacritics*, 12, no. 2 (Summer, 1982), p. 49.

10. LOUIS ALTHUSSER, 'Ideology and Ideological State Apparatuses', in *Essays in Ideology* (London and New York: Verso, 1984), p. 36.

11. For feminist critiques of the (largely male) new historical critics' general indifference to gender and women's writing, see Carol Thomas Neely, 'Constructing the Subject: Feminist Practice and New Renaissance Discourses', *ELR*, 18, no. 1 (Winter, 1988), pp. 5–10; and Ros Ballaster, 'New Hystericism: Aphra Behn's *Oroonoko*: The Body, the Text and the Feminist Critic', in *New Feminist Discourses: Critical Essays on Theories and Texts*, ed. Isobel Armstrong (London and New York: Routledge, 1992), pp. 286–7.

12. MICHEL FOUCAULT, *The Archaeology of Knowledge*, tr. A.M. Sheridan Smith (New York: Pantheon Books, 1972), pp. 107–8.

13. JEAN E. HOWARD, 'The New Historicism in Renaissance Studies', *ELR*, 16, no. 1 (Winter, 1986), p. 25.

14. See PETER STALLYBRASS, 'Patriarchal Territories: The Body Enclosed', in *Rewriting the Renaissance: The Discourses of Sexual Difference in Early Modern Europe*, ed. Margaret W. Ferguson, Maureen Quilligan and Nancy J. Vickers (Chicago and London: The University of Chicago Press, 1986), pp. 126–8.

15. STEPHEN GREENBLATT, 'Invisible Bullets: Renaissance Authority and its Subversion, *Henry IV* and *Henry V*', in *Political Shakespeare: New Essays in*

Cultural Materialism, ed. Jonathan Dollimore and Alan Sinfield (Manchester: Manchester University Press, 1985), pp. 18–47.

16. JONATHAN DOLLIMORE, 'Introduction: Shakespeare, Cultural Materialism and the New Historicism', in *Political Shakespeare: Essays in Cultural Materialism*, p. 12.

17. Ibid., p. 14.

18. KARL MARX and FREDERICK ENGELS, *Selected Works, In One Volume* (London: Lawrence and Wishart, 1968), p. 97.

19. ANN ROSALIND JONES, *The Currency of Eros: Women's Love Lyric in Europe 1540–1620*, p. 2.

20. ELAINE HOBBY, *Virtue of Necessity: English Women's Writing 1649–88* (London: Virago, 1988), p. 8.

21. CATHERINE BELSEY, *The Subject of Tragedy: Identity and Difference in Renaissance Drama* (London and New York: Routledge, 1985), pp. 192, 192–200.

22. LAWRENCE STONE, *The Family, Sex and Marriage in England 1500–1800* (London: Weidenfeld and Nicolson, 1977), pp. 270–1; Catherine Belsey, *The Subject of Tragedy: Identity and Difference in Renaissance Drama*, pp. 201–2.

23. T[HOMAS] E[DGAR], *The Lawes Resolutions of Women's Rights* (London: John More, 1632), pp. 124–5.

24. ELAINE HOBBY, *Virtue of Necessity: English Women's Writing 1649–88*, p. 81.

25. HILDA L. SMITH, *Reason's Disciples: Seventeenth-Century English Feminists* (Urbana, Chicago, London: University of Illinois Press, 1982), p. 75.

26. SUSAN DWYER AMUSSEN, *An Ordered Society: Gender and Class in Early Modern England* (New York: Columbia University Press, 1988), pp. 34–66.

27. CATHERINE BELSEY, *The Subject of Tragedy: Identity and Difference in Renaissance Drama*, pp. 149–60; 192–221.

28. FRANCIS BARKER, *The Tremulous Private Body: Essays in Subjection* (Ann Arbor: The University of Michigan Press, 1995), p. 28.

29. JANET TODD, *Feminist Literary History: A Defence*, pp. 99–102.

30. LAURA MULVEY, 'Visual Pleasure and Narrative Cinema', in *The Sexual Subject: A 'Screen' Reader in Sexuality*, ed. John Caughie and Annette Kuhn (London and New York: Routledge, 1992), p. 22.

31. KATHARINE M. ROGERS, *Feminism in Eighteenth-Century England* (Urbana, Chicago, London: University of Illinois Press, 1982), p. 98.

32. Other critics who see *Oroonoko* as a critique of Western culture include Frederick M. Link, *Aphra Behn* (New York: Twayne, 1968), pp. 140–1; Wylie Sypher, *Guinea's Captive Kings: British Anti-Slavery Literature of the Eighteenth Century* (New York: Hippocrene Books, 1969), pp. 113–6; and Katharine M. Rogers, 'Fact and Fiction in Aphra Behn's *Oroonoko*', *Studies in the Novel*, 20, no. 1 (Spring, 1988), pp. 1–15.

33. JANET TODD, *Feminist Literary History: A Defence*, p. 96. See also Ros Ballaster, 'New Hystericism: Aphra Behn's *Oroonoko*: The Body, the Text

and the Feminist Critic', in *New Feminist Discourses: Critical Essays on Theories and Texts*, ed. Isobel Armstrong, p. 286.

34. See GEORGE GUFFEY, 'Aphra Behn's *Oroonoko*: Occasion and Accomplishment', in *Two English Novelists: Aphra Behn and Anthony Trollope* (Los Angeles: William Andrews Clark Memorial Library, UCLA, 1975), pp. 3–41; and Anita Pacheco, 'Royalism and Honor in Aphra Behn's *Oroonoko*', *SEL*, 34, no. 3 (Summer, 1994), pp. 491–506.

35. ROS BALLASTER, 'New Hystericism: Aphra Behn's *Oroonoko*: The Body, the Text and the Feminist Critic', in *New Feminist Discourses: Critical Essays on Theories and Texts*, ed. Isobel Armstrong, pp. 290–4.

36. BELL HOOKS, 'Feminism: A Transformational Politic', in *Talking Back: Thinking Feminist*Thinking Black* (Boston: South End Press, 1989), p. 25. See also Margo Hendricks and Patricia Parker (eds.), *Women, 'Race', and Writing in the Early Modern Period* (London and New York: Routledge, 1994), Ania Loomba, *Gender, Race, Renaissance Drama* (Delhi and Oxford: Oxford University Press, 1992); Gayatri Chakravorty Spivak, 'Three Women's Texts and a Critique of Imperialism', in *'Race', Writing, and Difference*, ed. Henry Louis Gates, Jr. (Chicago: University of Chicago Press, 1986), pp. 262–80; Laura E. Donaldson, *De-Colonizing Feminism: Race, Gender, and Empire-Building* (London: Routledge, 1993); Jenny Sharpe, *Allegories of Empire: The Figure of the Woman in the Colonial Text* (Minneapolis: University of Minnesota Press, 1993); and Inderpal Grewal, *Home and Harem: Nation, Gender, Empire, and the Cultures of Travel* (Durham, N.C.: Duke University Press, 1996).

LADY MARY WROTH
(c.1587–1653)

1 'Shall I turne blabb?': Circulation, Gender, and Subjectivity in Mary Wroth's Sonnets*

JEFF MASTEN

Feminist criticism, with its interest in the cultural construction of human identity, especially gendered identity, has frequently joined forces with historicist criticism in attacking the modern humanist notion of the autonomous, self-creating subject, not least by tracing its own cultural construction in the course of the seventeenth century. Yet because the liberal humanist subject was male, and was defined by his difference from a female Other, the feminist critique of humanist subjectivity has a sexual political dimension, and feminist studies of seventeenth-century culture have recently sought to uncover signs of women's struggle to secure the same rights men were in the process of claiming for them-selves. This is Jeff Masten's project, in an essay which is both feminist and cultural materialist. The traces of the private, interiorized subject position he detects in Mary Wroth's sonnet sequence *Pamphilia to Amphilanthus* signal a woman writer's bid for self-determination by withdrawing her words and her marketable body from circulation. Masten stresses that this does not make Wroth a fully modern subject; to argue otherwise, as some feminist critics have, is to endorse the humanist belief in a transhistorical human nature.

1

What immediately strikes the modern reader of Mary Wroth's sonnet sequence *Pamphilia to Amphilanthus* is its sustained lack of reference. Trained to mine the Riches of the biographically thick Sidneian sequence, to register Stellas, Astrophils, Shakespearean Wills, and

* Reprinted from *Reading Mary Wroth: Representing Alternatives in Early Modern England*, ed. Naomi J. Miller and Gary Waller (Knoxville: University of Tennessee Press, 1991), pp. 67–87.

Spenser's three Elizabeths, we find within Wroth's sonnets little reference to their writer, no mention of the beloved by name (except in the title), few allusions to contemporary events (in the old-historical sense), and little attempt to engage outside interlocutors. Indeed, these sonnets center exclusively on, and are the intense poetic efflux of, a persona who claims she is in love. As such, they seem to speak an almost inscrutable private language.

What little we know about the sequence as material object – the 'external evidence' – replicates the privative experience of reading it. The sequence exists only in an undated holograph manuscript (Folger v.a. 104) and in the published *Urania*, where it occupies a separate section at the end; we do not know which version of the sequence is earlier. Josephine A. Roberts argues that, since the watermark of the Folger copy resembles those of two other manuscripts dated 1587 and 1602, the manuscript version of the sequence precedes its publication in 1621. This evidence, however, provides only a very tentative *terminus a quo* (since such a procedure attempts to date the paper not the sonnets), and could likewise support the argument that Wroth began writing the sonnets no earlier than the year of her birth, probably 1587; Gary Waller more tentatively dates them after Robert Wroth's death.[1] Furthermore, we know virtually nothing about the Folger manuscript's contemporary history, function, or readership, and the poems have not been discovered in published miscellanies or in manuscript commonplace books extant before 1621. Roberts cites Sylvester's *Lachrimae Lachrimarum* (1613) as evidence of circulation 'long before ... 1621', but the lines merely imply that Wroth was writing (something) by 1613 and mention no specific texts. Strangely, Roberts also cites Jonson's *Underwood* 28 as evidence of early circulation, though the poem was not published until 1640 and no prior date for it has been established, as Waller notes.[2] Jonson could just as well be 'exscribing' the sonnets after publication.

In an article surveying the movement of Renaissance poetry 'From Manuscript to Print', J.W. Saunders shows that such activities as the interpolation into manuscripts of commentary and verse in other hands, the transcription into one manuscript of another's poems, the circulation of manuscripts at four and five removes from the original writer, and the circulation of multiple copies (as many as twenty to thirty) were the common practice when Wroth was writing. Saunders sketches a picture of mobile, permeable texts which constantly gesture toward aspects of their own writing and widespread circulation in an open, collaborative setting. The manuscript of *Pamphilia to Amphilanthus* is notably at odds with this larger cultural practice. It contains no interpolations by, additions from, or transcriptions of others, and, in contrast to Margaret Ezell's description of the circulating writings of other women during the period, it has no title page, preface, dedication, or date and does not seem to be addressed to a family audience, friend, or patron.[3] There are no references to the sequence before 1621 and no multiple versions to indicate that the poems circulated before their publication.

In fact, the manuscript known as *Pamphilia to Amphilanthus* may not be a circulating sonnet sequence at all – or at least not in the way we have understood it to be. In her edition of Wroth's poems, Roberts asserts that the manuscript represents an early version of *Pamphilia to Amphilanthus* and assumes that Wroth circulated her sonnets among her friends. Roberts equates the Folger manuscript with the sequence *Pamphilia to Amphilanthus* – a possible interpretation of the evidence, if only because the first group of poems (and in the absence of a title page, apparently the whole manuscript) is designated by that title. But such a construal underplays the presence of other poems (some of which appear in *Urania*) and other important evidence. We might as easily read the manuscript as several distinct sequences of poems copied into a single manuscript, including *Pamphilia to Amphilanthus* (the first fifty-five poems) and the distinctly organized 'crowne of Sonetts'. This explains the manuscript's unusual numbering (which begins again with '1' at several points), the placement of blank pages between sets of poems, and the distinctive arrangement of these different sets on the page – as well as the regular alternation of sonnets and songs in the first set of poems in contrast to the rest of the groupings. In other words, rather than a circulating version of *Pamphilia to Amphilanthus* with a few *Urania* poems tacked on at the end, the manuscript may represent Wroth's own collection of several of her (more or less discrete) sonnet sequences, along with some other non-sequential poems. Both Roberts (whose structural analysis and continuous numbering impose unity and continuity upon the manuscript) and Elaine V. Beilin (whose novelistic narrative posits a totalizing structure) obscure discrete groupings within the manuscript. McLaren's and Paulissen's divisions of the manuscript into two and four parts respectively are, I think, conservative estimates. That the manuscript contains alterations in Wroth's hand and lacks dedication and title-page suggests it was a fair copy for her own use, not a presentation copy.[4]

In the following discussion, I suggest that interpreting this bibliographical evidence is part of, not simply prior to, the reading process, for the poems themselves – like the anomalous manuscript in which they are inscribed – encode a withdrawal from circulation. The sonnets stage a movement which is relentlessly private, withdrawing into an interiorized space; they foreground a refusal to speak in the public, exhibitionist voice of traditional Petrarchan discourse; in the context of the published portion of *Urania* they articulate a woman's resolute constancy, self-sovereignty, and unwillingness to circulate among men; they gesture toward a subject under self-control. In their insistent privacy and refusal to circulate, the poems reproduce the actual situation of their writing. And, as we shall see, privacy and circulation are tied closely to gender in this first sonnet sequence by an Englishwoman.

2

At the beginning of the seventeenth century, Francis Barker observes, 'the public and the private as strong, mutually defining, mutually exclusive categories, each describing separate terrains and distinct contents, practices, and discourses, are not yet extant'.[5] As twentieth-century readers of Wroth's texts, we must remind ourselves that concepts we may take as the organizing categories of existence are constructed in history, that the terms 'public' and 'private' are emergent in the discursive world we interrogate here. Wroth's texts, we shall see, are both documents and instruments of that construction; they do not merely reflect the emergence of a public/private distinction 'in the culture', but also work to create that distinction.

Arthur F. Marotti has asserted that the sonnet sequence was a public, courtly genre, circulating widely, expressing 'social, political, and economic suits in the language of love',[6] and from the outset *Pamphilia to Amphilanthus* seems to contest the place of a female speaker within that 'public' tradition of Petrarchan verse. In the initial sonnet Pamphilia watches as, in a dream vision, Venus inserts a Petrarchan burning heart into her breast, authorizing her position as a Petrarchan speaker: 'one hart flaming more then all the rest / The goddess held, and putt itt to my breast, / Deare sonne, now shutt sayd she . . .' (1/P1). The poem's final lines, with their ricochet of glosses for the speaking subject, emphasize that this sequence will contest woman's place in the Petrarchan lover's discourse: 'I, waking hop'd as dreames itt would depart / Yett since: O mee: a lover I have binn.'

But at the same time that these images place the fictional Pamphilia firmly within the Petrarchan tradition, the sonnet also represents a withdrawal from public signification. Like so many of these poems, it deploys images of night, blackness, darkness, and sleep to register privacy and privation. The heart transplant is, as Roberts notes, a recurrent image in the English tradition of Petrarchanism, but the insertion it signifies, the movement inward at this inaugural moment, recurs throughout the sequence as a withdrawal into an interiorized corporeal space: 'now shutt sayd she . . .'[7] In sonnet 22/P25, for example, Pamphilia memorably compares herself to 'the Indians,

scorched with the sunne . . . they doe as theyr God adore.' The Indians
are outwardly marked by their worship of the sun, but Pamphilia asks
to 'weare the marke of Cupids might / *In hart* as they *in skin* of
Phoebus light. . . .' The next sonnet makes this privatization more
explicit still:

> When others hunt, my thoughts I have in chase;
>   If hauke, my minde att wished end doth fly,
>   Discourse, I with my spiritt tauke, and cry
>   While others, musique choose as greatest grace.

Here the speaker appropriates public (and one might argue, male)
'pastimes' and brings them into a private space, 'free from eyes' (1, 5).
And what seems perhaps a merely metaphorical conversion of public
activity into private introspection is enacted in the couplet (indeed, in
the entire sonnet and the sequence at large), as the speaker explicitly
'discourses' with her 'spiritt'.[8]

Sonnet 36/P41 stages a comparison of the public lover and
Pamphilia's private love, not by appropriating the public but by
repudiating it. The inserted heart of the first sonnet again registers the
authenticity of this inward pain: 'How well poore hart thou wittnes
canst I love. . . .' But Pamphilia emphasizes her difference from the
Petrarchan tradition of displayed corporeality: 'Yett is itt sayd that sure
love can nott bee / Wher soe small *showe of passion* is descrid.' Wroth's
dismissal of the typical Petrarchan speaker's outwardly demonstrative
body accords with Barker's argument that the construction of the
public/private distinction 'in its modern form' occurs simultaneously
with the 'disappearance of the body from public view'.[9] The sonnet
concludes with a strong repudiation of love theatrically displayed,
positing instead a self-enclosed authenticity of expression: 'For know
more passion in my hart doth move / Then in a million that make
show of love.'

Here Pamphilia writes in Petrarchan discourse to write against it,
and the other sonnets are implicated in this strategy. Returning to
those poems, we can read the figures against which she establishes
herself (the Indians, the hunters and hawkers) as representations of
the male speakers of the popular English Petrarchan tradition – the
million that make elaborate textual show of love – as practiced most
significantly by Wroth's uncle in *Astrophil and Stella*. The worship of
the master/mistress as a sun and Wroth's citations of hunting, music,
and discourse recall dozens of other sonnets from the tradition.

Furthermore, Shakespeare's 'As an unperfect actor on the stage'
(Sonnet 23) and Spenser's 'Of this world's Theatre in which we stay'
(*Amoretti* 54) exploit the lover's theatrical 'shows'. In her sonnets, then,

Wroth transforms seemingly ungendered signs into markers of her gender-difference from the tradition in/against which she writes; moreover, in each case she displaces public, male exhibition with a discourse seeking to register a private authenticity of feeling. To put Hamlet's memorable phrase in a gendered context, Pamphilia explicitly refuses the 'actions that a man might play' (*Hamlet*, I.ii.84).

Read in this context, the speaker of sonnet 38/P44 becomes one 'bannish'd' from enjoying 'pastimes' the earlier poems gendered as male:

> What pleasure can a bannish'd creature have
>   In all the pastimes that invented arr
>   By witt or learning, absence making warr
>   Against all peace that may a biding crave:
> Can wee delight butt in a wellcome grave. . . .

The 'creature' of the first line and the 'wee' of the second quatrain read as signifiers for the banished and speechless female Other of the male-authored Petrarchan sequences (see *OED* definition 3b for gendered examples of 'creature'). Furthermore, the syntactically difficult lines 3–4 seem to connect 'absence' not with an absent lover but with the speaker herself, banished as she is from Petrarchan language as it is usually spoken. The next sonnet, one of the few which focus explicitly on writing, again takes up Pamphilia's position in relation to Petrarchan discourse: 'Nor can I as those pleasant witts injoy / My owne fram'd words, which I account the dross / Of purer thoughts, or recken them as moss . . .' (39/P45). Reflecting on her own elaborately fram'd sonnets, Pamphilia argues that her texts are the expression of inward emotion and distinguishes herself from the 'witt sick' 'witts', whom she views as (merely) playfully discursive. Admitting that her words are but pale reflections of an inward authenticity, she nonetheless argues that her poetry, unlike theirs, grounds itself in an emotional reality. Confronting them directly, she adds: 'Alas, think I, your plenty shewes your want, / For wher most feeling is, words are more scant. . . .' The sonnet thus sets up a number of oppositions important to the sequence at large: plenty versus want, empty Petrarchan discourse versus full emotion, show versus authenticity.

Addressing the 'witts' again, the next sonnet acts as a gloss on its predecessors, stressing in particular the inauthentic theatricality of stock Petrarchanism:

> Itt is nott love which you poore fooles do deeme
>   That doth *appeare* by fond, and *outward showes*
>   Of kissing, toying, or by swearings glose. . . .

'T'is nott a *showe* of sighes, or teares can prove
    Who loves indeed ... ;
Butt *in the soule* true love in safety lies. ...

(40/P46)

Pamphilia's anti-theatricality is strikingly similar to Hamlet's statement
in a different context that he has 'that within, which passeth show;
/ These, but the trappings, and the suites of woe' (I.ii.85–86). As in
Barker's reading of that play, Pamphilia here makes a decisive claim
'for qualitative distinction from the corporeal order of the spectacle';
however, to do so in her case is to foreground a gender difference –
to repudiate the rhetorical trappings and metaphorical suites of male
Petrarchan discourse.[10]

Interestingly, given Wroth's uncle's sequence, sonnet 41/P47
comments on the 'blessed starrs which doe heavns glory show' and
resonates with a later sonnet (6/P100) that subtly writes against
Sidney's star-struck sequence. Asking in that poem 'that noe day
would ever more appeere,' the speaker concludes:

Lett mee bee darke, since bard of my chiefe light ...
To mee itt seems as ancient fictions make
    The starrs all fashions, and all shapes partake
    While in my thoughts true forme of love shall live.

Pamphilia speaks at one level in a Platonic vocabulary, comparing the
mere 'shapes' of love to her own 'true forme', and at another level
about 'ancient' astrology, with its constellations of animal and human
shapes. But the mere mention of star-study by a member of the Sidney
family brings with it resonances of *Astrophil and Stella*, which might
have seemed by Wroth's time an 'ancient fiction'.[11] And the Petrarchist
discourse which makes its Stellas and Astrophils into 'all fashions
and all shapes' is here set against the interior private space – 'thes
haples rooms', playing on the Italian *stanza* – site of articulation for
the authentic version of love, spoken by an individual who claims
the traditionally non-discursive space of a 'darke' lady. As before,
the 'shapes' and 'fashions' are associated with the inauthenticity of
'stage play like disguised pleasures'.

The earlier set of sonnets culminates with a defence of interior
authenticity and the most strident anti-theatricality of the sequence:

If ever love had force in humaine brest?
    If ever hee could move in pensive hart?
    Or if that hee such powre could butt impart
    To breed those flames whose heart brings joys unrest.
Then looke on mee; I ame to thes adrest,
    I, ame the soule that feeles the greatest smart;

31

I, ame that hartles trunk of harts depart
And I, that one, by love, and griefe oprest;
Non ever felt the truth of loves great miss
Of eyes, till I deprived was of bliss;
For had hee seene, hee must have pitty show'd;
I should nott have bin made this stage of woe
Wher sad disasters have theyr open showe
O noe, more pitty hee had sure beestow'd.

(42/P48)

As in sonnet 36/P41, where the speaker claims 'more passion . . . /
Then in a million that make show of love,' this poem insists on interior
and superlative feeling, 'the soule that feeles the greatest smart'. If
interiority exists (and that existence is, in an important way to which
we will return, precisely what this sequence maps out), the speaker
claims with her repeated and emphatically punctuated 'I, ame' that she
is its exemplary embodiment. The poem's opening conditional clauses
(made doubly conditional by the unusually situated question marks)
contest the very existence of emotion 'in humaine brest', and the
insistence of the second quatrain ('Then looke on mee') indicates
the novelty of this discursive situation. Here the speaker does not
repudiate spectacle as she had in earlier sonnets but instead laments
that she has herself been made to participate in public, theatrical
signification, 'this stage of woe / Wher sad disasters have theyr open
showe . . .' Finally, this sonnet associates the emergent private space
with (de)privation and emptiness; in a way that resonates with the
opening sonnet, the speaker here is 'that hartles trunk of harts depart'.
Absence as a palpable presence pervades Wroth's verse, but as the
syntactically vexed 'bannish'd creature' sonnet shows, referents for this
absence are ambiguous or absent themselves. Does 'absence' refer to
the Amphilanthus present only in the title? to the speaker herself? to
'the hartles trunk of harts depart'? Or does the speaker use the absent
lover as a device for speaking of this newly postulated private discursive
space? In other words, does Wroth appropriate the machinery of
Petrarchanism, with its absent/distant lover, as a convenient discourse
for figuring a private self?[12]

These are questions to which we will return; sonnet 45/P52, one of
the few sonnets to engage an interlocutor, capitalizes on this ambiguity.
'Good now bee still, and doe nott mee torment,' the speaker exclaims,
and demands that she be allowed to withdraw into the interiority
valorized elsewhere in the sequence: 'only lett mee quarrell with
my brest.' The initial quatrains read as the attempted escape from
'Divell'-ish public discourse, with its 'toungue torture' and 'multituds of
questions', into the private domain. Read in this context, the sestet is

not so much a ruse to free the speaker from the interlocutor (a madness play-acted by sanity) as it is a gloss upon the lines which have preceded it, an attempt to explain a novel discursive position in terms the interlocutor can understand:

> Well then I see noe way butt this will fright
>> That Divell speach; Alas I ame possesst,
>> And mad folks senceles ar of wisdomes right,
> The hellish speritt absence doth arest
>> All my poore sences to his cruell might. . . .

Pamphilia appropriates the familiar discourse of demonic possession, but, importantly, she is 'possesst' not by some definitive intruding demon (this is not the earlier 'Divell') but rather by 'the hellish speritt absence'. And once again absence defers a referent.

The sonnets' insistent withdrawal – their repudiation of public Petrarchan discourse and its inauthentic 'open shows', 'shapes', and 'fashions' – registers at a number of levels a refusal to circulate. Pamphilia refuses to construct herself or circulate as a Petrarchan sign, eschewing the signifying body of both the Petrarchan master and mistress (though she could fill either role, as writer or as woman): 'Take heed mine eyes, how you your lookes doe cast / Least they beetray my harts most secrett thought . . .' (34/P39, 1–2). Furthermore, as Roberts's survey of 'The Biographical Problem' suggests, the sequence makes few particular references outside itself which would serve to draw in a reading 'public', and, with few exceptions, there is nothing here resembling the male Petrarchists' engagement of other public (courtly) personae – or of the master/mistress/other itself.[13] If, returning to Marotti's conclusions, we agree that Wroth's chosen genre was otherwise relentlessly public – circulating at large to express male 'social, political, and economic suits in the language of love' – then *Pamphilia to Amphilanthus* is a woman's privatization of that genre toward other ends. The published books of Wroth's *Urania* place this privatizing poetics within the context of romance narrative.

3

Pamphilia, noted by Maureen Quilligan as the *Urania*'s privileged poetfigure,[14] is also 'the most silent and discreetly retir'd of any Princesse' (50). In an extremely public narrative – detailing the wanderings of innumerable characters across a seemingly boundaryless Eurasian landscape – she is remarkably immobile, and her poetic process is closely linked with retirement. She writes sequestered in a 'fine wood, delicately contriu'd into strange, and delightfull walkes' (74), to which she alone has a key. The first of her many poems in the text is signalled by a vow (like the speaker of the sonnets) 'not to carry the tokens of her losse openly on her browes, but rather to weare them priuately in her heart' (76). Furthermore, in response to her suitor Leandrus's suggestion that she acquire the protection of a male lover, Pamphilia defends her garden 'walkes' as a distinctly independent domain: 'My spirit . . . as well guards me alone, as in company; and for my person, my greatnesse, and these walls are sufficient warrants and guardians for my safety . . . for strength I had rather haue these [walls], then ones power I could not loue' (178). Pamphilia effectively genders her garden, privileging the autonomy of this private female space over the protection of a male lover–guardian.[15]

A later break in the narrative makes emphatic the opposition of a public, male world and Pamphilia's withdrawal into a privatized locus of female poetic expression. The long-awaited conquest of Albania, in which almost every important male character participates, is abruptly interrupted by a mid-paragraph shift to Pamphilia 'in her owne Country', 'walk[ing] into a Parke she had adioyning to her Court . . .' (264). Talking to herself, she hears her words repeated by an echo, which she silences: 'Soft said she, shall I turne blabb? no Echo, excuse me, my loue and choyce . . . must not be named by any but my selfe. . . . As none but we doe truely loue, so none but our owne hearts shall know we loue' (264). Just as she remains embowered in her garden (and that embowerment is juxtaposed to the male boundary–transgressions of war), her thoughts remain enclosed; they must not circulate beyond herself.[16] Moreover, Pamphilia exercises self-containment even in 'public': 'shee could bee in greatest assemblies as priuate with her owne thoughts, as if in her Cabinet, and there haue as much discourse with her imagination' (391). Such physical and verbal discretion clearly recalls aspects of the sonnet sequence.

Pamphilia's hallmark, as the text makes clear at every available point, is her unflagging constancy to Amphilanthus. Constancy distinguishes her from virtually every other character; it is, she explains, the basis of her identity: 'I can neuer [let in that worthlesse humour change] till I can change my selfe, and haue new creation and another soule . . .' (391). Pamphilia's constancy and her identity as a female subject might thus seem to be based on Amphilanthus (that is, on a male being exterior to her self). But as both Quilligan and Miller have emphasized, Pamphilia, by citing the constancy of her love for Amphilanthus rather than the love itself, foregrounds autonomy.[17] Though her love is male-directed, her constancy (the privileged virtue) is self-maintained. In an important way to which we will return, then, Pamphilia's 'constancy' may represent the proto-virtue of a bourgeois subject only beginning to emerge at this point in history, for it is a virtue constructed as interior to the self, self-authorized and unchanging. Rather than subjecting herself to a protecting male lover as Leandrus suggests, Pamphilia constructs her own 'walls' in a prototypical gesture of subjection to the self.

Constancy is also a defense against circulating in the text as a marriageable female. Though Pamphilia constant/ly stresses her devotion to Amphilanthus, their marriage is always deferred, for no apparent reason – at least on the level of plot. She doesn't marry Amphilanthus through 558 pages of the published narrative, and, unlike other characters, she steadfastly refuses to marry any but her one true love. Pamphilia thus avoids what Gayle Rubin has called the basis of the 'sex/gender system' in patriarchal cultures: 'the traffic in women'. Men, Rubin argues, trade women as conduits of but not participants in patriarchal power. Women are thus subjected but are not subjects; that is, they are allowed no self-control, and a woman can begin to occupy a subject position only by blocking her trafficking.[18] By asserting her withdrawal from the 'traffic' that characterizes both the romance text and the culture in which Wroth wrote, by refusing to allow herself to be bestowed upon a husband by a father as a gift between men, Pamphilia establishes that she is 'subject' to her self.

Wroth figures this self-control in the discourse of female political sovereignty; Pamphilia tells her father that he 'had once married her before, which was to the Kingdome of Pamphilia, from which Husband shee could not bee diuorced, nor ever would have other . . .' (218). For her emergent female subject Wroth thus appropriates her culture's only available model of a sovereign female self (subjected only to herself, singularly able to control her own circulation within the traffic in women), the virgin queen Elizabeth. Urania makes the connection when she asks Pamphilia, 'how can you command others, that cannot master your selfe, or make laws, that cannot counsel, or soueraignise ouer a poore thought?' (398). Whereas a married woman would be governed by her husband, this queen withdraws into the political space she rules independently of patriarchy. Married only to her country, her name is appropriate for an emergent female subject: she 'soueraignises' over Pamphilia – her country and her self.

A refusal to circulate between men and the important ramifications for the formulation of a female subject are foregrounded in *Urania*'s treatment of poetic manuscripts. The narrative privileges manuscript protection, while manuscript circulation is often problematic. Love letters are forged and intercepted (231, 513–14), and circulating poems lead to a love triangle in which a woman is shared sexually by two men (384). Nereana circulates verses to a lover and goes mad when they fail to have the desired effect (417–20). Steriamus gives Urania a book of verses to explain his decision to love her; circulating verses rationalize an act of inconstancy, a change of love-object (276). In Pelarina's narrative, a woman's loss of control over her manuscript is worse than the loss of her virginity; her lover's reading of her poems motivates her conversion to virtuous constancy and a pilgrimage to Jerusalem (453–54).

Notably, Pamphilia's poetic practice is altogether different; her first verses in the text are 'buried' almost as soon as she writes them (51–52). Later, when Antissia discovers Pamphilia's poem carved on a tree in her private garden, Pamphilia coyly argues that the poem does not refer to her own situation – that it has no publicly significant referentiality. Furthermore, at an important moment in book 3, Pamphilia refuses to recite her verses and instead tells the prose tale of Lindamira – 'faign[ed]' to be written in a French Story' and detailing the life of the anagrammatically related Ladimari Wroth. The story culminates in Lindamira's public dishonor: 'her honour not touched, but cast downe, and laid open to all mens toungs and eares, to be used as they pleas'd' (425). Public/ation – the 'laying open' and 'use' of a woman's narrative – is figured in sexual terms, and this discursive violation occurs at the very point in *Urania* where the autobiographical Lindamira, the narrator of Lindamira's story, and the narrator of *Urania* (Lady Mary?) become indistinguishable in a narrative which describes all three: Lindamira 'complain'd, which complaint, because I [Pamphilia] lik'd it, or rather found her estate so neere agree with mine, I put into Sonnets . . . ; for thus the Booke leaues her, the complaint is this diuided into seauen Sonnets' (425). Who is speaking in the final clause, and about which Booke? Lindamira's tale? the French Story? book 3 of *Urania*, which concludes with these poems?

This complex juncture of autobiography and fictions – centered on the public/ation of a woman's story – produces *Urania*'s only interpolated sonnet sequence. Pamphilia's transcription of Lindamira's complaint displaces the 'laying open' and making public of Pamphilia's own verses. However, unlike the explicit prose narration introducing it, the surrogate sequence is seemingly non-referential, a sustained inscription of emotion suggestive of *Pamphilia to Amphilanthus*. Once again sonnets are deployed as a withdrawal into a privatized discursive space – deployed against the making public, the circulation, of a woman's story.

4

To assert that Pamphilia figures an 'emergent female subject', is not, as that term suggests, to argue that a female subject rises fully constituted from these texts. Several Wroth critics have indeed discerned or assumed a full-fledged modern subjectivity in the sonnets. Roberts finds that 'Wroth analyzes . . . universal psychological conflicts', while Beilin argues that Wroth 'explores the psychology of woman's passion'. Both read the sonnets as unproblematic transcriptions of a 'state of mind' and make Wroth inappropriately our psychological, psychoanalyzable contemporary. Such arguments, like Carolyn Ruth Swift's attempt to locate a 'feminine consciousness' in *Urania*, are perhaps both canonic and essentialist. To posit 'universalist' psychological conflicts in the texts of a heretofore unacknowledged woman writer is to prepare her for entrance into a humanist great-books canon. To read for evidence of an essential female psychology is to read gender at the expense of history – rather than gender through/across history.[19] Instead – and here I am following and gendering Stephen Greenblatt's provocative formulation – I think we can read *Pamphilia to Amphilanthus* as a text which gestures toward and contests the very notion of female subjectivity – the eventual construction of which has made such psychological interpretations possible. Like so many Renaissance texts, Wroth's sonnets speak a language which seems simultaneously to invite and deny our reading Pamphilia as a humanist subject.[20]

In the context of a larger argument detailing the emergence of the subject of 'bourgeois culture', Francis Barker argues that in the early seventeenth century subjection 'does not properly involve subjectivity at all, but a condition in which place and articulation are defined . . . by incorporation in the body politic. . . .' As a part of the larger spectacle, the typical character in *Hamlet* (Barker's example) has meaning not through 'an interiorized, self-recognition', but through its acting of certain roles within a publicly displayed hierarchy. In contrast, the atypical Hamlet can insist on his own exception from this rule, announcing he has 'that/Within, which passeth show'. But as Barker notes, Hamlet's 'Within' is never articulated, is always deferred 'as a central obscurity which cannot be dramatized'. Because it is historically 'premature', an interiorized subjectivity is imagined 'outside the limits of the text-world in which it is as yet emergent only in a promissory form'.[21] *Pamphilia to Amphilanthus* shares important aspects of this formulation. Pamphilia voices a refusal to signify publicly and insists instead upon a private authenticity beyond/beneath the text. Likewise, she denounces the courtly theatricality that constructs meaning in the world around her. But (as in Barker's formulation) the subjectivity mapped 'in' Pamphilia is not only private but privative; the text figures it in terms of emptiness, lack, loss, and absence. *Pamphilia to Amphilanthus* clears a space for a nascent subject without articulating what it is that fills that emergent private space. Pamphilia, though constant to herself, is 'possesst' by 'absence' (45/P52).

But Pamphilia differs from Hamlet in the crucial matter of gender, and, as Catherine Belsey has persuasively argued, the construction of the male subject in this period was accomplished against a female Other.[22] The question then becomes: How did Wroth, writing in a culture which generally denied women a stable place from which to speak, negotiate the gendered positions of speech and silence to construct an emergent subject's voice? Part of the answer lies in Wroth's remarkable personal history. Descending from a line of prolific poets, as Hannay and Waller argue in their essays, she continued even after her marriage to be associated closely with the Sidney family name and its poetic heritage. Wroth's class position and illustrious family precursors served as an authorization to write and to be read; the *Urania* title page announces Wroth as 'Daughter to the right Noble Robert Earle of Leicester. And Neece to the ever famous, and renowned Sr. Phillips Sidney knight. And to ye most exelent Lady Mary Countesse of Pembroke. . . .' Furthermore, as Miller and Quilligan have argued, Wroth created at least one of her texts as reaction to and rewriting of her uncle's; her romance begins by turning his inside out, making articulate in *The Countesse of Mountgomeries Urania* the voice of a woman prominently silent in *The Countess of Pembroke's Arcadia*.[23]

Wroth works a similar transformation in *Pamphilia to Amphilanthus*. If 'Petrarchism is one of the discourses in which a recognizably modern mode of subjectivity . . . is first articulated and actively cultivated',[24] Wroth's sequence appropriates that discourse to map the position of a female subject. But, as the initial lines of the sequence make clear, she can attest to the emergence of this subjectivity only in terms of its lack: 'When nights black mantle could most darknes prove, / And sleepe deaths Image did my senceses hiere / From knowledg of my self. . . .' Finally, unlike the male subject constituted by the writing and circulation of verses within a courtly Petrarchan context, Wroth's female subjectivity is predicated on a refusal to circulate.

Speaking of the decades around 1600, Saunders has noted that 'there must have been widespread traffic (and perhaps marketing, white and black) in poetic manuscripts, and a large number of people must have prized and collected them' (521). Given what we have seen in the *Urania*, it seems no mere coincidence that Saunders's observation applies equally to poetic manuscripts and to women in Wroth's culture. At this intersection of bibliography and gender, we can read *Pamphilia to Amphilanthus* – both the 'external' and 'internal' evidence – as a suggestion that Wroth's control over and containment of her poetic manuscripts figures control over herself as a potentially trafficable woman. Recognizing the risks involved for women who (like Elizabeth Cary's Mariam) 'with publike voyce runne on',[25] Wroth seemingly constitutes her distinctively private female subjectivity against the traffic in both women and words.

Pamphilia, we remember, is 'the most silent and discreetly retir'd of any Princesse', and the word *discreet*, wonderfully resonant in this context, recurs in descriptions of her. In the early seventeenth century, spelling was only beginning to differentiate meanings we now separate into 'discreet' and 'discrete'; as the *OED*'s glosses suggest, both meanings apply to Pamphilia and to Wroth's writing:

> *discreet* Showing discernment or judgement in the guidance of one's
> own speech and action; . . . circumspect, cautious; often esp. that can
> be silent when speech would be inconvenient.
> *discrete* Separate, detached from others, individually distinct.

In an era before lexical standardization, a single word fuses the construction of a female subject – a woman 'separate, detached from others, individually distinct' – with one who withdraws from public discourse into 'circumspect', even 'silent' speech.

To discuss *Urania* and *Pamphilia to Amphilanthus* in a context of 'privacy' and non-circulating silence, however, elides one of the few definitive facts one can state about these texts: they were made public and did circulate in the elaborate folio *Urania* of 1621. Unfortunately, this is virtually the end of certainty when one speaks of the volume's publication. Strangely, *The Countesse of Mountgomeries Urania*, written by one prominent noblewoman and named for another, contains 'no dedicatory epistles, poems, or prefatory material', as Roberts notes. The narrative ends with a provocative 'And', and the sonnets appear in a separately paginated and signed section at the end. We do not know whether Wroth initiated, assisted, or otherwise participated in the volume's printing, and she is on record in a letter to the then Marquess of Buckingham as both opposing and supporting its publication.[26]

What, then, are we to make of the sonnets' appearance in this cryptically published, ambiguously public volume? The answer lies in the project I have outlined thus far. To insert oneself into Petrarchan discourse in order to register one's subject position and (simultaneously) to keep private the texts which construct that position is at best a mute gesture. Dis/course runs to and fro; by definition it circulates. More simply: if a woman writes in a forest (or garden) and no one reads her, has she written anything? Wroth, as a woman-writer, must resist publication as a form of male trafficking, yet that resistance can only register if it is made public. It is ironically appropriate, then, that Pamphilia marries not in the published *Urania* but in the unpublished continuation. Paradoxically, the published texts must announce their resistance to public/ation, in the multiple senses of the word; they stage their own privatization.

Wroth's letter to Buckingham carefully balances such concerns: 'I have with all care caused the sale of [my booke] to bee forbidden, and the books left to bee shut up, for thos that are abroad, I will likewise doe my best to gett them in, if itt will please your Lordship to procure mee the kings warrant to that effect, without which non will deliver them to mee, besids that your Lordship wilbe pleased to lett mee have that which I sent you . . . what I ame able to doe for the getting in of books (which from the first were solde against my minde I never purposing to have had them published) I will with all care, and diligence parforme.'[27] Within the confines of a single sentence Wroth says both that she never meant to publish the volumes and that she sent a presentation copy to one of the most public figures in the kingdom. Indeed, by requesting the king's warrant, Wroth injects the controversy into the very arena she elsewhere seems most eager to avoid. At the same time, she stages her anxieties about publication; to publish is to set meaning loose, to allow the possibility of 'strang constructions' circulating 'abroad'.

To be sure, there is ample evidence of male aristocrats protesting their unwillingness to engage in publication and circulation, but the situation for women goes far beyond gestures of mere reluctance. Lord Denny's verses to Wroth following *Urania*'s appearance illustrate exactly what a woman risked in publishing her work. His gender-specific attack ('leave idle bookes alone / For wise and worthyer women have writte none') portrays Wroth in precisely the ways she repudiates in the sonnets; a 'Hermophradite in show,' she becomes in his view a sexual and theatrical 'monster' – indiscreet (in both senses) and open to the view of 'all men'.[28] Denny's attack thus reproduces the perceived correspondences in the period between a woman's sexual transgressiveness, 'her linguistic "fulness" and her frequenting of public space'.[29] In writing to Buckingham, Wroth stages anxieties of publication in comparable spatial metaphors; the offending books – like Pamphilia herself in the sonnets and romance – she promises to 'shut up' and 'gett in'.

To argue that Wroth 'stages' anything at all in so vehemently antitheatrical a text as *Pamphilia to Amphilanthus* may seem contradictory. And yet it is this very anti-theatricality and self-enclosure which Wroth must dramatize in her construction of the authentic, articulate subject. Returning to sonnet 42/P48, 'If ever love had force in humaine brest?,' we see that the poem makes an exhibition of its privacy, demanding that the reader 'looke on mee'; however, the drama the reader witnesses is the demonstrative Petrarchan body interiorized: 'in humaine brest', 'in pensive hart', in 'the soule'. Like a soliloquy, this sonnet presents itself as interior discourse, all the while alluding to its public performance. The speaker likewise asserts in order to register submission, expressing what will come to be the condition of bourgeois subjectivity – a freeing of the self from exterior constraints which becomes, instead, a subjection in and to the self, the self in and under control: 'I, ame the soule that feeles the greatest smart; / I, ame that hartles trunk of harts depart / And I, that one, by love, and griefe oprest. . . .' Finally, the speaker obscures her own agency in the anti-theatrical drama she stages: 'I should nott have bin made this stage of woe / Wher sad disasters have theyr open showe.'

Wroth's sonnets thus demonstrate several points crucial to our understanding of subjectivity, genders, and writing in the Renaissance. To withdraw from 'the traffic in women' is to imagine the possibility of female subjectivity; likewise, to withdraw from the traffic in manuscripts – to exercise control over one's words – is to imagine the possibility of a voice of one's own, a speaking female subject. And yet, ironically, the subject's 'mastery' over her words and her self can only be acknowledged by in some measure relinquishing absolute privacy and control. If the subject is constituted in and through discourse, she must speak to exist. 'Soft said she, shall I turne blabb?' Publish or perish.[30]

Notes

1. See ROBERTS's stemma in *The Poems of Lady Mary Wroth* (Baton Rouge and London: Louisiana State University Press, 1983), p. 65, and Waller's stemma in his edition of *Pamphilia to Amphilanthus* (Salzburg: University of Salzburg, 1977), pp. 22–23; for the question of dating, also see Waller, p. 8.

2. ROBERTS, *Poems*, pp. 62, 19; Waller, *Pamphilia to Amphilanthus*, p. 8.

3. See J.W. SAUNDERS, 'From Manuscript to Print: A Note on the circulation of poetic MSS in the sixteenth century', *Proceedings of the Leeds Philosophical and Literary Society* (1951), 507–28; Margaret J.M. Ezell, *The Patriarch's Wife: Literary Evidence and the History of the Family* (Chapel Hill: University of North Carolina Press, 1987), ch. 3.

4. ROBERTS, *Poems*, pp. 44–46; see Elaine V. Beilin, *Redeeming Eve: Women Writers of the English Renaissance* (Princeton: Princeton University Press, 1987), ch. 8; Margaret [Witten-Hannah] McLaren, 'Lady Mary Wroth's *Urania*: The Work and the Tradition', Ph.D. diss., University of Auckland, 1978, p. 143; May N. Paulissen, 'The Love Sonnets of Lady Mary Wroth: A Critical Introduction', Ph.D. diss., University of Houston, 1976, p. 191. That the 1621 *Urania* volume prints much of what appears in the ms. as if it were a single sequence cannot be construed as Wroth's intention. Because it is more accessible than the Folger ms., I follow (somewhat reluctantly) other

essays in quoting from Roberts's edition, giving both Wroth's and Roberts's numbering. All emphases are mine. Roberts's copy-text in most cases is the ms., though it is important to note that she rearranges the ms. sonnets in the order of the 1621 printed text. She asserts that the 1621 ordering of the sonnets is authorially intended, but that other aspects of the printed text are not. Waller prints the 1621 text in the 1621 order. Sonnet order is not crucial to my argument; I merely wish to point out that no printed edition reproduces the unusual and significant arrangement of the ms.

5. FRANCIS BARKER, *The Tremulous Private Body: Essays on Subjection* (London: Methuen, 1984), p. 34.

6. ARTHUR F. MAROTTI, ' "Love is not Love". Elizabethan Sonnet Sequences and the Social Order', *English Literary History* 49 (1982), 399.

7. ROBERTS, *Poems*, p. 85. I am grateful to Ann Rosalind Jones for pointing out to me the more contextually consistent reading of this line: Venus orders Cupid to shoot Pamphilia's heart. I would note, however, that, as the *OED*'s entries for both 'shoot' and 'shut' suggest, the spelling 'shutt' signified prolifically in the period; I am proposing here a more inclusive reading that does not preclude the possibility that the word aligns Pamphilia's entry into a lover's discourse ('shoot') with her corporeal enclosure ('shut').

8. See also Ann Rosalind Jones, 'Designing Women: The Self as Spectacle in Mary Wroth and Veronica Franco' and Nona Fienberg, 'Mary Wroth and the Invention of Female Poetic Subjectivity', in Naomi J. Miller and Gary Waller (eds), *Reading Mary Wroth: Representing Alternatives in Early Modern England* (Knoxville: University of Tennessee Press, 1991).

9. BARKER, *Tremulous Body*, p. 14.

10. BARKER, *Tremulous Body*, p. 35. Given the resemblance to Hamlet's speech in the presence chamber, Wroth's appearance in Jonson's *Masque of Blackness*, and her later removal from court, a probable target of Pamphilia's denunciation is courtly display. For the courtly context of Petrarchan poetry, see Marotti, 'Love', and Louis Adrian Montrose, 'The Elizabethan Subject and the Spenserian Text', in *Literary Theory/Renaissance Texts*, ed. Patricia Parker and David Quint (Baltimore: Johns Hopkins University Press, 1986), pp. 303–40.

11. See ALAN HAGAR, 'The Exemplary Mirage: Fabrication of Sir Philip Sidney's Biographical Image and the Sidney Reader', *English Literary History* 48 (1981), 1–16. See also Naomi J. Miller, 'Rewriting Lyric Fictions: The Role of the Lady in Lady Mary Wroth's *Pamphilia to Amphilanthus*', in *The Renaissance Englishwoman in Print: Counterbalancing the Canon*, ed. Anne M. Haselkorn and Betty S. Travitsky (Amherst: University of Massachusetts Press, 1990), pp. 295–310.

12. See QUILLIGAN, 'The Constant Subject: Instability and Female Authority in Wroth's *Urania* Poems', in *Soliciting Interpretation: Literary Theory and Seventeenth-Century English Poetry*, ed. Elizabeth D. Harvey and Katharine Eisaman Maus (Chicago: University of Chicago Press, 1990), pp. 311–12; Montrose, 'Elizabethan Subject', p. 325; and Jones's and Fienberg's essays in Miller and Waller (eds), *Reading Mary Wroth*.

13. JOSEPHINE A. ROBERTS, 'The Biographical Problem of *Pamphilia to Amphilanthus'*, *Tulsa Studies in Women's Literature* 1 (1982), 43–53. Sonnet 9/ P71 seems to record four significant words from an addressee (Amphilanthus?): 'I must bee gone.'

14. QUILLIGAN, 'Constant Subject', p. 315.

15. PETER STALLYBRASS notes the association of enclosed gardens, the state, and the female monarch: see 'Patriarchal Territories: The Body Enclosed', in *Rewriting the Renaissance: The Discourses of Sexual Difference in Early Modern Europe*, ed. Margaret W. Ferguson, Maureen Quilligan, and Nancy J. Vickers (Chicago: University of Chicago Press, 1986), p. 129. Margreta de Grazia has suggested to me the similarity of Urania's 'contriu'd walkes', seventeenth-century gardens, and the 'labourinth' enclosing the speaker of Wroth's 'Crowne of Sonetts'.

16. Women who do circulate (geographically and sexually) are compared to ill-kept gardens. Nereana, who goes on an international 'Knightlike' quest for her beloved, is 'a garden [which], neuer so delicate when well kept under, will without keeping grow ruinous' [279].

17. QUILLIGAN, 'Constant Subject', pp. 322–23; see also Miller's essay, 'Engendering Discourse: Women's Voices in Wroth's *Urania* and Shakespeare's Plays', in Miller and Waller (eds), *Reading Mary Wroth*, pp. 154–72.

18. GAYLE RUBIN, 'The Traffic in Women: Notes on the "Political Economy" of Sex', in *Toward an Anthropology of Women*, ed. Rayna Reiter (New York: Monthly Review Press, 1975), pp. 157–210.

19. ROBERTS, 'Biographical Problem', p. 51; Beilin, *Redeeming Eve*, pp. 233, 236; Carolyn Ruth Swift, 'Feminine Identity in Lady Mary Wroth's Romance *Urania*', *English Literary Renaissance* 14 (1984), 328–46.

20. STEPHEN GREENBLATT, 'Psychoanalysis and Renaissance Culture', in Parker and Quint, *Literary Theory/Renaissance Texts*, 210–24.

21. BARKER, *Tremulous Body*, pp. 31, 36.

22. CATHERINE BELSEY, *The Subject of Tragedy: Identity and Difference in Renaissance Drama* (London: Methuen, 1985).

23. QUILLIGAN, 'Constant Subject', p. 310; Naomi J. Miller, ' "Not much to be marked": Narrative of the Woman's Part in Lady Mary Wroth's *Urania*', *Studies in English Literature* 29 (1989), 126–27.

24. MONTROSE, 'Elizabethan Subject', p. 325.

25. ELIZABETH CARY, *The Tragedie of Mariam, the faire Queene of Iewry*, ed. A.C. DUNSTAN (Oxford: Malone Society Reprints, 1914), sig. A3.

26. See ROBERTS, *Poems*, pp. 69–70.

27. ROBERTS, *Poems*, p. 236. There may be a public/private distinction within the realm of print itself. Donne writes: 'I am brought to a necessity of printing my Poems, and addressing them to my L. Chamberlain. This I mean to do forthwith; not for much publique view, but at mine owne cost, a few Copies.' See Arthur Marotti, 'John Donne and the Rewards of Patronage', in *Patronage in the Renaissance*, ed. Guy Fitch Lytle and Stephen Orgel (Princeton: Princeton University Press, 1981), p. 232.

28. ROBERTS, *Poems*, pp. 32–33.

29. STALLYBRASS, 'Patriarchal Territories', p. 127.

30. With clarifying criticism of this essay's early versions, Margreta de Grazia, Jay Grossman, and Wendy Wall have in important ways saved me from turning blabb, and I thank them.

2 'Yet Tell Me Some Such Fiction': Lady Mary Wroth's *Urania* and the 'Femininity' of Romance*

Helen Hackett

Helen Hackett's study of Wroth's prose romance *The Countess of Montgomery's Urania* addresses two issues that figure prominently in feminist criticism of women's writing: the consequences of a female author's intervention in a male-constructed genre, and the political implications of women's reading of 'escapist' romantic fiction. The former question, while it preoccupies many of the critics in this collection, is especially relevant to Wroth's engagement with a genre which, although it was widely construed as 'feminine', had hitherto been written exclusively by men. Hackett's essay is too historically grounded to claim that the interaction of woman writer and feminine romance radically transforms the genre's male heritage. Yet while Hackett underlines the ways in which Wroth's romance reproduces even the most misogynist conventions and values of male-authored romances, she also demonstrates that the *Urania* differs significantly from these texts, particularly in its representation of female authorship and of women's reading of romances as a source of autonomy, consolation and pleasure. Hackett comes to a more measured conclusion about the oppositional value of women's escape into romance fiction, an activity which in Wroth's own narrative is distinctly double-edged, offering a private emancipation which inevitably serves to perpetuate the existing social order.

In late sixteenth- and early seventeenth-century England, it seems to have been thought that romances were mainly read by women. There is evidence for this in the fact that numerous romances were dedicated to women and included authorial asides addressed to female readers; and in satirical or moralistic writings which held up women's taste for

---

* Reprinted from *Women, Texts and Histories, 1575–1760*, ed. Clare Brant and Diane Purkiss (London and New York: Routledge, 1992), pp. 39–68.

romance to ridicule or opprobrium.[1] Yet the authors of Elizabethan and Jacobean romances were men. The only known exceptions to this were *The Mirror of Knighthood*, translated from Spanish by Margaret Tyler in 1578; and *The Countess of Montgomery's Urania*, written by Lady Mary Wroth, in 1621. These texts, and especially the latter, are therefore of great interest as interventions by women into a form hitherto aimed at women as consumers, but closed to women as writers.

The Renaissance romance was usually a long work of prose fiction, with a highly digressive structure and a highly rhetorical style, concerning improbable events taking place in a fantastic realm. These romances often shared with the modern romantic novel a central concern with love and courtship; but they added to this a concern with chivalry and martial exploits, which, in some cases, was the main narrative theme.[2] Old-established chivalric romances like *Guy of Warwick* and *Bevis of Hampton* circulated among the lower classes in cut-down chap-book form; but most new romances were either dedicated to 'gentlewomen', or, like the *Arcadia*, originated at a courtly level, then filtered down through the gentry and trading and servant classes. The material discussed in this essay under the term 'Renaissance romance' belonged mainly to these aristocratic or bourgeois milieux.[3]

These class distinctions, as well as generally low literacy rates, meant that Renaissance romance differed from the modern romantic novel in that it did not possess a mass market of the size that exists today. However, it was perceived as catering to a growing and commercially important female audience, and resembled modern romantic fiction in being denigrated as a 'women's genre'. For example, Barnaby Rich's *Farewell to Military Profession*, 1581, a collection of romance-type stories, and John Lyly's *Euphues and his England*, 1580, both contained separate dedications to male and female readers. The dedications to women employ irony and a patronizing tone to imply an underlying disdain for this newly lucrative market, to which the author is stooping reluctantly, out of economic necessity. The assumption seems to be that female readers will take the barbed compliments in such dedications at face value, while male readers are more sophisticated and are therefore in on the author's joke. Male readers are addressed 'straight' in their own dedications, as the author's equals and colluders.[4]

Such use of dual dedications suggests that women were not the only readers of romances, but that a professed intention to write for women serves as an announcement to readers of both sexes that the work in question is light and frivolous: 'but a toy', as Lyly puts it; or, in Sir Philip Sidney's words, 'but a trifle, and that triflingly handled'.[5] [. . .]

However, despite such evidence of a dual audience, and the anecdotal nature of much evidence of reading habits, so far as we can tell women readers did indeed derive great enjoyment from romance in this period.

Caroline Lucas, drawing on theories of the reader's participation in the construction of the text, suggests that Renaissance women may have derived pleasure from romances *in spite of* the restrictive examples of virtuous femininity expounded in many of these texts, and the inherently oppressive nature of the relationship between narrator and reader which many of them construct, by actively reading them against the grain. She draws on recent studies of the modern romantic novel,[6] a genre which resembles Renaissance romance not only in that both have been perceived by the dominant cultures of their time as 'women's reading', of low aesthetic merit, but also in that both genres appear to have appealed to female readers because they offered fantasy and escapism. Louis B. Wright posits this resemblance in conventional sexist terms, when he writes that romances were popular with female readers then as now, 'Since women in general have never subscribed to realism.'[7] While differing considerably from Wright in identifying serious social reasons for this, feminist critics might agree that escapism has had a value for women over the centuries.

In Janice Radway's 1984 study of the avidly romance-reading women of Smithton, a suburban community of the American midwest, her subjects' descriptions of what they enjoyed or valued in romantic novels repeatedly employed the word 'escapism'. Radway discusses how far such escapism is inherently politically repressive, providing women with 'compensatory literature' which distracts them from the injustices of their social situations; and how far it might be politically oppositional, enabling them to 'absent' themselves from their husbands in a realm of self-absorbed pleasure.[8] It is interesting to compare this with Renaissance depictions of women as romance-readers, particularly when the women concerned hold subordinate social positions. In the 1615 edition of Sir Thomas Overbury's *Characters*, 'A Chamber-Mayde' is shown as follows:

> Shee reads *Greenes* works over and over, but is so carried away with the *Myrrour of Knighthood*, she is many times resolv'd to run out of her selfe, and become a Ladie Errant.[9]

Her running 'out of her selfe' is lightly amusing provided it remains merely a distraction and an act of the imagination; but there is a subtext of anxiety that fantasy might not be enough to satisfy her, that the adventurous roles of women in romance might influence her behaviour and encourage her to 'run out of' her socially determined role. Such reading is therefore pre-emptively mocked as over-literal and naïve. The creation of a private female imaginative space has advantages for the patriarchal order, as long as it is marginalized as fantasy and delimited from 'real life'.

An anxiety that enjoyment of romance might lead to non–conformity and disobedience is more openly put in Thomas Powell's *Tom of All Trades. Or The Plaine Path-way to Preferment*, 1631. He gives the following advice on the bringing up of middle-class daughters:

> In stead of Song and Musicke, let them learne Cookery and Laundrie. And in stead of reading Sir *Philip Sidneys Arcadia*, let them read the grounds of good huswifery. I like not a female Poetresse at any hand.[10]

Both gender and class are at issue here: Powell is writing for the trading and professional classes, and he sees such arty pursuits as reading the *Arcadia* and writing poetry as the preserve of 'greater personages', not appropriate for 'a private Gentlemans Daughter'. The reading of romances, and, even more threateningly, literary creation by a woman, are feared as implying aspiration and autonomy, and deviation from the middle-class wife's 'proper' activities of attention and domestic service to a man.

Powell's fears that the female reader might grow into that even more threatening figure, the 'female Poetresse',[11] are striking in that they seem so ungrounded. Although romances were consistently aimed at female readers, by the date of Powell's writing (1631) hardly any of those readers had been fired to create their own romantic reading matter, at least not in published form. This was despite the fact that, besides the apparent existence of a sizeable female readership, romance seems to have been regarded as 'feminine' in other, more metaphoric ways. Patricia Parker has discussed how the 'dilation' of romance, its digressiveness and diffusiveness, were associated by Renaissance writers with the supposed garrulity and irrationality of women, and with the seductive dangers of female sexuality.[12] Roger Ascham, for instance, condemned 'fond books, of late translated out of Italian into English, sold in every shop in London', as being full of 'the enchantments of Circe';[13] they are distrusted as leading the masculine will astray into prodigal paths of pleasure. This was true not only for the male reader, but also for the male writer. Authors like Rich and Lyly in the dedications discussed above imply that they are effeminized and degraded by their excursion into romance. Sidney, for his part, seems virtually to step into female disguise with his hero:

> thus did Pyrocles become Cleophila – which name for a time hereafter I will use, for I myself feel such compassion of his passion that I find even part of his fear lest his name should be uttered before

fit time were for it; which you, fair ladies that vouchsafe to read this, I doubt not will account excusable.[14]

The phrase 'I will use' is ambiguous, and can suggest that, in entering the domain of 'fair ladies', an enchanted, enclosed circle where love, courtship and courtliness are chief concerns, the male author performs an act of literary transvestism. It is an effeminization which, it could be argued, is creative and liberating for Sidney, but is represented by Rich and others as a degrading dilution of manhood.

Within Renaissance prose fictions, story-telling was often the role of women. In Gascoigne's *The Adventures of Master F.J.*, Dame Pergo and Dame Frances both tell stories of the uneven course of love as part of the courtly game of *questioni d'amore*.[15] Greene's *Penelope's Web* was a sequence of tales told by Penelope and her nurse and maids as they unravel by night the work she had done on her web by day. The 'endlesse' labour of the web is identified with the 'prattle' by which the loquacious company of women 'beguyle the night'. The unweaving of the web becomes identified with the unwinding of the tales, representing both as women's work: Ismena, one of the maids, is shown 'applying as well her fingers to the web as her tongue to the tale'; and later the other women listen to Penelope, 'setting their hands to the Web, and their eares to hir talke'.[16] Outside fiction, there is evidence of the participation of women of all classes in oral narrative traditions, including the telling of folk-tales, fairy-tales, and bawdy jokes and stories, and the singing of ballads, often at the centre of a circle of listeners and co-participants.[17] The association of rambling or fantastical tales with female tellers persists in the proverbial expression 'an old wives' tale', current in the sixteenth century as now.[18] Yet, despite all these conditions which might have favoured female authorship of romance, it appears that no woman in England took on the role until Margaret Tyler's translation of *The Mirror of Knighthood*, published in 1578. Even then, she was the translator of the work of a male Spanish author, rather than the originator of the text.

Tyler's translation was highly successful and influential. Before it appeared, continental chivalric romances had been little known in England, but it set a trend, including numerous sequels to *The Mirror of Knighthood* itself, produced by other Spanish authors and English translators. It is cited in many of the satirical representations of women as romance-readers: it is the very text which inspired the chambermaid in Overbury's *Characters* to become 'a lady errant'.[19] Tyler's epistle to the reader[20] has become well-known among students of early modern women's writing, partly for its enjoyably feisty tone, but also because it poses exactly the question which occurs to the modern critic, namely:

if women were the main readers of romances, why did they not write them? Tyler writes,

> And if men may & do bestow such of their travailes upon gentlewomen, then may we women read such of their works as they dedicate unto us, and if we may read them, why not farther wade in them to the serch of a truth. And then much more why not deale by translation in such arguments, especially this kinde of exercise being a matter of more heede then of deep invention or exquisite learning.

She asserts, 'my perswasion hath bene thus, that it is all one for a woman to pen a story, as for a man to address his storie to a woman'.

Yet within the very terms she uses to assert the legitimacy of her role as writer, Tyler proffers some clues as to why other women might have been deterred from emulating her. First, it is notable that she only recommends the translation of books by women; this is acceptable and/or achievable by them because it only requires 'heede', carefulness, rather than 'deep invention or exquisite learning', creative powers or erudition. Second, she finds it necessary to defend her choice of a chivalric romance as her text for translation, which might be regarded as unfeminine material:

> Such delivery as I have made I hope thou wilt friendly accept, the rather for that it is a womans woork, though in a story prophane, and a matter more manlike then becommeth my sexe.

And third, Tyler feels obliged to defend her choice of a secular genre, in a period when the only genre which appears to have been socially sanctioned for women writers was the devotional.[21] She writes,

> But amongst al my il willers, some I hope are not so straight that they would enforce mee necessarily either not to write or to write of divinitie. Whereas neither durst I trust mine own judgement sufficiently, if matter of controversy were handled, nor yet could I finde any booke in the tongue which would not breed offence to some.

Tyler ingeniously employs a modesty *topos*, disclaiming the ability to meddle in religious matters. As with her recommendation of translation as a female activity, she is careful to circumscribe the radicalism of her stance with reassuringly conventional qualifications. Even so, she goes on to make a forceful assertion that romance-reading has moral value: it is pleasure seasoned with 'profitable reading', and the reader will find in her story 'the just reward of mallice & cowardise, with the good speed of honesty & courage'.

It seems clear that female authors were deterred from writing romance because it was seen as morally dubious. The notion of romance as a feminine genre was thus riddled with paradox. Romance was construed as feminine in that it was lightweight, not serious, the sort of thing women were assumed to enjoy; but because it was lightweight it was also morally disreputable, and therefore not fit for women to write. Thus women were fed with romance as consumers, while being simultaneously castigated for accepting it, and categorically excluded from its manufacture.

The Countess of Montgomery's Urania was, so far as we know, the first published romance in English which was authored by a woman. Lady Mary Wroth was the daughter of Sir Philip Sidney's brother Robert; she was born in 1586 or 1587, and married Robert Wroth in 1604. In her early adulthood she played a prominent part in court life: she danced twice before Elizabeth I, and she seems to have enjoyed the favour of Anne of Denmark, with whom she performed among other ladies in *The Masque of Blackness* in 1605. However, in 1614 Robert Wroth died, leaving his widow with enormous debts from which she never fully recovered. Her social as well as financial status now went into decline, and she seems to have fallen from her central place at court. She became involved in a long-running affair with her cousin, William Herbert, the third Earl of Pembroke, by whom she had two illegitimate children. Herbert was both married and notorious at court for his promiscuity.[22]

It was during this less fortunate period of her life that Wroth wrote the *Urania*. The published volume contains a romance in four books, 558 pages long, followed by a sonnet sequence. The central narrative thread is the love of Pamphilia for Amphilanthus, and her constancy in the face of his inconstancy. Amphilanthus' name, we are told, means 'the lover of two',[23] and we are shown Pamphilia's heroic patience as he repeatedly deserts her for chivalric quests and other mistresses. It was published in 1621, also the date of a new edition of Sir Philip Sidney's *Arcadia*. The *Arcadia* by now was an established best-seller, and it may have been that Wroth, or her publisher, hoped to cash in on its success by presenting the *Urania* as a companion volume.[24] Certainly Wroth's Sidney identity was hammered home on the title-page:

The Countesse of Mountgomeries URANIA. Written by the right honorable the Lady MARY WROATH. Daughter to the right Noble Robert Earle of Leicester. And Neece to the ever famous, and re:nowned Sr. Phillips Sidney knight. And to the most exelent Lady Mary Countesse of Pembroke late deceased.

51

It may be that Wroth's Sidney credentials gave her a confidence unavailable to other women writers, since she could lay claim to a legitimate identity as an author of romance as Sidney's literary heir.

However, the Sidney name did not protect Wroth from scandal. The *Urania* was widely construed as a *roman-à-clef* whose characters were based on Wroth's friends and acquaintances at court. In particular, Edward Denny, Baron of Waltham, was convinced that one of the *Urania*'s many sub-narratives was a slander upon himself and his family. An arranged marriage had taken place between Denny's daughter, Honora, and Lord James Hay, one of James I's favourites. When she was found to have continued an existing love affair after her marriage, Denny had threatened to kill her. Wroth's story of Sirelius was almost identical to this in its events, and it described the father as 'a phantastical thing, vaine as Courtiers, rash as mad-men, & ignorant as women' (p. 439). There was an exchange of bitterly sarcastic letters between Denny and Wroth, and, although Wroth vehemently denied any intended reference to the Denny family, their standing at court obliged her to withdraw all copies of the *Urania* a few months after its publication. Even so, twenty-seven copies are known to have survived.[25] Wroth also continued the story in manuscript, in a sequel of another two books.[26]

Although this scandal did not arise specifically from the supposed impropriety of a woman's writing a romance, such terms did enter Denny's attack on Wroth. His first letter to her contains some biting verses, which open, 'Hermophradite in show, in deed a monster/As by thy words and works all men may conster.' In his desire to retaliate against his perceived injury, Denny evidently finds easy ground in the assertion that Wroth's act of authorship was unfeminine and unnatural, and seems able to assume that his peer group, the Jacobean court, will concur. His verses conclude 'leave idle bookes alone/For wise and worthyer women have writte none.' Wroth's invocation on her title-page of her illustrious female literary forebear, the Countess of Pembroke, famous for her religious translations, is made to rebound on her by Denny: he urges her to 'repent you of so many ill spent yeares of so vaine a booke', and to:

> redeeme the tym with writing as large a volume of heavenly layes and holy love as you have of lascivious tales and amorous toyes that at the last you may followe the rare, and pious example of your vertuous and learned Aunt.[27]

Denny suppresses the fact that the Countess, as the dedicatee of the *Arcadia*, was also famous as a connoisseur of romance.[28] He perpetuates the view that, whereas religious writing by women was socially respectable, and women's reading of romance was a social fact, female authorship of romances was unfitting and immoral.

Despite Wroth's heated denials of any intention of personal reference to Denny, the story of Sirelius was uncannily close to recent Denny family history, and it is hard to resist the conclusion that the *Urania* was indeed a *roman-à-clef*. Other contemporaries who construed it as such included John Chamberlain, who reported that many people at court believed that Wroth 'takes great libertie or rather licence to traduce whom she please'; and George Manners, seventh Earl of Rutland, who, in a letter of 1640 to his 'noble cosin', very probably Wroth, seems to ask for authorial confirmation of his attempt to draw up a key:

> heere meetinge with your Urania I make bold to send this enclosed and begg a favor from you that I may read with more delight. If you please to interprete unto me the names as heere I have begunn them, wherein you shall much oblige me.[29]

There are numerous analogies between events and personages in the fiction and events and personages in the Sidney and Herbert families and at court. [. . .]

Beyond the title-page, there are numerous other details which keep Wroth's Sidney literary heritage in view. For instance, the romance opens with the appearance of the shepherdess Urania, possibly filling in the suggestive narrative absence which opens the revised *Arcadia*, where Claius and Strephon lament the fact that Urania is lost; and it ends, like the revised *Arcadia*, in broken mid-sentence. The inclusion of a sonnet sequence looks back to a form which, by 1621, was out of fashion and was associated with the Elizabethan period, and specifically with Philip Sidney's *Astrophil and Stella*.[30] Wroth's Sidney lineage is clearly important to her not only in legitimating her act of authorship, but also in defining generic conventions for her writing. Yet at the same time she appropriates and adapts Sidneian traditions in ways related to her gender. For instance, the sonnet sequence, entitled 'Pamphilia to Amphilanthus', innovates in being addressed from a woman to a man.[31] The full title of the whole volume, *The Countess of Montgomery's Urania*, is clearly imitative of Sidney's full title, *The Countess of Pembroke's Arcadia*, but with the significant difference that Wroth's book is dedicated to a woman by a woman, placing writer and reader on a level.[32] It is notable that Wroth's narrative voice is never explicitly gendered; though she sometimes steps forward to make authorial comment, and frequently exhibits sympathy with female characters, she never steps forward to identify herself overtly as female. Apart from the dedication, her audience is not explicitly gendered either; we do not find in the *Urania* Sidney's chivalrous asides to 'fair ladies', nor the patronizing or flirtatious addresses to their female readers of other male authors of romance. The relationship between author and reader in the *Urania* is an unusually asexual one.

Wroth was influenced by *The Faerie Queene, Orlando Furioso,* and other romances besides the *Arcadia*.[33] She was writing within a genre whose conventions had hitherto been shaped by male writers – yet one of those conventions was a concept of romance as 'feminine'. What happens, then, when a woman writer enters this 'feminine' genre, stepping into an already feminized authorial role? Does it produce a text which evinces a strongly feminine point of view? – perhaps, even, an early feminist text?

The contextual evidence which we have already considered indicates that Wroth's authorship was in itself a radical act. It is tempting on these grounds alone to lay claim to Wroth as a proto-feminist. Carolyn Ruth Swift is one critic who has sought a distinctively female and feminist consciousness in Wroth's works: she asserts that the theme of the *Urania* is that 'society limited women unreasonably and harmed them in the process'. In her view, Wroth's characters 'embody their author's awareness of real societal injustice to women'.[34] Maureen Quilligan, while acknowledging that we might have anachronistic expectations of the *Urania,* reads it as being primarily a critique of 'the traffic in women', the exchange of women in marital alliances by patriarchal authorities, whether fathers or brothers, which acts as the 'cultural glue' between men.[35] [. . .]

We may wish to read the *Urania* as an exposé of the patriarchal iniquities of Jacobean aristocratic society, but in doing so we are deploying a consciousness which Wroth may not share. The *Urania* is certainly concerned with women's sufferings; but the cause to which these are most often attributed is not patriarchal oppression, but men's inconstancy. This inconstancy is presented as a timeless and irremediable feature of male nature. Although women's sufferings are shown to be inflicted by men, they are not given an explicitly political interpretation or blamed on a particular social system. In Book III, a lady advises Amphilanthus' latest mistress:

> take heed brave Lady, trust not too much; for believe it, the kindest, lovingst, passionatest, worthiest, loveliest, valliantest, sweetest, and best man, will, and must change, not that he, it may bee, doth it purposely, but tis their naturall infirmitie, and cannot be helped.
>
> (p. 375)

There is radicalism here in the contradiction of the usual stereotypical association of fickleness with femininity; but in this ahistorical world of romance, the possibility of change or reform is not addressed. In the

Urania's own terms, women's chief remedy for the suffering inflicted upon them by men is to develop noble resignation and self-sufficiency, which is what Pamphilia does.[36]

However, even if the *Urania* is not an explicitly political social critique, this very representation of Pamphilia's self-sufficiency does open possibilities for a new, though limited, form of female autonomy. Pamphilia is determined to keep her love a secret, even, at first, from Amphilanthus. This secret is something which she prizes and takes pride in; as a possession which is hers alone, it gives her a sense of identity. She habitually resorts to deserted forests or her private chamber to muse upon her love; to a great extent, her primary affective relationship is with her own emotions, abstracted and held up to regard, rather than with Amphilanthus. Most importantly, Pamphilia derives not only a sense of selfhood, but also creative power from her secret passion: reading and, more significantly, writing figure largely as private forms for her emotional expression.

In her solitary wanderings in the woods, Pamphilia is frequently moved to carve sonnets on the bark of trees, a motif which alludes to the frequent inscribing of poems on natural objects in the *Arcadia*. But reading and writing specifically by female characters is of particular importance in the *Urania* as demarcating a private female space. For instance, in Book I, Pamphilia retires to her chamber alone to 'breath out her passions, which to none shee would discover'. She goes to bed,

> taking a little Cabinet with her, wherein she had many papers, and setting a light by her, began to reade them, but few of them pleasing her, she took pen and paper, and being excellent in writing, writ these verses following.
>
> (p. 51)

Here female reading engenders female writing, and both provide a private and autonomous space for Pamphilia's free and unconstrained expression of her emotions. Later, when Pamphilia and Amphilanthus declare their mutual affection, their companions leave them and they go 'into the next roome, which was a Cabinet of the Queenes, where her bookes and papers lay; so taking some of them, they passed a while in reading of them' (p. 217). Their love is consummated by Pamphilia's admittance of Amphilanthus to her private literary domain.

The incident reveals not only the prevalent literariness of the *Urania*, but also the importance in the text of the selective disclosure of secrets and the selective admission of chosen individuals to private spaces. Pamphilia takes on agency as a writer, and as arbiter of the boundary between concealment and revelation. In this the inner themes of the text mirror its outward form, as a female-authored *roman-à-clef*.

A secret which is completely secret can have no value; it is through its partial disclosure that it becomes powerful, just as the factual referents behind a *roman-à-clef* must be concealed but also partly revealed for it to have any force.[37]

In so far as Pamphilia's pride in her secrecy, and her literary pursuits, provide a model of female authority and self-expression, it is one which is circumscribed, fully enabled only in chambers and cabinets, in isolation from society. In her presentation of women's public roles, Wroth conforms with seventeenth-century prescriptions of silence as a feminine virtue. In public, Pamphilia is 'generally the most silent and discreetly retir'd of any Princesse' (p. 50). At the beginning of Book I, Perissus describes his visit to his mistress Limena and her family:

> Being there ariv'd ... her Father, a grave and wise man, discoursed with mee of businesse of State: after him, and so all supper time, her husband discoursed of hunting.... Neither of these brought my Mistris from a grave, and almost sad countenance, which made me somewhat feare, knowing her understanding, and experience, able and sufficient to judge, or advise in any matter we could discourse of: but modestie in her caus'd it, onely loving knowledge, to be able to discerne mens understandings by their arguments, but no way to shew it by her owne speech.
>
> (pp. 6–7)

This positive evaluation of feminine modesty and discretion is reinforced by the depiction of countertypes to Pamphilia. One of these in Antissia, who believes herself to be Amphilanthus' mistress when the story opens, but is abandoned by him for Pamphilia. Antissia suffers from bouts of emotional confusion, when she is 'a meere Chaos, where unfram'd, and unorder'd troubles had tumbled themselves together without light of Judgement, to come out of them' (p. 95 [numbered 85]). Intrinsic to Pamphilia's admirability as a heroine is her ability to govern her emotions; indeed, images of government are frequently employed, translating her public authority as a queen into a metaphor for her private self-control (e.g. pp. 188, 398). Antissia, on the other hand, eventually goes mad in the manuscript continuation of the *Urania*, and in her madness she produces raving and rambling poetry, in direct contrast with Pamphilia's elegant versifyings.[38]

A further countertype to Pamphilia is Nereana, who is in love with Steriamus, who in turn is unrequitedly in love with Pamphilia. Nereana makes the long journey to Pamphilia's father's court to inspect her rival. After being received there, she wanders in the woods, but, unlike Pamphilia who derives calm and solace from her solitary musings, Nereana drives herself into a frenzied rage. The main feature of her character is pride and a lack of self-knowledge, 'all good thoughts wholy bent to her owne flattery'; she therefore rails at others whom she blames for her predicament. She loses herself in the woods, and this is linked metaphorically to her emotional confusion and lack of self-direction. She encounters Allanus, a shepherd turned mad by love, who decides she is the goddess of the woods, ties her to a tree, and dresses her up in buskins and a quiver. This incenses her still further, and when she then encounters a knight, Philarchos, who assumes from her outlandish appearance that she is a madwoman and scorns her, she becomes almost wild with fury. This is presented as a highly comic scene: the more pompously Nereana, in her ridiculous costume, asserts her regal identity, the more Philarchos is convinced of her madness (pp. 164–8). Swift misses the comic tone of the episode:

> Wroth recognizes that Nereana is mad mainly in the eyes of an unreasonable world. . . . In the story of Nereana, women are justly angry at being idolized as women and then rejected when they use the wisdom for which they are revered.[39]

But if the story is read in context and with attention to the narrator's tone, it is clear that Nereana is being satirized for her pride and lack of emotional control, and is shown as receiving poetic justice.

The latter reading is supported by the beginning of the episode, Pamphilia's reception of Nereana at her father's court. She tells her,

> in truth I am sorry, that such a Lady should take so great and painefull a voyage, to so fond an end, being the first that ever I heard of, who took so Knight-like a search in hand; men being us'd to follow scornefull Ladies, but you to wander after a passionate, or disdainefull Prince, it is great pitie for you. Yet *Madam*, so much I praise you for it, as I would incourage you to proceede.
>
> (p. 163)

She tells Nereana that since she has no use for Steriamus' love, Nereana is welcome to it. Pamphilia is subtly mocking Nereana for taking on the inappropriate role of a 'lady errant', like the chambermaid in the 1615 *Characters*. This is confirmed by Nereana's reaction:

> These words were spoken so, as, though proud *Nereana* were nettled with them, yet could she not in her judgement finde fault openly with them, but rather sufferd them with double force to bite, inwardly working upon her pride-fild heart, and that in her eyes she a little shewed, though she suffered her knees somewhat to bow in reverence to her.
>
> (p. 163)

Pamphilia's speech is later referred back to by the narrator, who describes Nereana as 'exercising the part of an adventurous lover, as *Pamphilia* in jest had call'd her' (p. 165).

The 'double force' felt by Nereana is irony: just as Pamphilia only expresses her feelings freely in private, so, in public, she discreetly conceals her true opinion behind a veil of irony, at once saying and not saying, using its double-edged sword in cutting fashion without breaching the social code of feminine decorum. Thus irony, like private versifying, is presented in the *Urania* as a legitimate though circumscribed means of female expression. Indeed, it is frequently employed by the narrator, especially at the expense of male inconstancy, and, in particular, Amphilanthus. When a lady named Luceania declares her love for him, we are told that he is 'rather sorrie, then [i.e. than] glad', being pledged to Pamphilia; but he acquiesces out of chivalry: 'considering gratefulnesse is required as a chiefe vertue in everie worthie man. . . . Hee kindly entertain'd her favours, and courteously requited them.' We are left in no doubt that he does not find this duty to the knightly code particularly onerous (p. 136). Later, the narrator exclaims, '*Amphilanthus* I pittie thee . . . for inconstancy, was, and is the onely touch [i.e. fault] thou hast, yet can I not say, but thou art constant to love; for never art thou out of love' (p. 312). Just as Pamphilia uses 'double force' against Nereana, so the narrator frequently uses the form of compliment for teasing criticism of her hero.

In the mockery of Nereana for adopting the role of 'lady errant', Wroth reinforces stereotypical notions of appropriate masculine and feminine roles. There are other points in the narrative where women who appropriate masculine public roles are viewed with unease; in Book III, for instance, we encounter: 'a brave Lady, more manly in her demeanour, and discourse, then the modestest of her sexe would venture to be, and so much that fashion affected her, as she was a little too unlike a well governed Lady' (p. 351). Yet Pamphilia is sometimes praised for her 'brave and manlike spirit' (p. 483), when masculinity is being equated simply with emotional strength. There are places where Wroth seems anxious to revise feminine stereotypes, especially in the way she holds up women's private strengths for admiration. A knight describes his encounter with a bride whose lover has been slain:

You will say, she wept, tore her haire, rent her clothes, cri'd, sobd, groand; No, she did not thus, she onely imbraced him, kissed him, and with as deadly a palenesse, as death could with most cunning counterfeit, and not execute, She entreated me to conduct her to the next Religious house, where shee would remaine till she might follow him. I admird her patience, but since more wonder'd at her worth.

(p. 36)

Yet strength continues to be equated with masculinity, and weakness with femininity, sometimes producing paradox: Urania – a woman – forcefully urges Perissus – a man – to action, saying, 'Leave these teares, and woman-like complaints' (p. 13).

Swift rightly advises that we should not 'be antagonized by a woman writer's acceptance of the word "masculine" as synonymous with "strong" and "feminine" with "weak"'.[40] We must acknowledge the ideological and generic constraints upon Wroth's discourse, some of which she strains against, others of which she reproduces. For a modern feminist reader, one of the most problematic ways in which Wroth appears merely to reproduce conventions constructed by male authors is in the operation of the gaze in the *Urania*. Laura Mulvey has shown how, in traditional narrative cinema, a 'scopophilic' gaze operates, a 'determining male gaze', shared between male characters, camera and audience, which subordinates female characters and reduces them to a state of '*to-be-looked-at-ness*'. At the same time, the objectified woman is threatening, connoting castration, so that the feminine image is either fetishized, or subjected to sadistic voyeurism.[41] Nancy Vickers and Patricia Parker have shown that this model of the male gaze can be illuminating when applied to Renaissance texts, particularly those which use the blazon. They argue that the blazon, in analogy to the objectification of woman in narrative cinema, has less to do with the representation of women than with discursive display by a male speaker to a male audience.[42]

This model of the 'male gaze' creates problems in reading work like Wroth's. Though she is a woman writer, working in a genre of which a significant proportion of the readership was female, she introduces blazons at several points in the *Urania*'s narrative. One example is the Forest Knight's vision of Melasinda, the distressed Queen of Hungary: it runs through the conventional catalogue of hair, face, eyes, lips, a neck like marble and breasts like snow (p. 64). It is difficult to reconcile this with a concept of the workings of the male gaze as an exchange between male describer and audience. This is illustrated even more vividly in the representation of Limena. Limena is in love with Perissus, but her husband, Philargus, discovers this fact, and determines to kill her. [. . .]

Just as Philargus was about to kill Limena, Perissus burst in. He describes what happened next:

> then untying a daintie embrodered wastcoate; see here, said she, the breast, (and a most heavenly breast it was) which you so dearely loved, or made me thinke so, calling it purest warme snow . . . but now 'tis ready to receive that stroake, shall bring my heart blood, cherish'd by you once, to dye it. . . . Whether these words, or that

sight (which not to be seene without adoring) wrought most I knowe not, but both together so well prevaile as hee stood in a strange kind of fashion.

(p. 11)

This is a narrative act of voyeurism, which can be interpreted in terms of Mulvey's discussion of scopophilia as described above. The admiring focus on the breast is fetishization; while, at the same time, the imagined scene of the white breast stained with red blood invokes sadism. Both male responses to the threat of the female body seem to be in play here, although the physical outbreak of sadism is delayed by the paralysing and stupefying sight of the breast. This hiatus in the onslaught of male-inflicted violence ties in with Vickers's and Parker's discussions of the erotic display of the female body as creating a stasis which is disempowering for the male onlooker, and which he defensively shatters by turning violence against the female body, such as in Petrarch's conversion of the destruction of Actaeon into the descriptive dismemberment of Diana, and the destruction of Acrasia and the Bower of Bliss in *The Faerie Queene*.[43]

When Limena's story is picked up again later, the narrator describes the spectacle of a woman, as yet unnamed, whom a man has stripped to the waist and tied to a pillar by her hair to whip her (p. 68). These figures are identified as Limena and Philargus; Limena is rescued, then continues the narrative herself:

When I had put of all my apparell but one little Petticote, he opened my breast, and gave me many wounds, the markes you may here yet discerne, (letting the Mantle fall againe a little lower, to shew the cruell remembrance of his crueltie).

(p. 71)

Here we have the figure of a woman, in a woman-authored text, who tantalizingly invites our gaze upon her body, marked by male sadism, as an erotic object. The male gaze is supposed to operate by the collusion of a male audience in the erotic objectification of the female body by male characters in a male-authored text; but, here, such a gaze is shown to operate when a female character in a female-authored text describes herself to a largely female readership. E. Ann Kaplan has asked whether, in film, the gaze as an instrument of power might be by its very nature inherently and inevitably male, and her questions and conclusions seem relevant here:

Perhaps we can ... say that in locating herself in fantasy in the erotic, the woman places herself as either passive recipient of male desire, or, at one remove, positions herself as *watching* a woman who is

passive recipient of male desires and sexual actions.... The gaze
is not necessarily male (literally), but to own and activate the gaze,
given our language and the structure of the unconscious, is to be in
the male position.[44]

These examples of the male gaze in the *Urania* illustrate the
internalization by a female author of ways of seeing and representing
which are associated with masculine sexuality. Here is another
limitation upon the 'female consciousness' to be found in Wroth's
romance.

However, alongside these instances where Wroth writes 'as a man',
deploying a male or masculine gaze in ways which are oppressive to
her own sex, there are other ways in which the gaze operates in the
Urania. There are numerous episodes where an exchange of gazes,
especially between female characters, marks an epiphanic moment
of revelation and mutual affirmation. In Book II, Mellissea, a benign
sorceress, prophesies their future fate to Pamphilia and her closest
friend, Urania. Afterwards, 'they both stood gazing in each others face,
as if the shining day Starre had stood still to looke her in a glasse'.
Amphilanthus, who is with them, is excluded from this moment of
revelation and mutual female reflection: in characteristically cavalier
fashion, he forestalls Mellissea's attempt to prophesy to him: 'Nay, say
no more, cry'd he, this is enough, and let me this enjoy, Ile feare no ills
that Prophesies can tell' (p. 160). In a later episode, the shepherdess
Veralinda is wandering, lamenting the loss of her love when she
encounters a nymph of Diana, Leonia, who is also bemoaning her lost
love. Again, a bond of similitude and empathy between them is sealed
by a gaze. Veralinda has eyes 'so full of love, as all loving creatures
found a power in them to draw them to her call'. Leonia's eyes 'full
of teares were seeing themselves in the streame, shewing their watry
pictures to each other'. But her gaze is drawn by Veralinda's, and
the quest for solace in a reflection is redirected to her. They resolve
to live together and return to Veralinda's home, 'the Shepheard[es]s
passionately beholding *Leonia* in memory of her love, and the Nimph
amorously gazing on her in her owne passions' (pp. 369–72).

In these examples, the exchange of gazes between women provides
emotional solace and affirms their sense of self. It is analogous to
another sort of visual pleasure identified by Mulvey, drawing on
Lacan's description of the 'mirror stage' in infant development: that
of identification with the image seen, which operates as a superior,
perfected mirror-image, an ideal ego.[45] There is a further example
in Pamphilia's encounter with another nymph of Diana, Allarina.
Pamphilia and her ladies are hunting when they come across Allarina
bathing in a stream, with her quiver and bow on the bank. Allarina

tries to hide herself, but Pamphilia reassures her that she is no Actaeon: 'Sweete Nimph bee not thus dismaid, wee are none such as will give cause of any harme to you; wee are your friends, and following the sport which you oft do.' In an all-female company, the gaze does not intrude or engender violence; instead, it engenders empathy and communion. Like the confrontation between the male gaze and the female body, this encounter creates stasis, and Allarina is momentarily dumbstruck: 'when I did see you first I was amas'd'. But this is the stasis not of a disempowerment of the intratextual viewer which provokes defensive violence, but of wonder and revelation; as for Lacan's infant, visual recognition is the moment preceding language. Pamphilia, in drawing attention to the fact that she is hunting, indicates her likeness to the nymph; Allarina in turn confides that she has often secretly watched Pamphilia when she was hunting. Their mutual gaze encapsulates a mutual fascination and identification. The obvious echo of the myth of Diana and Actaeon makes this episode a direct all-female revision of the operation of the male gaze, converting its dominance and violence to peaceful reciprocity.

Allarina explains to Pamphilia that, having been abandoned by a faithless lover, she has 'wedded my selfe to chast *Dianas* life', changed her name to Silviana, and embraced solitude and self-reliance: 'I love my selfe, my selfe now loveth me.' The parallels between her and Pamphilia are evident, but she has gone further in achieving a complete renunciation of love, for which Pamphilia admires her. Her story presents a striking and positive example of total female autonomy (pp. 181 [numbered 281]–8). However, Wroth does not leave the story here. Over two hundred pages later, Pamphilia returns to Silviana's country, eager to see her again, only to find to her dismay that Silviana has reverted to her persona of Allarina and is getting married. Her explanation is simply that her old lover returned to her, which reduces her earlier dedication to chastity to mere hypocrisy or expediency (pp. 409–11). Likewise, the story of Veralinda and Leonia, apparently a celebration of passionate affection between women, is revised by the later course of the narrative: it turns out that all along Leonia was actually Leonius, Veralinda's male lover, in disguise (p. 389).[46] In these sub-plots, potentially radical models of female community or autonomy are asserted, but are ultimately reversed or contained.

It is necessary to stress the plurality of romance, and especially Wroth's romance. As I have said, Wroth's narrative voice differs from that of male-authored romance in that it is not explicitly gendered. In fact, Wroth's narrator is often in the shadows, on the sidelines, as narratives are framed within narratives. Whenever two characters meet, they tell each other their stories, or those of others, and such recessed narratives make up the bulk of the text. This means that there is a plethora of narrative voices, of both genders; and the multiplicity of voices and points of view render it an inaccuracy to assert that the story is simply about the constancy of women and inconstancy of men; rather, constancy is a theme which is explored dialectically. The character of Urania and her story propose an alternative to Pamphilia's fixed constancy as a response to the changefulness of men and of the world in general. Urania changes lovers, with no slur on her virtue, and is identified with variety, flexibility and common sense. She debates the value of constancy with Pamphilia, and exposes the sterility and excessiveness of Pamphilia's creed: love 'is not such a Deity, as your Idolatry makes him', and 'Tis pittie said *Urania*, that ever that fruitlesse thing Constancy was taught you as a vertue' (pp. 399–400).[47] Furthermore, in the many sub-narratives, women are as often inconstant as men.[48] There are many debates between characters on the themes of love and constancy: the Prince of Thiques reports of his encounter with the Lady of Rhodes, 'shee could say nothing against men, that I had not as much, or more to speak against women'. She 'at last agree'd with mee, that Man was the constanter of the two uncertainties' (p. 464). Earlier, Dolorindus and Steriamus engage in 'deep, and almost collerick dispute, against, and for the worth of women kinde'. Dolorindus has been deserted by his mistress, and Steriamus accuses him of bias: 'Love in aboundance made you too farre crost, blame Love then, not her scorne' (p. 159). This suggests that we should regard all the various voices in the *Urania* as subjective and relative.

However, despite these many counterpoints to the central narrative of Pamphilia and Amphilanthus, constant woman and inconstant man, it remains central, and the narrator seems to have a particular sympathy with her heroine. Indeed, many of Wroth's contemporaries assumed that she was representing herself in Pamphilia. This reading is sustained by the fact that Pamphilia is herself a writer, and the representation of women's reading and writing within a piece of women's writing sets up a complex sequence of narrative frames. For instance, at one point we see Pamphilia, characteristically, sitting alone in a thick wood reading a romance:

> the subject was Love, and the story she then was reading, the affection of a Lady to a brave Gentleman, who equally loved, but being a man, it was necessary for him to exceede a woman in all things, so much as inconstancie was found fit for him to excell her in, hee left her for a new.
>
> (p. 264)

This sounds uncannily like a description of the *Urania* itself: Pamphilia is reading her own story. Ironically, she doesn't enjoy the book, and throws it away. Later, Pamphilia tells Dorolina the story of Lindamira, 'faigning it to be written in a French Story'. In fact, the events of Lindamira's life bear a striking resemblance to Wroth's own; for instance, she abruptly falls from her Queen's favour, 'remaining like one in a gay Masque, the night pass'd, they are in their old clothes againe, and no appearance of what was' (pp. 423–4). Dorolina admires the story, 'which shee thought was some thing more exactly related then a fixion' (p. 429). So, here, Lady Mary tells the story of Pamphilia who in turn tells the story of Lady Mary/Lindamira.

In this story of Lindamira, and in the whole *Urania* as a *roman-à-clef*, Wroth attempts to use fiction as a veil, a coded means of telling 'real-life' stories, at once revealing and concealing them. Intensifying the effect of Chinese boxes, her heroine does the same. In Book I, Antissia finds some of Pamphilia's verses carved on a tree; she triumphantly confronts Pamphilia with the information that she has discovered her secret love: 'You cannot thus dissemble (replied *Antissia*), your owne hand in yonder faire Ash will witnes against you. Not so (said *Pamphilia*) for many Poets write aswell by imitation, as by sence of passion' (p. 77 [numbered 67]). This sounds very like Wroth defending the *Urania* against Denny's charge of libel. Both the author and her heroine disclaim a connection between life and art in order to protect themselves. Fiction, like irony, has a 'double force', at once saying and not saying; and, like irony or private versifying, Wroth seeks to appropriate fiction as a means of 'safe' female expression. Both she and her female characters attempt to use fiction as an outlet for personal grievances and a means of achieving desired ends, without risking the breach of social codes of courtesy and femininity. In book IV, Elyna gets rid of an unwanted suitor by telling him: 'a tale before him of himselfe, his wooing so dully, her scorne, and affection to another, all in the third parsons, but so plainely and finely, as he left her to her pleasures' (p. 508).

Unfortunately, for Wroth, fiction was not so efficacious. [. . .]

John Chamberlain's letter to Sir Dudley Carleton at the height of the *Urania* scandal said that Wroth 'takes great libertie or rather licence to traduce whom she please, and thincks she daunces in a net'.[49] The expression 'to dance in a net' seems to have been proverbial, with the primary sense that the dancer exposes her/himself while thinking s/he is concealed.[50] It may therefore have the sense here that Wroth, by straying too far into the recognizably real and personal, had exposed herself improperly, in a manner analogous to physical self-exposure. The veil of fiction behind which she presumed to hide was deemed too thin for decency.[51]

Zurcher has eloquently shown how aptly the phrase 'dancing in a net' describes Wroth's predicament, on many grounds:

As an author who relies on her own position inside society at the same time she pitches herself outside it, Wroth is thus bound by the same ambivalence that liberates her, dancing a teetering dance on the lines of a net.... In a precarious and not-quite-definable position socially, financially, literarily because of both her gender and her family, the author was caught between past and present, action and inaction, meaning and non-meaning, and her romance is the reflection both of the power and the paralysis this predicament brought her as a writer.[52]

From this unstable position, Wroth engages ambivalently with the conventions of male-authored romance. Sometimes she merely reproduces masculine conventions, even when they are oppressive to women. Sometimes she overturns them only to reinstate them at later stages of the narrative, enacting a form of contained transgression. But she performed an act of outright radicalism in her very authorship of a romance; and in her bold and repeated assertion throughout her book that literary activity, whether the writing of poetry or the reading of romances, is appropriate, indeed, invaluable for women. In debate with Urania, Pamphilia declares,

> yet I must say some thing in loves defence ... that I have read in all stories, and at all times, that the wisest, bravest, and most excellent men have been lovers, and are subject to this passion.
>
> (p. 399)

Her reading of romances provides her with an authorization of her way of life; and, in particular, it authorizes the primacy of the private, emotional and personal, the 'feminine' domain. Just as the reciprocal gaze between women can be a source of support and self-affirmation, so fiction is also a kind of mirror in which the female reader can see her experiences duplicated and thereby, paradoxically, made more real.[53] Elsewhere, Pamphilia asks Limena to tell her a story, hoping that, by measuring her experiences against those of the characters, she will be able to raise herself from a despairing mood:

> let me but understand the choice varieties of Love, and the mistakings, the changes, the crosses; if none of these you know, yet tell me some such fiction.
>
> (p. 188)

Fiction is at once a guide to life, consolation for heartache, and a private pleasure.

In this Pamphilia resembles the modern women readers of romantic fiction studied by Janice Radway, and some of the questions raised by

Early Women Writers

Radway become relevant. Could Renaissance romance subvert the patriarchal order in its demarcation of private, autonomous, imaginative, female space? Or, by enabling women to escape from their daily lives, and by its presentation of iniquitous relations between the sexes as timeless and 'natural', did it distract them from protest or resistance and reinforce the status quo? Pamphilia finds solace and self-reliance in her reading and writing, but they perpetuate her passive resignation to Amphilanthus's mistreatment. Wroth's negotiations of the conventions of romance illustrate how the supposed 'femininity' of the genre held both positive and negative aspects for female writers and readers.

Notes

(Place of publication for works printed before 1800 is London unless otherwise stated. Original spellings have been retained, apart from u/v and i/j, and book titles, which have been modernized, and quotations from modernized sources.)

I am indebted to Clare Brant, Katherine Duncan-Jones, Dennis Kay, Diane Purkiss, Josephine Roberts and Sophie Tomlinson for their extremely helpful comments on this piece.

1. See LOUIS B. WRIGHT, *Middle-Class Culture in Elizabethan England*, Chapel Hill, University of North Carolina Press, 1935, pp. 111–17; Tina Krontiris, 'Breaking the Barriers of Genre and Gender: Margaret Tyler's Translation of *The Mirrour of Knighthood*', in *English Literary Renaissance*, 1988, vol. 18, no. 1, pp. 24–5.

2. For a definition of romance, see Gillian Beer, *The Romance*, London, Methuen, 1970, pp. 1–12. Lennard J. Davis, *Factual Fictions: The Origins of the English Novel*, New York, Columbia University Press, 1983, p. 40, lists characteristic differences between the novel and the romance.

3. On the class and gender of the readership of Renaissance romances, see Wright, pp. 111–17; Margaret Spufford, *Small Books and Pleasant Histories: Popular Fiction and its Readership in Seventeenth-Century England*, Cambridge, Cambridge University Press, 1985, pp. 34–6, 50–1, 233–4; Caroline Lucas, *Writing for Women: The Example of Woman as Reader in Elizabethan Romance*, Milton Keynes, Open University Press, 1989, pp. 8–18.

4. BARNABY RICH, *Rich's Farewell to Military Profession*, 1581, ed. Thomas M. Cranfill, Austin, University of Texas Press, 1959, pp. 3–19; John Lyly, *Euphues: The Anatomy of Wit, Euphues and his England*, ed. M.W. Croll and H. Clemons, London, Routledge, 1916, pp. 191–204.

5. LYLY, p. 201; Sir Philip Sidney, *The Countess of Pembroke's Arcadia (The Old Arcadia)*, ed. Katherine Duncan-Jones, Oxford, Oxford University Press, 1985, p. 3.

6. LUCAS, pp. 18–26.

7. WRIGHT, p. 110.

8. JANICE A. RADWAY, *Reading the Romance: Women, Patriarchy and Popular Literature*, Chapel Hill and London, University of North Carolina Press, 1984,

66

pp. 86–118, 209–22; and see also Lucas, pp. 22–6; Tania Modleski, *Loving with a Vengeance: Mass-produced Fantasies for Women*, New York, Methuen, 1984; Jean Radford, 'Introduction', in *The Progress of Romance: The Politics of Popular Fiction*, London, Routledge Kegan Paul, 1986, pp. 1–20.

9. SIR THOMAS OVERBURY, *New and Choise Characters of Severall Authors*, 6th edn, 1615, sigs G4V–5R. For discussion of the phrase 'lady errant', see Hero Chalmers', '"The Person I am, or What They Made me to Be": The Construction of the Feminine Subject in the Autobiographies of Mary Carleton', in Clare Brant and Diane Purkiss (eds), *Women, Texts and Histories 1575–1760*, London and New York, Routledge, 1992, pp. 164–94.

10. THOMAS POWELL, *Tom of All Trades. Or the Plaine Path-Way To Preferment*, 1631, p. 47.

11. 'Poetresse' is simply an obsolete term for 'poetess'; see the *Oxford English Dictionary*, 2nd edn, Oxford, Clarendon, 1989.

12. PATRICIA PARKER, *Literary Fat Ladies: Rhetoric, Gender, Property*, London, Methuen, 1987, pp. 8–35, especially pp. 10–11.

13. ROGER ASCHAM, *The Schoolmaster*, 1570, ed. Lawrence V. Ryan, Ithaca, NY, Cornell University Press, 1967, p. 67.

14. SIDNEY, p. 25.

15. GEORGE GASCOIGNE, *The Adventures of Master F.J.*, 1573, in Paul Salzman (ed.), *An Anthology of Elizabethan Prose Fiction*, Oxford, Oxford University Press, 1987, pp. 54–8, 67–73.

16. ROBERT GREENE, *Penelope's Web*, 1587, in Alexander B. Grosart (ed.), *The Life and Complete Works of Robert Greene*, 15 vols, N.P. Huth Library, 1881–6, vol. V, pp. 194, 233, 154–5, 162.

17. SPUFFORD, pp. 4–6, 12–13, 59, 62, 79–80, 172.

18. e.g. GEORGE PEELE's play, *The Old Wives' Tale*, 1595.

19. See also PHILIP MASSINGER, *The Guardian*, in Philip Edwards and Colin Gibson (eds), *The Plays and Poems of Philip Massinger*, vol. IV, Oxford, Oxford University Press, 1976, I. ii. 66–71.

20. MARGARET TYLER, 'To the Reader', in Diego Ortuñez de Calahorra, *The Mirrour of Princely Deedes and Knighthood*, trans. M[argaret] T[yler], Thomas East, 1578, sigs A3R–4V. Subsequent quotations from Tyler are taken from her epistle to the reader.

21. See MARGARET PATTERSON HANNAY (ed.), *Silent But for the Word: Tudor Women as Patrons, Translators, and Writers of Religious Works*, Kent, Ohio, Kent State University Press, 1985, especially 'Introduction', pp. 1–14.

22. For further biographical detail, see Lady Mary Wroth, *The Poems of Lady Mary Wroth*, ed. Josephine A. Roberts, Baton Rouge and London, Louisiana State University Press, 1983, pp. 3–40.

23. LADY MARY WROTH, *The Countesse of Mountgomeries Urania*, 1621, p. 250. All further references to this work will be referred to by page number in the text. Josephine A. Roberts was due to complete a new edition of the *Urania* in 1992.

24. WROTH, *Poems*, p. 70, n. 15. Dale Spender thinks that Wroth wrote the *Urania* in order to rescue herself from debt, and may therefore have been the first woman to write for money (Dale Spender, *Mothers of the Novel: 100 Good Women Writers before Jane Austen*, London, Pandora, 1986, pp. 11–22).

25. I am grateful to Josephine A. Roberts for this information.

26. The manuscript is in the Newberry Library, Chicago, call no. Case MS f.Y1565.W95.

27. WROTH, *Poems*, pp. 31–5, 238–9.

28. See ELAINE V. BEILIN, *Redeeming Eve: Women Writers of the English Renaissance*, Princeton, Princeton University Press, 1987, p. 212.

29. WROTH, *Poems*, quotes Chamberlain on p. 36 and Manners's letter on pp. 29, 244–5. Other analogies are discussed on pp. 29–31. Margaret Hannay also discusses possible family references in the *Urania* in ' "Your vertuous and learned Aunt": the Countess of Pembroke as a Mentor to Lady Wroth', in Naomi J. Miller and Gary Waller (eds), *Reading Mary Wroth: Representing Alternatives in Early Modern England*, Knoxville, University of Tennessee Press, 1991, pp. 15–34. I am grateful to Professor Hannay for allowing me to read this piece prior to publication.

30. AMELIA ZURCHER lists echoes of the *Arcadia* in the *Urania* in ' "Dauncing in a Net": Representation in Lady Mary Wroth's *Urania*', unpublished M.Phil. thesis, Oxford University, 1989, p. 8. I am very grateful to the author for permission to quote from this thesis. Beilin, p. 215, points out that the name Pamphilia is an amalgam of Pamela and Philoclea. In Wroth, *Poems*, Roberts's notes on Wroth's poems point out numerous correspondences between her work and that of Philip and other Sidneys.

31. See ELAINE V. BEILIN, ' "The Onely Perfect Vertue": Constancy in Mary Wroth's *Pamphilia to Amphilanthus*', *Spenser Studies*, 1981, vol. 2, pp. 229–45; Beilin, *Redeeming Eve*, pp. 232–43.

32. The Countess of Montgomery was Susan Vere, a close neighbour and friend of Wroth's; she was married to Wroth's cousin, Sir Philip Herbert, brother of William Herbert. See Wroth, *Poems*, p. 27.

33. See MAUREEN QUILLIGAN, 'Lady Mary Wroth: Female Authority and the Family Romance', in George M. Logan and Gordon Teskey (eds), *Unfolded Tales: Essays on Renaissance Romance*, Ithaca, NY, Cornell University Press, 1989, pp. 257–80, for discussion of specific incidents in the *Urania* which rewrite episodes from the *Arcadia* and *The Faerie Queene*.

34. CAROLYN RUTH SWIFT, 'Female Identity in Lady Mary Wroth's Romance *Urania*', *English Literary Renaissance*, 1984, vol. 14, no. 3, pp. 330, 331. See also Carolyn Ruth Swift, 'Feminine Self-definition in Lady Mary Wroth's *Love's Victorie (c. 1621)*', *English Literary Renaissance*, 1989, vol. 19, no. 2, pp. 171–88.

35. QUILLIGAN, p. 261 and *passim*.

36. This description does not quite fit Pamphilia's strategies in the manuscript continuation, but for brevity's sake this discussion is confined to the published 1621 *Urania*.

37. For a fuller discussion of the importance of secrets and their selective disclosure as a source of female strength and identity in the *Urania*, see Zurcher, pp. 17–26.

38. WROTH, Newberry MS, ff. 11R–12R, 15V–16V.

39. SWIFT, 'Female Identity', p. 345.

40. ibid., p. 346.

41. LAURA MULVEY, 'Visual Pleasure and Narrative Cinema', *Screen*, 1975, vol. 16, no. 3, pp. 6–18.

42. NANCY J. VICKERS, '"The blazon of sweet beauty's best": Shakespeare's *Lucrece*', in Patricia Parker and Geoffrey Hartman (eds), *Shakespeare and the Question of Theory*, New York and London, Methuen, 1985, pp. 95–115; Nancy J. Vickers, 'Diana Described: Scattered Woman and Scattered Rhyme', in Elizabeth Abel (ed.), *Writing and Sexual Difference*, Brighton, Harvester, 1982, pp. 265–79; Parker, pp. 65–6, 126–54.

43. VICKERS, 'Diana Described'; Edmund Spenser, *The Faerie Queene*, ed. A.C. Hamilton, London, Longman, 1977, II. xii; Parker, pp. 65–6.

44. E. ANN KAPLAN, 'Is the Gaze Male?', in Ann Snitow, Christine Stansell and Sharon Thompson (eds), *Desire: The Politics of Sexuality*, London, Virago, 1984, pp. 328, 331.

45. JACQUES LACAN, 'The Mirror Stage as Formative of the Function of the I', in *Ecrits: A Selection*, trans. Alan Sheridan, London, Tavistock, 1977, pp. 1–7; Mulvey, pp. 9–10, 12.

46. Indeed, the first encounter between Veralinda and 'Leonia' and their mutual gaze strongly resembles the meeting between Philoclea and 'Cleophila' in the *Old Arcadia* which culminates in an embrace and Pyrocles' revelation of his identity (Sidney, pp. 104–5).

47. For further discussion of Urania as representing a positive alternative to Pamphilia's constancy, see Zurcher, pp. 57–9, 67–80. Zurcher also suggests that Urania is identified with the plurality and prose of romance narrative, while Pamphilia is identified with the emotional directness of lyric poetry.

48. See, for example, the Lady-of-May-type figure who is satirized for her inability to choose between two lovers (pp. 382–6); and Lady Fancy in the manuscript continuation (Wroth, Newberry MS, ff. 12R–V).

49. WROTH, *Poems*, p. 36.

50. See ZURCHER, pp. 2–3, 81–2, n. 4.

51. See ROSALIND BALLASTER's chapter in Brant and Purkiss (eds), *Women, Texts and Histories 15–1760* on Delariviere Manley, a later woman writer who caused scandal through her use of the *roman-à-clef*: 'Manl(e)y Forms: Sex and the Female Satirist', pp. 217–41.

52. ZURCHER, pp. 9–13.

53. See HERO CHALMERS's chapter in Brant and Purkiss (eds), *Women, Texts and Histories 1575–1760* on Mary Carleton, a woman of the later seventeenth century who used the discursive models of romance in 'real life' for both the authorization of female subjectivity and the disruption of masculine definitions of identity.

KATHERINE PHILIPS
(1632–64)

3 Orinda and Female Intimacy*

ELAINE HOBBY

A seventeenth-century female poet whose work found its way into print, Katherine Philips, 'the matchless Orinda', nonetheless secured a reputation among her contemporaries for exemplary femininity. Elaine Hobby explains this historical curiosity as the result of a carefully devised strategy: the Philips who wrote apparently unobjectionable poems about love and friendship and modestly denied any desire for or entitlement to public recognition was a self-representation through which the poet turned contemporary constructions of femininity into a license to write. Hobby's formulation of the relationship between early women's writing and the ideologies of gender which disallowed it foregrounds human agency: within the limits of the patriarchal world she inhabited, Philips managed to negotiate a small space of self-determination. Indeed, Hobby's theory of strategic self-construction, while persuasively argued, endows Philips with a degree of psychic autonomy which contrasts with Celia A. Easton's study of the poet.

Katherine Philips, 'the Matchless Orinda', the author of a book of poetry, two play translations and some published correspondence, has long been perceived as a model lady poetess, dabbling in versification in a rural Welsh backwater, confining her attention solely to the proper feminine concerns of love and friendship. It is generally agreed that she was modestly alarmed at the prospect of any public attention for her work. By briefly examining her *Letters from Orinda to Poliarchus* (her correspondence with the Master of Ceremonies at Charles II's court, Charles Cotterell) and the images of constraint and retirement found in her poetry, I will suggest that the 'Orinda' persona who appears in modern critical accounts is a creation made necessary by the particular

---

* Reprinted from Elaine Hobby, *Virtue of Necessity: English Women's Writing 1649–88* (London: Virago, 1988), pp. 128–42.

circumstances confronting this seventeenth-century woman poet. Through 'Orinda', Philips gained acceptance in her own period, and has a reputation that has survived into our own. I will then go on to examine more closely Philips's best-known work, her poetry celebrating women's friendship, and how it engages with the conventions of the courtly love tradition to produce an image of female solidarity (and, perhaps, of lesbian love) that could be sustained within the tight constraints of marriage.[1]

Since her death in 1664, Katherine Philips's writings have never dropped entirely from the public eye.[2] There is a certain significant irony in this, since she is remembered as the archetypal blushing poetess, who shied away from any public recognition of her works. She never desired publication, and was horrified when a surreptitious edition of her poetry appeared in 1664, the story goes. The figure who appears in her poetry and her *Letters to Poliarchus* is 'the matchless Orinda', the self-effacing lady poet who thoroughly understands that she is inferior to the male sex. As such, she has been allowed a tiny and peripheral place in the literary canon.

In part, the image of Orinda that has come down to us is dependent on the belief that her writing was really a secret and private affair, her poems passed around only in manuscript form to a few trusted friends. This is an anachronistic distortion of the method of 'publication' that she used: circulation of manuscripts was the normal way to make writing public before the widespread use of printed books, and was a method that continued to be popular in court circles throughout the reign of Charles II, at least.[3] Such a description also fails to consider the fact that, as a royalist poet married to a leading parliamentarian, she had positive reasons for avoiding too much public attention during the 1650s, which was when she did most of her writing. Bearing these factors in mind, we find that the evidence suggests that she was actually a well-known writer.

As early as 1651, when she was nineteen years old, Philips's writing was sufficiently well thought of for a poem of hers to be prefaced to the posthumous edition of William Cartwright's plays, and a poem written in praise of Philips by Henry Vaughan was included by him in his collected works in that same year. She must already have been circulating some of her writings. In 1655, a song of hers was printed by Henry Lawes in his *Second Book of Ayres*. Although Katherine Philips's identity was not revealed in Cartwright's text, both Vaughan and Lawes printed her full name. It is clear that her achievements were well known, at least among prestigious royalists. She addressed poems to Francis Finch, John Birkenhead and Sir Edward Dering, and the fact that they were also involved with the publication of Cartwright's plays and the *Second Book of Ayres* could indicate that her acquaintance with them dated from 1651 or even earlier. It is not surprising to find that by 1657, when Jeremy Taylor answered in print Katherine Philips's enquiries about the nature of friendship, his complimentary address to her should have heralded her as someone known to be 'so eminent in friendships'.[4] And after the Restoration, she sought out recognition from aristocracy and royalty, sending poems to the Duchess of York, the Archbishop of Canterbury, and to King Charles himself, and dedicating her translation *Pompey* to the Countess of Cork. Her skill as a translator had a sufficiently high public profile for John Davies to praise her by name when dedicating his 1659 translation of *Cléopatre* to her in 1662, and for Lord Roscommon to claim to have undertaken a translation from French purely in compliment to her.[5] Any assessment of Philips's writing that suggests that she was of a shy and retiring spirit, forced into the public eye in 1664 against her strongest inclinations, is choosing to ignore her involvement with this then more traditional form of public recognition. The 'public' she was interested in reaching was the coterie of court and leading poets, not the wider world.

The assertion that Philips did not wish her works published is based on the letters she wrote to Sir Charles Cotterell between 1661 and 1664, published in 1705 after his death as *Letters from Orinda to Poliarchus*. The correspondence deals in part with her preparing a translation of Corneille's *Pompée*, and seeing it onto the stage and through the press in 1663, and her attempts to suppress an unofficial edition of her poems in 1664. The established judgement of these letters' significance is that they demonstrate Katherine Philips's blushing horror at the thought of her works and name becoming public property. They are used to reconfirm the image of her that has come down to us from posterity. The fact that *Pompey* was published without identifying the translator is seen as proof that Philips held a suitably modest assessment of her own abilities. What is not noticed is that the prologue to the play, written by the Earl of Roscommon, and its epilogue by Sir Edward Dering, both identify the author as female.[6] Given Philips's reputation as a translator, and the fact that she was living in Dublin during the play's much-acclaimed performance there, it is likely that her identity was common knowledge, at least among those whose opinion of her she valued. In the copy that she sent to the Countess of Roscommon she certainly made no attempt to hide her name, and the stationer Henry Herringman knew whom to contact when he wanted to bring out a London edition of *Pompey* (see Chapter Five).

The *Letters to Poliarchus* have been read as if they give straightforward access to 'the real Katherine Philips', her personal doubts and fears, and that they can therefore tell us the 'truth' about her identity as an author.[7] Such a reading discounts the fact that all writing is governed by specific conventions, and that in the case of a mid-seventeenth-century woman these conventions included the requirement that she apologise for daring to take up the pen, and find ways to excuse her boldness. We would therefore expect to find, as we do, that the *Letters*, written to her important political ally and sponsor Charles Cotterell, are preoccupied largely with finding ways to justify writing as a 'female' activity. The *Letters to Poliarchus* indeed provide material for a fascinating study of the process through which 'Orinda' is constructed and refined throughout the correspondence, making it possible for Philips to write and gain wide public acclaim while disavowing any desire to do either. Orinda can also humbly request advice and guidance from Cotterell with her translation of *Pompée*, whilst blithely continuing to follow her own judgement when he disagrees with her.

There are many examples of this in the *Letters*. The most extended is found in a long-drawn-out discussion of one word in her translation: the word 'effort', at that time seen as a French term not an English one. Cotterell counselled her to omit the word, and the subsequent correspondence continued for some months. There was every reason for Philips to take Cotterell's advice and change her text. He was, after all, a recognised linguist and translator. However, although she finally asks Cotterell to change the text himself, the word appears unaltered in the published version. Part of the justification for her consistency, which might have been seen as unfeminine stubbornness, is that she is leaving the word alone at the insistence of another eminent man and writer, Roger Boyle. She tells Cotterell,

> I would fain have made use of your correction, and thrown away 'effort', but my Lord Orrery would absolutely have it continued; and so it is, to please his humour, though against my will and judgement too.
>
> (*Letters*, p. 123)

There is no need to assert her own opinion against Cotterell's. She can cite another male authority instead.

Translation, as defined by Philips in the *Letters*, was a suitably modest undertaking for a woman, the task being to produce a text that kept well within the specific and narrow bounds of the original. This restrictive format could then be used, however, to vindicate her own expertise, and to criticise judiciously the work of others. This is demonstrated strikingly in Philips's detailed analysis of 'what chiefly disgusts me' (p. 179) in a rival translation of *Pompée* undertaken by a group of men. Her comments become so scathing as to strain the limits of self-effacement, and her letter criticising the men's translation ends with the necessary retraction: 'I really think the worst of their lines equal to the best in my translation' (p. 180). [. . .]

The best-known of Philips's *Letters to Poliarchus* is the one most centrally concerned in producing the image of the poetess that has come down to us. It appears as part of the preface to the posthumous, 1667 edition of the poems, having been written after Richard Marriot had brought out a surreptitious edition from an imperfect manuscript early in 1664. Cotterell hurried to suppress the edition, and Philips's letter refers to this with gratitude. The letter has been read, as the editor of the posthumous edition no doubt designed, as clear proof of the poet's diffidence.[8] In the 1667 edition of *Poems* the letter lies framed by his assertion of her bashfulness and self-effacement, directing the reader how to interpret it. Much is made of her description of herself as someone 'who never writ any line in my life with an intention to have it printed'. Printing Philips might have been nervous about: it could in no way be construed as a feminine act. She was not, however, averse to having her writings published in a more traditional way. This letter, which finally was printed, was not the 'private' communication it is presented as, but was designed for a public audience. In a covering note, which is not included in the 1667 preface, Philips urges Cotterell to 'show it to anybody that suspects my ignorance and innocence of that false edition of my verses' (p. 34).[9] The greatest danger, indeed, was that she might be suspected of the same kind of scheming that many male authors practised: of having arranged the appearance of this incomplete edition as a way of testing how it would be received, before fully committing herself to it in public. Those with long memories would know, after all, that some of her works had already appeared in print, in 1651 and 1657. If her identity as the acclaimed translator of *Pompey* was also known or suspected despite its anonymous publication, such a consequence was likely, and would do irreparable damage to her carefully sculpted public image.

It is worth noting that Katherine Philips had other objections to the surreptitious printing of her poems, which she also mentions in the published letter. Since she died before the 1667 *Poems* appeared, it is impossible to know how she would have re-edited the text, but it is clear that there are many variants between the editions. The most obvious change is that the 1667 edition contains some fifty-five poems, and the two play translations, not found in the earlier text. Many of the omitted poems were written in Ireland, which suggests that the manuscript used by Marriot was an early one, perhaps an early draft, since some verses also scan badly. In addition, the absence of some lines and inclusion of nonsense verses suggests that it was illegible in places. The reader of the surreptitious edition would get an impression of the poet's skill far inferior to that provided by the amended text.[10]

So what kind of poetry was written under the name of Orinda? Katherine Philips was a royalist and High Church Anglican whose immediate family included many important parliamentarians and Independents. Having been born and educated in London, the daughter of a wealthy merchant, John Fowler, she had moved to Wales to join her mother by the time she was fifteen. Her father had died, and her mother was remarried to a prominent parliamentarian, Richard Phillipps. In August 1648, at the age of sixteen, Katherine was wedded to a fifty-four-year-old relative of Sir Richard's, James Philips of Tregibby and The Priory, Cardigan.[11] James was called to the Barebones Parliament in 1653, and served locally as a commissioner for sequestration.

During the 1650s, the political differences between husband and wife seem to have become known, and Colonel John Jones apparently attempted to discredit James Philips by publishing some writing of Katherine's. Her poem addressed to her husband on this occasion is fascinating. While expressing remorse and admitting she had undermined her spouse's reputation, she in no way promises to alter her opinions. Indeed, the poem is in fact a statement of her separateness from him, and a call for her to be assessed as an independent being, not as a part of her husband. At one level, there is nothing indecorous in these lines, as she is asking that her husband be considered free from her guilt. At another, she asserts that from the first, from the time of Adam and Eve, women and men should be regarded as autonomous, each responsible for their own actions. Even her enemy's wife, she maintains, need not be treated as though she agreed with Colonel Jones's opinions (Jones's wife indeed differed from him politically).[12] Under a legal system where the husband and wife were assumed to be one person, the husband, this is a quietly radical statement.

To Antenor, on a Paper of mine which J.J.
threatens to publish to prejudice him.
Must then my crimes become thy scandal too?
Why, sure the devil hath not much to do.
The weakness of the other charge is clear,
When such a trifle must bring up the rear.
But this is mad design, for who before
Lost his repute upon another's score?
My love and life I must confess are thine,
But not my errors, they are only mine.
And if my faults must be for thine allowed,
It will be hard to dissipate the cloud:
For Eve's rebellion did not Adam blast,

Until himself forbidden fruit did taste.
'Tis possible this magazine of hell
(Whose name would turn a verse into a spell,
Whose mischief is congenial to his life)
May yet enjoy an honourable wife.
Nor let his ill be reckoned as her blame,
Nor yet my follies blast Antenor's name.

(Poems, 1667, p. 47)

This poem to Antenor was not the only one Philips wrote on this
occasion. She also addressed one to her close friend, Anne Owen,
'the truly competent judge of honour, Lucasia', asking her to believe in
her untainted honesty. This appeal to Lucasia's support is unsurprising.
Philips's solution to finding herself surrounded by those whose political
and religious beliefs contrasted sharply with her own had been to
establish her Society of Friendship. The friends admitted to this select
band were all royalists, and their correspondence and companionship
must have done much to offset her isolation. Naming herself 'Orinda',
she gave similar pastoral-sounding names to her friends, and addressed
poetry to them which uses the language and imagery of courtly love
conventions.[13] Some of the Society's members have not been identified,
but their number seems to have included Anne Owen (Lucasia),
Mary Aubrey (Rosania), Francis Finch (Palaemon) the brother of the
philosopher Anne Conway, John Birkenhead (Cratander), Sir Edward
Dering (Silvander), Lady Mary Cavendish (Policrite), James Philips
(Antenor) and Sir Charles Cotterell (Poliarchus). (Those added after
the Restoration, when the Society of Friendship presumably changed
somewhat, included Anne Boyle – Valeria – and Elizabeth Boyle –
Celimena – relatives of the diarist and autobiographer Mary Rich.)

In general, the extant poems that she addresses to these friends make
few overt comments on state politics. (Almost all her explicitly royalist
poems were written after the Restoration.) During the 1650s, addressing
issues of state politics was far more common among women sectaries
than their more conservative sisters. Affairs of government were
supposed to be beyond the realm of proper female concern, and in
her lines deploring the execution of Charles I Philips found it necessary
to assert that, in general, women should leave public issues well alone.
Only with the whole world order upset by the 'murder' of the monarch,
she asserts in 'Upon the Double Murther', could the unfeminine act of
commenting on affairs of state be excused.

Philips's poems on solitude, retreat and the country life, however,
also reveal her royalism. Maren-Sofie Røstvig has shown how the
defeated royalists in their rural exiles took up classical images of
contentment and virtue in the countryside.[14] The controlled and

balanced happy man, contemptuous of the fervent battles of the
political world, was their answer to the Puritan image of the committed
Christian warrior. Henry Vaughan and Abraham Cowley both wrote
in this vein, and both men were known by Philips. The writings of
Saint-Amant were also incorporated into this tradition in England, and
Philips was familiar with his work, translating his 'La Solitude'.

Her poetry shows many signs of commitment to this philosophy
of retirement, wherein submission and acceptance of limitations are
heralded as positive and necessary virtues. Many of the poems which
in other respects are widely different from one another are characterised
by advocacy of contentment or confinement or restriction, and the
assertion that true freedom and choice can be found through this.
(These include, for instance, 'A Sea-Voyage from Tenby to Bristol',
'To my dear Sister Mrs C.P. on her Marriage', 'Happiness' and 'Upon
the Graving of her Name Upon a Tree in Barnelmes Walk'.) These
sentiments would have been deeply familiar to Philips's royalist
contemporaries.

There is, however, a radical difference between Katherine Philips's
situation and that of her fellow-poets. They were men, and their
retirement from affairs of state was a recent change in circumstances,
and in some cases self-imposed. Philips was a woman. Her residence
in the countryside was due to the fact that she had to be with her
husband. She had no choice in the matter, and no hope that this
apparently natural state of affairs had ever been different, or could
ever be changed. This is most poignantly apparent in the many
poems written on parting from one of her close women friends.
Orinda recommends a stoical acceptance of separation, claiming that
only through such a resignation of will can true self-determination be
found. The way in which the parting is experienced, she argues, is
something that friends do have control over, and this is where their
freedom lies. This gives a very special inflexion to the traditional
courtly love motif of separation from a beloved. Only by giving this
particular extension to notions of self-control and contentment under
compulsion could Katherine Philips find a way to maintain some
autonomy, living as she was surrounded by her political enemies,
people who had legal control over her existence. In 'Parting with
Lucasia: A Song' this theme is especially interesting because Philips
suggests that through resignation women can become 'conquerors at
home'. The double meaning in this phrase – it can be read both as
'conquerors of ourselves' and 'conquerors in the house' – shows how,
for this woman poet, a measure of self-determination could be achieved.
If women can control their grief at being separated from one another,
she argues, any task is slight by comparison, and can be performed.
The poem ends

Nay then to meet we may conclude,
  And all obstructions overthrow,
Since we our passion have subdued,
  Which is the strongest thing I know.

(pp. 65–6)

About half of Philips's poems are concerned with love and friendship.
The great majority of these address the theme of intimacy between
women, exploring its delights and problems. This anatomisation
and celebration of female closeness is made in direct defiance of the
accepted view of women. Although from its earliest days the language
and themes of courtly love poetry had been used to glorify friendships
between men, women's relationships with one another had never been
treated to such serious consideration in print.[15] Orinda's response to
this nonsense is unequivocal.

If souls no sexes have, for men t'exclude
  Women from friendship's vast capacity,
Is a design injurious or rude,
  Only maintained by partial tyranny.
Love is allowed to us and innocence,
And noblest friendships do proceed from thence.

(p. 95)

It is entirely characteristic that she should argue that qualities normally
attributed to women are the very features that most fit them to move
outside the conventional requirements.

The courtly love conventions are an important and frequent feature
of Orinda's poetry. In some poems, she adopts wholesale the stance
and language of the frustrated lover, wooing a merciless mistress.
An integral part of this tradition was the poem renouncing love,
and Philips's works include a wholly conventional example of this
kind, 'Against Love'. Addressed to Cupid, the poem includes stock
references to lovers burning and raving and the 'killing frown' of the
mistress who provides only diseased joys. What is unusual is for such
a renunciation of love to be made by a woman. By writing from the
position usually reserved for the male lover, the woman poet gains
access for herself to the power and freedom that were usually enjoyed
only by men in love relationships. Traditionally, this poetry, while
lamenting the control wielded by the mistress over her lover through
her 'killing frown', nonetheless gives voice only to the lover, who
explores and revels in his (usual) 'subjugation' to the mistress's gentle
charms. The price that Philips pays for this access to male speech in
at least some of her poems is that she is limited thereby to the kinds

of relationship allowed by this essentially male tradition. Some of the poems addressed to Mary Aubrey include a great deal of this conventional language, and are restricted to situations taken directly from the courtly love tradition. Since one of the fundamental assumptions of this poetry is that the beloved object is an exception to the general run of womankind and infinitely superior to other females, this can have the result of deprecating other women. Such is the case in 'Rosania shadowed whilst Mrs Mary Aubrey'.

> Unlike those gallants which take far less care
> To have their souls, than make their bodies fair;
> Who (sick with too much leisure) time do pass
> With these two books, pride and a looking-glass:
> Plot to surprise men's hearts, their power to try,
> And call that love, which is mere vanity.
> But she, although the greatest murtherer,
> (For every glance commits a massacre)
> Yet glories not that slaves her power confess,
> But wishes that her monarchy were less.
>
> (pp. 48–9)

Many of Orinda's poems, however, rigorously rework these conventions, giving them new meanings that express a particularly female perspective. In 'A Dialogue betwixt Lucasia, and Rosania, Imitating that of Gentle Thyrsis', Lucasia is a shepherdess and Rosania the wooer who tries to persuade her to leave the flocks and go away with her (pp. 126–7). Lucasia explains that she would much rather leave with Rosania, given the choice, but must stay where her duty lies. The poem presents loving friendship between women as the part of their lives that is characterised by choice and freedom, but prevented from blossoming by the duties of female existence: 'Lucasia: Such are thy charms, I'd dwell within thine arms / Could I my station choose.' The poem, like many in the tradition from which it springs, looks forward to a final union after death.

> Rosania: Then whilst we live, this joy let's take and give,
>   Since death us soon will sever.
> Lucasia: But I trust, when crumbled into dust,
>   We shall meet and love for ever.

These lines echo another dialogue, 'A Dialogue of Absence 'Twixt Lucasia and Orinda, set by Mr Henry Lawes', which ends in a chorus anticipating a future where women will no longer be forced to part by other concerns: 'But we shall come where no rude hand shall sever,/ And there we'll meet and part no more for ever' (p. 26).

Some of the most interesting of Katherine Philips's poems take particular images from the received patterns and rework them. In doing so, Philips both shows that relationships between women are different from those between men and women, and implicitly criticises her male poetic sources. A notable instance of this is her reworking of John Donne's famous 'compasses' image in his 'A Valediction: forbidding Mourning'.

> If they be two, they are two so
>   As stiff twin compasses are two,
> Thy soul the fixed foot, makes no show
>   To move, but doth, if th'other do.
>
> And though it in the centre sit,
>   Yet when the other far doth roam,
> It leans, and hearkens after it,
>   And grows erect, as that comes home.
>
> Such wilt thou be to me, who must
>   Like th'other foot, obliquely run;
> Thy firmness makes my circle just,
>   And makes me end, where I begun.

This has been praised as the expression of all-transcendent love. A quick and simple feminist reading, however, would point out how the compasses actually celebrate woman's immobility and fixity in 'the centre', and man's freedom to move and still be loved. It is the male 'foot' that roams: the female can only lean in sympathy with it. Katherine Philips's response to these lines seems to involve the same analysis. 'To my dearest Lucasia' celebrates love between women. It describes an emblem that could be used to represent the relationship, and uses an image of compasses to describe equal freedom and equal control.

> The compasses that stand above
> Express this great immortal love:
> For friends, like them, can prove this true,
> They are, and yet they are not, two.
>
> And in their posture is expressed
> Friendship's exalted interest:
> Each follows where the other leans,
> And what each does, this other means.
>
> And as when one foot does stand fast,
> And t'other circles seeks to cast,

The steady part does regulate
And make the wanderer's motion straight:

So friends are only two in this,
T'reclaim each other when they miss:
For whosoe'er will grossly fall,
Can never be a friend at all.

Katherine Philips's poetry provides a developing definition of female friendship. One of its most fundamental characteristics – and one which by implication must exclude men from this greatest intimacy with women – is that women friends are so alike that they mirror one another. This idea appears explicitly, for instance, in 'A Friend'.

Thick waters show no images of things;
  Friends are each other's mirrors, and should be
Clearer than crystal or the mountain springs,
  And free from clouds, design or flattery,
For vulgar souls no part of friendship share:
Poets and friends are born to what they are.

(p. 94)

A comparison with a poem addressed to her husband, 'To my dearest Antenor, on his Parting', illustrates how very different this essentially equal relationship is from marriage. Philips-as-wife is her husband's image, passively reflecting him. There is no equal mirroring here.

And besides this thou shalt in me survey
Thyself reflected while thou art away . . .
So in my breast thy picture drawn shall be.
My guide, life, object, friend, and destiny:
And none shall know, though they employ their wit,
Which is the right Antenor, thou, or it.

(pp. 76–7)

Even though she calls Antenor her friend, the relationship defined here is quite different from the one she celebrates with women who are close to her.

Orinda's most extended exposition of the argument that women's friendship has a special and superior quality is the poem 'To my Excellent Lucasia, on our Friendship'. This moves from the opening 'I' of the first stanzas to the exultant, united 'we' of the final one. The friendship, through mirroring and recognition of similarity, gives joy and peace that is found in no other relationship – certainly not in the 'bridegroom's mirth'.

I did not live until this time
   Crowned my felicity,
When I could say without a crime,
   I am not thine, but thee.

This carcase breathed, and walked, and slept,
   So that the world believed
There was a soul the motions kept:
   But they were all deceived.

For as a watch by art is wound
   To motion, such was mine:
But never had Orinda found
   A soul till she found thine;

Which now inspires, cures and supplies,
   And guides my darkened breast:
For thou art all that I can prize,
   My joy, my life, my rest.

No bridegroom's nor crown-conqueror's mirth
   To mine compared can be:
They have but pieces of this earth,
   I've all the world in thee.

Then let our flames still light and shine,
   And no false fear control,
As innocent as our design,
   Immortal as our soul.

(pp. 51–2)

Marriage contains elements of duty and compulsion. Struggling
to resolve the conflict between wifely submission and passionate
friendship, and accept that she cannot change her situation, Katherine
Philips asks her dearest friend to be patient with her imperfections.
She reflects on the divine essence of friendship, claiming that in its
origins the relationship is superhuman. True friendship should
consist of harmony and freedom, and she laments that, in her human
imperfection, she is seeking to control and possess her friend. In a
world where so many imperative demands were made of them, women
seek, she says, to allow perfect liberty to one another in this most perfect
of relationships. Having described the state she aspires to, she sighs,

But what's all this to me, who live to be
Disprover of my own morality?
And he that knew my unimproved soul,
Would say I meant all friendship to control
But bodies move in time, and so must minds;

And though th'attempt no easy progress finds,
Yet quit me not, lest I should desperate grow,
And to such friendship add some patience now.

(pp. 58–9)

The range and themes of Katherine Philips's poetry show the ways in
which a woman whose religious and political allegiances placed her
outside the sisterhood of the radical sects could negotiate a space of
autonomy for herself and her female friends. She was a tremendously
important reference point for contemporary High Church women.
Her translation *Pompey* was greeted with overwhelming joy by an
Irishwoman who signs herself simply 'Philo-Philippa'. The terms of
this praise illustrate the fact that Orinda's spirited defence of women's
friendship was not lost on the women of her times.

Let the male poets their male Phoebus choose,
Thee I invoke, Orinda, for my muse;
He could but force a branch, Daphne her tree
Most freely offers to her sex and thee,
And says to verse, so unconstrained as yours,
Her laurel freely comes, your fame secures:
And men no longer shall with ravished bays
Crown their forced poems by as forced a praise.
. . .
    That sex, which heretofore was not allowed
To understand more than a beast, or crowd;
Of which problems were made, whether or no
Women had souls; but to be damned, if so;
Whose highest contemplation could not pass,
In men's esteem, no higher than the glass;
And all the painful labours of their brain,
Was only how to dress and entertain:
Or, if they ventured to speak sense, the wise
Made that, and speaking ox, like prodigies.
From these thy more than masculine pen hath reared
Our sex; first to be praised, next to be feared.
And by the same pen forced, men now confess,
To keep their greatness, was to make us less . . .
Ask me not then, why jealous men debar
Our sex from books in peace, from arms in war;
It is because our parts will soon demand
Tribunals for our persons, and command.
. . .
    That noble friendship brought thee to our coast,
We thank Lucasia, and thy courage boast.

Death in each wave could not Orinda fright,
Fearless she acts that friendship she did write:
Which manly virtue to their sex confined,
Thou rescuest to confirm our softer mind;
For there's required (to do that virtue right)
Courage, as much in friendship as in fight.
The dangers we despise, doth this truth prove,
Though boldly we not fight, we boldly love . . .
Thus, as the sun, you in your course shine on,
Unmoved with all our admiration:
  Flying above the praise you shun, we see
  Wit is still higher by humility.[16]

Philips's poetry was also an essential reference point for women poets
who followed her. Many of those writing later in the seventeenth
century, including Aphra Behn, Anne Killigrew, Ephelia and Jane
Barker, refer to her as their guide. In the post-Restoration world, where
acceptable female behaviour was again being narrowly defined, she was
an important example that it was possible for a woman to be praised
for her writing, as long as she was sufficiently modest in her claims.
While helping to open a pathway into print for women, therefore, she
also staked it out as a strait and narrow way. Through the critics'
appraisals, 'the matchless Orinda' became the scourge of such followers
as the 'incomparable Astrea', Aphra Behn.

Notes

1. The author was working in 1988 on a study of seventeenth-century women's
   sexuality. It is acknowledged that the use of the term 'lesbian' when
   discussing this period is contentious.

2. *Letters from Orinda to Poliarchus* was published in 1705, 1714, 1729. An
   anonymous poem of Philips's appeared in Tottel's *Miscellany* in 1716 and
   1727. She is praised in Dryden's poem to Anne Killigrew, which was
   published in 1693, 1701, 1716, 1727, and reference was made to her in 1743
   by the anonymous satirist who wrote *The Crooked Sixpence*. Her poems
   appear in *Poems by Eminent Ladies*, 1757. In 1764 her achievements were
   noted by David Erskine in *Biographia Dramatica*. In 1776 William King
   praised her in *The Art of Love*, and in 1780 John Nicolls reprinted William
   Temple's *Elegy* on her, appending a biographical note. Articles also
   appeared in *Theatrum Poetarum* 1800 and 1812, and *Biographia Dramatica*
   1782, 1812. In 1861 she was mentioned in Jane Williams's *The Literary
   Women of England*. Edmund Gosse's *Seventeenth-Century Studies* mentioned
   her in 1883, and John Aubrey's *Brief Lives* in 1898. 1904 saw the beginning
   of the 'Orinda Booklets', a series which opened with L.I. Guiney's edition of
   a selection of Philips's poems. Thorn-Drury's *A Little Ark*, 1921, included

J.C.'s *Elegy* on her. In many of these instances, some familiarity with her work is assumed, so reference to her was clearly much wider than this.

3. MARJORIE PLANT, *The English Book Trade: An Economic History of the Making and Sale of Books* (London: Allen and Unwin, 1965); David Vieth, *Attribution in Restoration Poetry: A Study of Rochester's 'Poems' of 1680* (New Haven and London: Yale University Press, 1963).

4. JEREMY TAYLOR, *A Discourse of the Nature, Offices, and Measures of Friendship*, 1657, p. 9.

5. WILLIAM ROBERTS, 'The Dating of Orinda's French Translations', *Philological Quarterly*, 49, 1970.

6. PHILIPS chose this prologue and epilogue from many others offered to her, *Letters from Orinda to Poliarchus*, pp. 119–20.

7. See, for example, Philip Souers, *The Matchless Orinda* (Cambridge, Mass.: Harvard University Press, 1931).

8. The editor was probably Charles Cotterell. The edition was entered in the *Stationers' Register* on the same day as Cotterell's *Relation of the Defeating of Cardinal Mazarin* (21 January 1667).

9. She also refers to an earlier surreptitious edition of some of her poetry in *Letters to Poliarchus*, p. 127: 'I am sure it [*Pompey*] will be as false printed as was my copy of verses to the queen'. I have been unable to identify this text, and believe it might have been a Dublin imprint.

10. Lines were omitted in 1664 from 'On the Fair Weather just at the Coronation'; 'To the Noble Palaemon on his Incomparable Discourse of Friendship'; 'To My Dear Sister Mrs C.P. on her Marriage'. Significant variations between editions affect, for instance, 'Friendship'; 'To the Queen's Majesty'; 'In Memory of F.P.'; 'In Memory of that Excellent Person, Mrs Mary Lloyd'. See also Paul Elmen, 'Some Manuscript Poems by the Matchless Orinda', *Philological Quarterly*, 30, 1951; Catherine Mambretti, '"Fugitive Papers": A New Orinda Poem', *Papers of the Bibliographical Society of America*, 71, 1977.

11. I suspect she was brought in as a stepmother for James's nine-month-old daughter, Frances.

12. RICHARD GREAVES and ROBERT ZALLER, *Biographical Dictionary of English Radicals* (Brighton: Harvester, 1982).

13. SOUERS, op. cit., argues that the Society of Friendship was limited to women, but a letter to Lucasia from Dering quoted in William Clark, *The Early Irish Stage: the Beginnings to 1720* (Oxford: Clarendon Press, 1955), p. 51, shows that men were included. I agree with Souers, though, that relationships with women are celebrated with more intensity than those with men.

14. MAREN-SOFIE RØSTVIG, *The Happy Man: Studies in the Metamorphoses of a Classical Ideal* (Oslo: Norwegian Universities Press, 1962).

15. JEREMY TAYLOR, op. cit., pp. 88–9 and Martin Kornbluth, 'Friendship and Fashion: The Dramatic Treatment of Friendship in the Restoration and Eighteenth Century', unpublished PhD thesis, Pennsylvania State University, 1956.

16. In *Letters to Poliarchus*, p. 124, Philips reports receiving an adulatory poem by an unknown woman; this is probably that one.

4 Excusing the Breach of Nature's Laws: The Discourse of Denial and Disguise in Katherine Philips' Friendship Poetry*

CELIA A. EASTON

Both Easton and Hobby uncover in Philips' friendship poetry a disguised female discourse which privileges emotional and perhaps erotic bonds between women. Hobby's reading accords with her theory of Philips's carefully sculpted public persona: by deploying an acceptably 'feminine' subject matter, Philips constructed an escape route from marital subjection without appearing to do so. Easton's theory of two rival textual voices leaves less room for autonomy. Femininity in her reading is less a strategic role than a powerful, constraining discourse imprinted on Philips's poetry, which seeks (and fails) to suppress any engagement with the political and physical world. The tension of repression which Easton detects in Philips's verse points to both the ideological pressures which shaped her identity and her resistance of those culturally assigned meanings. While Hobby's reading facilitates Philips's enlistment into the ranks of early feminists, Easton's underlines a more ambivalent relationship to the patriarchal dictates which Philips struggled to embody and strained against.

In his preface to the first authorized edition of Katherine Philips' *Poems*, her editor and confidant, Charles Cotterell, praises the poems that follow by attempting to situate them beyond gender, beyond history, beyond language, beyond geography, and beyond mortal existence:

Some of them would be no disgrace to the name of any man that amongst us is most esteemed for his excellency in this kind, and there are none that may not pass with favour, when it is remembered that they fell hastily from the pen but of a Woman. We might well have

---

* Reprinted from *Restoration: Studies in English Literary Culture, 1660–1700*, 14, no. 1 (Spring, 1990), pp. 1–14.

call'd her the English *Sappho*, she of all the female Poets of former
Ages, being for her Verses and her Vertues both, the most highly to
be valued; but she has called her self ORINDA, a name that deserves
to be added to the number of the Muses, and to live with honour as
long as they. Were our language as generally known to the world
as the Greek and Latine were anciently, or as the French is now, her
Verses could not be confin'd within the narrow limits of our islands,
but would spread themselves as far as the Continent has Inhabitants,
or as the Seas have any shore. And for her Vertues, they as much
surpass'd those of *Sappho* as the Theological do the Moral, (wherein
yet *Orinda* was not her inferiour) or as the fading immortality of an
earthly Lawrel, which the justice of men cannot deny to her excellent
Poetry, is transcended by that incorruptible and eternal Crown of
Glory where with the Mercy of God hath undoubtedly rewarded her
more eminent Piety.

This urging for transcendence typifies the neo-platonism espoused by
Philips and her circle of friends; the movement toward the 'eternal
Crown of Glory' fittingly acknowledges Philips' recent, untimely death.
The condescending 'pen but of a Woman' is echoed by women and
men alike in the seventeenth century. But Cotterell's introduction
to the poems of 'The Matchless Orinda' reveals more than sexist
commonplaces and conventions of praise. The areas of transcendence
Cotterell outlines are precisely those that trigger what I shall call a
'discourse of denial and disguise' in Katherine Philips' poetry. Orinda's
poems, in fact, insist upon their ties to gender, history, and language,
although they often seem to follow the path to a superior realm
Cotterell maps out both for the collection and its author. At times,
Philips draws her reader beyond history while she herself is covering
up her royalist politics prior to the Restoration; at other times, she
appeals to a transcendent, non-physical notion of friendship while
creating exclusive, affectionate bonds with other women.[1]

I do not focus on the categories of politics and affection arbitrarily.
One of the interests of this essay is the way in which the poems from
one category draw upon the other for their metaphors. Philips is best
known for her poems on friendship, though the first poem in the 1667
collection defends the memory of Charles I against the satirical pen of a
man who would 'murder' the king again, in print.[2] The poet protests in
the opening line of this poem, 'I think not on the State', then proceeds
to chastise Vavasor Powell for libelling the dead king. The lines in
which Orinda explains why she must speak out – though it is irregular
for her to do so as a woman and an apolitical person – tellingly parallel
her protests against – and partial reconciliation with – the physical
world in her friendship poems:

> ... this is a cause
> That will excuse the breach of Nature's laws.
> Silence were now a sin, nay Passion now
> Wise men themselves for Merit would allow.
>
> (*Poems*, 1)

'Nature's laws', a phrase that echoes the popularity of the new science of the seventeenth century, here refers to rules of decorum and propriety rather than principles of physics. A woman's 'natural' condition is silence; passion most grievously violates that nature. But a 'cause' can invert the natural order, transforming 'whatever is' into 'whatever's not'.

The poetry of Mrs. Katherine Philips, the Matchless Orinda, whether political or affectionate, struggles with 'nature' and its contradiction. To sort out the conflicting voices in the poetry, we might think of 'Philips' as the voice of the woman whose proper place is guarded, 'Orinda' as the voice of the poet for whom silence is a sin. For Orinda, the medium for violating the natural order is the language of poetry. It is Philips who needs transcendence, who dares not acknowledge a political, public, or physically affectionate life; it is Orinda who circumvents the censor, whose metaphors return the subjects of her poetry to the physical world.

These voices may overlap, and yet are separate from the biographical Katherine Philips. Katherine Fowler, age sixteen, married James Philips, age fifty-four, in 1648. During the Commonwealth, while James Philips served the Cromwell government by quelling Royalist uprisings, she lived both in her husband's home in Wales and in their London lodgings (Souers, 24–28). Her acquaintances in London, mostly Royalist sympathizers, included childhood friends, the poets Henry Vaughan and Abraham Cowley, and the theologian Jeremy Taylor.[3] Philips' 'Society of Friends', described in her poetry as a group of close friends, each assigned classical names and addressed with the hyperbolic conventions of friendship literature (Charles Cotterell, for example, was 'Worthy Poliarchus'), may or may not have met regularly. Souers casts doubt on the theory that Philips headed a salon for intellectuals, pointing to the infrequency of her visits to London. More likely, he asserts, the Society's 'members' kept in touch through correspondence and the circulation of poems in manuscript (43–44).

In the eighteenth century, the English equivalent of the *salon* was the 'Bluestocking party', a gathering run by one of several intellectual women for the purpose of drawing together men and women for 'serious' (i.e., regarding art and literature) conversation. Souers argues that Philips would not have been sponsoring such parties in the seventeenth century, since the focus on friendship in her poetry (and

91

there is very little other evidence for the 'Society') is almost exclusively
female 'Orinda's Society was not a salon', he asserts, 'it was the official
order of Friendship in the kingdom of feminine sensibility' (44). It is
possible that Professor Souers, whose 1931 biography of Philips is the
only book-length study of her life and work, might startle at Lillian
Faderman's observation that had Orinda 'written in the twentieth
century, her poetry would undoubtedly have been identified as
"lesbian"', but there is no critical dispute that Orinda desires to define
her friendships in exclusively female terms. The poems make clear that
whatever respect the biographical Philips received from her husband
and male acquaintances, the poet, Orinda, felt compelled to defend
women's friendships as, alternatively, equal to and superior to men's.

Katherine Philips consulted Jeremy Taylor in the 1650s on the nature
of friendship. Taylor dedicated to her his 1657 'Discourse of the Nature,
Offices and Measures of Friendship', 'Written in answer to a Letter from
the most ingenious and vertuous M.K.P.,' i.e., Mrs. Katherine Philips.
Taylor's acknowledgment of his friendship with his correspondent
certifies both that Philips' friendship society was well known and that
Taylor believed friendship could extend across gender – as far as the
limits of gender allowed. Much of Taylor's book depends upon Cicero's
De Amicitia, with two major exceptions in the argument. In Cicero's
dialogue, Laelius insists that one never think of one's friend as 'useful',
and he is explicit in declaring that friendship is possible only between
two good (virtuous) men. Taylor explains that he does not mean to
sound 'mercenary' (28), but that he believes a sign of a worthy man is
his ability to do the most good; a man who loves him will do him 'all
the good he can' (30).

Taylor's other break with the classical conception of friendship, which
speaks most directly to Philips' concerns, is his slight admission of
women to friendship's realm. First of all, they may enter through
marriage: 'Marriage is the Queen of friendships, in which there is a
communication of all that can be communicated by friendship . . . being
made sacred by vows and love, by bodies and souls, by interest and
custome, by religion and by laws . . .' (72). Taylor concludes that
marriage is the archetype of friendship, friendships being marriages
of the soul (74). Even when he considers women outside marriage,
he continues to view them in relation to or in comparison with men.
Since Taylor's conception of friendship begins with Christian charity,
he is willing to admit that women are capable of generous acts.
He addresses the subject explicitly in an aside (for which he later
apologizes, seeming to have lost sight of his argument):

> But by the way (Madam) you may see how much I differ from the
> morosity of those Cynics who would not admit your sex in to the

communities of a noble friendship. I believe some Wives have been
the best friends in the world. . . .

(86)

But Taylor's sense of women is that they are imperfect men:

I cannot say that Women are capable of all those excellencies by
which men can oblige the world; and therefore a femal[e] friend in
some cases is not so good a counsellor as a wise man, and cannot so
well defend my honour; nor dispose of reliefs and assistances if she
be under the power of another. . . .

(88)

These defects, he admits, are no reason to exclude women from
friendship. Women may never be wise men, but, then again, neither
will many men.

Orinda's poetry consciously swerves from several points of Taylor's
wisdom. Although she does write a handful of epithalamiums,[4] most
of the poems celebrate the friendship of women. When Taylor contends
that a woman cannot 'defend my honour', his examples are explicitly
military, of men sacrificing themselves for others in battle. Philips, the
voice of restraint, acknowledges that woman's place is not in warfare,
but Orinda will often adopt military metaphors when addressing
another woman, simultaneously imitating and defying the poetic
practices of men.

Orinda expresses affection in military language most explicitly in her
poem, 'To the truly Noble Mrs. Anne Owen, on my first Approaches'.
The language is a convention of male speech, as Taylor's document
reveals. But Orinda does not merely adopt military metaphors for her
own seductive purposes. The poem's simultaneous distance from and
embrace of the language of conquerors makes it clear that the speaker
is a woman self-consciously appropriating a language that is not hers,
not merely imitating male conventions:

Madam,
As in a Triumph Conquerors admit
Their meanest Captives to attend on it,
Who, though unworthy, have the power confest,
And justifi'd the yielding of the rest:
So when the busie World (in hope t'excuse
Their own surprize) your Conquests do peruse,
And find my name, they will be apt to say,
Your charms were blinded, or else thrown away.
There is no honour got in gaining me,

93

Who am a prize not worth your Victory.
But this will clear you, that 'tis general,
The worst applaud what is admir'd by all.
But I have plots in't: for the way to be
Secure of fame to all posterity,
Is to obtain the honour I pursue,
To tell the World I was subdu'd by you.
And since in you all wonders common are,
Your Votaries may in your Vertues share,
While you by noble Magick worth impart:
She that can Conquer, can reclaim a heart.
Of this Creation I shall not despair,
Since for your own sake it concerns your care.
For 'tis More honour that the World should know,
You made a noble Soul, than found it so.

(Poems, 33–34)

The conceit of the poem is a simple one: Anne Owen is a 'Conqueror', and Orinda is her 'Captive'. Orinda effects a self-deprecating voice, praising her friend by disparaging herself. According to the poem, Anne Owen wins no glory in conquering Orinda, since Orinda is not worth Anne's attentions; but she is honored, in the world's eyes, by ennobling Orinda's soul, by imparting the conqueror's virtues to the conquered.

The metaphor is familiar in the romance tradition, echoed in the Cavalier poems of Orinda's male contemporaries. But Orinda, intimately addressing Anne Owen from the beginning of the poem, explicitly subverts conventional sex roles. Can one argue that this poem, by the 'English Sappho', is meant to be read, as many of Sappho's lyrics were through the nineteenth century, as a fictional, male persona addressing a woman? I believe there is no mistaking that this is a poem about the conquering of one woman's heart by another. The traditionally feminine tokens 'honour' and 'prize' are associated with the speaker. Anne is compared to a triumphant military leader, yet she retains certain conventionally female attributes: her 'charms' and her 'Vertues'. Orinda is no passive captive, however; she plots and pursues and creates. Not only has Orinda challenged the conventional male/female structure of a conquest poem, she has also created a woman's voice that can be simultaneously submissive and aggressive. In this way, Orinda does not merely imitate a tradition of heterosexual conquest. Rejecting the static positions of conqueror and conquered through a fluidity of roles, she dismantles the power relations of erotic expression.

If this is a 'breach of Nature's laws', it is not without a 'cause'. Ostensibly, Orinda can push beyond the boundaries of gender's commonplaces because, as she has presented the problem in the poem, she must preserve Anne Owen's reputation, lest 'the world' believe it has been sullied by an unworthy conquest. Blame me, says Orinda: let the world understand the pursuit as mine, satisfying my desire to be 'subdu'd by you'. If Orinda merely proposed this plot and let go of it, Anne would be relieved of her connections with male metaphors, since Orinda has asserted herself as the true aggressor. But the fiction is too pleasurable to renounce. She is not ashamed of the lie she has produced: 'Of *this Creation* I shall not despair.' She will pretend, for the world's sake, that Anne is not responsible for her conquest, but in the end Orinda wants both women to be seen as both 'Conquerors' and 'Captives'.

The strange part of this poem is that even though it turns upon the imagined opinion of 'the World', it ends transcendently. Orinda becomes Anne's 'Votary'; Anne ennobles Orinda's Soul. This is the tension between what I have called, for shorthand purposes, the voices of Philips and Orinda. Orinda's language is, after all, not merely military but also sexual: the title refers to her 'first Approaches'; line 9 refers to Anne 'gaining me'; and in line 16 Orinda admits she desires to be 'subdu'd'. In steering the subject away from the physical and into a transcendent realm, Philips echoes Jeremy Taylor's definition of friendship as a marriage of souls. But that definition does not have the ultimate voice in this poem. The last lines, 'For 'tis more honour that the World should know,/You made a noble Soul, than found it so,' remind the reader that even though it is desirable to have a 'noble soul', Orinda, living in a fleshly world, does not gain hers without external intercession.

In a strategy of denial, Philips appeals to a neo-platonic, spiritual notion of friendship. Orinda circumvents this denial by imposing the physical world, through metaphor, upon the transcendent. This suggests to me two separate concerns in the poetry. The first is simply repression: politics, public life, homoeroticism and physicality make Philips nervous, so she admits them only as vehicles to a 'higher' truth. The inevitable return of the repressed, however, is staged through Orinda's metaphors. They insist, no matter how much *Philips* cries, 'I think not on the State', *Orinda* does.

The second concern of the poetry, as I read it, relates to this tension of repression. It is the implicit exploration in Orinda's work of the nature and power of poetic language. In the Anne Owen poem I have been describing above, Orinda defends her 'Creation', which is to say, her fiction or her lie, which she enacts in the course of the poem. Composed of language, this creation opposes the ideal realm of friendship, where souls ought to be able to merge without mediation. But if Philips – the voice that favors *soul* over body – wishes to celebrate her friendships, she is dependent upon Orinda's mediating language. Another poem to Anne Owen, 'To my Lucasia, in defence of declared Friendship,' seems to suggest that, though friendship is discovered in the ideal realm, it is maintained by its verbal celebration. The following lines are selected from the twenty-stanza poem:

1

O My Lucasia, let us speak our Love,
    And think not that impertinent can be,
Which to us both doth such assurance prove,
    And whence we find how justly we agree.

7

Think not 'tis needless to repeat desires;
    The fervent Turtles always court and bill,
And yet their spotless passion never tires,
    But does encrease by repetition still.

8

Although we know we love, yet while our Soul
    Is thus imprison'd by the Flesh we wear,
There's no way left that bondage to controul,
    But to convey transactions through the Ear.

9

Nay, though we read our passions in the Eye,
    It will oblige and please to tell them too.
Such joys as these by motion multiply,
    Were't but to find that our Souls told us true.

16

If I distrust, 'tis my own worth for thee,
    'Tis my own fitness for a love like thine;
And therefore still new evidence would see,
    T' assure my wonder that thou canst be mine.

17

But as the Morning-Sun to drooping Flowers;
    As weary Travellers a Shade to find,
As to the parched Violet Evening-showers;
    Such is from thee to me a Look that's kind.

18

But when that Look is drest in Words, 'tis like
    The mystick pow'r of Musick's unison;
Which when the finger doth one Viol strike,
    The other's string heaves to reflection.

(Poems, 82–85)

Insecurity commonly motivates demands for written expressions of devotion: some lovers declare their affection in poetry, others in newspaper advertisements, still others in death-defying graffiti, spray-painting 'I love you Carol always' across highway overpasses. Many a love affair is over, however, before an author has time to develop the metaphysical justification for announced love that Philips produces in this poem.

Her justification is logically flawed, though sentimentally attractive. Philips first attempts to tiptoe around the physical world in stanza 7: how does one explain 'desires' and 'passion' in the context of transcendent friendship? The turtle doves seem to provide a safe metaphor. Although they are 'fervent', their passion is 'spotless'. Yet we are left with an image of Orinda and Lucasia contentedly cooing and cooing and cooing. Orinda will not be satisfied with a single declaration. As she echoes the 'repeat' of the first line of this stanza in the 'repetition' of the fourth, one senses that this is another occasion on which 'silence were now a sin'.

Her logic breaks down more explicitly in stanza 8. Here we are invited by Philips' Christian neo-platonism to consider 'the Flesh' a prison house for 'the Soul'. As prisoners, we desire to control this 'bondage', and we might expect to do so through an appeal to an outside force, i.e., the warden, God, Grace, or some other unfleshly power. There seems to be a bit of corruption in the prison house, however, since our resource is an insider: 'the Ear'. Or perhaps this sense organ is a privileged prisoner. Promoted, though not freed, for good behavior, the Ear sympathizes with the soul's desire for freedom. The Ear loosens the soul's bonds. The Ear enables one soul to pass a message of affection to another.

Before discussing how the Ear might have gained its favored status, I want to contrast it with the other privileged portion of the flesh that appears in stanza 9: 'the Eye'. The Eye has traditionally held a superior office as the conveyor of the soul's intentions. Through the Eye, Orinda says, friends can read each other's passions. Lucasia's look, she admits in stanza 17, is like sunshine, an oasis, a resuscitating shower. But 'that Look' is improved as a token of affection, she contends in stanza 18, if it is 'drest in Words'. In this cause, Orinda will not settle for silence. The Ear has greater control over the flesh than the Eye does.

Katherine Philips died several years before Milton's Satan stigmatized the Ear by tempting rather than liberating Eve's soul with a few well placed whispers in her innocent aural cavity. We have no reason to be suspicious of this sense organ in this poem to Lucasia. On the contrary, the Ear assumes the special role of being the part of the flesh that can affect our control over the bondage of the flesh because it is the organ that receives language – at least spoken language. Orinda commands in the first line of the poem, 'let us speak our Love'. Her poem, while commanding, is also her speech-act, for here Orinda does 'speak her love'. Creating by speaking is action with precedents no one need be ashamed of, the most famous of which is recounted in the first two chapters of Genesis. So Philips treads on safe ground poetically, and in an extended sense, theologically (the creation of the world producing a harmonious music of the spheres), when she suggests in the 18th stanza that composed ('drest in') words are like harmonious music, 'reflecting' one note with another through sympathetic vibration. This is to say, language is creative, language, like music, creates special relationships, and language improves understanding that depends merely upon visual impressions.

But something is wrong with the Eyes and Ears of this work; Philips ignores language's written, rather than spoken, capacities, an odd position to take in a composed poem. Is she practicing denial? writing sloppily? composing cleverly? The synaesthesia of stanza 18 curiously directs us to this problem. I read the musical simile two ways. The first is that there are two musicians; one responds to the performance of the other as each contributes separate lines of a duet. The second interpretation is that the sounding of one string on one instrument effects the sounding of a second string on that instrument through sympathetic vibration, though that string is not played by the musician. I will not dispute there may be other readings of these lines. My quibble is over the word 'reflection', a word borrowed from the sense world of the Eye rather than the Ear. Even allowing for changes in English pronunciation since the 17th century, 'reflection' is not a particularly strong rhyme for 'unison'. I believe it is purposefully chosen. Orinda seems to have invented *aural* reflection to describe her relationship with Lucasia.

The relationship is as contradictory as the mixing of Ear and Eye because it resists seventeenth-century expectations of women's behaviour. Orinda must convince Lucasia that declared love is not 'impertinent'. She gives permission for a woman to 'oblige and please' (stanza 9) not a man, but another woman. She intimates a physical dimension to their friendship when she claims the Viol string (stanza 18) does not merely echo or respond but *'heaves* to reflection'. Here, as in the earlier poem to Anne Owen, Orinda calls for performance within the corporeal world rather than transcendence of it.

The third contradiction of this poem is its denial of its graphic dimension. This contradiction actually consolidates the poem's contradiction of senses (Eye/Ear) and contradiction of behaviors (expected/resisted). I have been trying to suggest in the discussions of these two poems to Anne Owen that 'Philips'' desires contradict 'Orinda's.' Orinda situates her friendships in a public, political,

physical world. Philips retreats from this world through an appeal to
an ideal of friendship between souls rather than bodies. Orinda resists
Philips' denial by disguising her physical desires as metaphors, rather
than subjects, in her poetry. Philips seems to reply that if poetry is
the vehicle by which she will 'speak her Love', she will make it as
transcendent as possible by denying its relation to the *visible* world.

Although Katherine Philips' poems circulated in manuscript
throughout the interregnum, she refused to have them published
until her friends convinced her that she must do so in order to refute
the faulty, pirated edition of her work, which appeared in 1664.
Unpublished poems might seem more likely to appeal to the aural
rather than visible world. But even they leave their graphic trace on
handwritten pages. The written poem is an 'aural reflection.' It is the
means by which Orinda and Lucasia can coo and coo and coo together,
even though they are separated in Wales and London. It is a fiction,
of course. Orinda is not 'speaking' but *writing* her love. But it is an
acceptable 'Creation', as Orinda says in the earlier poem, one which
pretends merely to give forth invisible sounds.

Philips repeats the idea that real poetry, verse that will be eternal, is
voiced rather than inscribed in her poem, 'To my Lady Elizabeth Boyle,
Singing now affairs, &c'. Here again are political and military
metaphors; here again are sounds of sexual submission. And here
again is an explicit denial of the power of the pen:

> Subduing fair! what will you win
>   To use a needless Dart:
> Why then so many to take in
>   One undefended heart?
> I came expos'd to all your Charms,
>   'Gainst which the first half hour
> I had no will to take up Armes,
>   And in the next no Power.
> How can you chuse but win the Day,
>   Who can resist your Siege,
> Who in one action know the way
>   To Vanquish and Oblige?
> Your Voice which can in melting strains
>   Teach Beauty to be blind,
> Confines me yet in stronger Chains,
>   By being soft and kind.
> Whilst you my trivial fancy sing,
>   You it to wit refine,
> As Leather once stamp'd by a King
>   Became a Current Coin.

By this my Verse is sure to gain
  Eternity with men,
Which by your voice it will obtain,
  Though never by my Pen.
I'd rather in your favour live
  Then in a lasting name,
And much a greater rate would give
  For Happiness then Fame.

(Poems, 107)

This poem of praise and gratitude to a woman who, with others of
Katherine Philips' acquaintance, learned and privately performed songs
from Philips' *Pompey* (a translation of Corneille), is another poem from
a vanquished lover to her conqueror. It too depends on contrasts: the
oxymoronic 'Subduing fair' suggests an androgynous Elizabeth Boyle;
chains are made stronger 'By being soft and kind.' Will contrasts with
power, voice with pen, and happiness with fame. Yet even these
contrasts are of two sorts: paradoxes and choices. The paradox of
the aggressive woman or the soft chain is acceptably unreconciled, but
choices must be decided. Orinda's duel of will and power dissolves in
a double defeat, but voice wins out over pen and happiness over fame.
Philips consistently selects the least physical and least visible quality or
object, but Orinda equally consistently undermines that choice. Philips
may be thinking of transcendent friendship, but Orinda's poem is still
panting from Elizabeth Boyle's obliging siege.

    The siege's success, according to the poem, depends neither on the
pen nor on another superfluous, long, pointed object, the 'needless dart'.
The third line of the poem clarifies the complaint: Boyle's quantity of
erotic arrows is excessive; Orinda's heart puts up no defense. There
really is no question of Boyle shooting too many phallic weapons
against Orinda; there is no need for any dart at all. Orinda claims that
she cannot resist the woman 'Who in one action know(s) the way/To
Vanquish and Oblige.' I find nothing unusual in Orinda's use of
military metaphor: she draws equally from poetic convention and her
own adult life in England during the Civil Wars. But she emasculates
the convention. The 'Dart' is needless.

    And so, for the same reasons perhaps, the pen is also needless.
Charles Cotterell's introduction to the *Poems* makes it clear that most
verses are the products of the pens of men. He also tellingly notes
that Orinda's poems 'fell hastily' from her pen, as if she wanted to rid
herself of that tool as quickly as possible. To have a poem and not a
pen is paradoxical, but paradoxes do not upset this poet. Although
Orinda knows the power of poetic language and Philips knows the
harmony of souls fed by linguistic communication, there are serious

objections from both perspectives to the symbolism of the pen. Its mark is too physical for Philips. Its connections are too masculine for Orinda.

Orinda's rejection of masculine symbolism contributes to her 'Sapphic', if not 'feminist' identity. Hilda Smith cites Katherine Philips as an early feminist role model because of her 'retreat' poems, which promote pastoral escape with other women from a male world of politics, war, and sexuality (Smith 154–155).[5] Since Katherine Philips' concerns about gender difference led her to no political action, nor even to question the sexist commonplaces spoken by her husband and male friends, 'feminist' sounds as anachronistic as Faderman's label, 'lesbian'. Her poetic vision is one of separatism and a rejection of phallocentrism. Her poetic passions are lesbian, whether or not they accurately describe physical consummation. The seventeenth-century provides no descriptive erotic vocabulary for such female discourse, unless we expand the customarily asexual label, 'The English Sappho', that Katherine Philips shared with Anne Killigrew and others. By validating women's friendship as a theme that combines Katherine Philips' contradictory voices, the poems represent a Sapphic discourse produced by a rejected pen.[6]

Despite Jeremy Taylor's concession that wives make good friends, the words flowing from the pens of most men Orinda knew of, since Aristotle and Cicero, claimed that women did not have the capacity to be friends – whether with men or (had it been thought of) with other women. Theological opinion admitted, by the seventeenth century, that women did indeed have souls, but having less power of reason, women's souls were more vulnerable than men's to corruption and wickedness. Orinda disputes both classical wisdom and theological prejudice. She argues in a didactic, fifteen stanza poem, 'A Friend', that such biases are based on faulty premises. Gender distinctions are part of the material world; souls are only temporarily imprisoned in that world. It is the 'Philips' voice that appeals to transcendence as an argument for equality in the fourth stanza:

> If Souls no Sexes have, for Men t'exclude
>   Women from Friendship's vast capacity,
> Is a design injurious or rude,
>   Onely maintain'd by partial tyranny.
> Love is allow'd to us and Innocence,
>   And noblest Friendships do proceed from thence.
>
> (*Poems*, 95)

This is another safe argument: Philips takes the tyrant's own words and throws them back at him. Having granted (Christian) women the capacity to love – as daughters, wives, and mothers – and having acknowledged women's 'innocence' by their ready protection of it, Philips' male contemporaries have already granted women the vital ingredients of friendship. Moreover, if they truly believe in the separation of the body and the soul, they must dismiss their idea that women's souls are as encumbered as their bodies by their gender. Friendship, being the merging of souls, is gender neutral.

'A Friend' asserts that when women are defined in terms of their relations with men, as daughters, mothers, or wives, they love on a less pure level than they do as friends. Friendship is, the third stanza claims,

> Nobler th[a]n Kindred or th[a]n Marriage-band,
>   Because more free; Wedlock-felicity
> It self doth only by this Union stand,
>   And turns to Friendship or to Misery.
> Force or Design Matches to pass may bring,
> But Friendship doth from Love and Honour spring.

Relationships, this poem explains, can be created by family, formality, or force, but these are not inherently felicitous joinings. The stanza concludes with Philips' appeal to the abstract ideals of Love and Honor, which produce friendship. If earthly relationships are to produce any happiness at all, they must include friendship. But why is friendship 'more free' than 'Kindred' or 'Marriage-band'? From a seventeenth-century woman's perspective, it is the only relationship over which she has control, having no choice over the family into which she is born and little choice in the man she must marry. But women's friendships are also freer from obligations and consequences than family or marriage. As a daughter, a mother, or a wife, a woman must serve someone else; in friendships between women, love is mutually exchanged.

Another poem, 'Friendship', argues that friendship is not merely more free but also more pure than heterosexual union:

> All Love is Sacred, and the Marriage-tie
> Hath much of Honour and Divinity.
> But Lust, Design, or some unworthy ends
> May mingle there, which are despis'd by Friends.

(78–79, ll. 29–32)

Not only does Katherine Philips fret over the corruptibility of marriage, she also clings to an ideal notion of friendship unblemished by desire, manipulation, or expectation. Yet these are certainly attributes – positive attributes – of the friendships Orinda reveals in her poems to other women. Perhaps coming exposed to Elizabeth Boyle's charms is not 'lust'; perhaps creating a fiction of desiring to be subdued by

Anne Owen is not 'design'; perhaps demanding a declaration of love is a 'worthy end' unto itself. But this is a philosophical poem, not specific in its address. It holds back the very physical tokens Orinda offers her intimates.

Curiously, Philips' rejection of the physical also rejects a belief in equality of the sexes. She measures men and women by different standards, degrading men and idealizing women. The poems suggest that men degrade themselves by seeking material conquests. For Philips, women's friendships prove that their values are superior to men's. Many feminists would reject this view of women's nature. It fails to query whether or not women, in general, would object more than men to war, violence, ambition, and politics if greater opportunity for participation in so called 'men's activities' had been available to them. Philips accepts the seventeenth-century commonplaces: with fewer ties to the world, women can more easily transcend it. By idealizing women as superior peace-makers, Orinda validates the lesbian discourse of her poems addressed to women: appeals to women's 'nature' provide a socially acceptable excuse for preferring women to men.

In her philosophical, defining poems, like 'A Friend' and 'Friendship', Orinda proves that the pen can nearly murder a subject by cramming it into lengthy, laborios stanzas. But when she addresses her friends, when her poem becomes not merely a description but also an act of friendship, it delights with lyrical freshness, the aural reflection of unaffected affection. In 'To my Excellent Lucasia, on our Friendship', Orinda combines commonplaces with the gushing of an enamored individual. Here, again, body contrasts with soul, men's happiness contrasts with women's. Here, again, Philips situates friendship in an ideal realm. But here again, as well, Orinda's worldly, poetic language steals back the subject: friendship does not entirely abandon the earth.

> I did not live until this time
>   Crown'd my felicity,
> When I could say without a crime,
>   I am not thine, but Thee.
>
> This Carcass breath'd, and walkt, and slept,
>   So that the World believ'd
> There was a Soul the Motions kept;
>   But they were all deceiv'd.
>
> For as a Watch by art is wound
>   To motion, such was mine:
> But never had *Orinda* found
>   A Soul till she found thine;

103

Which now inspires, cures, and supplies,
    And guides my darkned Breast:
For thou art all that I can prize,
    My Joy, my Life, my Rest.

No Bridegrooms nor Crown-conquerors mirth
    To mine compar'd can be:
They have but pieces of this Earth,
    I've all the World in thee.

Then let our Flames still light and shine,
    And no false fear controul,
As innocent as our Design,
    Immortal as our Soul.

Without Lucasia, Orinda was a soulless automaton, a cadaver imitating human life. Since they have become friends, Orinda's previously empty shell has found joy, life, and rest. This is no mere marriage of souls, however; Orinda seems to have consumed Lucasia, to have become Lucasia, to have absorbed Lucasia's soul. The last stanza explains that their souls are like flames: Orinda's appropriation of Lucasia's soul intensifies rather than consumes it.

Nevertheless, 'To my Excellent Lucasia, on our Friendship' does not abandon its reader, disembodied, in friendship's transcendent realm. Men's happiness, as 'Bridegrooms' or 'Crown-conquerors', is admittedly a material happiness scorned by Philips. But it is also inferior to the speaker's because it is produced by mere 'pieces of this Earth', in contrast with having 'all the World in thee'. Philips is slipping here: her preference is not for the spiritual over the temporal, but for the whole over a part. Admittedly, 'this Earth' is a subset of 'the World', the latter including both the tangible and the intangible. An automaton plus a soul equal a self. Correspondingly, the Earth plus the transcendent realm equal the World. Totality is not merely in the transcendent realm of friendship. Orinda has *all the world* 'in thee', in the person of Lucasia.

In her poem, 'A Friend', the word 'design' was part of a tyrannical toolkit, wielded by rude men who wanted to exclude women from the delights of friendship. In the last stanza of this poem to Lucasia, however, both the women's 'Flames' and their 'Design' are 'innocent'. Design, in Orinda's woman-identified world, is prelapsarian, creative, uncorrupt.

Yet her design is physical. She rejects the 'crown-conquerors', conveniently displacing her political allegiances to both the crown-conquering Puritans and the crown-conquered Royalists. But the eliminated subject returns as metaphor. The first two lines of the poem confess, 'I did not live until this time/Crown'd my felicity.' Philips pretends to be apolitical, but Orinda adorns her messages of affection with political imagery. She also situates that affection in the temporal world: 'this time' crowns her felicity. The ideal realm is eternal, beyond time; Orinda's friendships are here and now.

In the third stanza, she compares her former self to a watch, underscoring this concern with time. The simile is unfavorable: a watch is mechanically driven, and so was Orinda before she received Lucasia's soul. The difference between the mechanical and the inspired life Orinda desires is the difference between an individual and a community. The watch is a creation, designed to perform a task. It is functional and observable, but not – in the terms of 1980s' tech toys – interactive. Lucasia's soul, in contrast, inspires, cures, supplies and guides. Once again, it is the interchange of friendship that most attracts Orinda. But the watch has been enhanced, not replaced. The interchange of friendship occurs in mortal time.

I want to return now to Charles Cotterell's list of praise, with which I began this essay. He says Orinda's poems would not disgrace 'the name of any man'. He claims her poems are timeless, for her name should 'live with honour as long as' the Muses. He laments the isolation of the English language, for he believes Orinda's verses speak beyond the concerns of national boundaries. And finally, her poetry, which he claims reflects her 'Vertues', surpassing Sappho, he compares to heavenly glories. Cotterell's goal is not consistent literary criticism. He confuses the poet and her poetry as he shifts his praise of the virtues of each, but his interests are appropriate for discussing a poet whose poems extol transcendence.

The physical side of Orinda's poetry does not reach Charles Cotterell; she excludes it through denial and disguise. According to seventeenth-century social conventions, the poet, Katherine Philips, respects 'Nature's Laws': she marries, she mothers, she muses. Her Sapphic persona, Orinda, who forms bonds outside marriage, who renames her friends, and who writes – with a pen – unconventional verses, breaks the Laws. The tension of voices in the poems includes the kind of writer Cotterell describes: a virtuos, timeless, universal, woman poet. But Orinda's voice also insists on poetry not merely in thought but in deed, as she physically reinscribes herself in morality, history, and place.

Notes

1. Her topics have ultimately cost her a readership. Lucy Brashear has argued persuasively that Katherine Philips' poems recognize 'society's restrictions

against a serious woman poet' (69), and that Philips' poems ceased to be read, after the eighteenth century, because they are women's friendship poems.

2. 'Upon the Double Murther of K. Charles I, in Answer to a Libellous Copy of Rimes by Vavasor Powell,' *Poems*, 1–2. Souers (82) estimates the date of this attack on the versifier Powell to be 1653. Although the poem indicates some sympathy for the executed king, it focuses on Powell's maliciousness in print. This poem, like the rest of Philips' work, would have circulated privately prior to the Restoration, inoffensive to her royalist friends and discreetly shielding her Puritan family from anti-Commonwealth publicity.

3. Thomas cracks some of Orinda's code names and discusses several of Orinda's relationships with male poets before the Restoration. He detects echoes in several poems between Orinda and Vaughan. Cowley wrote a tribute poem for the introduction of the posthumous *Poems*.

4. Elizabeth Hageman discusses Philips' wedding poems (for relatives and friends) briefly in her 1986 pamphlet, and has expanded on this topic in 'In England: Katherine Philips and the Epithalamion', a paper delivered at the Medieval and Renaissance Conference, Binghamton, NY, October 1987. See also Hageman's introduction to Orinda, 'The Matchless Orinda: Katherine Philips' in Wilson (especially 567–569).

5. Mulvihill strongly disagrees with Smith's assessment of Philips, suggesting that Smith imposes her own ideology upon the seventeenth-century poet (126).

6. The struggle with labels may be less important for our subjects than for our sense of ourselves as critics and the readings we thereby produce. The physical nature of Katherine Philips' homoeroticism is even more disguised than the 'spiritual' friendships Martha Vicinus describes (noting the inadequacy and inaccuracy of the word, 'lesbian') in her study of economically independent women in the nineteenth century. Yet their paradoxical relationships, as Vicinus explains them, resemble the tension in Katherine Philips' poetry: 'No matter how much women, and especially religious women, might call their friendship "spiritual", they were keenly alive to its earthly component' (Vicinus, 160). Just as 'sexual' meant 'heterosexual' for women in the nineteenth century, Philips' homoeroticism does not explicitly replace the heterosexual erotic. She may be identified with Adrienne Rich's concept of a 'lesbian continuum', if not 'lesbian history', regardless of her 'genital experience with another woman' (Rich, 648). Yet I also respect Bonnie Zimmerman's urging for expanded identification of lesbian writing. I intend my chosen phrase, 'Sapphic', to focus on the homoeroticism of the discourse rather than the poet or her subjects.

References

BRASHEAR, LUCY. 'The Forgotten Legacy of "The Matchless Orinda"'. *The Anglo-Welsh Review* 65 (1979): 68–76.

FADERMAN, LILLIAN. *Surpassing the Love of Men*. New York: William Morrow, 1981.

HAGEMAN, ELIZABETH. *Katherine Philips: 'The Matchless Orinda'*. Saskatoon, Canada: Peregrina Publishing Co., 1986.

MULVIHILL, MAUREEN E. 'Essential Studies of Restoration Women Writers: Reclaiming a Heritage'. *Restoration: Studies in English Literary Culture, 1660–1700* 11 (1987): 122–131.

PHILIPS, KATHERINE. *Poems of the Most Deservedly Admired Mrs. Katherine Philips, The Matchless Orinda. To which is added Monsieur Corneille's Pompey & Horace, Tragedies. With Several other Translations out of the French*. London: Printed by J.M. for H. Herringman, at the Sign of the Blew Anchor in the Lower Walk of the New Exchange, 1667.

RICH, ADRIENNE. 'Compulsory Heterosexuality and Lesbian Existence'. *Signs: Journal of Women in Culture and Society* 5 (1980): 631–660.

SMITH, HILDA L. *Reason's Disciples: Seventeenth-Century English Feminists*. Urbana: University of Illinois Press, 1982.

SOUERS, PHILIP. *The Matchless Orinda*. Cambridge: Harvard University Press, 1931.

THOMAS, PATRICK. 'Orinda, Vaughan and Watkyns: Anglo-Welsh Literary Relationships during the Interregnum'. *The Anglo-Welsh Review* 26 (1976): 96–102.

VICINUS, MARTHA. *Independent Women: Work and Community for Single Women. 1850–1920*. Chicago: University of Chicago Press, 1985.

WILSON, KATHARINA, ed. *Women Writers of the Renaissance and Restoration*. Athens: University of Georgia Press, 1987.

ZIMMERMAN, BONNIE. 'What Has Never Been: An Overview of Lesbian Feminist Criticism'. In *The New Feminist Criticism: Essays on Women, Literature & Theory*, ed. Elaine Showalter. New York: Pantheon, 1985: 200–224.

MARGARET CAVENDISH, DUCHESS OF NEWCASTLE (1623–73)

5 'The Ragged Rout of Self': Margaret Cavendish's *True Relation* and the Heroics of Self-Disclosure*

SIDONIE SMITH

The autobiographical writings of seventeenth-century women are among the most important early women's texts to have been recovered for study in recent years. While many of these works are conversion narratives which afforded their female authors a well-established pattern of spiritual experience in which to represent themselves, Margaret Cavendish sought to integrate the story of her life into the androcentric conventions of secular autobiography, which understood 'life' to mean 'public life'. Sidonie Smith's essay focuses on the contradictory self-representations which emerge as Cavendish's claim to public significance clashes with the imperatives of the feminine ideal, and, like Easton, she illuminates the depth of a seventeenth-century woman's commitment to the patriarchal definitions she simultaneously resists. Smith's essay intersects with Masten's and Gallagher's in its interest in the formation of modern subjectivity during the early modern period. She argues that the tension between Cavendish's two selves generates a 'protomodern preoccupation with the self qua self', although she also stresses the lack of conceptual space available during this period in which to figure an independent female subject.

When the rumour spread that the crazy Duchess was coming up from Welbeck to pay her respects at Court, people crowded the streets to look at her, and the curiosity of Mr. Pepys twice brought him to wait in the Park to see her pass. But the pressure of the crowd about her coach was too great. He could only catch a glimpse of her in her silver coach with her footmen all in velvet, a velvet cap on her head, and her hair about her ears. He could only see for a

---

* Reprinted from Sidonie Smith, *A Poetics of Women's Autobiography: Marginality and the Fictions of Self-Representation* (Bloomington and Indianapolis: Indiana University Press, 1987), pp. 84–101.

moment between the white curtains the face of 'a very comely woman,' and on she drove through the crowd of staring Cockneys, all pressing to catch a glimpse of that romantic lady, who stands, in the picture at Welbeck, with large melancholy eyes, and something fastidious and fantastic in her bearing, touching a table with the tips of long pointed fingers, in the calm assurance of immortal fame.

Virginia Woolf, *The Common Reader*

Margery Kempe tested for her culture the boundaries between madness and divinest sense, to paraphrase an Emily Dickinson poem. A mother of fourteen children who wore white to symbolize her chastity, an illiterate middle-class woman who conversed with holy men about Scripture, a worldly adventurer who spread herself on the floor of her neighborhood church to weep and wail at the suffering of Christ made her presence felt and her voice resonate throughout the medieval world, if not throughout the centuries to follow. Domesticating Christ, Kempe facilitated her own empowerment in the larger arena of public debate. Two hundred years later Margaret Cavendish also tested the boundaries of madness for her culture. Mad Madge, as her contemporaries sometimes called her, was no extroverted woman like Kempe. Painfully shy and retiring, she nonetheless acknowledged the same desire for public significance as Kempe did. She, too, sought empowerment within the public arena of heroism; and like Kempe she achieved both public praise and notoriety. With more self-consciousness and less volubility, Cavendish was another 'eccentric' woman who went about shaping her life and her life story for posterity.

Critics of seventeenth-century autobiography, when they have discussed Cavendish's autobiography, *A True Relation of My Birth, Breeding, and Life*, have remarked on the surprising and unprecedented self-scrutiny evident in her work. Paul Delany states that 'it would be giving the Duchess more than her due to describe her as a penetrating self-analyst, but in her ingenuous way she does reveal much more about her personality than most autobiographers of her time'; and he goes so far as to trace her autobiographical lineage to Rousseau: 'The line of development is unbroken from her work to a modern, subjective autobiography like Rousseau's – his kind of preoccupation with his own singularity is already implicit in the Duchess's *Relation*.'[1] Suggesting that the duchess's narrative 'adumbrates, if it does not achieve, a scientific emphasis', Wayne Shumaker concludes that it is 'full of psychological significance – more so, perhaps, for the modern than for the seventeenth-century reader – and, whatever the motivating purpose, can properly be regarded as a study of character in a broadly sketched environmental setting'.[2] Recently, Cynthia S. Pomerleau contends that autobiographies by women in the century, Cavendish's included, 'seem more modern, more subjective, more given to self-scrutiny, more like what we have come to know as autobiography' than those works by men that have been conflated with the autobiographical tradition of the seventeenth century.[3] All three, motivated by different critical scenarios, identify in Cavendish's narrative, even if they do not stop to explore it, a protomodern preoccupation with the self qua self that promotes a thickness of self-representation distinguishing her autobiography from others of the period.

'That romantic lady,' as Virginia Woolf describes her, would have reveled in such recognition of her 'true' distinction, though not perhaps at its failure until recently to command serious attention.[4] She was born Margaret Lucas about 1624 at St. John's in Essex, the youngest of eight children. Her father, a landed gentleman, died when she was two, after which she was raised in an apparently sheltered, even idyllic environment by her mother and older siblings. With the advent of the Civil War, the circumstances of the young woman's life altered dramatically. Two of her brothers died as a result of the fighting. Family property was confiscated. Then she left home to serve, from 1643 to 1645, as maid of honor to Queen Henrietta-Maria. In 1645, she accompanied the queen into exile in Paris, where she met and married William Cavendish, then marquis, but later duke, of Newcastle. They spent seventeen years in exile in Paris, Rotterdam, and Antwerp, during which time Cavendish turned to writing as a 'profession'. During the fifteen years between 1653 and 1668, she wrote and published fourteen works: five scientific treatises, five collections of poetry and fantasies, two collections of essays and letters, and two collections of plays, as well as a biography of her husband and an autobiography. With the Restoration she and her husband returned to England and retired from court to live on their country estate at Welbeck, where she died in 1674. Before her death Cavendish became a controversial figure, as the passage from Woolf so sympathetically suggests. She wrote. She wore theatrical costumes. She promoted the importance of a chaste life. She thereby gained a reputation for madness. And yet she received the adulation of some prominent writers and scholars of the period.[5]

Cavendish wrote her autobiography at the relatively young age of thirty-two; she thus looked back, not on a long life, but on a short span covering childhood, young adulthood, early marriage, and the beginning of a 'career'. She had, in fact, only just begun to write and had not yet achieved public recognition of her talents. But she had married well; and the duke was himself a celebrity. Earlier she had written a biography of her husband, an occasion to idealize him and to defend him against detractors. Her decision to write her own story suggests that Cavendish also wanted to immortalize herself and to defend herself against her own detractors.

113

Men and women writing autobiographies in the seventeenth century – Cavendish particularly – would have grappled with complex problems of self-representation in a fragmented tradition. They would have struggled with the contours of individual experience, personal intentions, the formal options, and the expectations of their readers, influenced by a cultural ambiance that encouraged exploration of all kinds, including self-exploration, but offered few clearly defined models, in part because many of the autobiographies written during the period remained unpublished for several hundred years.[6] There were, however, two generalized conventions that provided provisional topographical opportunities: the narrative of religious conversion tracing its roots to Augustine's *Confessions* and the secular *res gestae* tracing its roots back to the classical period.[7] Yet in both nascent conventions the figures of selfhood would have complicated the autobiographical project for a woman. Religious autobiographers tended to be members of formal church hierarchies who perceived the significance of their lives to derive from their status as members of the 'militant elite' or 'spiritual aristocracy'.[8] While the Protestant sects that emerged from the Reformation validated woman's authority to read her life for the signs of God's grace, except for the Quakers, they continued to deny her access to public roles and responsibilities. Excluded from the ministry because of patriarchal notions about her 'natural' subordination to the authority of her husband and her suspect relationship to language, a woman could not claim membership in the church hierarchy and could not, therefore, claim her life's significance to derive from that kind of activity. Nor did the conventions of secular autobiography offer unequivocal guidance, for they depended in the seventeenth century on the premise that the sum of public acts constituted an individual's 'life'.[9] In other words, formal 'autobiography' remained clearly androcentric.

When Cavendish initiated her autobiographical project, neither sacred nor secular figures promised to conform comfortably to the experience of her life. Whatever her relations to and ideas about the other world, they remained outside the purview of her narrative, which she grounds exclusively in the world of people, education, individual characteristics, not in the exploration of divine providence and personal salvation. Moreover, since her only relationship to public events came from her ascribed status as the daughter of Master Lucas and the wife of the duke of Newcastle, she could not write in the tradition of *res gestae* unless she wrote about the men who had given her her names. (She did so, of course, when she wrote the biography of her husband, to which her own autobiography was appended soon after its first publication. But she originally separated her autobiography from his biography, in 1656 publishing her 'life' in a folio entitled *Natures Pictures drawn by Fancies Pencil to the Life.*)

As did other educated and predominantly aristocratic women who wrote secular autobiography during the century, Cavendish turned to her private experience for the matter of her narrative. Pomerleau argues that 'for women, and not for men, the domestic choices were, partly by default, a medium for self-expression; and as men began gropingly to write about their public lives, so, amazingly, did a few women write about their private lives'. She goes on to contend that 'the idea that oneself, one's feelings, one's spouse and domestic relations were properly and innately worth writing about was essentially a female idea, however tentatively conceived at the time'.[10] For that reason, Donald A. Stauffer finds women's autobiographies of the period 'more personal, informal, and life-like' since the women are 'engrossed in the more enthralling problems of their own lives'.[11] Moreover, educated women writing their lives approached autobiography with a different orientation toward rhetoric and writing than educated men did. Denied the classical training offered to young men, a training built on imitation and repetition of classical models, elaborated through the structure of argumentation and agonistic combat, articulated in the voice of 'objectivity', women often wrote in a style and with a rhetorical voice more fluid and familiar.[12]

Evidence suggests, however, that other women did not presume, as Cavendish did, to garner for themselves significance beyond that attached to conventional figures of women's selfhood, so that they shunned formal autobiography, never writing expressly about themselves for the public. Some, such as Lucy Hutchinson, based their claim to significance on their domestic roles as mothers and as companions to men of public stature, whose biographies they wrote. For instance, Hutchinson abandoned her autobiographical project after describing her parentage and early years, and turned instead to the biography of her husband in a release of great and skillful verbosity as if her own life story ended after adolescence when marriage subsumed her identity in her husband's.[13] Ann Lady Fanshawe wrote specifically for her son's edification and assumed an appropriately self-abnegating stance as she focused on her husband's career.[14] In both purpose and design these texts served to enhance the image of man. Others may have written of their own, rather than their husbands', exploits in the larger social and political arena, but they limited the audience for their work to family members as Anne Lady Halkett did.[15] Consequently, such works by women fell well within cultural expectations governing women's relationship to self-writing and reaffirmed an ideology of autobiography as a male preserve.

Cavendish, having dutifully written the biography of her husband and having had no children whom she could edify, journeyed well beyond those other autobiographers by publicizing her life. She usurped the authority to write her own story for the world, authoring her autobiography as she authored scientific treatises and works of poetry, philosophy, utopian fantasy, drama, biography. She recognized, however, that her readers would read her as 'woman', inflecting their response to her narrative with patriarchal expectations of woman's identity, condemning her 'unfeminine' desire to use her intelligence and ambition in pursuit of public acclaim. For, as Hilda Smith suggests, Cavendish 'understood, better than any of her sisters, the multifaceted nature of women's oppression. She noted their poor education, exclusion from public institutions, political subordination within the home, physiological dictates of childbirth, and society's pervasive vision of women as incompetent, irresponsible, unintelligent, and irrational.'[16] A self-consciousness about her identity and status as a woman therefore dominated her works and prompted her critique of the ideology of gender. Yet, as Smith also notes, her critique, while extensive and even radical, was not without its contradictions: 'She often suggested that society's perception was correct; women had made few contributions to past civilization, not because they were ill educated but because they had less ability than men.'[17] Such contradictions worry the autobiography itself. Influenced by the discourse on man and its empowering narratives, Cavendish wanted to become not merely an ascriptive footnote in the course of history but a person of acknowledged achievements and historical distinction whose eminently 'readable' life would gain her 'fame in after ages'.[18] Yet as she pursued this vision she threatened herself with still another kind of exile, not from the court, not from England, but from that larger domain of 'womanhood' with its privileged stories of selfhood. Moreover, she was herself a product of that discourse and so, as she grew accustomed to seeing herself reflected in 'the looking-glass of the male-authored text', internalized the narrative of feminine goodness, a silent plot of modesty, naïveté, virtue, dependency, innocence, and self-concealment.[19] The anxiety occasioned by such doubling of narrative purpose manifests itself in the fundamental ambiguity at the heart of Cavendish's self-representation.[20] Indeed, there are in *A True Relation* two competing self-representations: that of the woman who fulfils the patriarchal imperatives of female selfhood and who defends the integrity of her innocence; and that of the woman who demands from the world recognition of her own independent achievements. The tension that drives Cavendish's narrative and that leads to the unprecedented self-scrutiny noted by critics of her work, is the tension generated as Cavendish struggles to reconcile, if in the end she only fails to do so, her desire to maintain the silence of the ideal woman and her desire to give voice to her own unconventional and heroic narrative.

Cavendish begins her story with a brief biography of her father, revealing the degree to which she located her identity in his status and character: 'My father was a gentleman,' she writes, 'which Title is grounded and given by Merit, not by princes.'[21] Probably because he was dead before Cavendish turned three, she invests the slim biography with such mythic resonances. He represents the ideal hero who 'did not esteem Titles, unless they were gained by Heroick Actions'. But he represents also the hero robbed of heroic possibilities. The critical moment around which the lost possibility coalesces is the scene of the duel her father fought when a young man. A sign of masculine bravery and integrity, the duel reveals her father's allegiance to the 'Laws of Honour'. And yet the times are not conducive to that particular expression of heroism: Because of political complications, her father is exiled from England by Queen Elizabeth. When he finally returns after Elizabeth's death, 'there was no Employments for heroick Spirits' since the times of 'wise' King James remain peaceful. In the end, her father never gains a 'title' and never, as a result, gains a historically prominent lineage or a heroic story such a title would command. The story she tells of her father is one of exile and frustrated desire.

In its themes of heroism and of exile, this paternal biography resonates with the daughter's desire for story and her own sense of confusion and frustration about self-representation. In many ways Cavendish is her father's daughter. Like her father before her, she would leave behind the legitimate trace of her 'Heroick Actions', those 'manly' accomplishments that would ensure her 'fame in after ages'. Like him, she suffers from frustrated desire, as political, social, and cultural circumstances deny her access to the realm of public activity and significance that lie outside the womb. Like him, she suffers 'exile' for her attentiveness to that androcentric code of honor. And just as her father's life is lived out in a heroic eventlessness that silences his claims to titles, so too Cavendish's life of inactivity threatens to silence her claim to a cultural story of her own. Thus, as she begins her narrative, Cavendish confronts the cultural silence of the very life she would represent.

In this context it is interesting to consider the relationship of Cavendish's autobiography to the biography she wrote of her husband. Since her husband had been a central (and controversial) leader of the Royalist forces and a companion to the king, his life provided the material and the occasion for Cavendish to engage in heroic storytelling. (Unlike her father, her husband gained esteem and public titles from his

heroic feats during fiercely troubled times.) Cavendish organized
her story in four parts. The first two parts tell of her husband's
participation in the Civil War; but more than that, they offer a
partisan's defense of the hero's actions as a way of answering his
critics and enhancing his reputation. Thus she presents him as the
hero-warrior devoted to his sovereign, abused by the mediocre people
around him; and her story appropriates conventional features of the
classical *res gestae*. In the third part she turns to a description of his
character, humor, disposition, birth, breeding, and education, in an
apparent attempt to flesh out the details of the inner, the personal, life
of the hero. The fourth part introduces the voice of the hero himself
as she assembles a collection of his own writings and commentaries.
Ultimately, Cavendish creates in the story of her husband an ideal
figure who enacts 'the heroic ethic of the masculine world'.[22]

While Cavendish desires to place heroic action in the plot of her
own life, she can in fact replicate only the third part of the biography's
structure in her story, the personal rather than the public story. Thus
she amasses rather disjointed descriptions of her birth, education,
family, disposition, and humor, and winds them around a slim
chronological narrative of her personal development from childhood
to young adulthood. Yet Cavendish does introduce brief narratives of
male heroism into her story as she digresses with adulatory descriptions
of the characters and adventures of father, brothers, brother-in-law,
and husband. Of her brothers she affirms that 'they loved Virtue,
endeavoured Merit, practic'd Justice, and spoke Truth; they were
constantly loyal, and truly Valiant' (272). Of her brother-in-law: 'He
was nobly generous, wisely valiant, naturally civill, honestly kind, truly
loving, Virtuously temperate' (286). Of her husband: 'my Lord is a
person whose Humour is neither extravagantly merry, nor unnecessarily
sad, his Mind is above his Fortune, as his Generosity is above his purse,
his Courage above danger, his Justice above bribes, his Friendship above
self-interest, his Truth too firm for falsehood', and on and on (296). Such
passages clearly evince not only Cavendish's desire to defend her family
but also her obvious admiration of quintessentially male-identified
values and qualities of character. They also provide a parallel story of
masculine activity alongside her own story of public silence.

Such 'male' stories seem to add value, authority, and legitimacy to
Cavendish's 'life' by a process of association. She enhances her own
figure and status as a result of the ideal figures of such male relatives.
Yet ironically, such privileging of male biography and ideals of
personality in the story effectively subverts a central quality of character
she would claim for herself: Like her father, who refuses to buy the
status of nobility and who would only earn it through significant heroic
action, Cavendish seeks to earn her recognition and fame through

significant public action and merit of her own, not to purchase it
ascriptively through the heroic feats of men. By incorporating those
'masculine' stories so fully into her own, she partially undermines her
effort to follow in her father's footsteps. Moreover, she turns her
woman's autobiography into a biography of men.

The attentiveness to males – to father, brothers, husband – testifies
simultaneously to a very 'feminine' orientation to storytelling and to
the world in that it pays homage to the superior value and virtue of
male-identified activities. Such an orientation becomes particularly
critical for Cavendish since, as certain passages in the text reveal, she is
acutely aware of the reputation she is gaining as an 'unwomanly', even
a somewhat 'mad', woman. She alludes to rumors and 'false reports',
projecting throughout her text a public and a reader critical of her
desire for public display of her person (in the ostentatious clothes she
wears), of her word (in the court appeals she makes, in the books she
writes), and of her ambition. Responding to the pressure of those
cultural voices, Cavendish struggles to defend her identity as an ideal
woman, thereby assuring her reader that she has followed, not in her
father's, but in her mother's footsteps. And so, interweaving throughout
the digressive narratives of male relatives (and the idealization of the
masculine ethic) is the story of her 'maternal' inheritance with its
idealization of true womanhood – the story, as Mary C. Mason
suggests, 'of an emerging young woman'.[23]
 If her father as exemplar of masculine integrity sits at the threshold
of her autobiography, her mother, the exemplar of the true feminine,
inhabits the center of her story – literally and figuratively. The daughter
represents her mother as the embodiment of perfect beauty: 'She was
of a grave Behaviour, and had such a Magestic Grandeur, as it were
continually hung about her, that it would strike a kind of awe to the
beholders, and command respect from the rudest' (282). She is also the
'affectionate Mother, breeding her children with a most industrious care,
and tender love, and having eight children, three sons and five daughters,
there was not anyone crooked or any ways deformed, neither were they
dwarfish, or of a Giant-like stature, but every ways proportionable'
(283). And finally, she is the model wife and widow, who

> never forgot my Father so as to marry again; indeed, he remain'd
> so lively in her memory, and her grief was so lasting, as she never
> mention'd his name, though she spoke often of him, but love and
> grief caused tears to flow, and tender sighs to rise, mourning in sad
> complaints; she made her house her Cloyster, inclosing her self, as it
> were therein, for she seldom went abroad, unless to Church.
>
> (282)

119

Read in tandem these descriptive passages pay empassioned tribute to a remarkable woman, an ideal of timeless beauty and devotion, an image of female perfection that is cloistered, quiescent, eternal.

Throughout *A True Relation*, Cavendish tenaciously insists that she has imitated the maternal model of the ideal feminine and that she has achieved the sanctity and aristocratic gentility of inner life on which the imitation depends. She does so by characterizing herself as 'the sheltered innocent' who lives 'the cloistered life', drawing repeatedly on the language and imagery of both figures to sustain that narrative identity. For instance, as Cavendish nostalgically represents it, her childhood was lived out in an idyllic, protected, totally innocent world. Here mother and older siblings created for her a conventual environment closed off from the public realm where males acted heroically; and in that enclosed space the child and young woman was bred 'according to ... the Nature of my Sex ... Virtuously, Modestly, Civilly, Honourably, and on honest principles' (268). Her education included 'singing, dancing, playing on musick, reading, writing, working, and the like' (271). Yet intellectual accomplishment and independence of mind were discouraged to such an extent that she can write of her sisters that they 'did seldom make Visits, nor never went abroad with Strangers in their Company, but onely themselves in a Flock together agreeing so well, that there seemed but one Minde amongst them' (276–77).

Describing her entrance as a young woman into the world of the court, Cavendish identifies herself as the sheltered innocent leaving the virtuous life of the cloister to confront a 'fallen' world where cunning, sophistication, intrigue, debauchery proclaim the reign of evil. Deprived of the guidance of her siblings, she was 'like one that had no Foundation to stand, or Guide to direct me, which made me afraid, lest I should wander with Ignorance out of the waies of Honour, so that I knew not how to behave myself' (278). As a result, she 'durst neither look up with my eyes, nor speak, nor be any way sociable, insomuch as I was thought a Natural Fool' (278). Thus, although she might have gained an education, she clings to innocence, maintaining that 'being dull, fearfull, and bashfull, I neither heeded what was said or practic'd, but just what belonged to my loyal duty, and my own honest reputation; and, indeed, I was so afraid to dishonour my Friends and Family by my indiscreet actions, that I rather chose to be accounted a Fool, then to be thought rude or wanton' (279). When she describes her later attempt to petition the English courts for access to her husband's lands (which had been confiscated during his exile), she again characterizes herself as 'unpracticed', 'unlearned', 'ignorant', 'not knowing'. And when she analyzes her bashfulness (292–93) and her way of living (300), she emphasizes again and again her isolation from the fallen multitude and her 'aversion to such kinds of people'. For Cavendish, the representation of herself as foolish, uncomfortable, ignorant, fearful, bashful, and speechless in public testifies to her superior virtue, the basis on which her true merit as model woman rests.

Cavendish also establishes that her virtue derives from her chaste relationship to men and to sexual passion. During her childhood, she tells her reader, her mother 'never suffered the vulgar Servingmen to be in the Nursery among the Nurse Maids, lest their rude love-making might do unseemly actions, or speak unhandsome words in the presence of her children, knowing that youth is apt to take infection by ill examples, having not the reason of distinguishing good from bad' (270–71). She describes herself as a young woman who 'did dread Marriage, and shunn'd mens companies as much as [she] could' (280). And she maintains that she 'never was infected [with amorous love], it is a Disease, or a Passion, or both, I only know by relation, not by experience' (280). These passages taken together reveal her vision of sexuality as a form of 'infection' and of men's company as conducive to another kind of dis-ease. Adding chastity to the catalog of goodness, Cavendish reveals, by the way, the degree to which the life story of the ideal woman demands the repression of sexual desire. In fact, in her relationship to the duke, she represents herself as totally without desire, as a kind of clean slate waiting to be written on: 'My Lord the Marquis of Newcastle did approve of those bashful fears which many condemn'd, and would choose such a Wife as he might bring to his own humours, and not such an one as was wedded to self-conceit, or one that had been temper'd to the humours of another, for which he wooed me for his Wife' (280). Here she joins the imagery of sexual purity, religious devotion, and self-effacement when describing her vision of marriage, recapitulating the metaphor of the cloistered life (associated with her mother) with obvious rhetorical flamboyance: 'though I desire to appear to the best advantage, whilest I live in the view of the public World, yet I could most willingly exclude myself, so as Never to see the face of any creature, but my Lord, as long as I live, inclosing myself like an Anchoret, wearing a Frize gown, tied with a cord about my waste' (309).

The powerful appeal of feminine 'silence' for Cavendish may have derived in part from her profound experience of displacement during exile from England and her desire to reclaim her rightful place in the order of English society. Thus a preoccupation with traditional patterns of social arrangements, and with the sexual arrangements at the center of them, characterizes her autobiography as it does much of secular autobiography of the late Renaissance. As Delany notes, 'secular autobiographers were often unusually concerned with their social status, either because it had changed significantly for better or worse, or because they had perceived a shift in the relative standing of the class to which they gave allegiance'.[24] The very identity of Cavendish's family had altered dramatically, irrevocably: two of her brothers had perished as a result of the Civil Wars; her mother had been stripped of her lands and assets; her husband had been exiled. In such a context Cavendish seems to cling to the old, the established, the fundamental patterns of sexual relationships that root her personal identity. Pomerleau, writing of women's autobiographies in the century, suggests that 'the old patterns may actually have provided an element of serenity and stability in a world where the sanctity of these patterns could no longer be taken for granted'.[25] A proud supporter of the authority of the monarch and a critic of the democratic impulses of the opposition (and of democracy generally, evidenced by her aristocratic scorn of the fallen multitude), Cavendish maintained, despite her acute recognition of the oppression of women, despite her often strong condemnations of the institution of marriage, a commitment to the authority of the familial patriarch as well as to that of the royal one.[26]

Cavendish's insistence before the reader on identifying discomfort with virtue, bashfulness with merit, childlike fear with ideal feminine purity and ignorance testifies to the intensity of her desire to imitate the self-abnegating model of ideal womanhood represented by her mother and thereby to secure the love and acceptance of the world. Yet her rhetoric in key passages betrays another vision of that model of womanhood. If we return to the central passages describing her mother and read them once again, we see that the language evokes, however subtly, images of feminine enclosure and physical and psychological entombment. Of her mother, Cavendish writes that

> her beauty was beyond the ruin of time, for she had a well favoured loveliness in her face, a pleasing sweetness in her countenance, and a well-temper'd complexion, as neither too red nor too pale, even to her dying hour, although in years, and by her dying, one might think death was enamoured with her, for he imbraced her in a sleep, and so gently, as if he were afraid to hurt her.
>
> (283)

Cavendish obviously wants to testify to her mother's perfection and mystical power. Yet in doing so she testifies to much more. Forever devoted to a dead husband, willingly cloistered in her womb-like convent, marvellously preserved from the physical ravages of time, and caressed easily by death, this mother is also the figure of frozen stillness, a necromantic presence whose real power derives from the hold her memory has on the daughter. Paradoxically, the daughter subverts the grasp of this mother, whose image commands obedient imitation, by betraying in the very language of entombment a fundamental dissatisfaction with the ideal. For to be cloistered in such an ideal, however well preserved and comfortable it may be, is to be dead to independent expression, knowledge, and heroic possibilities. Ultimately, that ideal of self-representation is unmasked as a 'fiction', compellingly prescriptive yet untruthful and invalid. While Cavendish would duplicate her mother's story, her language reveals the desire for a duplicitous transgression of its lines.

The language of the text subverts the representation of her mother as ideal woman in yet another way. Cavendish acknowledges that, however much her mother might have emphasized 'being' and deemphasized 'doing' in her educational scheme, she embraced a socially acceptable practical role foisted upon her by widowhood: 'though she would often complain that her family was too great for her weak Management, and often prest my Brother to take it upon him, yet I observe she took a pleasure, and some little pride, in the governing thereof: she was very skilful in Leases, and setting of lands, and Court-keeping, ordering of Stewards, and the like affairs' (285). In this telling description, Cavendish notes the deference and self-abnegation of her mother's public mask and the private sense of satisfaction and power concealed by that mask. In other words, she identifies the fictional nature of her mother's public persona: Before her, her mother, too, masked her pleasure in power.[27] In this characterization, therefore, Cavendish captures her own dilemma – how to maintain the virtuous woman's silence and simultaneously pursue public power. Moreover, she reveals her strategy for negotiating the dilemma – the fabrication of a self-effacing mask. But in doing so she calls into question the very truthfulness of her representation of herself as the virtuous, silent woman.

Of course, the first evidence of a self-asserting protagonist is the autobiography itself. The title announces the very desire for public acknowledgment Cavendish tries unsuccessfully to mute; for once she commits herself to the autobiographical project, she dissociates herself from the figure of the self-abnegating woman. By writing she authorizes her own story: she speaks publicly. Then the opening of the narrative, discussed earlier, reveals her strong identification with the father and the heroic values of the world of men. Male heroics are denied her, however; thus she takes up the pen, a choice that seems natural to her as the preface to one of her other works suggests: 'That my ambition of extraordinary Fame, is restless, and not ordinary, I cannot deny: and since all Heroick Actions, Publick Employments, as well Civill as Military, and Eloquent Pleadings, are deni'd my Sex in this Age, I may be excused for writing so much.'[28] While she does not turn her autobiography into a conscious exploration of her development as an artist, she does provide, if only unconsciously, a thin strand of a story tracing her emerging authorship.

The figure of an empowered and ambitious self becomes visible in such passages as the one in which she describes her early fascination with dress: 'I never took delight in closets, or cabinets of toys, but in the variety of fine clothes, and such toys as onely were to adorn my person' (302). She thus grounds in early childhood her preoccupation with fashioning herself in her own representations, albeit in a conventional script of women's lives:

> My serious study could not be much, by reason I took great delight in attiring, fine dressing, and fashions, especially such fashions as I did invent myself, not taking that pleasure in such fashions as was invented by others: also I did dislike any should follow my Fashions, for I always took delight in a singularity, even in accoutrements of habit.
>
> (303–304)

Unique, 'loud' clothes break the silence and the anonymity at the core of feminine goodness, publicly distinguishing her from all other girls by giving original lines to her body. Through such fashioning, the young woman gives form to her fantasies of creative selfhood, and the autobiographer, recalling such moments, unmasks her desire for 'making up' in both senses of the phrase: making up stories about herself and making herself up for public exposure.[29]

Suzanne Juhasz, in an essay on contemporary autobiographies by women, alludes to the dynamic relationship of literary women to the realm of fantasy, suggesting that 'because there is usually a profound discrepancy between the options that society offers to women and the potential that they find within themselves, women frequently have complex inner lives, worlds of fantasy'.[30] Cavendish's autobiography reveals that fantasy became a means she early developed to mediate between the cultural imperative of self-annihilating silence and more heroic possibilities of selfhood. Shy, contemplative, yet ambitious – as she tells her reader a number of times – in fantasy and later in writing Cavendish can become the empowering author of her own story and fashion herself as a protagonist of heroic proportions, thereby wresting greatness and distinction from insignificance. Unable to grasp the sword or to ride a horse into battle as her husband (and male relatives) can, she can grasp the pen and ride words across pages. And she can create in her writing women of heroism who take on all the roles of men, including fighting, ruling, discovering, as they do in such works as *Bell in Campo* and *The Description of a New World*. Thus writing, with its promise of regenerative, capacious, galvanizing selfhood, not the 'Lord' of her text, represents life itself to Cavendish, since it enables her to exercise her reason and imagination, and to body forth her originality by shaping interpretations.[31] (In fact, the marquis, at least as he is represented in the autobiography, performs a function much like the woman 'in some corner' of Freud's male daydreams.[32] He becomes a kind of male muse who acknowledges, who seems even to inspire, her writing.) What Stephen Jay Greenblatt claims for the prominent literary men of the Renaissance applies as well to Cavendish: 'the Renaissance figures we have considered understand that in our culture to abandon self-fashioning is to abandon the craving for freedom, and to let go of one's stubborn hold upon selfhood, even selfhood conceived as a fiction, is to die'.[33]

Cavendish's language and imagery suggest the degree to which she imagined writing as a female equivalent to male warfare, a heroic arena in which women might gain access to distinction through merit. In describing her method of writing and her handwriting, she appropriates a trope from the dominant discourse, noting that

> when some of those thoughts are sent out in words, they give the rest more liberty to place themselves in a more methodicall order, marching more regularly with my pen, on the ground of white paper, but my letters seem rather as a ragged rout, than a well armed body, for the brain being quicker in creating than the hand in writing, or the memory in retaining, many fancies are lost, by reason they ofttimes outrun the pen; where I, to keep speed in the Race, write so fast as I stay not so long as to write my letters plain.
>
> (298)

Yet this language also reveals the degree to which she felt ambiguous about the presumption inherent in such an analogy. Having established the analogy, Cavendish associates herself with the routed and defeated rather than with the heroic and victorious. Hers is a battle lost, at least in terms of the orderliness of her ideas and her handwriting, which by the end of this passage is what her 'writing' has been reduced to. Or more precisely, she is really an interloper on the field of battle as the distinction she draws between her husband's writing and her own attests. While the marquis 'recreates himself with his pen, writing what his Wit dictates to him', she 'pass[es] [her] time rather with scribbling than writing, with words than wit' (297). This disclaimer recapitulates the earlier rhetoric of ignorance and reaffirms – at the moment she would reveal her desire for significant action and accomplishment – her continued allegiance to the conventions of ideal female gentility, in

particular the modesty that forbids the assertion of female authority and
authorship.

Elsewhere Cavendish takes pains to distinguish herself from other,
less virtuous women who speak publicly in their own behalf as
'Pleaders, Attornies, Petitioners, and the like, running about with their
several Causes' (290). Such women

> doth nothing but justle for the Preheminence of words, I mean not for
> speaking well, but speaking much, as they do for the preheminence
> of place, words rushing against words, thwarting and crossing each
> other, and pulling with reproaches, striving to throw each other down
> with disgrace, thinking to advance themselves thereby.
>
> (290)

Again Cavendish appropriates the combat trope, but with an intriguing
difference. Here she would accuse other women of unfeminine activity
and self-asserting public display, and so doing reaffirm her own
modesty in public. But ironically, while she means to mark the
difference between herself and other women who use language publicly,
the imagery in the passage identifies her with them. Like them, she
would through writing enter the world of male combat and seek
distinction on the field of battle. Like them, she seeks preeminence.
That confusion in her recourse to the combat trope betrays the
confusion at the heart of her project and betrays the 'fictionality'
of both self-asserting and self-effacing representations.

The problematic nature of Cavendish's public exposure is represented
both literally and figuratively in her relationship to her carriage. Twice
in the narrative she alludes to the pleasure she feels in riding about and
reveals her motives for such public exposure: 'because I would not
bury myself quite from the sight of the world, I go sometimes abroad,
seldome to visit, but only in my Coach about the Town' (300). Reality
beyond the cloister must be engaged in order for her to enlarge the
experiential bases of her fantasies and to feed her vanities: 'I am so
vain, if it be a vanity, as to endeavor to be worship't, rather than not to
be regarded' (309). Like the hero who rides through the streets in his
triumphal chariot, Cavendish would be worshipped by the populace.
Yet the 'fallen' public, that awesome, often truculent, intractable,
vulgar reality, threatens to shatter the fantasy of purity and distinction.
Thus, for an 'ideal' woman cloistered within the protective walls of
bashfulness but desiring an audience larger than her Lord to validate
her true originality, the carriage becomes the vehicle that promises both
assertive self-display and the requisite self-concealment emblematic of
an inner goodness so critical to the chaste, virtuous woman. If the

public is allowed to see but not to touch, Cavendish is allowed to be
seen but not to be touched by the fallen multitude.

The autobiography is itself a metaphorical carriage, a vehicle that
parades the body of Cavendish's life before the public, allowing her
to escape the confinement of silence. But that secular gesture of
self-display threatens to take her on a transgressive ride beyond
the conventional path of woman's selfhood. The final passage of
Cavendish's autobiography captures the central dilemma in its poignant
self-reflexiveness. In the first clause she acknowledges a prominent
motif embedded in the ideology of gender: Women manifest a natural
tendency to vanity, and vanity in woman is evil. Thus the public
display of the woman who would write autobiography marks her as
a true daughter of Eve. The scene of autobiography is no place for
woman. Just as she earlier acknowledges public censorship of her
sartorial fashioning, Cavendish here recognizes the inevitability of
public censorship of her literary self-fashioning, of the very
autobiography she has just written. In response, she assumes a
defensive posture, strategically citing authoritative precedents: 'but I
hope my readers will not think me vain for writing my life, since there
have been many that have done the like, as Cesar, Ovid, and many
more, both men and women, and I know no reason I may not do it as
well as they' (309). In a gesture of petulance, she would bring the
authority of Caesar and Ovid to bear on her enterprise. Perhaps she
identifies with the betrayal of the former and the exile of the latter,
since as a Royalist she is living through just such betrayal and exile.
Certainly, she identifies her autobiographical authority with the literary
authority of the man of public action and the poet. But, as Patricia
Meyer Spacks notes, the models to whom she refers are male – her
reference to female precedents notwithstanding – and their deeds a
matter of public significance.[34] She can cite no female models of
significance, no tradition of women's autobiography. Moreover, the text
betrays Cavendish's own ambivalence about such comparisons. The
very next clause speaks to the lack of public significance in women's
lives and by implication in their narratives: 'but I verily believe some
censuring Readers will scornfully say, why hath this Lady write her
own Life? since none cares to know whose daughter she was, or whose
wife she is, or how she was bred, or what fortunes she had, or how she
lived, or what humour or disposition she was of?' (310). The catalog of
content, a summation of her own autobiographical material, betrays the
absence of heroic action and public deeds, the conventional subject
matter of formal autobiography.

Her defensive posture intensifies: 'I anser that it is true, that 'tis to
no purpose to the Reader, but it is to the Authoress, because I write it
for my own sake, not theirs' (310). While she declares that the reader's

expectations are insignificant to her, the pose remains more rhetorical than convincing. For the next and final passage reveals powerfully the fundamental motivation of the effort:

> Neither did I intend this piece for to delight, but to divulge; not to please the fancy, but to tell the truth, lest after-ages should mistake, in not knowing I was daughter to one Master Lucas of St. Johns, near Colchester, in Essex, second wife to the Lord Marquis of Newcastle; for my Lord having had two Wives, I might easily have been mistaken, especially if I should dye and my Lord Marry again.
>
> (310)

These closing words of her text testify eloquently to her desperate need to be 'read' accurately by those readers who will, if they so choose, distinguish her for posterity from her husband's other wives. Ultimately, then, the issue is one of identity versus anonymity. Cavendish is writing for her very life. Ironically, however, only her identity as daughter and wife will differentiate her from her husband's other wives. So for all her effort to follow her father's example and to maintain the value of merit as the source of 'fame in after ages', Cavendish can rely only on her ascriptive status as wife and daughter to place her historically. In that light it is interesting to note again that originally the autobiography appeared by itself in her collection of her writings, *Natures Pictures drawn by Fancies Pencil to the Life*; only later was it appended to the second edition of the biography of her husband, a kind of historical footnote. Thus her story becomes a satellite revolving around the body of man's story. Paradoxically, while she authors his life, his life, in fact, authors and authorizes hers.

Cavendish could not tell her autobiographical story the way her culture had come to expect it to be told. She could not discover in her life the plot for *res gestae* or for spiritual quest. Somehow, she had to make the private story suffice instead of the public one. Decked out in those 'odd' autobiographical clothes, she insisted on being regarded, if only by a public bent on laughing at her. However flawed, however entangled as it inevitably was in the very patriarchal plots that mocked her attempts at self-fashioning, her autobiographical carriage ride is in its own way as frustratedly heroic as her father's youthful duel. Like her father, she was doomed to 'die' in the realm of feminine silence and the repetitive anonymity that characterized women's narrative possibilities in the seventeenth century or to become an exile from the autobiographical conventions of her culture. Engaged as she is in that effort, she cannot help but be more self-revealing than contemporary autobiographers who inscribed their self-representations in the more 'impersonal' conventions of *res gestae* or spiritual awakening or in the narratives of domestic drama that provided the autobiographer more comfortable, because more clearly delimiting, narrative personae. Cavendish can give neither us nor herself those comfortable masks. She gives us, instead, a woman struggling uncomfortably with an androcentric genre.

In its narrative chaos the prose surface of Cavendish's *True Relation* reveals the desperate pleasure the very act of writing must have offered her. Suppressed energy and vitality permeate the text and its constant transformations. Sentences start in one direction, shift, scatter, reconvene, then go off suddenly elsewhere. That may be, as some critics remark, the sign of her undisciplined mind, the mind of a woman denied the intellectual training reserved exclusively for men. As such it reveals the price she paid for being a woman. But it also reveals the fierce desire for power at the heart of Cavendish's personal struggle for 'fame in after ages'. And so, out of all the mutability and the mobility, the interpenetration of story lines, the proliferation of digressive details, Cavendish constitutes both her 'character' and her 'life', representing herself as a woman of desire and of potentially unbounded imagination. For all her confusions and ambivalences, for all her protestations of cloistered selfhood, she evinces that unenclosed originality she so admired.

Notes

1. PAUL DELANY, *British Autobiography in the Seventeenth Century* (New York: Columbia University Press, 1969), p. 160. Although Delany admits that Cavendish's preoccupation with herself 'ensures that we come into unobstructed contact with her, instead of being blocked by the multiple defences erected by so many male autobiographers', he nevertheless finds this preoccupation 'tedious', which may explain why, after making such interesting claims for the work, he does not bother to analyze it. Since he does not, he has not the opportunity to reconsider his easy dismissal of the defenses she does erect.

2. WAYNE SHUMAKER, *English Autobiography: Its Emergence, Materials, and Form* (Berkeley and Los Angeles: University of California Press, 1954), p. 92. But, having said this, he too moves on without further exploring the intricacies of the work.

3. CYNTHIA S. POMERLEAU, 'The Emergence of Women's Autobiography in England' in *Women's Autobiography: Essays in Criticism*, ed. Estelle C. Jelinek (Bloomington: Indiana University Press, 1980), p. 22. Pomerleau's article draws general comparisons among women's autobiographies of the seventeenth and eighteenth centuries; she does not consider Cavendish's *True Relation* in any detail either. Bottrall briefly discusses the works

by women of the seventeenth century, but only alludes in passing to Cavendish's life in Margaret Bottrall, *Every Man a Phoenix* (London: John Murray, 1958). The historian Hilda L. Smith discusses the life and works in Hilda L. Smith, *Reason's Disciples: Seventeenth-Century English Feminists* (Urbana: University of Illinois Press, 1982). Two literary critics have, however, given the work serious and more detailed consideration: Patricia Meyer Spacks, *The Female Imagination* (New York: Knopf, 1975), esp. ch. 6; and Mary C. Mason, 'The Other Voice: Autobiographies of Women Writers', in *Autobiography: Essays Theoretical and Critical*, ed. James Olney (Princeton: Princeton University Press, 1980), pp. 207–235. Though I do not always agree with the details of Spacks's analysis, I do agree with the general outlines of her reading of the autobiography. Mason's essay, although it offers an interesting theoretical framework, is ultimately too limited.

4. VIRGINIA WOOLF, 'The Duchess of Newcastle', in *The Common Reader: First Series* (New York: Harcourt, Brace & World, 1925), p. 79.

5. This biographical material comes from *Dictionary of National Biography*, ed. Sir Leslie Stephen and Sir Sidney Lee (London: Oxford University Press, 1917), vol. 3, pp. 1264–65.

6. The fact that a good many of the English autobiographies written during the seventeenth century remained unpublished for as long as two hundred years suggests one reason why the autobiographer, especially the secular one, confronted, as Delany notes, a 'difficult and confusing task, for he had to organize his "performance" without much help from literary tradition, unless he was using a particular religious convention' (p. 115). See also Waldo H. Dunn, *English Biography* (New York: E.P. Dutton, 1916), pp. 139–40; and Donald A. Stauffer, *English Biography before 1700* (Cambridge: Harvard University Press, 1930), pp. 175–76.

7. See SIDONIE SMITH, *A Poetics of Women's Autobiography* (Bloomington and Indianapolis: Indiana University Press, 1987), chapter two, for further discussion of the historical forces encouraging the emergence of these modes of self-representation.

8. DELANY, pp. 17–18.

9. SHUMAKER, p. 57.

10. POMERLEAU, p. 28.

11. STAUFFER, p. 209.

12. For an analysis of the difference of men's and women's rhetorical style in biographies, Cavendish's biography of the duke included, see PATRICIA A. SULLIVAN, 'Female Writing beside the Rhetorical Tradition: Seventeenth Century British Biography and Female Tradition in Rhetoric', *International Journal of Women's Studies* 3 (March/April 1980): 143–60.

13. LUCY HUTCHINSON, *Memoirs of the Life of Colonel Hutchinson* (London: Oxford University Press, 1973). The work was written about 1670–1675 and first printed in 1806.

14. *Memoirs of Anne, Lady Halkett and Ann, Lady Fanshawe*, ed. John Clyde Loftis (Oxford: Oxford University Press, 1979). The work was first published in 1907.

15. Ibid. The work was written in 1678.

16. Hɪʟᴅᴀ L. Sᴍɪᴛʜ, pp. 75–76.

17. Ibid., p. 76.

18. As Hɪʟᴅᴀ L. Sᴍɪᴛʜ remarks, 'She wanted to be read, to be popular, to be remembered. Her social position brought her attention, but the duchess wanted the world to admire her for her own talents and works, not because she married well. This desire for personal recognition inspired her repetitious defense of the originality of her work. Her writings, she reiterated, came not from her husband nor others, but solely from her own rational powers' (p. 78).

19. Sᴀɴᴅʀᴀ M. Gɪʟʙᴇʀᴛ and Sᴜsᴀɴ Gᴜʙᴀʀ, *The Madwoman in the Attic: The Woman Writer and the Nineteenth-Century Literary Imagination* (New Haven: Yale University Press, 1979), p. 20. See also Spacks, *The Female Imagination*, pp. 190–92.

20. For their discussion of the 'anxiety of authorship' the woman writer must inevitably experience in patriarchal culture, see Gilbert and Gubar, ch. 2. Spacks explores the struggle in Cavendish's *Life* between 'the desire to assert and the need to deny the self' in Spacks, *The Female Imagination*, p. 195; and Patricia Meyer Spacks, 'Reflecting Women', *Yale Review* 63 (Autumn 1973): 36–37. While I, too, pose this general thematics in the work, I see other complexities and emphasize other entanglements in her self-representation.

21. *The Lives of William Cavendish, duke of Newcastle, and of his wife, Margaret, duchess of Newcastle. Written by the thrice noble and illustrious princess, Margaret, duchess of Newcastle*, ed. Mark Antony Lower (London: J.R. Sᴍɪᴛʜ, 1872), p. 309. Subsequent citations appear in the text. Hilda L. Smith suggests that '[t]his emphasis on her family status may have grown from her resentment toward those who cautioned the duke against marrying beneath himself'. 'Yet,' she goes on to note, 'the emphasis was similar to that which she was to pursue in her own life and writings; socially granted status mattered little compared to that which was awarded for intellectual contribution or personal merit. Her literary labors and her desire for fame grew out of a belief that merited worth, of the kind she believed her parent possessed, mattered more than the titled position her marriage brought her' (p. 86).

22. Discussing recurrent themes in Cavendish's plays, poetry, and prose pieces, Dᴇʟᴏʀᴇs Pᴀʟᴏᴍᴀ suggests that 'the ideals and ambitions Cavendish sought to realize in her own life were appropriated from and expressed in terms borrowed from the heroic ethic of the masculine world' (Delores Paloma, 'Margaret Cavendish: Defining the Female Self', *Women's Studies: An Interdisciplinary Journal* 7 [1980]: 55–56).

23. Mᴀsᴏɴ, p. 223.

24. Dᴇʟᴀɴʏ, p. 169.

25. Pᴏᴍᴇʀʟᴇᴀᴜ, p. 23.

26. Hɪʟᴅᴀ L. Sᴍɪᴛʜ, p. 202.

27. As Hɪʟᴅᴀ L. Sᴍɪᴛʜ suggests, 'Practical accomplishment, which her mother inherited with widowhood, the daughter pursued in a less socially accepted form during the life of her husband' (p. 86).

28. *Natures Pictures*, 2nd edn (London, 1668), sig. Cv.

29. 'If . . . female creativity has had to express itself within the confines of domesticity (in part because of the emphasis on the personal in female socialization), women could at least paint their own faces, shape their own bodies, and modulate their own vocal tones to become the glass of fashion and the mold of form. To make up, for such women, means not only making up stories but making up faces. In terms of the Pygmalion myth with which I began, the woman who cannot become an artist can nevertheless turn herself into an artistic object' (SUSAN GUBAR, ' "The Blank Page" and the Issues of Female Creativity', *Critical Inquiry* 8 [Winter 1981]: 249).

30. SUZANNE JUHASZ, 'Towards a Theory of Form in Feminist Autobiography: Kate Millett's *Flying* and *Sita*; Maxine Hong Kingston's *The Woman Warrior*', in *Women's Autobiography*, ed. Jelinek, p. 230.

31. Mason is only partially accurate when she claims that 'for all her singularity, for all her strong individuality and distinctiveness of personality, for all her fantasticalness, Margaret Cavendish required a substitute figure or other – an alter ego really – with and through whom she might identify herself. . . . [She] found in the Duke of Newcastle both her husband and her Lord, but remarkably enough she succeeds in making this of him without ever dimming the bright light of her own personality' (p. 222). Actually the duke functions much like the woman in Freud's male daydreams. He becomes a kind of male muse who sanctions and even inspires her writing.

32. For a discussion of the dynamics of male and female daydreams and writing, see NANCY K. MILLER, 'Emphasis Added: Plots and Plausibilities in Women's Fiction', *PMLA* 96 (January 1981): 40.

33. STEPHEN JAY GREENBLATT, *Renaissance Self-Fashioning: From More to Shakespeare* (Chicago and London: University of Chicago Press, 1980), p. 257.

34. SPACKS, *The Female Imagination*, p. 194.

6 Embracing the Absolute: Margaret Cavendish and the Politics of the Female Subject in Seventeenth-Century England*

CATHERINE GALLAGHER

Feminism's political project of combatting patriarchy and gender inequality seems logically incompatible with a broadly conservative political stance. That this was conspicuously not the case in the seventeenth century, when early feminist thought was almost invariably accompanied by royalist political allegiances, is an historical anomaly explored by Catherine Gallagher in her essay on Cavendish. This investigation leads her to consideration of Cavendish's self-construction as an autonomous female subject. While Sidonie Smith foregrounds the absence of female models for this project of self-fashioning, Gallagher contends that it was, paradoxically, in the ideology of absolute monarchy that Cavendish found a model of the absolute, sovereign private self. Gallagher emphasizes the historical and social conditions which facilitated the formation of this absolutist female identity: the royal retreat into exile during the Interregnum, and women's exclusion from any public role but that of monarch. We reproduce here only the first half of the essay, which goes on to examine Mary Astell's integration of Cavendish's sovereign female self into a reformist feminist politics.

It is an odd but indisputable fact that the seventeenth-century women whom we think of as the forerunners and founders of feminism were, almost without exception, Tories.[1] Since seventeenth-century Tory ideology is often associated with the radical patriarchalism of Robert Filmer, a patriarchalism equating the family and the kingdom and asserting the divinely granted absolute power of the father-king,[2] historians have been understandably puzzled by the fact that Tory ladies and gentlewomen wrote the earliest extended criticisms of

---

* Reprinted from Catherine Gallagher, 'Embracing the Absolute: The Politics of the Female Subject in Seventeenth-Century England', *Genders*, 1, no. 1 (Spring, 1988), pp. 24–33.

the absolute subordination of women in marriage and the earliest systematic assertions of women's rational and moral equality with men.

Some historians have, to be sure, questioned the facile equation of Tory ideology with Filmerian patriarchalism and Whig ideology with Locke's objections to Filmer.[3] Their revisions of the ideological history, however, are no help in explaining the surprising predominance of Tories among seventeenth- and early eighteenth-century feminist writers. It may be the case that there were no consistent differences between monarchists and parliamentarians or between Tories and Whigs on the issues of family organization and women's political rights, but then one would expect early feminists to be equally divided between the parties. If there were no gender issues at all on the agenda of either party, then the deep affinity between Toryism and feminism is still buried in obscurity.

In one of the most sustained attempts to shed some light on the relationship, Hilda Smith has suggested that it resides not so much in the ideological as in the sociological dimension of Toryism.[4] She argues that women of the classes whose interests were represented by the Tories were relatively deprived of certain opportunities and privileges during the seventeenth century, and this relative deprivation made them conscious of the unfair restrictions placed on the lives of all women. As the privileges of rank were called into question, and as middle-class men acquired new political, economic, and educational advantages, aristocratic ladies and gentlewomen may have felt a relative erosion of their social power, even if no actual loss of position can be substantiated. A sensed loss of status, her argument goes, would have led certain especially perceptive women of these classes to the painful revelation that their femaleness (and not their rank) determined their social power and to the concomitant wish that distinctions of rank would override those of gender. Hence their Toryism, by giving political articulation to their desire to restore or protect a stable social hierarchy, both encouraged the general habit of critically reflecting on social arrangements and linked their interests as ladies and gentlewomen to the restoration of that hierarchy.

This explanation seems plausible as a first step, but it is not quite adequate to dispose of some troubling counterevidence. The emphasis on social class fails first of all to explain why many very prominent aristocratic ladies of the period found it easy to maintain and even extend the privileges of their rank within the context of Whig politics. Especially in the very late years of the century when the Tory Party properly speaking came into being and the country underwent an unprecedented politicization, social class does not seem to have been a reliable indicator either of which women became politically active or of what their party affiliation was. In other words, there was an across-the-board increase in upper-class women's partisan political activities during this period[5] that belies the claim that a general class experience created a bond between the interests of upper-class women as a group and Toryism. The sociological model will, therefore, require considerable refinement before it can give us such an accurate account of the differences between Whig and Tory ladies that we would be able to see what special factors in the social experience of monarchist women might have inclined them toward feminism or what some writers have called proto-feminism.[6]

In the meantime, those of us who are not social historians might look to the texts of the Tory feminists themselves for pieces of the puzzle. That is what I will be doing in this essay. Several of the works of Margaret Cavendish (1626–1673) and Mary Astell (1666–1730) will provide the evidence for my contention that Toryism and feminism converge because the ideology of absolute monarchy provides, in particular historical situations, a transition to an ideology of the absolute self. It is the paradoxical connection between the *roi absolu* and the *moi absolu* that I wish to trace in the early history of feminism.

Margaret Cavendish was a notorious eccentric, and hence it is difficult to argue for her representativeness even within the tiny sorority of seventeenth-century women writers. By her own account she was an isolated child, painfully shy.[7] As a teenager, during the Civil War, she became a maid of honor to the queen, and at court she met William Cavendish, thirty years her senior, then marquis of Newcastle and leader of the loyalist forces in the north of England. She married William in 1645, and, like the rest of the English court, they spent the next fifteen years in exile. When they returned to England with the restoration of the monarchy, the Cavendishes lived a retired life. Margaret dressed in an outlandish fashion and published books that most of her contemporaries found simply incomprehensible.

If it is difficult to see Margaret Cavendish as representative of seventeenth-century women writers, it is even harder to imagine her as a typical early feminist. Indeed, historians of feminism have found her a troublesome ancestress,[8] embarrassingly apt to deliver such sentences as the following, which opens her 1655 book *The World's Olio*: 'It cannot be expected I should write so wisely or wittily as Men, being of the Effeminate Sex, whose Brains Nature hath mix't with the coldest and softest Elements.'[9] Histories of feminism, nevertheless, routinely include her (even though they have a difficult time finding appropriate quotations), for in Cavendish's works about her self and her writing, feminists have seen early assertions of a woman's need for self-inscription.

Such assertions are bound up with Cavendish's wilful eccentricity, the very characteristic that also links her protofeminism and her absolutist rhetoric. In her proclamations of what she calls her 'singularity', she insists that she is an autotelic, self-sufficient being, not a secondary creature, a satellite orbiting a dominant male planet, but a self-centered orb, eccentric because outside of anyone else's circle. In describing and justifying this absolute singularity, Cavendish repeatedly invokes the model of the absolute monarch. At first glance, these two absolutes, the absolute monarch and the autotelic woman who claims to rule herself, seem logically incompatible. But Cavendish's works manifest their interdependence and especially their interdependence for a woman seeking preeminence through writing.

Cavendish's Toryism largely consists of her commitment to absolute monarchy, but most of her defenses of this form of government turn into defenses of singularity itself. The monarch becomes a figure for the self-enclosed, autonomous nature of any person. In her writings, there are dozens of instances of this figural use of the monarch, but one of the most instructive is in her preface to her biography of her husband:

> Although there be many sorts of histories yet these three are the chiefest: (1) a general history. (2) A national history. (3) A particular history. Which three sorts may, not unfitly, be compared to the three sorts of governments, Democracy, Aristocracy, and Monarchy. The first is the history of the known parts and people of the world; the second is the history of a particular nation, kingdom or commonwealth. The third is the history of the life and actions of some particular person. ... The last [the history of the single person which corresponds to monarchy] is the most secure; because it goes not out of its own circle, but turns on its own axis, and ... keeps within the circumference of truth.[10]

The comparison made here between any particular life history and monarchy stresses the security that is gained by staying within the bounds of singularity, and the comparison relies on a third metaphorical term, that of planetary motion. The book that centers on a single self, like the state that centers on a single ruler, comprises a self-contained world that 'turns on its own axis' and makes its own circle. Inside the history of the particular individual is epistemological security (it keeps within the circumference of truth), just as within the absolute monarchy is political security. What is imagined here is a plurality of worlds, each based on that model of singularity, the monarchy. Each individual, each book, becomes whole, true, distinct, a world unto itself, only by virtue of the authoritative metaphor of absolute monarchy. Hence, what at first appears to be an absolutism that would merely lead to the subjection of all individuals except the monarch was actually for

Cavendish the foundation for a subjectivity that would make its own absolute claims.

Cavendish frequently urges these claims against those who would limit her intellectual activity on the basis of her sex. In describing her fitness for authorship, she claims, 'my minde is become an absolute Monark, ruling alone, my thoughts as a peaceable Commonwealth'.[11] Moreover, Cavendish explicitly links her gender to this absolutist model of subjectivity, claiming at the beginning of her book *The Blazing World*, for example, that restrictions on her worldly ambitions have directed her inward, toward the microcosm of the self:

> I am . . . as Ambitious as ever any of my Sex was, is, or can be; which is the cause, That though I cannot be Henry the Fifth, or Charles the Second; yet, I will endeavour to be, Margaret the First: and, though I have neither Power, Time, nor Occasion, to be a great Conqueror, like Alexander, or Cesar [*sic*]; yet, rather than not be Mistress of a World, since Fortune and the Fates would give me none, I have made One of my own . . . thus believing, or, at least, hoping, that no Creature can, or will, Envy me for this World of mine.[12]

I will return to this text and to the problematic self that ultimately emerges from it, but for now I simply want to stress its feminization of the writing subject, who is isolated and complete unto herself. The desire for absolute power is circumscribed, qualified, according to this passage, by Cavendish's sex. Not having been born a monarch, she cannot, like a man, gain empire through conquest. Hence she retreats to the empire of the mind, where her absolute rule is undisputed ('unenvied' because there can be no shortage of such worlds).

We should not be misled by this passage, though, into concluding that Cavendish presents herself as a woman whose ambition has simply been defeated or diverted by her femaleness. Her emphasis on the microcosm of the self does suggest a compensatory withdrawal; because her sex conflicts with her ambitions, she retreats to the domain of subjectivity. And such a narrative implies that the absolutist desire, the ambition, exists prior to the gender awareness that thwarts it. However, much in Cavendish's texts suggests that the absolutist desire, the desire to be the sovereign monarch, itself derives from a certain female disability: not from her inability to be a monarch but from her inability to be a full *subject* of the monarch. Of the two available political positions, subject and monarch, monarch is the only one Cavendish can imagine a woman occupying. And this, of course, accorded with her historical experience; women were excluded from all state offices except that of monarch. Even in her fantasy worlds, Cavendish keeps recreating these all-or-nothing political alternatives for women; in *The Blazing World*, for example, an extended fantasy of imperial power, the empress rules alone, her ministers are eunuchs, and no other woman is allowed to have 'employment in Church or State' (p. 18). Since the only model of political being available to women in Cavendish's writings is that of monarch, a woman's ambition can only take the absolute form. Her mode of constructing her gender, then, not only directs her absolutism toward the domain of the self but also generates that desire for absolute domain in the first place by obviating the alternative – political subjecthood.

Thus, as the following passage from her *Sociable Letters* emphasizes, women come to occupy the position of monarch because of their exclusion from the polity:

> As for the matter of Governments, we Women understand them not; yet if we did, we are excluded from intermedling therewith, and almost from being subject thereto; we are not tied, nor bound to State or Crown; we are free, not Sworn to Allegiance, nor do we take the Oath of Supremacy; we are not made Citizens of the Commonwealth, we hold no Offices, nor bear we any Authority therein; we are accounted neither Useful in Peace, nor Serviceable in War; and if we be not Citizens in the Commonwealth, I know no reason we should be Subjects to the Commonwealth: And the truth is, we are no Subjects.[13]

It is this extraordinary assertion, 'we are no Subjects', that forms the logical foundation for that ambitious statement quoted earlier: 'I will endeavour to be Margaret the First.' Exclusion from political subjecthood allows female subjectivity to become absolute.

Cavendish, then, feminizes her absolutism from the outset. This is most clearly seen when she contrasts it to her husband's absolutism. She presents William Cavendish as circumscribed always by the terms of political subjection and hence unable to escape a self-sacrificing subordination:

> I have heard him say several times, that his love to his gracious master King Charles the Second, was above the love he bore to his wife, children, and all his posterity, nay to his own life: and when, since his return into England, I answered him, that I observed his gracious master did not love him so well . . . ; he replied, that he cared not whether His Majesty loved him again or not; for he was resolved to love Him.[14]

The subjectivity of the male absolutist is here presented as impaired by the need to choose between the self and the monarch. Since only one can be absolute, William Cavendish must constantly choose against himself. During their long exile, Margaret reports that she suggested to William that he, like her, find satisfaction and a sense of his own complete being in political nonsubjection. But to the royalist male, Margaret implies, such nonsubjection is simply nonbeing: 'My Lord being in banishment, I told him, that he was happy in his misfortunes, for he was not subject to any state or prince. To which he jestingly answered, that as he was subject to no prince, so he was a prince of no subjects.'[15]

A perfectly constituted subject of the king, William Cavendish becomes merely abject in the monarch's absence, whereas Margaret becomes absolute. According to Margaret, the monarch for women is always a simultaneous presence / absence. He is the cynosure, the guiding star, that directs her to her own selfhood. But the very completeness of her selfhood, modelled on him, then makes the monarch irrelevant. Cavendish writes as if banishment is every woman's natural political condition and one that allows her to be in miniature what Charles II was on a grander scale during the years of their shared exile: an absolute monarch without a country. The beheading of Charles I may have spelled the end of dynastic rule in England, just as it showed that the country had never had a truly absolutist state. Nevertheless, the royal martyrdom and exile also confirmed the faith of many absolute monarchists, and certainly the loss of the state created an important imaginative opening for Cavendish. During the years when the Cavendishes, like the rest of the English court, were exiled in France and Holland, Charles II was himself the ruler of a kind of fantasy kingdom. In a sense, the exile literalized the monarch's metaphoric significance. The real king had become the ruler of what amounted to a microcosm, had almost been reduced to a private kingdom, and hence had practically enacted the metaphorical equivalence of sovereign monarch and sovereign private person. Margaret Cavendish's loyalty to her monarch did not preclude this identification, as her husband's did. She, like the king, was no subject; the king, like her, had no 'terrestrial realm'. According to *The Blazing World*, this lack should only have made his rule more perfect:

> For every human Creature can create an Immaterial World fully inhabited by Immaterial Creatures, and populous of Immaterial subjects . . . and all this within the compass of the head or scull; nay, not onely so, but he may create a World of what fashion and Government he will, and give the Creatures thereof such motions, figures, forms, colours, perceptions . . . as he pleases. And since it is in your power to create such a World, What need you to venture life, reputation and tranquility to conquer a gross material World? For

you can enjoy no more of a material world than a particular Creature
is able to enjoy, which is but a small part, considering the compass of
such a world . . . for it is impossible, that a Kingdom, nay, a Country,
should be injoyed by one person at once, except he take the pains to
travel into every part, and endure the inconveniencies of going from
one place to another.[16]

Thus, we might infer, Charles II's deprivation, the reduction of his
realm to private dimensions, should have been the perfection of his
absolute control.

The monarch in the interregnum, then, serves as a convenient
historical pivot for a metaphoric reversal in Cavendish's work: the
private woman, completely retired, turns into a figure for the emperor:

I by this retirement live in a calm silence, wherein I have my
contemplations free from disturbance, and my mind lives in peace,
and my thoughts in pleasure. . . . My mind is entertained [with my
own thoughts] and takes as much Delight as Augustus Caesar did
to have his Mecaenas, the Patron of Poets, sit and hear Virgil and
Horace read their Works unto them; so my Mind takes Delights in
its dear Mecaenas, which is Contemplation, and to have its Poetical
Thoughts . . . Repeat their Poems, and other Works which they make;
and those my Mind likes best, it sends them forth to the Senses to
write down, and then to send them out to the publick view of the
World. . . . So that the Mind and Thoughts imploy the Senses, and
the Senses imploy the Mind and Thoughts, and thus I take . . .
Pleasure within my self.[17]

The private and the courtly depend on one another in this conceit. The
court (rather than the empire) is that which serves as an analogue for
the self because the private woman has already been imagined as a self-
sufficient court, complete with monarch, patron, poets, ministers, and
heralds. And this utterly private self then becomes the optimal, indeed
the only, site of true sovereignty: 'But this Retired Life is so Pleasing to
me, as I would not change it for all the Pleasures of the Publick World,
nay, not to be Mistress of the World, for I should not desire to be
Mistress of that which is too Big to be Commanded, too Self-willed to
be Ruled, too Factious to be Govern'd too Turbulent to live in Peace.'[18]

In Cavendish's writings, then, the absolute is reimagined as that
which she conceives to be the private and the feminine. But this entails
the concomitant reimagining of the feminine as absolutely private,
subjective, and yet nonsubjected. This idea of femininity maintains its
immemorial association with a private, sequestered place. However,
the significance of these texts lies in their transformation of the idea of

privacy for women. In Cavendish's works, the private realm is not
simply country retirement, nor is it the sphere of the family, nor the
scene of domestic productivity, nor the space of erotic encounter. It is,
rather, absolute privacy, void of other bodies and empty even of other
minds. The frontispiece to her *Philosophical and Physical Opinions* shows
Cavendish sitting in a study completely empty of books, and the legend
reads:

> Studious She is and all Alone
> Most visitants, when She has none,
> Her Library on which She looks
> It is her Head, her Thoughts her Books.
> Scorninge dead Ashes without fire
> For her owne Flames doe her Inspire.[19]

This utter solitude, complete and autotelic, is strikingly different from
traditional ways of imagining feminine privacy and subjectivity. The
woman here is in no sense a relative creature. However, as the legend
of the frontispiece also stresses, this is a strangely haunted and even
feverish solitude. There is a sense of alarm raised especially by the
image of the flaming head. And this is just one of numerous instances
in which Cavendish seems imperiled by her total self-referentiality. For,
paradoxically, self-fragmentation is entailed in her very metaphors of
absolute sovereignty.

Throughout her writings, when a kingdom of the self is invoked, it
carries with it implications of multiplicity: one is a commonwealth.
And the more grandiose the metaphor of the microcosmic monadic self,
the more pluralized an entity the individual becomes:

> This Lady only to her self she Writes,
> And all her Letters to her self Indites;
> For in her self so many Creatures be,
> Like many Commonwealths, yet all Agree.
> Man's Head's a World, where Thoughts are Born and Bred,
> But in all Heads doth not a Caesar Reign,
> A Wise Augustus hath not every Brain,
> And Reason in some Brains from Rule's put out
> By Mad, Rebellious Thoughts, and Factious Rout;
> And Great Disorder in such Brains will be,
> Nor any Thought with Reason will Agree;
> But in her Brain doth Reason Govern well,
> Not any Thought 'gainst Reason doth Rebell.[20]

Here the link between absolute subjectivity ('Man's Head's a World')
and the need for an absolute emperor is explicit, but so too is the

141

slippage of both from figures of singularity to images of almost infinite plurality ('For in her self so many Creatures be'). The subject, in order to be absolute, must have subjects. Thus the model of the self based on absolutism, with its implicit image of the self as a microcosm, leads in Cavendish's works to a multiplicity of subjectivities.

Nowhere is this logic more elaborately ramified than in her extended fantasy *The Blazing World*, and nowhere is its connection to her gender more apparent. That book, as I remarked earlier, begins by revealing the bond between the feminization of the absolute and the new absolutism of the private female. Because Cavendish is not a man, the opening epistle claims, her ambition takes an absolute form and her absolutism takes a private form. This private dominion of the self, though, requires some external articulation; its proof lies in the creation of an imaginary world; that is, the world of the book.

The desire to be a singular authority leads first to an insistent, militant subjectivity, and then to a multiplication of worlds belonging to the self, each of which circumscribes yet another self. The self is a world, and the proof of its self-sufficiency is that it can make a world in fiction, utterly fantastic and 'singular', the 'world' of the text we are reading. However, it turns out that the textual microcosm of *The Blazing World* depicts not just one but several worlds. According to this fantasy, an infinity of worlds is arranged in two different dimensions. First, an infinite number of them, we are told, are strung together like beads on a chain. Joined at their poles, each turns on its own axis. The blazing world of the title is only one of these. Second, the text gives us another dimension of multiplication by imaging the infinite recessing of worlds within worlds. And these two directions of multiplication intersect. The most important world in the chain of worlds, the blazing world of the title, has an empress, seemingly a figure of the ambitious author's wish-fulfilment, who rules absolutely. However, by recreating the self as a fantasy empress inside the world that is, according to the preface, supposedly inside herself, the text begins a process of infinite regression. The self is no longer coextensive with its microcosm, just as the blazing world is not coextensive with the microcosm of the text. Hence, frustration enters the fantasy. For, we are told, 'the Empress here, which although she possesses a whole World, yet enjoys she but a part thereof; neither is she so much acquainted with it, that she knows all the places, Countries, and Dominions she Governs' (p. 97).

The fantasy of absolute power over a world which figured itself in absolute monarchy is hence no sooner articulated than it finds monarchy an inadequate figure for absolute power. In a movement we have already noted as characteristic of Cavendish's thought, the story then explores the superior alternative of making worlds in the mind; it depicts the privatization of the absolute, which the epistle told us was the origin of the text in the first place. 'Why,' asks one of the guiding spirits in the blazing world, 'should you desire to be Empress of a Material World, and be troubled with the cares that attend Government? when as by creating a World within your self, you may enjoy all both in whole and in parts, without controle or opposition; and may make what World you please and alter it when you please, and enjoy as much pleasure and delight as a World can afford you?' (p. 97). Thus, inside the story, both the empress and her scribe – who is named Margaret Cavendish and who says, like the author of the book, 'my Ambition is, That I would be . . . an Empress of a World, and I shall never be at quiet until I be one' (p. 94) – adopt the superior alternative of creating 'Worlds within themselves' (p. 98). Presumably the character Cavendish's world will, like the blazing world, also contain a Margaret Cavendish who wishes to be empress of a world and decides instead to create a microcosm, etc. *ad infinitum.*

These imaginary worlds, therefore, display the same infinite recessiveness that Cavendish, anticipating Leibniz, believed existed in every particle of nature. As Leibniz expresses it, 'Each part of matter can be thought of as a garden full of plants or as a pond full of fish. But each branch of the plant, each member of the animal, each drop of its humors, is also such a garden or such a pond.'[21] Cavendish had arrived at this vision as early as 1653, when she began exploring how 'Small Atomes of themselves a World may make' (beginning of *Poems and Fancies*). The epistemological implications of such a vision are various. Cavendish, like Aphra Behn, who was the first English translator of Fontenelle's *Plurality of Worlds*, seems to have been fascinated by the radical perspectivalism of the New Science, its destruction of a hierarchy of knowers. Because she assumes that each unit of matter englobes a self-sufficient and radically distinct consciousness, she is able to imagine that there is no privileged perspective of universal knowledge, such as that which might earlier have been attributed to the topmost position on the great chain of being, the position occupied by the male human being. In Cavendish's poetry, for example, we are invited to see the hunt from the perspective of the hunted animal, the feast from the perspective of the food, the ball from the perspective of the microscopic inhabitants of a lady's earring. Absolutism and relativism, then, become two sides of one logic in her works; she uses perspective to decenter the universe by insisting on the eccentricity – the absoluteness – of all knowing.

However, when this decentering is accomplished on the writer herself, when the divisibility of matter becomes the divisibility of the self, subjectivity begins a regressive self-pursuit. In *The Blazing World*, for example, absolutism entails the elusiveness of subjectivity: (1) the absolutist imagines the self as microcosm; (2) the microcosm requires

an absolute ruler, a figure of the self in the world of the self; (3) the
ruler of the microcosm, finding herself to be but a part of the microcosm
she inhabits, must create yet another microcosm in order to meet the
demands of absolutism. Such a text finally imagines subjectivity as an
infinite, unfathomable regression of interiority.

We are by now perhaps overly familiar with this structure: it is a
classic *mise en abîme*. Indeed, we might call Cavendish the seventeenth-
century's Ms. en abîme. The character, Margaret Cavendish in the
microcosm who is determined to create a microcosm, functions like
the escutcheon on the escutcheon. When the representation of the
whole is reiterated as a part of the whole, it unsettles the very identity
it was intended to anchor. And the absolute monarch, of course, as
representation of the whole functions in just the same way. This vision
of subjectivity is clearly a splendid generator of texts, and although it
may dizzy the reader, it does not necessarily presage 'the death of the
subject', about which we hear so much. Indeed, Cavendish's texts show
that the infinitude of selfhood accompanies the birth of the subject.
Specifically in this case, it is connected with the birth of the woman as
subject. That which seems the undoing of the stability of the self is that
which allows subjectivity to come into existence as an excessiveness of
consciousness in relationship to all objects but especially in relationship
to itself as object.

But useful as such a vertiginous self may be in textual production
and compelling as it may seem in its elusive inexhaustibility, this
aspect of Cavendish's model of the self was ultimately unsuited to
the needs of the Tory feminists who followed her. Those women who
argued at the end of the century for the reform of female education
and the elevation of women's social status retained Cavendish's stress
on the autotelic woman but removed her from the vortex of solipsistic
regression. They freed woman's sovereign self from the complete
political and social isolation in which Cavendish had placed her.

Notes

1. HILDA L. SMITH, *Reason's Disciples: Seventeenth-Century English Feminists*
    (Urbana: University of Illinois Press, 1982), pp. 3–17; Joan K. Kinnaird,
    'Mary Astell and the Conservative Contribution to English Feminism',
    Journal of British Studies 19, no. 1 (Fall 1979): 53. For accounts of individual
    Tory feminists, see *First Feminists: British Women Writers 1578–1799*, ed. and
    with an introduction by Moira Ferguson (Bloomington: Indiana University
    Press, and Old Westbury: The Feminist Press, 1985).

2. GORDON J. SCHOCHET, *Patriarchalism in Political Thought: The Authoritarian
    Family and Political Speculation and Attitudes Especially in Seventeenth-Century*

England (Oxford: Basil Blackwell, 1975), chaps. 7 and 8. Schochet asserts that 'Filmer's books became the backbone of Tory ideology', p. 120. See also Smith, *Reason's Disciples*, pp. 57, 202.

3. Among those who question Filmer's centrality to Tory thought are James Daly, in *Sir Robert Filmer and English Political Thought* (Toronto: University of Toronto Press, 1979), pp. 159–63, and J.G.A. Pocock in *Virtue, Commerce, and History: Essays on Political Thought and History, Chiefly in the Eighteenth Century* (Cambridge: Cambridge University Press, 1985), pp. 95, 222–23.

4. Smith, *Reason's Disciples*, chap. 1.

5. Geoffrey Holmes and W.A. Speck, *The Divided Society: Party Conflict in England 1694–1716* (London: Edward Arnold, 1967), pp. 82–87; Ruth Perry, *The Celebrated Mary Astell* (Chicago: Chicago University Press, 1986), p. 188.

6. Kinnaird, for example, uses 'protofeminism' to avoid implying that these women held a set of beliefs corresponding to those of modern feminists.

7. Biographical material on Margaret Cavendish comes from her own autobiographical writings published with her *Life of the First Duke of Newcastle & Other Writings* (London, 1916) and from Douglas Grant, *Margaret the First. A Biography of Margaret Cavendish, Duchess of Newcastle, 1623–1673* (London: Rupert Hart-Davis, 1957).

8. See, for example, Smith, *Reason's Disciples*, pp. 75–95.

9. 'Preface to the Reader', *The Worlds Olio* (London, 1655), n.p.

10. *Life of the Duke*, pp. 10–11.

11. *World's Olio*, p. 46.

12. 'To All Noble and Worthy Ladies', *The Description of a New World, Called the Blazing World* (London, 1668), n.p.

13. *Sociable Letters* (London, 1664), p. 27.

14. *Life of the Duke*, p. 165.

15. Ibid., p. 167.

16. *Blazing World*, pp. 96–97.

17. *Sociable Letters*, pp. 57–59.

18. Ibid., p. 62.

19. Reproduced in Grant, *Margaret the First*, opposite p. 166.

20. *Sociable Letters*, d.

21. Gottfried Wilhelm Leibniz, 'The Monadology', sec. 67, in *Gottfried William Leibniz: Philosophical Papers and Letters*, trans., ed., and with an introduction by Leroy E. Loemker, 2nd edn (Dordrecht, Holland, 1969), p. 650.

APHRA BEHN
(1640–89)

7 'Once a Whore and Ever'? Whore and Virgin in *The Rover* and Its Antecedents*

NANCY COPELAND

Aphra Behn's *The Rover* is a key text in the gender/genre debate, for the sexual politics of a play which rewards its sexually rapacious rake–hero with marriage to the wealthy virgin may not necessarily be any more enlightened (any may indeed be less) than those of male-authored Restoration comedies. Nancy Copeland addresses this problem by relating Behn's 'happy' ending to her treatment of the play's central comic *topos*: the hero's choice between virgin and whore. Behn repeatedly blurs the moral distinction between chaste comic heroine and prostitute which obtains in her male-authored source play, refusing to demonize the woman whose sexuality does not serve patriarchy's dynastic ends. The emergence of the traditional distinction in the play's dénouement would, in a new historicist reading, signal the dominant discourse's containment of subversion; in Copeland's feminist reading, the abrupt reversals work to reinforce the play's social critique and undermine comic resolution.

In her Postscript to *The Rover*, Aphra Behn claimed, in response to accusations of plagiarism, that 'the sign of Angellica' was 'the only stolen object' that she had appropriated from Thomas Killigrew's *Thomaso* (1.13, 130). She had, in fact, borrowed considerably more, and her debt has been duly documented.[1] Nevertheless, her disingenuous claim does point to an 'object' that is of particular significance to her play. The courtesan Angellica Bianca, 'stolen' from *Thomaso*, is the vehicle for meanings that suggest the difficult position of the female subject in a period when, in the words of Harold Weber, 'sexual change could both elevate and degrade women at the same time' (152). Thanks to the presence of this unusual character derived from an earlier comic

* Reprinted from *Restoration: Studies in English Literary Culture 1660–1700*, 16, no. 1 (Spring, 1992), pp. 20–27.

tradition, a courtesan is brought together with the 'gay' heroine of
Carolean comedy to produce a conjunction that, by complicating both
the progress and the resolution of the action, exposes an inherent
contradiction in contemporary attitudes toward female sexuality. While
Killigrew's Angellica demonstrates the simple truth of the adage 'once a
whore and ever', in Behn's play the resemblance between Angellica and
Hellena, the momentary idealization of Angellica's libertinism, and the
lack of closure in the play's treatment of her, call into question the
value of female chastity and challenge her consignment to the status
of 'whore'.

1

The main plot of *The Rover* is, like *Thomaso*'s, built around the comic
topos of the hero's choice between *virgo* and *meretrix*. *Thomaso* is the
successor of the many Jacobean city comedies that represent the same
subject. Of these, Marston's *Dutch Courtesan* (1605) is exemplary: the
'*Fabulae Argumentum*' announces that '*The difference betwixt the love of
a courtesan and a wife is the full scope of the play . . .*' (3); further, the
play is, according to Richard Horwich, in many respects, 'a sort of
encyclopedia of popular attitudes toward courtesans . . .' (272 n. 8).
The view of the subject finally endorsed by the plot is expressed in
Act V by the hero, Freevill, in a comparison of his virtuous wife-to-be,
Beatrice, with his vengeful cast-off whore, Franceschina:

> O heaven,
> What difference is in women and their life!
> What man, but worthy name of man, would leave
> The modest pleasures of a lawful bed,
> The holy union of two equal hearts,
> Mutually holding either dear as health,
> The undoubted issues, joys of chaste sheets,
> The unfeigned embrace of sober ignorance,
> To twine th'unhealthful loins of common loves,
> The prostituted impudence of things
> Senseless like those by cataracts of Nile,
> Their use so vile takes away sense! How vile
> To love a creature made of blood and hell,
> Whose use makes weak, whose company doth shame,
> Whose bed doth beggar, issue doth defame!
>
> (V.i.65–79)

Inscribed in this passage is the absolute distinction between virgin and whore that is a commonplace of Elizabethan and Jacobean drama (see, for example, Leggatt 99 and Weber 133). Although Killigrew subdivided his prostitutes into 'good courtesans and bad courtesans' (Harbage 230), this distinction is preserved in *Thomaso*, whose hero repeats Freevill's discovery of 'the difference between a vertuous passion', whose object is the chaste Serulina, 'and a lustful flame' directed toward Angellica. Again like Freevill, Thomaso comes to identify his rejection of the courtesan in favor of the virgin as a sign of his maturity (2 *Thomaso* IV.ix, 438).[2]

In *The Rover*, Behn rewrites *Thomaso* in the light of the post-Restoration comedies that focus on the love duel between the members of a 'gay couple'. The antecedents of Hellena, the heroine of *The Rover*, include Florimell in *Secret Love*, Jacinta in *An Evening's Love*, and their precursor, Beatrice's witty sister, Crispinella, rather than the passive, idealized Beatrice herself, or the 'noble mind[ed]' Serulina, who becomes the romantic Florinda in Behn's play (2 *Thomaso* IV.ix, 438).[3] The juxtaposition of this character type with Angellica results in a narrowing of the distance between virgin and whore that complicates the final rejection of the courtesan and her ultimate exclusion from the play's comic conclusion.

Like other 'gay' heroines, Hellena acknowledges and acts on her desire, and risqué, potentially libertine sentiments form an important part of her discourse. '[O]ur business as well as our humours are alike,' she tells Willmore, the genuinely libertine 'rover' of the title: 'yours to cozen as many maids as will trust you, and I as many men as have faith' (III.i.198–200). Like her predecessors, she represents the new female ideal identified by Lawrence Stone, which fused formerly distinct 'archetypes of sexual conduct' in the figure of the wife who could both provide 'sensual pleasure' and guarantee a legitimate male heir by her chastity (Stone 326–27).[4] Indeed, the similarity between the prostitute and the chaste woman that is implicit in this ideal is inscribed in Hellena. Jones DeRitter has noted that '[m]uch of Hellena's background and even a few of her lines are culled from the speeches of the good courtesans in *Thomaso* – that is, from Angellica and Paulina' (89).

Within *The Rover* itself, the proximity of the 'good' prostitute and the 'gay' mistress underlines their resemblance, a resemblance only latent in Serulina, which is successfully obscured by her idealization. In contrast to Serulina, Hellena enters into direct competition with Angellica for Willmore. To satisfy her desire for a man 'that will spoil [her] . . . devotion' and save her from a convent (I.i.37–38), Hellena is drawn out of her father's house and into the realm of commerce, the realm that Angellica inhabits by virtue of her profession. More explicitly than the Serulina–Angellica rivalry, Hellena's competition with Angellica includes not only love but also money on both sides: Willmore, who has persuaded Angellica to give herself to him for love, emerges from his free night with her *'Jingl[ing] gold'* (III.i.115); Hellena is an heiress, with 'two hundred thousand crowns' to offer the man who marries her (IV.ii.185).[5] Both women also enter into a competition with Willmore himself in their courtship. Behn's Angellica is like her predecessor in debating the relative merits of love and prostitution with her would-be lover (II.ii); after her capitulation, she is compelled to defend constancy against his libertine doctrine. Hellena differs from Serulina in also competing directly with her gallant: she engages in the conventional 'gay' battle of wits with Willmore, a battle in which Horwich, writing of its early use by Middleton, has identified a competitiveness and profit-seeking ('two people, each attempting to extract from marriage more than he or she puts into it') that turn marriage into 'a marketplace' (270).

The central point of similarity is, however, the women's advertising of themselves: it is not only Angellica who does so. The 'sign of Angellica', the picture of herself that she hangs outside her house, is an advertisement of her professional status; Hellena's description of herself in the first scene of the play similarly puts her on display. 'Prithee tell me,' she asks her sister Florinda, 'what dost thou see about me that is unfit for love? Have I not a world of youth? A humour gay? A beauty passable? A vigor desirable? Well shaped? Clean limbed? Sweet breathed? And sense enough to know how all these ought to be employed to the best advantage?' (I.i.43–48).

Patricia Parker identifies the commercial character of the blazon, of which this description is an example. She quotes Nancy Vickers to assert that the 'relationship so constructed involves an active buyer, an active seller, and a passive object for sale'.[6] Conventionally the seller, the speaker of the blazon, and the buyer, the audience, are male, while the 'passive object' is the woman whose body is described. 'The inventory or itemizing impulse of the blazon . . . would seem to be part of the motif of taking control of a woman's body . . . ,' Parker continues (131). The usual relationship is exemplified in the famous blazon in one of Behn's sources, *Secret Love*, in which Celadon, played by Charles Hart, itemizes the beauties of Florimell's body in terms which are believed to be a description of Nell Gwyn, who first played the role (I.ii.48–49, 56–62, 332). Hellena's blazon has a similar self-reflexive character: in it Elizabeth Barry – who was indeed young, vigorous and desirable, although only passably beautiful – advertised herself near the beginning of her career.

The fictive implications of Hellena's blazon are suggested in an article by Catherine Gallagher on Behn's use of the whore-persona. Gallagher argues for a connection (at the metaphorical level) between prostitution and identity that 'fits into the most advanced seventeenth-century ideas about selfhood' and property (29): the sale of the self is proof of the existence of a self to be sold, or, the 'proof of self ownership is self sale' (33). Her explication of the trope of prostitution helps us to see Hellena's (self-)blazon as a further instance of her similarity to Angellica (a similarity reinforced by Barry's notorious reputation), both in her selling of herself and in the construction of her fictive identity.

There is, nevertheless, a crucial difference between Hellena's blazoning of herself and Angellica's sign: Angellica advertises herself publicly; Hellena's self-advertisement, within the play's fictive world, takes place in the privacy of her home. This difference is eroded, however, when Hellena is blazoned by Willmore at the beginning of Act V. Having badgered Hellena into showing him her face, which has been masked, he takes possession of her beauty in a blazon: 'Oh, the charms of those sprightly black eyes! That strangely fair face, full of smiles and dimples! Those soft round melting cherry lips and small even white teeth!' (III.i.203–06). In the process, Hellena's private self-advertisement not only becomes public, but passes into the hands of another. Again, Gallagher proves illuminating. Writing of *The Lucky Chance*, she observes: 'to lose honor is to give away control over one's public representations' (37). The ambiguity of Hellena's position now extends to a loss of control over her 'public representations' that brings her yet closer to Angellica.

2

Angellica herself differs from her many demonized predecessors in Jacobean comedy: already in *Thomaso*, she is represented with a tolerance that recalls the treatment of courtesans in some of Middleton's plays for the private theatre, among them *A Mad World, My Masters*.[7] Harold Weber, in *The Restoration Rake Hero*, has noted the difference between Killigrew's Angellica and the Jacobean portrayal of prostitutes as 'monstrous expressions of our fallen state' (153). Weber interprets Killigrew's character as an idealized representation of the female libertine, although one with which 'Killigrew . . . has little sympathy . . . ,' since the 'ideal' relationship she establishes with Thomaso is 'no sooner . . . formulated than undercut' (156). Behn's Angellica, however, exhibits the consequences of the higher valuation of female sexuality that is also visible in Hellena. A comparison of Behn's character with Killigrew's demonstrates the extent to which the later Angellica's relationship with Willmore is presented more favorably than her predecessor's with Thomaso.

I will focus my comparison of the two Angellicas on the crucial
scenes in which they are persuaded to give themselves to their
respective rakes for love rather than money: 1 *Thomaso* II.iv. and 1
Rover II.ii. Thomaso and Willmore are alike in their desire to convert
their courtesans from mercenary to free love; the difference essential to
my argument lies in the representation of Angellica herself. Killigrew's
Angellica thinks of herself as a 'whore': her status as an immoral
outcast is central to her identity. Reproached by Thomaso for 'sell[ing]'
her 'blood' (338), she says: 'your truths are a knowledge I have learn'd
too late: And to afflict my self with the consideration of that which
cannot be remedied is second folly; Onely (once a whore and ever) is
the world adage; yet there may be degrees of ill; and I am vain
enough to believe, though I am not a good woman, I am not an ill
Mistress' (339). Later, having offered him 'love for love', despite her
wish that 'thy purse [were] as great as thy heart' (340), she portrays
herself as a victim. Asking 'if thou be'st kind, forget and forgive my
faults that are past, which are crimes of the Nation, not mine; sold by
a Mother, oppres'd with misery when I knew no better then to obey
her . . .', she weeps at the thought of her condition. She concludes her
appeal for Thomaso's love with the wish that tears 'could make me as
pure a Virgin as I am now a perfect Lover; then I would beg to be thy
wife; but that must not be; for love bids me not ask that which
honour forbids thee to grant . . .' (341).

Behn's Angellica makes her proposal to Willmore in these words:

Thou'rt a brave fellow! Put up thy gold, and know,
That were thy fortune as large as is thy soul,
Thou shouldst not buy my love
Couldst thou forget those mean effects of vanity
Which set me out to sale,
And as a lover prize my yielding joys.
Canst thou believe they'll be entirely thine,
Without considering they were mercenary?

(II.ii.99–106)

She shows no sign of regret or repentance for her loss of her virginity:
her only fault is in being mercenary, a vice that can, apparently, be
separated from her sexuality. Nor, unlike her predecessor, is she
immediately weakened by her admission of love. Her relationship with
Willmore is still a bargain: 'will you pay me then the price I ask?' she
says; but it is negotiated between (apparent) equals, and the price she
asks is the same that Hellena expects: 'thy love for mine' (148, 154).

The absence of any sense that Angellica does, or should, feel shame
because she is no longer a virgin is only one of many elements that

contribute to the idealization of libertinism in the scene. It is also lent glamor by its association with Willmore (who has already been established as an attractive figure), by its opposition by Angellica's 'bawd', Moretta, and by the language of the scene. While in *Thomaso* the diction of the scene is somewhat elevated, *The Rover* uses the language and verse form of serious drama. Willmore appeals to Angellica in these terms:

> Throw off this pride, this enemy to bliss,
> And show the power of love: 'tis with those arms
> I can be only vanquished, made a slave.

To which she replies:

> Is all my mighty expectation vanished?
> No, I will not hear thee talk; thou hast a charm
> In every word that draws my heart away,
> And all the thousand trophies I designed
> Thou hast undone. . . .

(II.ii.130–37)

The blank verse invests the dialogue with the prestige associated with the form, as well as conveying the passionate nature of the exchange (Easthope 65 f.; Creizenach 330).

In sum, Behn's version of the scene portrays the relationship between Willmore and Angellica in terms that resemble the libertine Golden Age she describes in her poem of that title, in which the banishment of 'cursed Honour! thou who first didst damn, / A Woman to the Sin of shame' will 'let the Golden age again, / Assume its Glorious Reign' in which women and men will be rendered free and equal in the enactment of desire (141, 143). While Thomaso's dalliance with Angellica is an expression of his humor, one of the 'follies' of his youth (2 *Thomaso* IV.ix.438), Willmore's with Angellica seems, momentarily, to present a serious threat to the amatory ambitions of Hellena.

3

Nevertheless, this situation is temporary. When Willmore, like most other theatrical rakes (Hume 172), marries the virgin, the disruptive consequences of Behn's 'theft' make themselves felt as Angellica is consigned to the position of the conventional whore in order to facilitate

the conventional ending.[8] Her initial difference from her predecessor in
Thomaso is erased when, following her unsatisfactory interrogation of
Willmore, she adopts the language of the fallen woman, lamenting her
loss of 'honour':

> ... I had forgot my name, my infamy,
> And the reproach that honor lays on those
> That dare pretend a sober passion here.
> Nice reputation, though it leave behind
> More virtues than inhabit where that dwells,
> Yet that once gone, those virtues shine no more.

(IV.ii.406–11)

Convinced that she is 'not fit to be beloved' (IV.ii.412), Behn's
Angellica, again like Killigrew's, resolves on revenge; but while
Killigrew's character merely facilitates a plot against Thomaso's life
that has been planned by the 'bad' whores, Behn's is transformed from
an idealized libertine into an avenging fury who undertakes to shoot
Willmore herself. She now resembles the demonized Franceschina of
The Dutch Courtesan in the violence of her resentment, in the high-flown
language in which she expresses her rage, and, also, in the ridicule to
which it exposes her. In these changed circumstances, the heroic
language of II.ii is liable to construction as rant and posturing which
prevent her from being taken seriously. Confronting Willmore at pistol
point in the last act of the play, she asks: 'Does not thy guilty blood
run shivering through thy veins? Hast thou no horror at this sight, that
tells thee thou hast not long to boast thy shameful conquest?' To which
Willmore unconcernedly replies: 'Faith, no, child. My blood keeps its
old ebbs and flows still, and that usual heat too, that could oblige thee
with a kindness, had I but opportunity' (V.222–27). His refusal to
recognize her 'pain' undermines the heroic stature to which she aspires.[9]

The alteration in Angellica's character reopens the space between the
virgin and the whore, but it simultaneously produces gaps in the text.
Although she becomes a more conventional figure in the latter part of
the play, the essential contradictions in the role – the resemblances
between Angellica and Hellena and Angellica's contradictory subject
positions – remain unthematized. The situation is exacerbated by
Willmore's persistent libertinism. When Angellica declines to 'do the
drudgery' of his 'virtuous mistress' (IV.ii.173), Willmore responds by
disclaiming any interest in virtuous women: 'Virtue is but an infirmity
in woman ...' (IV.ii.177). Behn allows this denial to stand, where
Killigrew, in keeping with the less ambiguous moral stance of his
play, portrays his protagonist's similar sentiments as a bare-faced lie
(2 *Thomaso* IV.i., 430–31). With this conventional reason for the hero's

choice done away with in favor of libertine sentiment, the rejection of the courtesan becomes problematic.

The result of these contradictions is 'negation', in Iser's sense of blanks 'which bring to the fore the problematical aspects [of norms] and so point the way to the reassessment of the norms' (213). In this case, the relevant norm is the sexual double-standard. The narrowing of the gap between virgin and whore and the momentary idealization of female libertinism in the figure of the prostitute make the whore's eventual rejection seem arbitrary: the hero's choice between *virgo* and *meretrix* raises questions about the importance of female 'honour' at the moment that such honor is apparently affirmed as essential.

This negation is emphasized by the completeness with which Angellica is excluded from the comic ending. Behn's Angellica is last seen in the middle of Act V when she leaves Willmore with a parting curse:

... to show my utmost of contempt,
I give thee life ...
. . .
Live to undo someone whose soul may prove
So bravely constant to revenge my love.

(V.351–55)

Following her departure, Willmore and Hellena come to their agreement to marry and the play is brought to a celebratory close as the gay couple dare to '*venture in the storms o'th' marriage bed*' (V. 576). Nothing further is heard of Angellica. In Killigrew's play, in contrast, while Angellica is finally judged to be 'a common Whore' (2 *Thomaso* IV.ix, 438), she is nevertheless incorporated into the comic ending, although *in absentia*, by an apology to Thomaso for her part in the conspiracy against him delivered by the other 'good' whore, Paulina, and by her plan to go to Venice in the company of Paulina and one of her erstwhile lovers (2 *Thomaso* V.vii, 459; V.x, 462). Even Franceschina is less isolated at the conclusion of the play in which she appears than Behn's Angellica: her sentence to 'severest prison' (V.iii.55) is evidence, albeit repressive, of society's interest in her fate.

Killigrew's and Marston's endings emphatically reaffirm their characters' status as whores and permit the spectator or reader to incorporate this figure easily into their concretization of the action, but the final position of Behn's Angellica is much more ambiguous. She cannot simply be typed as a whore: at the conclusion she remains, as she has been throughout, separated from the play's 'bad' prostitute, the duplicitous Lucetta; nor is she shown returning to her trade. No other place is provided for her, however: she is not only isolated, but left in

157

Early Women Writers

limbo. Because of this lack of closure, Behn's Angellica resists inclusion
in a coherent concretization of the action: the 'stolen object' remains
a troubling source of difficult questions about the position allotted by
society to a female sexuality that is neither demonized, nor secured by
marriage, nor uniquely linked to the marketplace.

Notes

1. See, for example, Link's introduction to *The Rover* xi–xii and DeRitter.

2. The somewhat different attitudes toward prostitutes in Marston's and
   Killigrew's plays may perhaps be owing to the different approaches of
   the private and public theatres. Marston's play belongs to the 'tradition of
   moralizing comedy' of the public stage; a more tolerant, 'joking' attitude was
   characteristic of the private theatres (Leggatt 101 n. 5, 104).

3. See Loftis 140 for *The Rover*'s debt to Dryden's plays and Haselkorn 65 for
   Crispinella.

4. Cf. Tysefew's marriage contract with Crispinella: 'My purse, my body, my
   heart is yours: only be silent in my house, modest at my table, and wanton
   in my bed . . .' (Marston IV.i.76–78).

5. Elin Diamond notes that Angellica's money and Hellena's have the same
   source: Hellena's and Pedro's uncle (533).

6. Nancy Vickers, ' "The blazon of sweet beauty's best": Shakespeare's *Lucrece*',
   in Patricia Parker and Geoffrey Hartman, eds, *Shakespeare and the Question of
   Theory* (New York and London: Methuen, 1985) 97, quoted in Parker 129.

7. See also Haselkorn 75.

8. Cf. Canfield's brief description of Angellica in terms of the 'stereotypes of the
   fallen woman' and the 'termagant' (160).

9. For Franceschina's ludicrousness see Horwich 260 and Haselkorn 60.

References

BEHN, APHRA. 'The Golden Age'. *The Works of Aphra Behn*. Ed. Montague
Summers. 6 vols. 1915. New York: Phaeton, 1967. 6: 138–44.
——. *The Rover*. Ed. Frederick M. Link. Regent's Restoration Drama.
Lincoln: University of Nebraska Press, 1967.

CANFIELD, J. DOUGLAS. 'Female Rebels and Patriarchal Paradigms in Some
Neoclassical Works'. *SECC* 18 (1988): 153–66.

CREIZENACH, WILHELM. *The English Drama of the Age of Shakespeare*. 1916.
New York: Russell and Russell, 1967.

DERITTER, JONES. 'The Gypsy, *The Rover*, and the Wanderer: Aphra Behn's
Revision of Thomas Killigrew'. *Restoration* 10 (1986): 82–92.

DIAMOND, ELIN. '*Gestus* and Signature in Aphra Behn's *The Rover*'. *ELH* 56 (1989): 519–41.

DRYDEN, JOHN. *Secret Love. The Works of John Dryden*. Vol. 9. Ed. John Loftis and Vinton A. Dearing (Berkeley: University of California Press, 1966): 113–203, 331–51.

EASTHOPE, ANTHONY. *Poetry as Discourse*. London: Methuen, 1983.

GALLAGHER, CATHERINE. 'Who was that masked woman?' *Women's Studies* 15 (1988): 23–42.

HARBAGE, ALFRED. *Thomas Killigrew: Cavalier Dramatist, 1612–83*. Philadelphia: University of Pennsylvania Press, 1930.

HASELKORN, ANNE M. *Prostitution in Elizabethan and Jacobean Comedy*. Troy, New York: Whitston, 1983.

HORWICH, RICHARD. 'Wives, Courtesans, and the Economics of Love in Jacobean City Comedy'. *Drama in the Renaissance: Comparative and Critical Essays*. Ed. Clifford Davidson, C.J. Gianakaris, John H. Stroupe. New York: AMS Press, 1986. 255–73.

HUME, ROBERT D. 'The Myth of the Rake in "Restoration Comedy"'. *The Rakish Stage*. Carbondale: Southern Illinois University Press, 1983, 138–75.

ISER, WOLFGANG. *The Act of Reading: A Theory of Aesthetic Response*. Baltimore: Johns Hopkins University Press, 1978.

KILLIGREW, THOMAS. *Thomaso. Comedies and Tragedies*. 1664. New York: Benjamin Blom, 1967. 310–464.

LEGGATT, ALEXANDER. *Citizen Comedy in the Age of Shakespeare*. Toronto: University of Toronto Press, 1973.

LOFTIS, JOHN. *The Spanish Plays of Neoclassical England*. New Haven: Yale University Press, 1973.

MARSTON, JOHN. *The Dutch Courtesan*. Ed. M.L. Wine. Regents Renaissance Drama. Lincoln: University of Nebraska Press, 1965.

PARKER, PATRICIA. 'Rhetorics of Property: Exploration, Inventory, Blazon'. *Literary Fat Ladies: Rhetoric, Gender, Property*. London: Methuen, 1987. 126–54.

WEBER, HAROLD. *The Restoration Rake-Hero*. Madison: University of Wisconsin Press, 1986.

8 *Gestus* and Signature in Aphra Behn's *The Rover**

ELIN DIAMOND

A complex analysis of the sexual politics of representation, particularly theatrical representation, Elin Diamond's essay centres on the prostitute Angellica Bianca's portrait. When the hero Willmore, invested with the patriarchal authority of king and court, appropriates the portrait before even seeing the woman it represents, his treatment of Angellica as a fetishized, male-owned object is linked metonymically to the commodification of the Restoration actress, comparably reduced to an enticing representation for male consumption. Thus, in Diamond's gendered version of Brecht's gestic moment, when the social meaning of a character's action is laid bare, the Restoration theatre is exposed as a microcosm of the patriarchal exchange economy which even the play's virgins, bent on marriage for love, cannot escape. Diamond's essay, while drawing extensively on Marxist and French feminist psychoanalytic theory, nonetheless affirms the importance of authorial signature: Angellica's portrait also encodes Behn's own position in a culture of gender which equated her professional status with prostitution. Within the context of the debate between Anglo-American and French feminism over women's writing, Diamond's essay represents an attempt to combine a post-humanist critical method with an Anglo-American woman-centred politics.

Where the dream is at its most exalted, the commodity is closest to hand.

(THEODOR ADORNO, *In Search of Wagner*)

Near the end of act 2 of *The Rover*, after the wealthy virgins and hungry gallants have been introduced, and the reader–spectator is made aware

---

* Reprinted from *ELH*, 56, no. 3 (Fall, 1989) pp. 519–41.

that comic symmetry is pressing toward chase and final reward, mention is made of a beautiful courtesan whom the gallants, including the affianced ones, are trying to impress. Angellica Bianca would seem to be a supplement to the intrigue plot – a supplement since one need not intrigue to visit a whore. Yet before the virgins are rewarded with the husbands they desire, they will traverse this whore's marketplace. In 'scenes' and 'discoveries', they will market themselves as she does, compete for the same male affection, suffer similar abuse. The courtesan herself enters the play not in the way the audience might expect, behind an exotic vizard, or 'discovered' in her bedchamber after the parting of the scenes, but as a portrait, as *three* portraits, a large one hung from the balcony and two smaller ones posted on either side of the proscenium door designating her lodging. Willmore, the play's titular rover, arrives at her door, and in the absence of the courtesan he cannot afford, he appropriates her in representation – he reaches up and steals a portrait.

Willmore's gesture, I will suggest, contains information beyond the local revelation of one character's behavior. We might read Willmore's gesture as a Brechtian *Gestus* or 'gest', a moment in performance that makes visible the contradictory interactions of text, theater apparatus, and contemporary social struggle.[1] In the unraveling of its intrigue plot, Aphra Behn's *The Rover* not only thematizes the marketing of women in marriage and prostitution, it 'demonstrates', in its gestic moments, the ideological contradictions of the apparatus Behn inherited and the society for which she wrote. Brecht's account of the *Gestus* is useful for alerting us to the vectors of historical change written into dramatic texts, but he makes no provision for gender – an unavoidable issue in Aphra Behn's own history. Educated but constantly in need of money, with court connections but no supporting family, Aphra Behn wrote plays when female authorship was a monstrous violation of the 'woman's sphere'. Since the reopening of the theaters in 1660, Frances Boothby and the Duchess of Newcastle each had had a play produced, but no woman had challenged the Restoration theater with Behn's success and consistency.[2] Indeed, that she could earn a living writing for the theater was precisely what condemned her. The muckraking satirist Robert Gould wrote typical slander in a short piece addressed to Behn that concluded with this couplet: 'For Punk and Poetess agree so Pat, / You cannot be This and not be That.'[3]

In her suggestive 'Arachnologies: The Woman, The Text, and the Critic', Nancy Miller implicitly proposes a feminist version of the *Gestus*; texts by women writers, says Miller, encode the signs or 'emblems of a female signature' by which the 'culture of gender [and] the inscriptions of its political structures' might be read.[4] In a woman-authored text, then, the gestic moment would mark both a convergence of social actions and attitudes, and the gendered history of that convergence. Robert Gould's verse, with its violent, unequivocal equation of 'poetess' and 'punk', provides some evidence of the culture of gender in Restoration London. Like her male colleagues, Behn hawked her intrigue comedies and political satires in the literary and theatrical marketplace, and like them, she suffered the attacks of 'fop-corner' and the sometimes paltry remuneration of third-day receipts. In her case, however, the status of professional writer indicated immodesty: the author, like her texts, became a commodity.

Deciphering Behn's authorial 'signature' obliges us to read the theatrical, social, and sexual discourses that complicate and obscure its inscription. I am aiming here to open the text to what Brecht calls its 'fields of force' (30) – those contradictory relations and ideas that signify in Behn's culture and are, as this reading will indicate, symptomatic of our own. Like Brecht, in his discussion of Shakespeare's *Coriolanus* (252–65), I am interested less in interpretative truth than in exploring a complex textual system in which author, apparatus, history, and reader–spectator each plays a signifying role. The following section will consider Behn's authorial contexts, the Restoration theater apparatus, with its proto-fetishist positioning of 'scenes' and actresses; the next two sections focus on multivalent signs of gender in *The Rover*; and the final section, returning to the theater apparatus by way of Behn's unique obsessions, poses the question of the woman dramatist's signature: How does Aphra Behn encode the conditions of her literary and theatrical production? How does she stage the relationship between female creativity and public calumny – between what Robert Gould, in darkly humorous euphemisms, refers to as 'this' and 'that'?

1. The Apparatus

The term 'apparatus' draws together several related aspects in theater production: the hierarchy of economic control, the material features of machinery and properties, and, more elusively, the social and psychological interplay between stage and audience. When Aphra Behn wrote her seventeen plays (1670–1689), the theatrical hierarchy, like all cultural institutions, was patriarchal in control and participation. Charles II invested power in the first patentees, Thomas Killigrew and William D'Avenant; aristocratic or upper-class males generally wrote the plays, purchased the tickets, and formed the coteries of critics and 'witlings' whose disruptive presence is remarked on in countless play prologues and epilogues. In its machinery and properties, the Restoration stage was not unlike Wagner's theater in Adorno's critique:

dreamlike, seductive, and commodity-intensive. Though the technology was well established in Italian and French courts, and in English court masques before the Interregnum, the two new Restoration theaters gave Londoners their first view of movable painted 'scenes' and mechanical devices or 'machines', installed behind the forestage and the proscenium arch. Actors posed before elaborately painted 'wings' (stationary pieces set in receding rows) and 'shutters' (flat painted scenes that moved in grooves and joined in the center). When the scenes parted, their characters were 'discovered' against other painted scenes that, parting, produced further discoveries.[5] Built in 1671, The Duke's Theater, Dorset Garden, the site of most of Behn's plays, was particularly known for its 'gawdy Scenes'.[6]

The movement of painted flats, the discoveries of previously unseen interiors, introduced a new scopic epistemology. Seated and unruly in semicircular areas of pit, boxes, first, middle, and upper galleries, Restoration spectators, unlike their Elizabethan counterparts, were no longer compelled to imagine the features of bed-chambers, parks, or battlefields. Like Richard Flecknoe, they could rely on scenes and machines as 'excellent helps of imagination, most grateful deceptions of the sight.... Graceful and becoming Ornaments of the Stage [transport] you easily without lassitude from one place to another, or rather by a kinde of delightful Magick, whilst you sit still, does bring the place to you.'[7] Assuming that Flecknoe's reaction is typical, and there is evidence that it is, Restoration stagecraft seems to have created a spectator-fetishist, one who takes pleasure in ornaments that deceive the sight, whose disavowal of material reality produces a desire for the 'delightful Magick' of exotic and enticing representations.[8]

I am deliberately conflating two uses of 'fetishism' in this account of Restoration reception: one, Freud's description of the male impulse to eroticize objects or female body parts, which derives from a disavowal of a material lack (of the penis on the mother's body); and two, Marx's account of the fetishization of the commodity: at the moment of exchange, the commodity appears to be separate from the workers who produce it; the 'specific social character of private labors' is disavowed.[9] Nowhere are these meanings of fetishism more relevant than in discourse generated by that other ornament of the stage, the Restoration actress. In his preface to *The Tempest*, Thomas Shadwell links the new phenomenon of female performers with painted theatrical scenes, both innovative commodities for audience consumption:

Had we not for yr pleasure found new wayes
You still had rusty Arras had, and thredbare playes;
Nor Scenes nor Woomen had they had their will,
But some with grizl'd Beards had acted Woomen still.

That female fictions were to be embodied by beardless women would, Thomas Killigrew promised, be 'useful and instructive'.[10] What the signifying body of the actress actually meant in the culture's sexual economy is perhaps more accurately suggested by metatheatrical references in play prologues and epilogues. The actress playing Flirt in Wycherley's *The Gentleman Dancing Master* satirically invites the 'good men o' th' Exchange' from the pit into the backstage tiring-room: 'You we would rather see between our Scenes'; and Dryden, in the Prologue to *Marriage A-la-Mode*, has the actor Hart refer to passionate tyring-room assignations.[11]

The private writings of Samuel Pepys are even more suggestive of the sinful pleasures afforded by actresses. On October 5, 1667, he visited the Theatre Royal in Bridges Street:

> and there, going in, met with Knipp [Mrs. Knep], and she took us up into the Tireing-rooms and to the women's Shift, where Nell [Gwyn] was dressing herself and was all unready; and is very pretty, prettier than I thought; and so walked all up and down the House above, and then below into the Scene-room.... But Lord, to see how they were both painted would make a man mad – and did make me loath them – and what base company of men comes among them, and how lewdly they talk – and how poor the men are in clothes, and yet what a show they make on the stage by candlelight, is very observable.
>
> (834)

Candlelight has the ideological function of suturing contradictions between 'lewd' actors and an alluring 'show', and even a habitual playgoer like Pepys is disturbed when the seams show. That actresses were pretty women was not surprising, but the transformation of women into painted representations beautifully exhibited by candlelight was both fascinating and disturbing. Pepys went behind the painted scenes, but the paint was still there. He hoped to separate the pretty woman from the painted actress, but it was the actress he admired – and fetishized – from his spectator's seat.[12]

For Pepys and other Restoration commentators, the actress's sexuality tended to disavow her labor. Rather than produce a performance, she is a spectacle unto herself, a painted representation to lure the male spectator. In her professional duplicity, in her desirability, in her often public status of kept mistress, she is frequently equated with prostitutes or 'vizard-masks' who worked the pit and galleries of Restoration theaters during and after performances. In Wycherley's *The Plain Dealer*, Mrs. Hoyden is disparaged for being 'As familiar a duck ... As an Actress in the tiring-room' (407).

The epistemological link between the theater apparatus and illicit female signs is not of course new to the Restoration. Jonas Barish, documenting the antitheatrical prejudice, notes that Patristic condemnation of the theater, typified in tracts from the third-century Tertullian's to those of Renaissance Puritans Phillip Stubbes and William Prynne, builds on the Platonic condemnation of mimesis as the making of counterfeit copies of true originals. Actors in paint and costume contaminate their true God-given identities: 'Whatever is *born*,' writes Tertullian, 'is the work of God. Whatever ... is *plastered on* is the devil's work.'[13] To the Puritan mind the presence of women on stage was an affront to feminine modesty, but more damning was the fact that the means of illusionism – use of costume, paint, masking – involved specifically female vices. The nature of theatrical representation, like the 'nature' of woman, was to ensnare, deceive, and seduce.

Given this cultural legacy, and the metonymic connection between painted female performer and painted scenes, it is not surprising that the first woman to earn money circulating her own representations had a combative relationship with the theater apparatus. As we will see, Aphra Behn, more than any other Restoration playwright, exploits the fetish/commodity status of the female performer, even as her plays seek to problematize that status. She utilizes the conventional objects of Restoration satire – the marriage market, sexual intrigue, masquerade, libertine flamboyance – even as she signals, in 'gestic' moments, their contradictory meanings for female fictions and historical women.

2. Virgin Commodities

The Rover (1677) and *The Second Part of The Rover* (1681), both drawn from Killigrew's *Thomaso, or The Wanderer* (1663), are Behn's only plays to label a character a courtesan; in her wholly original *The Feigned Curtezans* (1679), witty virgins impersonate famous Roman courtesans and near-debauches occur, but, as befits the romantic intrigue, marriages settle the confusion of plots and the financial stink of prostitution is hastily cleared away.[14] If courtesans figure by name in only three plays, however, the commodification of women in the marriage market is Aphra Behn's first and most persistent theme. Beginning appropriately enough with *The Forced Marriage; or The Jealous Bridegroom* (1670), all of Behn's seventeen known plays deal to some extent with women backed by dowries or portions who are forced by their fathers into marriage in exchange for jointure, an agreed-upon income to be settled on the wife should she be widowed.

There was a lived context for this perspective. The dowry system among propertied classes had been in place since the sixteenth century, but at the end of the seventeenth century there were thirteen women to every ten men, and cash portions had to grow to attract worthy suitors. As the value of women fell by almost fifty per cent, marriage for love, marriage by choice, became almost unthinkable.[15] Women through marriage had evident exchange value; that is, the virgin became a commodity not only for her use-value as breeder of the legal heir but for her portion, which, through exchange, generated capital. If, as Marx writes, exchange converts commodities into fetishes or 'social hieroglyphics', signs whose histories and qualitative differences can no longer be read (161), women in the seventeenth-century marriage market took on the phantasmagoric destiny of fetishized commodities; they seemed no more than objects or things. As Margaret Cavendish observed, sons bear the family name but 'Daughters are to be accounted but as Movable Goods or Furnitures that wear out.'[16]

Restoration comedy, from the earliest Etherege and Sedley through Wycherley, Dryden, Vanbrugh, D'Urfey, and Congreve, mocked the market-place values of marriage, promoting the libertine's aesthetic of 'natural' love, verbal seduction, and superiority over jealous husbands and fops. But Aphra Behn concentrated on exposing the exploitation of women in the exchange economy, adding vividly to contemporary discourse on the oppressions of marriage. 'Wife and servant are the same / But differ only in the name,' wrote Lady Mary Chudleigh.[17] 'Who would marry,' asks Behn's Ariadne (*The Second Part of the Rover*), 'who wou'd be chaffer'd thus, and sold to Slavery?'[18] The issue arises repeatedly in plays and verse of the period: not only are marriages loveless, but once married, women lose both independent identity and control of their fortunes. Ariadne again:

> You have a Mistress, Sir, that has your Heart, and all your softer
> Hours: I know't, and if I were so wretched as to marry thee, must
> see my Fortune lavisht out on her; her Coaches, Dress, and Equipage
> exceed mine by far: Possess she all the day thy Hours of Mirth, good
> Humour and Expence, thy Smiles, thy Kisses, and thy Charms of Wit.
> (1:152)

The feminist philosopher Mary Astell would have had no sympathy for the sensuous appetites of Behn's females, but Ariadne's sentiments receive astute articulation in Astell's *Some Reflections Upon Marriage*. The money motive for marriage produces in the man contempt and 'Indifferency' which 'proceeds to an aversion, and perhaps even the Kindness and Complaisance of the poor abused'd Wife, shall only serve to increase it'. Ultimately, the powerless wife ends up 'mak[ing] court to [her husband] for a little sorry Alimony out of her own Estate'.[19] Two centuries later Engels merely restates these comments in his observation that forced marriages 'turn into the crassest prostitution – sometimes of both partners, but far more commonly of the woman, who only differs from the ordinary courtesan in that she does not [hire] out her body on piecework as a wage worker, but sells it once and for all into slavery'.[20]

Yet in order to launch *The Rover*'s marriage plot and to provoke sympathy for her high-spirited aristocrats, Behn dissimulates the connection between virgin and prostitute. When Florinda, Hellena, and Valeria don gypsy costumes – assume the guise of marginal and exotic females – to join the carnival masquerade, they do so explicitly to evade the patriarchal arrangement of law and jointure laid down by their father and legislated by their brother Pedro: Florinda shall marry a rich ancient count and Hellena shall go into a convent, thus saving their father a second dowry and simultaneously enriching Florinda. The opening dialogue of *The Rover* is also implicitly 'gestic', raising questions about women's material destiny in life as well as in comic representation:

Florinda: What an impertinent thing is a young girl bred in a nunnery! How full of questions! Prithee no more, Hellena; I have told thee more than thou understand'st already.
Hellena: The more's my grief. I would fain know as much as you, which makes me so inquisitive.[21]

Hellena dons masquerade because she desires not a particular lover but a wider knowledge. Given the conventions of Restoration comedy, this wish to know 'more than' she already understands is troped as a wish for sexual adventure. But if we hear this dialogue dialogically – in its social register – other meanings are accessible.[22] Women's lack of access to institutions of knowledge spurred protest from writers as diverse as Margaret Cavendish, Bathsua Makin, Mary Astell, and Judith Drake. Aphra Behn mocks a university fool in *The City Heiress* and a learned lady in *Sir Patient Fancy*; she criticizes neoclassical aesthetics in 'Epistle to the Reader', appended to *The Dutch Lover* (1 : 221–25), for having nothing to do with why people write or attend plays.[23] When she translates Bernard de Fontenelle's *A Discovery of New Worlds*, however, she reveals as passionate a hunger for esoteric knowledge as these early English feminists. Unfortunately, the controlling conceit of Fontenelle's work – a mere woman is informally taught the complexities of Copernican theory – produces an untenable and revealing contradiction for Behn: 'He [Fontenelle] makes her [the Marchionness] say a great many silly things, tho' sometimes she makes observations so learned, that the greatest Philosophers in Europe could make no better.'[24] Insightful yet silly, wise yet a *tabula rasa*, Fontenelle's Marchionness oscillates between intellectual independence and slavish imitation. She is perhaps less a contradictory character than a projection of a male intellectual's ambivalence about female education.

Aphra Behn's Hellena seeks knowledge 'more than' or beyond the gender script provided for her. She rejects not only her brother's decision to place her in a nunnery, but also the cultural narrative of portion, jointure, and legal dependency in which she is written not as subject but as object of exchange. Yet Hellena, too, oscillates – both departing from and reinforcing her social script. Her lines following those cited above seem, at first, to complicate and defer the romantic closure of the marriage plot. To have a lover, Hellena conjectures, means to 'sigh, and sing, and blush, and wish, and dream and wish, and long and wish to see the man' (7). This thrice-reiterated wishing will result in three changes of costume, three suitors, and three marriages. As with the repetitions of 'interest', 'credit', and 'value' – commodity signifiers that circulate through the play and slip like the vizard from face to hand to face – this repetition invokes the processes underlying all wishing, to desire that will not, like a brother's spousal contract, find its 'completion'.

If we incorporate insights from feminist psychoanalytic theory, the virgins' masquerade takes on added significance, or rather this discourse helps us decode what is already implied – namely, that in an economy in which women are dependent on male keepers and traders, female desire is always already a masquerade, a play of false representations that covers over and simultaneously expresses the lack the woman exhibits – lack of the male organ and, concomitantly, lack of access to phallic privileges – to material and institutional power. Unlike the theatrical mask, which conceals a truth, the masquerade of female sexuality subverts the 'Law-of-the-Father' that stands 'behind' any representation.[25] Underneath the gypsy veils and drapes of Behn's virgins, there is nothing, in a phallic sense, to see; thus no coherent female identity that can be co-opted into a repressive romantic narrative. Willmore, titillated by Hellena's witty chatter, asks to see her face. Hellena responds that underneath the vizard is a 'desperate . . . lying look' (56) – that is, she, like her vizard, may prevaricate; represented may mingle with representer – for the spectator (Willmore) there will be no validating stake.

Yet, as Behn well knew, there is means of validation, one that guarantees patriarchy's stake in portion, jointure, and the woman's body: the hymen. In Restoration comedy no witty unmarried woman was really witty unless she had property *and* a maidenhead. Behn's virgins may re-'design' their cast of characters but they cannot change their plot. Ultimately their masquerade is dissimulation in the classic representational sense, a veil that hides a truth. Hellena's mask merely replicates the membrane behind which lies the 'true nature' of woman:

the equipment to make the requisite patrilineal heir. Thus Willmore's masterful response to Hellena's 'lying look' is a mock-blazon of her facial features, ending in a fetishistic flourish: 'Those soft round melting cherry lips and small even white teeth! Not to be expressed, but silently adored!' (56). The play in Hellena's discourse between knowing and desiring, which extends through the masquerade, completes itself in the marriage game. She exercises her will only by pursuing and winning Willmore, for as it turns out he has the 'more' she 'would fain know'.

Willmore acts not only as the rover but as signifier for the play's phallic logic. His name metaphorizes the trajectory of desire as he roves from bed to bed 'willing more', making all satisfactions temporary and unsatisfying. Desire's subject, Willmore never disguises himself (he comes on stage *holding* his mask); until enriched by the courtesan Angellica Bianca, he remains in 'buff' or leather military coat. In another sense, though, Willmore is already in disguise, or rather the entity 'Willmore' covers a range of linguistic and social signifiers. Behn's model for Willmore (like Etherege's for Dorimont) was reputedly the womanizing courtier, the Earl of Rochester, whose name, John Wilmot, contains, like the rover's, the word ('mot') 'will'. Rochester was also the lover and mentor of Elizabeth Barry, the actress who first played Behn's Hellena. In Tory mythology Charles II, on the verge of fleeing England, disguised himself in buff – a leather doublet.[26] Indeed, Willmore's first lines refer to the offstage Prince who, in exile during the Commonwealth, was also a rover. Doubled mimetically and semiotically with both Rochester and the Merry Monarch (who attended at least one performance of *The Rover* before the play was restaged at Whitehall), Willmore needs no mask to effect his ends: his libertine desire is guaranteed and upheld by patriarchal law. Hellena's playful rovings, on the other hand, and her numerous disguises, signal both ingenuity and vulnerability.[27] Ironically, the virgins' first costume, the gypsy masquerade, represents their actual standing in the marriage market – exotic retailers of fortunes (or portions). Their masquerade defers but does not alter the structure of patriarchal exchange.

3. Painting(s), person, body

In contrast to the virgins' 'ramble' are the stasis and thralldom that attend the courtesan Angellica Bianca. While the virgins are learning artful strategies of concealment, Angellica's entrance is a complicated process of theatrical unveiling. She arrives first through words, then through painted representation, then through the body of an actress who appears on a balcony behind a silk curtain. She is also the site of a different politics, one that explores desire and gender not only in the text but in the apparatus itself.

The first references to Angellica situate her beyond the market in which we expect her to function. According to Behn's gallants, she is the 'adord beauty of all the youth in Naples, who put on all their charms to appear lovely in her sight; their coaches, liveries and themselves all gay as on a monarch's birthday' (28). Equated thus with sacred and secular authority, Angellica gazes on her suitors and 'has the pleasure to behold all languish for her that see her' (28). This text in which desire flows from and is reflected back to a female subject is immediately followed by the grouping of the English gallants beneath the courtesan's balcony. They wait with the impatience of theater spectators for Angellica to appear – not in person but in representation, as 'the shadow of the fair substance' (29).

At this point the problematic connection between shadow and substance preoccupies them. Blunt, the stock country fool, is confused by the fact that signs of bourgeois and even noble status – velvet beds, fine plate, handsome attendance, and coaches – are flaunted by courtesans. Blunt is raising an epistemological issue that Behn and her colleagues often treat satirically – the neoclassical assumption regarding mimesis that imitated can be separated from imitator, nature from representation, truth from falsehood, virgin from gypsy. By suggesting that whores are indistinguishable from moral women, Behn revives the problematic of the masquerade, casting doubt on the connection/separation of sign and referent. Significantly, when Hobbes constructed his theory of sovereign authority, he employed theater metaphors to distinguish between *'natural'* and *'feigned* or *artificial'* persons. But he noted that 'person' was itself a slippery referent:

The word Person [persona] is Latin . . . [and] signifies the *disguise,* or *outward appearance* of a man, counterfeited on the stage; and sometimes more particularly that part of it, which disguiseth the face, as a mask or vizard: and from the stage, hath been translated to any representer of speech and action, as well in tribunals, as theatres. So that a *person* is the same that an *actor* is, both on stage and in common conversation.[28]

Since, as Christopher Pye notes, everyone is already a 'self-impersonator, a mediated representation of himself', the difference between 'natural' and 'feigned' rests on highly unstable assumptions about identity which, both 'on stage' and 'in common conversation' are capable of shifting.[29] Blunt's confusion about the true status of apparently noble women may also be read as an extratextual reference to the Restoration actress and her female spectators. As kept mistresses, actresses often displayed the fine clothing and jewels of aristocrats like the notorious Duchess of Cleveland, who regularly watched the play in vizard-mask from the king's box. Yet the respectable Mrs. Pepys also owned a vizard-mask, and on her frequent visits to the theater occasionally sat in the pit near the 'real' vizards.[30]

Given the theatricality of everyday Restoration life, and the ambiguity of signs representing the status and character of women, Angellica's three portraits allow Aphra Behn to comment on the pleasures and politics of theatrical signification. Though I have ignored the specifics of Behn's adaptation of her source play, it is helpful here to compare her handling of the paintings with that of Killigrew in his ten-act semiautobiographical closet drama, *Thomaso, or The Wanderer*. In both plays, one portrait is prominent and raised, and two smaller versions are posted below, one of which is snatched by the rake – Thomaso in the source play, Willmore in Behn's. But there is an important difference in the disposition of the paintings vis-à-vis the woman they represent. In *Thomaso*, 2.1, anonymous parties of men pass in front of the paintings, react scornfully to the courtesan's high price, and wander on. But in 2.2, with the arrival of Killigrew's main characters, Angellica Bianca is sitting on the balcony in full view of her prospective buyers. Her bawd challenges the men to 'compare them [the paintings and the woman] together'.[31] With neoclassical correctness, the men agree that the woman exceeds her representation: 'That smile, there's a grace and sweetness in it Titian could never have catch'd' (333). By the time the English Thomaso and his friends arrive, the viewing of the paintings and the viewing of Angellica are almost simultaneous:

> *Harrigo*: That wonder is it I told you of; tis the picture of the famous Italian, the Angellica; See, shee's now at her Window.
> *Thomaso*: I see her, 'tis a lovely Woman.

> (Killigrew, 334)

Aphra Behn's Angellica Bianca never invites such explicit comparison. In fact, Behn prolongs the dialogue between titillated suitors and suggestive portraits: Angellica's simulacra, not Angellica, preoccupy her male audience. When the English cavaliers first view the paintings, Belvile, the play's fatuous moral figure, reads them as 'the fair sign[s] to the inn where a man may lodge that's fool enough to give her price' (33). That is, the iconicity of the paintings, their likeness to Angellica, which so impresses Killigrew's cavaliers, is in Behn's text suppressed. Gazing on the portraits, the gallants rewrite the courtesan's monarchial description, now figuring her as a thing, a receptacle for depositing one's body. To underscore the point, Behn has Blunt ask the ontological question to which there is a ready answer in commodity discourse: 'Gentlemen, what's this?' Belvile: 'A famous courtesan, that's to be sold' (33). The infinitive phrase is curious. To be sold by whom? Released by her earlier keeper's death, Angellica and her bawd seem to be in business for themselves. At this point, however, Blunt reminds us again of the object status of the woman, as of her painted signs: 'Let's be gone; I'm sure we're no chapmen for this commodity' (33).

Willmore, however, monarchy's representative, succumbs to the lure of the signs, believing not only in their iconicity but in their value as pleasurable objects – for the original one must pay one thousand crowns, but on the portraits one can gaze for nothing. Penury, however, is not the real issue. Willmore seems to understand that the appeal of the paintings is precisely that they are not the original but an effective stand-in. After the two Italian aristocrats draw swords in competition for Angellica, Willmore reaches up and steals one of the small paintings, in effect cuts away a piece of the representation for his own titillation. His intentions, like his actions, are explicitly fetishistic:

This posture's loose and negligent;
The sight on't would beget a warm desire
In souls whom impotence and age had chilled.
This must along with me.

(38)

This speech and the act of appropriation occur *before* Willmore sees Angellica. Only in Behn's text do the paintings function as fetishes, as substitute objects for the female body. When challenged why he has the right to the small portrait, Willmore claims the right 'of possession, which I will maintain' (38).

At the outset of this paper I described Willmore's acquisitive gesture as a Brechtian 'gest' – that moment in theatrical performance in which contradictory social attitudes in both text and society are made heuristically visible to spectators. What does this gest show? Willmore removes Angellica's portrait the way a theater manager might lift off a piece of the set – because without buying her, he already owns her. Her paintings are materially and metonymically linked to the painted scenes, which were of course owned, through the theatrical hierarchy, by patentee and king – who, in Behn's fiction, validates and empowers Willmore. This 'homosocial' circuit, to use Eve Sedgwick's term, extends into the social realm.[32] As innumerable accounts make clear, Restoration theater participated in the phallic economy that commodified women, not in the marriage market, but in the mistress market: the

king and his circle came to the theater to look, covet, and buy.
Nell Gwyn is the celebrated example, but Behn's biographer Angeline
Goreau cites other cases. An actress in the King's Company, Elizabeth
Farley, joined the royal entourage for several months, then became
mistress to a Gray's Inn lawyer, then drifted into prostitution and
poverty.[33] The answer to the question, 'Who is selling Angellica?' is,
then, the theater itself, which, like Willmore, operates with the king's
patent and authorization. When Angellica sings behind her balcony
curtain for her Italian admirers, and draws the curtain to reveal a bit
of beautiful flesh, then closes it while monetary arrangements are
discussed, she performs the titillating masquerade required by her
purchasers *and* by her spectators. This is mastery's masquerade, not
to demonstrate freedom, but to flaunt the charms that guarantee and
uphold male power.

If Angellica's paintings stand for the theater apparatus and its
ideological complicity with a phallic economy, what happens when
Angellica appears? Is illusionism betrayed? Interestingly, Aphra Behn
chooses this moment to emphasize presence, not only of character but
of body; Angellica emerges in the flesh and offers herself, gratis, to
Willmore, finding his scornful admiration ample reason for, for the first
time, falling in love. In their wooing/bargaining scene it becomes clear
that Angellica wants to step out of the exchange economy symbolized
by the paintings: 'Canst thou believe [these yielding joys] will be
entirely thine, / without considering they were mercenary?' (45).
The key word here is 'entirely'; Angellica dreams of full reciprocal
exchange without commerce: 'The pay I mean is but thy love for mine.
/ Can you give that?' (47). And Willmore responds 'entirely'.[34]

A commodity, Marx writes, appears as a commodity only when it
'possess[es] a double form, i.e. natural form and value form' (138).
Angellica's name contains 'angel', a word whose meaning is
undecidable since it refers simultaneously to the celestial figure and to
the old English coin stamped with the device of Michael the archangel,
minted for the last time by Charles I but still in common circulation
during the Restoration. By eliminating her value-form, Angellica
attempts to return her body to a state of nature, to take herself out of
circulation. While the virgins of the marriage plot are talking 'business'
and learning the powers of deferral and unveiling, Angellica is trying
to demystify and authenticate herself. She wants to step out of the
paintings, to be known not by her surface but by her depth.[35] As she
'yields' to Willmore upstairs, the portraits on the balcony are removed
– a sign that the courtesan is working. In this case, not only does
the (offstage) 'natural' body supplant its painted representation, but the
courtesan, who has been in excess of, now makes up a deficiency in, the
marriage plot: Angellica (with Willmore) labors for love.

Though the paintings disappear in act 3, however, the signs of
commodification are still in place, or are metonymically displaced
through properties and scenes to other characters in the marriage plot.
We learn that Hellena's portion derives from her uncle, the old man
who kept Angellica Bianca; thus the gold Willmore receives from the
courtesan has the same source as that which he will earn by marrying
the virgin. Like Angellica, too, the virgin Florinda uses a portrait as a
calling card, and at night in the garden, *'in undress'*, carrying a little box
of jewels – a double metonym for dowry and genitals – she plans to
offer herself to Belvile (65). Unfortunately Willmore, not Belvile, enters
the garden and nearly rapes her.

Florinda's nocturnal effort at entrepreneurship takes place in the
upstage scenes, where Aphra Behn, like her fellow Restoration
dramatists, situated lovers' trysts and discoveries. The thematic link
between commodified 'Scenes' and females is particularly crucial,
however, in *The Rover*. In 4.4, a disguised Florinda flees from Willmore
by running in and out of the scenes until she arrives in Blunt's
chamber, where another near-rape occurs. Blunt has just been cozened
by a prostitute and dumped naked into the city sewer; he emerges
vowing to 'beat' and 'kiss' and 'bang' the next woman he sees, who
happens to be Florinda, but now all women appear to be whores. In
fact Willmore, Frederick, and even Belvile arrive soon after to break
open the door and 'partake' of Florinda. If Angellica Bianca makes a
spectacle of herself through balcony curtains and paintings, Florinda's
'undress' and her proximity to the painted scenes signify a similar
reduction to commodity status.

4. 'I . . . Hang out the sign of Angellica'

Angellica's paintings, I have argued, are the bright links in a metonymic
chain joining the text of *The Rover* to the apparatus of representation.
Angellica's portraits represent the courtesan in the most radical sense.
They produce an image of her and at the same time reduce her to that
image. Notwithstanding her passionate address, Angellica cannot
exceed her simulacra. In effect she is doubly commodified – first
because she puts her body into exchange, and second because this
body is equated with, indeed interchangeable with, the art object.
When Willmore performs the 'gest' of appropriating the painted image
of Angellica, he makes visible, on the one hand, the patriarchal and
homosocial economy that controls the apparatus and, on the other hand,
the commodity status of paintings, of their model, and, by metonymic
extension, of the painted actress and the painted scenes.

Flecknoe and Pepys, we noted earlier, testify to the intensity of visual pleasure in Restoration theater. It is a fascinating contradiction of all feminist expectation to discover that Aphra Behn, more than any of her Restoration colleagues, contributed to that visual pleasure by choosing, in play after play, to exploit the fetish/commodity status of the female performer. The stage offered two playing spaces, the forestage used especially for comedy, where actor and audience were in intimate proximity, and the upstage or scenic stage, where wing-and-shutter settings, as much as fifty feet from the first row of spectators, produced the exotic illusionistic discoveries needed for heroic tragedy. Writing mostly comedies, Aphra Behn might be expected to follow comic convention and use the forestage area, but as Peter Holland notes, she was 'positively obsessive' about discovery scenes (41). Holland counts thirty-one discoveries in ten comedies (consider that Sedley's *The Mulberry Garden*, 1668, uses one; Etherege's *The Man of Mode*, 1676, uses two), most of which are bedroom scenes featuring a female character '*in undress*'. Holland reasons that such scenes are placed upstage so that familiar Restoration actresses would not be distractingly exposed to the audience (41–42). We might interpret Behn's 'obsession' differently: the exposed woman's (castrated) body must be obscured in order to activate scopic pleasure. Displayed in 'undress' or loosely draped gowns, the actress becomes a fetish object, affording the male spectator the pleasure of being seduced by and, simultaneously, of being protected from the effects of sexual difference.

Is it also possible that this deliberate use of fetishistic display dramatizes and displaces the particular assault Behn herself endured as 'Poetess/Punk' in the theater apparatus? The contradictions in her authorial status are clear from the preface to *The Lucky Chance* (1686). Behn argues that 'the Woman damns the Poet' (3:186), that accusations of bawdy and plagiarism are levied at her because she is a woman. On the other hand, the literary fame she desires derives from a creativity that in her mind, or rather in the social ideology she has absorbed, is also gendered: 'my Masculine Part the Poet in me' (3:187).[36] In literary history, the pen, as Gilbert and Gubar have argued, is a metaphorical penis, and the strong woman writer adopts strategies of revision and disguise in order to tell her own story.[37] In Behn's texts, the painful bisexuality of authorship, the conflict between (as she puts it) her 'defenceless' woman's body and her 'masculine part', is *staged* in her insistence, in play after play, on the equation between female body and fetish, fetish and commodity – the body in the 'scenes'. Like the actress, the woman dramatist is sexualized, circulated, denied a subject position in the theater hierarchy.

This unstable, contradictory image of authority emerges as early as Behn's first play prologue (to *The Forced Marriage, or The Jealous*

Bridegroom, 1670). A male actor cautions the wits that the vizard-masks sitting near them will naturally support a woman's play and attempt to divert them from criticism. He is then interrupted by an actress who, pointing *'to the Ladies'* praises both them and, it would seem, the woman author: 'Can any see that glorious sight and say / A woman shall not prove Victor today?' (3:286) The 'glorious sight' is, once again, the fetishized, commodified representation of the female, standing on the forestage, sitting in the pit, and soon to be inscribed as author of a printed play. If this fascinating moment – in which a woman speaking a woman's lines summons the regard of other women – seems to put a *female* gaze into operation, it also reinforces the misogynist circuitry of the theater apparatus: that which chains actress to vizard-mask to author.

At the outset of this essay we asked how Aphra Behn encodes the literary and theatrical conditions of her production. Behn's 'Postscript' to the published text of *The Rover* provides a possible answer. She complains that she has been accused of plagiarizing Killigrew simply because the play was successful and she a woman. Yet while claiming to be 'vainly proud of [her] judgment' in adapting *Thomaso*, she 'hang[s] out the sign of Angellica (the only stolen object) to give notice where a great part of the wit dwelt' (130). This compliment to Killigrew may also indicate what compelled Behn to embark on this adaptation. The 'sign[s] of Angellica' both constitute and represent the theater apparatus, serving as metacritical commentary on its patriarchal economy, its habits of fetishistic consumption. They may also constitute Behn's authorial signature, what Miller calls the 'material . . . brutal traces of the culture of gender' (275). As a woman writer in need of money, Behn was vulnerable to accusations of immodesty; to write meant to expose herself, to put herself into circulation; like Angellica, to sell her wares. Is it merely a coincidence that Angellica Bianca shares Aphra Behn's initials, that hers is the only name from *Thomaso* that Behn leaves unchanged?

The 'signs of Angellica' not only help us specify the place of this important woman dramatist in Restoration cultural practice, they invite us to historicize the critique of fetishization that has informed so much feminist criticism in the last decade.[38] Certainly the conditions of women writers have changed since the Restoration, but the fetishistic features of the commercial theater have remained remarkably similar. Now as then the theater apparatus is geared to profit and pleasure, and overwhelmingly controlled by males. Now as then the arrangement of audience to stage produces what Brecht calls a 'culinary' or ideologically conservative spectator, intellectually passive but scopically hungry, eager for the next turn of the plot, the next scenic effect. Now as then the actor suffers the reduction of Angellica Bianca, having no existence except in the simulations produced by the exchange economy. The practice of illusionism, as Adorno points out above, converts historical performers into commodities which the spectator pays to consume.

If Restoration theater marks the historical beginning of commodity-intensive, dreamlike effects in English staging, Aphra Behn's contribution to contemporary theory may lie in her demonstration that, from the outset, dreamlike effects have depended on the fetish-commodification of the female body. When Willmore, standing in for king and court, steals Angellica's painting, Behn not only reifies the female, she genders the spectatorial economy as, specifically, a male consumption of the female image. Reading that confident gesture of appropriation as a *Gestus*, the contemporary spectator adds another viewpoint. Angellica Bianca's paintings appear to us now as both authorial 'signature' and 'social hieroglyphic', signs of a buried life whose careful decoding opens up new possibilities for critique and contestation.

Notes

1. JOHN WILLETT's translation of *Gestus* as 'gest' (with the adjective 'gestic') has become standard English usage (see *Brecht on Theatre; The Development of an Aesthetic* (New York: Hill and Wang, 1964, 42). Further references will appear in the text. Like many concepts in Brecht's epic theater theory, *Gestus* is terrifically suggestive and difficult to pin down. Words, gestures, actions, tableaux all qualify as gests if they enable the spectator to draw conclusions about the 'social circumstances' (105) shaping a character's attitudes. The gest should be understandable, but also dialectical, incomplete: '[the] expressions of a gest are usually highly complicated and contradictory . . .' (198). In an excellent essay the semiotician Patrice Pavis describes *Gestus* as 'the key to the relationship between the play being performed and the public, [as well as] the author's attitude [toward] the public'. See *Languages of the Stage* (New York: Performing Arts Journal Publications, 1982), 42.

2. MARGARET CAVENDISH's play was produced under her husband's name. See Maureen Duffy, *The Passionate Shepherdess: Aphra Behn 1640–1689* (London: Jonathan Cape, 1977), 95–104, and Angeline Goreau, *Reconstructing Aphra: A Social Biography of Aphra Behn* (New York: Dial, 1980), 115 ff.

3. ROBERT GOULD, cited in George Woodcock, *The Incomparable Aphra* (London: Oxford University Press, 1977), 103.

4. The full citation from Nancy K. Miller is as follows: 'When we tear the web of women's texts, we may discover in the representations of writing itself the marks of the grossly material, the sometimes brutal traces of the culture of gender; the inscriptions of its political structures.' See

'Arachnologies: The Woman, The Text, and the Critic' in *The Poetics of Gender*, ed. Nancy K. Miller (New York: Columbia University Press, 1986), 275. Further references appear in the text.

5. I am indebted to the detailed discussion of Restoration theater practice in Peter Holland's *The Ornament of Action: Text and Performance in Restoration Comedy* (Cambridge: Cambridge University Press, 1979), particularly the first three chapters. Further references will appear in the text.

6. See DRYDEN's Prologue *to Marriage A-la-Mode* in *Four Comedies*, ed. L.A. Beaurline and F. Bowers (Chicago: University of Chicago Press, 1967), 284.

7. RICHARD FLECKNOE, 'A Short Discourse of the English Stage' in *Critical Essay of the Seventeenth Century*, vol. 2, ed. J.E. Spingarn (Oxford: Clarendon Press, 1908), 96.

8. The Prologue to *Tunbridge-Wells*, produced at Dorset Garden, February–March, 1678, chastises the audience:

> And that each act may rise to your desire
> Devils and Witches must each Scene inspire,
> Wit rowls in Waves, and showers down in Fire....
> Your souls (we know) are seated in your Eies....

Cited in Montague Summers, *The Restoration Theatre* (London: Kegan Paul, Trench, Trubner & Co., 1934), 42. Pepys remarks frequently on Scenes and costumes. On March 8, 1664, he saw *Heraclius* at Lincoln's Inn Fields (the home of the Duke's Company before Dorset Garden was built): 'But at the beginning, at the drawing up of the Curtaine, there was the finest Scene of the Emperor and his people about him, standing in their fixed and different postures in their Roman habits, above all that ever I yet saw at any of the Theatres' (*The Shorter Pepys*, ed. Robert Latham [Berkeley: University of California Press, 1985], 362). Further references will appear in the text. See also Hugh Hunt, 'Restoration Acting', in *Restoration Theatre*, ed. John Russell Brown and Bernard Harris (London: E. Arnold, 1965), 178–92, on competition between theater companies over spectacular displays. Hunt makes the point, too, that as comedies often closed after one day, or ran no more than eight or ten performances, scenery was restricted to what was available (187). I comment on Behn's use of scenes and discoveries in the final section of this essay.

9. KARL MARX, *Capital*, trans. Ben Fowkes (New York: Vintage, 1977), 167. Further references will appear in the text.

10. SHADWELL and KILLIGREW are cited in Arthur H. Avery and Arthur H. Scouten, 'The Audience', in *Restoration and Eighteenth-Century Comedy*, ed. Scott McMillin (New York: W.W. Norton, 1973), 445, 442.

11. WILLIAM WYCHERLEY, *The Gentleman Dancing Master*, in *The Complete Plays of William Wycherley*, ed. W.C. Ward (London: T. Fisher Unwin, 1902), 242. Further references to *The Complete Plays* will appear in the text. John Dryden, *Marriage A-la-Mode*, 283. More damning are Dryden's lines to the playhouse 'gallants' (probably a mixture of country squires, London aristocrats, and young professionals) in the epilogue 'To The King And Queen, At The Opening Of Their Theatre Upon The Union Of The Two Companies In 1682' (Summers [note 8], 56):

> We beg you, last, our Scene-room to forbear
> And leave our Goods and Chattels to our Care.

Alas, our Women are but washy Toys,
And wholly taken up in Stage Employs:
Poor willing Tits they are: but yet I doubt
This double duty soon will wear them out.

12. On March 2, 1667, Pepys admired Nell Gwyn as Florimell, a 'breeches part' in Dryden's *Secret Love, or The Maiden Queen*, which allowed her to show her legs. He was so impressed he saw the play two more times. Breeches grant Behn's heroines the independence to fulfill their romantic destiny and simultaneously encourage the processes of fetishism. As Hugh Hunt (note 8) so quaintly puts it: 'to the Restoration gallants the public display of a woman's calf and ankle was little less than a "bombshell"' (183).

13. JONAS BARISH, *The Anti-Theatrical Prejudice* (Berkeley: University of California Press, 1981), 158.

14. *The Town Fop* (1676) and *The City Heiress* (1682) contain two practicing bawds, and Behn creates several adulterous wives; the latter, however, all claim a prior love attachment that was cut off by a forced marriage. *The Lucky Chance* (1686) is most concerned with what Eve Kosofsky Sedgwick calls the homosocial bonds between husbands and lovers. See *Between Men: English Literature and Homosocial Desire* (New York: Columbia University Press, 1982).

15. See ANGELINE GOREAU, *Reconstructing Aphra*, 77–78. See also Lawrence Stone, *The Family, Sex, and Marriage in England, 1500–1800* (New York: Harper and Row, 1979), 77–78.

16. MARGARET CAVENDISH, cited in Hilda Smith, *Reason's Disciples: Seventeenth-Century English Feminists* (Urbana: University of Illinois Press, 1982), 79.

17. LADY MARY CHUDLEIGH, 'To the Ladies', from *Poems on Several Occasions*, in *First Feminists: British Women Writers 1578–1799*, ed. Moira Ferguson (Bloomington: Indiana University Press, 1985), 237.

18. APHRA BEHN, *The Second Part of the Rover*, in *The Works of Aphra Behn*, ed. Montague Summers, 6 vols. (London: Heinemann, 1915), 1 : 152. With the exception of *The Rover*, all references to Behn's plays are cited from this edition.

19. MARY ASTELL, cited in Smith (note 16), 133, 135.

20. FREDERICK ENGELS, *The Origin of the Family, Private Property and the State* (New York: International Publishers, 1985), 134.

21. APHRA BEHN, *The Rover*, ed. Frederick Link (Lincoln: University of Nebraska Press, 1967), 7. All subsequent references are to page numbers in this edition.

22. 'Dialogism', associated with the writings of M.M. Bakhtin and V.N. Vološinov (a cover name for Bakhtin), implies that utterance is always social; any single utterance interacts with meanings in the larger discursive field. As Vološinov puts it: 'A word is a bridge thrown between myself and another.... A word is a territory shared by both addresser and addressee, by the speaker and his interlocutor.' (See *Marxism and the Philosophy of Language*, trans. L. Matejka and I.R. Titunik [Cambridge: Harvard University Press, 1986], 86.) Though Bakhtin has little to say about theater texts, the notion of shared verbal territory has obvious relevance for

speaker–audience interaction. How to describe and analyze the relationship between text and cultural context has long been the preoccupation of cultural materialists. See especially Raymond Williams, *Marxism and Literature* (London: Oxford University Press, 1977), Jonathan Dollimore, *Radical Tragedy: Religion, Ideology and Power in the Drama of Shakespeare and His Contemporaries* (Chicago: University of Chicago Press, 1984), Peter Stallybrass and Allon White, *The Politics and Poetics of Transgression* (Ithaca: Cornell University Press, 1986), and essays in *Rewriting the Renaissance: The Discourses of Sexual Difference in Early Modern Europe*, ed. M.W. Ferguson, M. Quilligan, N.J. Vickers (Chicago: University of Chicago Press, 1986), particularly feminist readings of women writers, for example, Ann Rosalind Jones's 'City Women and Their Audiences: Louise Labe and Veronica Franco', 299–316.

23. Until act 5 of *Sir Patient Fancy*, the prevailing view of the learned Lady Knowall seems to be best expressed by the real Sir Patient: 'that Lady of eternal Noise and hard Words . . . she's a Fop; and has Vanity and Tongue enough to debauch any Nation under civil Government' (4:32); indeed, like a female version of the old senex, Lady Knowall pursues her daughter's lover. Act 5, however, reveals her 'design': she has been testing the lovers and scheming to wrest from Sir Patient a fabulous jointure for them. The signs of Lady Knowall's learning (such as abstruse vocabulary) remain in place to the end but are rendered benign through her assumption of her proper gender role.

24. Cited in SMITH, 63.

25. According to Lacanian psychoanalyst Michele Montrelay, masquerade has always been considered 'evil' because, in flaunting the absent-penis, it sidesteps castration anxiety and repression, thus threatening the Father's law (incest taboo) and all systems of representation. See Montrelay, 'Inquiry Into Femininity', *m/f* 1 (1978): 83–101.

26. See SUSAN STAVES, *Players' Scepters: Fictions of Authority in the Restoration* (Lincoln: University of Nebraska Press, 1979), 2.

27. My view that Hellena is fully recuperated into the economy she rebels against contrasts with, among others, Frederick M. Link's interpretation in his Introduction to *The Rover* (note 21) and, more recently, to DeRitter Jones's in 'The Gypsy, *The Rover*, and the Wanderer: Aphra Behn's Revision of Thomas Killigrew', *Restoration* 10 (Fall 1986): 82–92. Both Link and Jones argue that Hellena represents a positive alternative to both the ingenuous Florinda and the rejected Angellica; her contract with Willmore is 'no marriage for "portion and jointure", no marriage arranged to perpetuate a family's name or increase its wealth, but a contract between two free and like-minded people' (Link, xiv). Even from a humanist perspective, this view is dubious: Hellena's freedom is inconceivable outside the market economy; from a historical or gestic perspective, Hellena's 'identity' is at the very least divided and ambivalent.

28. THOMAS HOBBES, *Leviathan*, ed. Michael Oakeshott (New York: Collier, 1962), 125.

29. CHISTOPHER PYE, 'The Sovereign, the Theater, and the Kingdome of Darknesse: Hobbes and the Spectacle of Power', *Representations*, 8 (Fall 1984): 91.

30. Cited in SUMMERS (note 8), 85–86. The self-theatricalizing nature of the audience produced enormous chaos, as indicated in this satirical speech from Betterton's *The Amorous Widow; or The Wanton Wife*: 'to see a Play at the Duke's House, where we shall have such Sport. . . . 'Tis the pleasant'st Thing in the whole World to see a Flock of wild Gallants fluttering about two or three Ladies in Vizard Masks, and then they talk to 'em so wantonly, and so loud, that they put the very Players out of countenance – 'Tis better Entertainment than any Part of the Play can be' (Summers, 68). See also the often-cited passage in Pepys in which he complains that dialogue between Sir Charles Sedley and two vizarded women both entertained – one was 'exceeding witty as ever I heard woman' – and distracted him from viewing the play (Pepys [note 8], 728).

31. THOMAS KILLIGREW, *Thomaso, or the Wanderer*, parts 1 and 2, in *Comedies and Tragedies* (London: Henry Herringman, 1663), 333. All references in the text are to this edition.

32. See SEDGWICK's *Between Men* (note 14), particularly her analysis of Wycherley's *The Country Wife* (49–66). Interestingly, when cuckoldry drives the plots of a Behn play, as in *The False Count*, the wife's passion, trammeled by her forced marriage, is given as much weight as homosocial competitiveness.

33. See GOREAU (note 15), 174.

34. What Angellica desires is the fantasy described by Luce Irigaray in 'Commodities among Themselves' (*This Sex Which is Not One*, trans. Catherine Porter with Carolyn Burke [Ithaca: Cornell University Press, 1985], 192–97): 'Exchanges without identifiable terms, without accounts, without end'. But such nonmaterialist exchange is possible, Irigaray implies, only in a lesbian sexual economy, while Behn's Angellica remains (and fails) within the heterosexual economy of the intrigue plot. Compare these representations to Margaret Cavendish's utopia for aristrocratic women in *The Convent of Pleasure* (pub. 1668). Cavendish bans husbands but offers her women unlimited access to commodities – 'Beds of velvet, lined with Sattin . . . Turkie Carpets, and a Cup-board of Gilt Plate' (see Ferguson, *First Feminists* [note 17], 91).

35. Behn intensifies the motif of the honest whore in *The Second Part of The Rover*. In the sequel, Hellena has died and Willmore is once again a free rover. Angellica's counterpart, La Nuche, is pursued by Willmore precisely because to deal with a prostitute is plain dealing, yet he also berates her: 'Damn it, I hate a Whore that asks me Mony' [sic] (1:123). Nevertheless, in this play the 'women of quality' envy the courtesan; Willmore and La Nuche reject marriage but swear undying love, while the virgin and gallant accept the less interesting but pragmatic fate of marriage.

36. The Prologue to *The Rover*, 'Written by a Person of Quality', dramatizes that ambivalence; the lines indirectly addressed to Behn use the pronoun 'him': 'As for the author of this coming play, I asked him what he thought fit I should say' (4). This is unusual. In Behn's prologues the masculine pronoun is used only as a general referent for poets/wits, as in the last line to the prologue to *Sir Patient Fancy*: 'He that writes Wit is the much greater Fool' (4:9).

181

37. See SANDRA M. GILBERT and SUSAN GUBAR, *The Madwoman in the Attic: The Woman Writer and the Nineteenth-Century Literary Imagination* (New Haven: Yale University Press, 1979), 3–92.

38. Feminist film theorists have taken the lead, with Laura Mulvey's path-breaking article on the fetishist position produced by Hollywood narrative cinema ('Visual Pleasure and Narrative Cinema', *Screen* 16, no. 3 [1975]: 6–19. For a full elaboration of this and other psychoanalytic concepts in film, see Mary Ann Doane's *The Desire to Desire: The Woman's Film of the 1940s* (Bloomington: Indiana University Press, 1987). In literary study, see Naomi Schor's 'Female Fetishism: The Case of George Sand' (in *The Female Body in Western Culture: Contemporary Perspectives*, ed. Susan R. Suleiman [Cambridge: Harvard University Press, 1986], 363–72). For fetishism in theater as well as in film and fiction, Roland Barthes's work is particularly useful; see 'Diderot, Brecht, Eisenstein' in *Image, Music, Text*, trans. Stephen Heath (New York: Hill and Wang), 69–78.

9 Aphra Behn's *Oroonoko* and Women's Literary Authority*

JANE SPENCER

Because women are not the only group to have been constructed as marginal to the dominant culture, the analysis of the relationship between gender, class and racial oppression is a crucial part of feminist criticism's political project. Behn's early colonial narrative *Oroonoko* invites such an analysis, for it is a woman-authored text with a female narrator which is centrally concerned with the issues of race and slavery. Jane Spencer's influential essay interprets Behn's novel as a politically progressive text which undermines European claims to superiority by transferring civilized values to its African hero and establishes, through its female narrator, a link between the marginal positions of the European woman and the African slave which makes possible a sympathetic identification with the racial Other. While not all critics of *Oroonoko* would agree that the novel is as critical of white colonial culture as Spencer suggests, her focus on Behn's use of a female narrator enhances our understanding of the way gender and race intersect in a text which privileges the female point of view.

What people thought about women writers changed with the times, and so did what women writers thought about themselves. Before the 1690s they were maverick figures, hesitant or bold according to individual temperament, with little sense of group identity despite the appeal back to Sappho and ancient female tradition. Delariviere Manley, Mary Pix and Catharine Trotter changed that, but some of the claims that they, especially Manley, made for women's special talents began to look more like accusations before very long. Once the belief in naturally chaste womanhood was established as a foundation of the bourgeois world view, the only way for a woman writer to be acceptable to herself and her society was to fit herself and her writing into the new mould.

---

* Reprinted from Jane Spencer, *The Rise of the Woman Novelist: From Aphra Behn to Jane Austen* (Oxford: Basil Blackwell, 1986), pp. 41–52.

Female literary authority was built up in various ways: one of the most intriguing, as well as most important ones was women writers' self-portraits. In autobiographies women explained why they thought themselves special, why they were learned and articulate. As often as not they apologized for this too, being conscious, with Margaret Cavendish, that readers might ask, 'why hath this Lady writ her own Life?',[1] or indeed why had she presumed to write at all? Perhaps the most interesting, because freer-ranging, self-portraits are those where the writer mingled fiction with autobiography, simultaneously projecting herself in fantasy and trying to justify herself to the world. The late seventeenth and early eighteenth centuries are rich in semi-autobiographical fiction. This mode suited women because in it they could become their own heroines... Romanticized autobiography, or fantastic fiction starring an idealized version of the author, provided a means not just of self-projection but of creating one's identity and authority as a woman writer. [...]

Aphra Behn's comments on herself as a writer are sprinkled liberally in the prefaces to her plays. She had to struggle for recognition of her right to a professional role – hence her tart remarks that women were equally entitled to write bawdy, and that people would have admired her plays more if they had thought a man had written them. To someone so determined to be accepted on equal terms with men, a good deal of the praise she was given must have been more galling than gratifying. Her admirers were busy building her a reputation as a writer of love, praising her poems for being erotic, even suggesting that reading Behn was tantamount to being seduced by her. Thomas Creech's poem to her announced:

> ... thy Pen disarms us so,
> We yield our selves to the first beauteous Foe;
> The easie softness of thy thoughts surprise,
> And this new way Love steals into our Eyes; ...
> In the same trance with the young pair we lie,
> And in their amorous Ecstasies we die...[2]

Using another common assumption about femininity, one eulogist saw her work as evidence of her delicate understanding of the mysteries of nature, women and love.

> What Passions does your Poetry impart?
> It shows th'unfathom'd thing a Woman's Heart,
> Tells what Love is, his Nature and his Art,
> Displays the several Scenes of Hopes and Fears,
> Love's Smiles, his Sighs, his Laughing and his Tears.[3]

A posthumous edition of her poems was introduced with similar claims: 'The Passions, that of Love especially, she was Mistress of, and gave us such nice and tender Touches of them, that without her Name we might discover the Author.'[4] Behn was certainly not above exploiting this image of herself when it came to selling her poems and her translation of Balthazar de Bonnecourse's *La Monstre, The Lover's Watch: or, the Art of making love*. Love was her subject here, and the encomium poems printed at the beginning of these volumes served as advertisements of the fact. Moreover, it is certainly fair that she should be remembered as a poet of love, when we consider such deservedly celebrated lyrics as 'Love in Fantastic Triumph sate' and 'A Thousand Martyrs I have made'. To Behn, though, love was not an especially feminine subject, it was simply an important poetic theme; and it was as a poet, simply, that she wanted to be remembered. 'Poetry (my Talent)', she wrote in proud parentheses, deceptively casual.[5] In the preface to one of her comedies, *The Lucky Chance* (1687), she asked for a very different kind of recognition from the kind she got:

> All I ask, is the Priviledge for my Masculine Part the Poet in me,
> (if any such you will allow me) to tread in those successful Paths
> my Predecessors have so long thriv'd in, to take those Measures that
> both the Ancient and Modern Writers have set me, and by which
> they have pleas'd the World so well: If I must not, because of my
> Sex, have this Freedom, but that you will usurp all to your selves; I
> lay down my Quill . . . for I am not content to write for a Third day
> only [i.e. just for money: playwrights took the proceeds of the third
> performance]. I value Fame as much as if I had been born a *Hero* . . .[6]

Instead of placing herself in the tradition of Sappho and Orinda, Behn is appealing here to the precedent of all the 'Ancient and Modern Writers', mostly men, and defining her poetic talent as masculine. The freedom she is demanding here is the freedom to write without any special restraints because of her sex.

Behn tended to compromise her claim for the freedom to write as men wrote by simultaneously denying that she wrote bawdy plays as they did: 'they charge [*The Lucky Chance*] with the old never failing Scandal – That 'tis not fit for the Ladys: As if (if it were as they falsly give it out) the Ladys were oblig'd to hear Indecencys only from their Pens and Plays.'[7] However, the fact that her comedies were successful on the stage in the 1670s and 1680s indicates that she escaped the requirements of 'decency' soon to bear especially hard on women. Her success in Restoration comedy has been held against her by some recent critics who find her work *too* 'masculine': reproducing the attitudes

185

of male libertines, so that the hero of her comedy *The Rover* (1677) is rewarded for his philandering by marriage to the chaste heroine, who (as it transpires in the sequel to the play) soon dies, leaving him free to rove once more.[8] Behn is not without general concern for her sex and for women's freedom, as her plays' treatment of arranged marriages and her heroines' criticisms of various masculine tyrannies demonstrate.[9] Still, it is outside the plays themselves that she supports women most thoroughly, through her claims for women's abilities as writers.

Her novels are particularly interesting from this point of view, because in them she tackles the problem of the woman writer's authority by creating an explicitly female narrator. Fiction formed a large part of Behn's output in her later years. First to be published was *Love Letters Between a Nobleman and his Sister*, in three volumes from 1784 to 1787. Based on the contemporary scandal of Lord Grey of Werke's elopement with his sister-in-law Lady Henrietta Berkeley, and containing much anti-Monmouth sentiment at the time of Monmouth's rebellion, it contained enough sexual and political intrigue to be very popular. Behn published several other works of fiction during her lifetime, the most important being *The Fair Jilt* (1688) and *Oroonoko* (1688), and there are several stories written probably about 1685 but not published until after her death.

Her experiments with narrative technique are notable. The first part of *Love Letters* is as the title suggests, epistolary, and the heroine's passionate letters have led to comparisons with the Portuguese nun, though here the man replies and the lovers are united. But emphasis on epistolary passion obscures the political and satirical slant of the work. Some of Silvia's letters to Philander are attempts to dissuade him from joining Monmouth in the Rye House Plot against Charles II. Philander's response shows that his adoration of Silvia is a cloak for political ambition. 'I design no more by this great enterprize, than to make thee some glorious thing', he tells her, but soon adds, 'in going on, Oh *Silvia*! When three Kingdoms shall lie unpossest, and be exposed, as it were, amongst the raffling Crowd, who knows but the chance may be mine, as well as any others . . . ?'[10]

In the second and third parts, Behn turned to third-person narration, which allowed her to develop more clearly her own ironic comments on Silvia and Philander. Her narrator undercuts any claim Silvia has to be a passionate heroine in the tradition of the Portuguese nun: Silvia has 'no other design on [Octavio, another admirer], bating the little Vanity of her Sex, which is an Ingredient so intermixt with the greatest Vertues of Womenkind, that those who endeavour to cure 'em of that disease, rob them of a very considerable pleasure . . . whatever other Knowledge they want, they have still enough to set a price on Beauty'.[11]

Generalizing from Silvia, the narrator comments on all female behaviour: Eve's 'love of Novelty and Knowledge has been intail'd upon her Daughters ever since, and I have known more Women rendred unhappy and miserable from this torment of Curiosity, which they bring upon themselves, than have ever been undone by less villainous Men'.[12] Such narrative comments seem to reiterate standard views of false womankind from a male perspective. The reason for this may be that Behn was modelling her narrative voice on that of Paul Scarron, whose *Comic Novels* were popular at this time in England as well as in his native France. Scarron's intrusive, sardonic and obviously masculine narrators place his work in a comic tradition later developed further by Le Sage and Fielding. Aphra Behn's story *The Court of the King of Bantam*, published posthumously in 1698, was said to have been written as 'a Trial of Skill, upon a Wager, to shew that she was able to write in the Style of the celebrated *Scarron,* in Imitation of whom 'tis writ',[13] and its facetious wit suggests that she must have won her bet. Already, though, Behn was moving away from the implicitly male viewpoint imitation of Scarron encouraged in her. The narrator of *The Court of the King of Bantam*, identified as a friend of the heroine, Philibella, rather than the more central male characters, might best be envisaged as a woman. In most of the other stories the narrator is clearly female.

In *The Unfortunate Happy Lady*, the narrator, describing the talk of a procuress and her girls, comments, 'our Sex seldom wants matter of Tattle'.[14] The narrator of *The History of the Nun: or, the Fair Vow-Breaker* (1689), confides to the reader that she was once encouraged to become a nun (*Works*, V, 265). Describing a duel between the heroine's rival lovers in *The Nun: or, The Perjur'd Beauty* (1698), the narrator exclaims, 'Ah! how wretched are our Sex, in being the unhappy Occasion of so many fatal Mischiefs, even between the dearest Friends!' (V, 341). In *The Unfortunate Bride: or, The Blind Lady a Beauty*, she tells us, ''tis the Humour of our Sex, to deny most eagerly those Grants to Lovers, for which most tenderly we sigh, so contradictory are we to our selves' (V, 404). In these stories the narrator identifies herself as a woman with the authority to make general statements about female nature – which are essentially the same as the stereotyped views she offered from a man's perspective in *Love Letters*.

There are times when Behn develops her narrative comments in the direction of that specifically feminine authority to comment on women's experience and on love, which her admirers were ready to grant her, but which in the prefaces to her plays she ignored so as to claim the same authority as men. In *The History of the Nun: or, the Fair Vow Breaker*, the narrator professes to offer new insights into love that are not available to most people:

Love, like Reputation, once fled, never returns more. 'Tis impossible to love, and cease to love, (and love another) and yet return again to the first Passion, tho' the Person have all the Charms, or a thousand times more than it had, when it first conquer'd. This Mistery in Love, it may be, is not generally known, but nothing is more certain.

(V, 313)

She also offers her experience as authority for advice on how to treat young women, explaining:

I once was design'd an humble Votary in the House of Devotion, but fancying my self not endu'd with an obstinacy of Mind, great enough to secure me from the Efforts and Vanities of the World, I rather chose to deny my self that Content I could not certainly promise my self, than to languish (as I have seen some do) in a certain Affliction.

She adds that she now thinks it a mistake to prefer the 'false ungrateful World' to the peaceful cloister, but:

nevertheless, I could wish, for the prevention of abundance of Mischiefs and Miseries, that Nunneries and Marriages were not to be enter'd into, 'till the Maid, so destin'd, were of a mature Age to make her own Choice; and that Parents would not make use of their justly assum'd Authority to compel their Children, neither to the one or the other.

(V, 265)

Claiming a woman's right to advise and slanting her advice in the direction of young women's freedom to choose their destiny, Behn here is very close to many of the woman novelists of the eighteenth century.

Often Behn makes her narrator not simply a woman but specifically the self-portrait of a well-known author, referring in passing to her own works. In *The Dumb Virgin* she is so pleased with the hero's assumed name of Dangerfield that 'being since satisfied it was a Counterfeit, I us'd it in a Comedy of mine' (V, 429). In *Oroonoko* she mentions meeting 'Colonel *Martin*, a man of great Gallantry, Wit, and Goodness, and whom I have celebrated in a Character of my new Comedy, by his own Name, in Memory of so brave a Man' (V, 198).[15] The events of *The Fair Jilt* are said to have taken place in Antwerp, 'about the Time of my being sent thither by King *Charles*' (V, 98), referring to a spying mission she undertook in 1666 to obtain information from a former friend William Scot, son of one of the regicides. Clearly one purpose of references like this was to impress upon her readers the literal truth of her narratives, whose events she claimed to have witnessed; and recent research shows that *Oroonoko* and *The Fair Jilt*, at least, have their basis in truth.[16] Another reason for putting her self-portrait into her novels is to include in them her vindication of the woman writer's ability and authority.

This is most evident in *Oroonoko*, where the autobiographical element means that Behn's interest in the narrator's position develops into an examination of her own role as woman and as writer. This fascinating novel marks an important stage in the history of women's quest for literary authority. Writing before the full establishment of the convention that love is the woman writer's subject and a moral aim her excuse, Behn has a freedom denied to most of her eighteenth-century descendants. She ranges widely over different societies, to investigate the meaning of civilized values in a story beyond the scope of many more polished later novelists. *Oroonoko* is the story of an African prince tricked into boarding a slave vessel and taken to Surinam while it is under English occupation. Because of his royal bearing Oroonoko (or Caesar, as the English appropriately rename him) is treated with respect by the Cornish gentleman, Trefry, who becomes his master. In Surinam he meets his long-lost love, Imoinda, also a slave, and they marry and conceive a child. Unwilling to have his child born into slavery, Oroonoko foments and leads a slave rebellion, which is suppressed. He is cruelly beaten. Vowing revenge, he takes his wife into the forest and kills her to prevent her falling into his enemies' hands; but after her death he loses his resolution and remains by her body. When he is recaptured he inflicts horrible injuries on himself, and then on the orders of General Byam, Deputy Governor of Surinam, he is executed. The tale affords a picture of an exotic colony (lost to the Dutch by the time of *Oroonoko*'s publication), and shows the English in their relations with its native people and with the African slave-trade. Three very different cultures – the European, the native Surinam, and that of Coramantien, Oroonoko's African home – are compared to one another. Thus it is a novel of ideas as well as action, and the narrator's comments are crucial to the rendering of these.

She is a narrator of a type especially common in the early novel – herself a character within the tale, relating it with the authority of an eye-witness. Neither omniscient and outside the action, nor central to it, she provides her commentary on the events she narrates.[17] Having travelled out to Surinam, as we know Aphra Behn herself did, she meets the enslaved Oroonoko, hears the story of his past life and adventures, and either sees or hears of the rest of his story up to his dreadful end. Trefry, she tells us, once intended to write the hero's life, but died before he could do it, and so the task fell to her, which, she says modestly, is a pity for Oroonoko. 'His Misfortune was, to fall in an obscure World, that afforded only a Female Pen to celebrate his

Fame' (V, 169). Yet as events unfold we realize that her gender is an important part of her authority: what she knows, and the comments she is able to make, depend on it. The female pen is vindicated.

The scene is set for Oroonoko's story by the narrator's description of Surinam. The Surinam natives represent 'an absolute *Idea* of the first State of Innocence, before Man knew how to sin: And 'tis most evident and plain, that simple Nature is the most harmless, inoffensive and virtuous Mistress (V, 131). Civilization could only bring repression, and 'Religion would here but destroy that Tranquillity they possess by Ignorance; and Laws would but teach 'em to know Offences, of which now they have no Notion' (V, 132). Their simplicity contrasts markedly with the duplicity shown by the white community throughout the story.

The story of Oroonoko's Coramantien life provides another contrast to Europe. Here it is not so much a case of the noble savage against civilization, as that of the truly civilized man against a decadent society. The young prince Oroonoko embodies the Restoration's heroic ideal: proud, honourable, superhuman in his prowess in battle, and 'as capable of love, as 'twas possible for a brave and gallant Man to be; and in saying that, I have named the highest Degree of Love: for sure great Souls are most capable of that Passion' (V, 137). His wit, his judgement, and his character all in all are as great 'as if his Education had been in some *European* court' (V, 135). His experiences show those Europeans whose highest values he has adopted in a very poor light. From the captain who tricks him aboard the slave-ship, to Byam, Deputy-Governor of Surinam, who tricks him into surrender after the slave rebellion, they fail to live up to their own code of honour.

The contrast between the African prince and the English people is used to expose what Behn saw as the recent betrayal of civilized values by the English. Oroonoko, royal himself, echoes his creator's royalist sentiments when he expresses horror at the execution of Charles I, 'with all the Sense and Abhorrence of the Injustice imaginable' (V, 135). He and his countrymen 'pay a most absolute Resignation to the Monarch, especially when he is a Parent also' (V, 139), most unlike the English, with Monmouth's plot against his father Charles II in their recent history by the time Behn was writing Oroonoko's story. The Coramantiens' attitudes to sexual relationships compare well with the Europeans', too. Oroonoko's early passion for Imoinda 'aimed at nothing but Honour, if such a Distinction may be made in Love; and especially in that Country, where Men take to themselves as many as they can maintain; and where the only Crime and Sin against a Woman, is, to turn her off, to abandon her to Want, Shame and Misery: such ill Morals are only practis'd in *Christian* countries' (V, 138–9).

As narrator, Behn has two assets which enable her to make Oroonoko's story serve this critique of her own society: her intimate acquaintance with and sympathy for the hero himself and her own identity as one of the Europeans, but not so completely at one with them that she cannot take a detached view of them.

Both these narrative assets are enhanced because of her social position and her sex. She has travelled out to Surinam with her father, who was to be Lieutenant-Governor of the colony, but died on the voyage. She lives in the best house on the plantation and has, she claims, 'none above me in that Country'.[18] She thus has status but no occupation, and no permanent stake in the colony; so she is well-placed to observe and comment freely. As a woman she can comment with authority on Oroonoko's gallantry and attractiveness. When she first saw him, she explains, he 'addressed himself to me, and some other Women, with the best Grace in the World' (V, 136). She gets to know him well because 'he liked the Company of us Women much above the Men' (V, 175). In fact 'we [women] had all the Liberty of Speech with him, especially my self, whom he call'd his *Great Mistress*; and indeed my Word would go a great Way with him' (V, 175–6). Thus she hears his story from his own lips and is able to report his noble sentiments.

The narrator also enters the action, exploiting Oroonoko's gallantry and his attachment to her in order to keep him under the control of the white settlers. Oroonoko is suspicious of their promises to set him free when the Lord Governor arrives, an attitude justified by his former experience of the Christian word of honour and by the narrator's comment that they 'fed him from Day to Day with Promises' (V, 175). The settlers, fearing a slave mutiny, ask the narrator to use her influence to persuade Oroonoko to wait till the Lord Governor makes his appearance. This she does, and it is hard to tell whether she does so in good faith or not. Her admiration for his heroic scorn of slavery sits oddly with her actions: 'I neither thought it convenient to trust him much out of our View, nor did the Country, who fear'd him', she reports (V, 177), relating how she and the other settlers surround Oroonoko with 'attendants' who are really spies. She encourages the royal slave to take several pleasant 'Diversions' – hunting tigers, fishing, visiting the Surinam Indians – the real purpose of which is to divert his thoughts from rebellion. She seems to be acting entirely, and with typical duplicity, as a European; but once the rebellion breaks out the narrator's ability to detach herself from her society's crimes becomes evident.

The whites, it now transpires, are split. Byam, 'a Fellow, whose Character is not fit to be mentioned with the worst of the Slaves' (V, 194), is for taking strong measures against the rebels, but 'they of the better sort', including the narrator, believe that Oroonoko has been badly treated and should not be harshly dealt with now (V, 193). Trefry joins in the pursuit of the rebels, meaning to act as mediator;

but, duped by Byam's promises of leniency, he persuades Oroonoko to surrender, and unwittingly leads him into a trap. The narrator now separates herself from the Europeans responsible for Oroonoko's downfall. She neither sides with Byam's cruelty nor shows Trefry's gullibility. If the reader wonders why someone of her high social position did nothing to protect Oroonoko from the vicious treatment he gets, the answer lies in her sex. As a woman, she has had to flee from the scene of action:

> You must know, that when the News was brought on *Monday* Morning, that *Caesar* had betaken himself to the Woods, and carry'd with him all the *Negroes*, we were possess'd with extreme Fear, which no Persuasions could dissipate, that he would secure himself till Night, and then would come down and cut all our Throats. This Apprehension made all the Females of us fly down the River, to be secured; and while we were away, they acted this Cruelty; for I suppose I had Authority and Interest enough there, had I suspected any such Thing, to have prevented it.
>
> (V, 198)

The trust between the royal slave and his 'Great Mistress' has been shattered by their racial differences, and yet her ignominious flight reveals similarities in the positions of the European woman and the enslaved African man. Like Oroonoko, who is given the outward respect due to a prince but kept from real power, the narrator is under the illusion that she has high status in the colony; but when it comes to a crisis the men are the real rulers, and being the daughter of a man who would have governed Surinam if he had lived does not help her. Ironically, she still seems to believe in her 'Authority and Interest' as she tells a story which reveals how illusory these were.

The narrator's gender is now her alibi. It saves her from sharing the guilt of her countrymen's treatment of the noble black prince, and, by implication, from sharing in the general corruption of the European society she criticizes. She is absent at other key moments too. She has to leave the hero when she sees his self-inflicted wounds, being 'but sickly, and very apt to fall into Fits of dangerous Illness upon any extraordinary Melancholy' (V, 207). She is still away when he is executed. Her mother and sister (scarcely mentioned in the story up to this point) witness the event in her stead, but they are 'not suffer'd to save him' (V, 208). Their position here is like the narrator's throughout: a spectator, but because of her femininity, a helpless one.

This feminine position, though, is an appropriate one for a narrator. On the fringes of her world, she is unable to act in the decisive scenes, but she observes, records, and eventually hands the story down to posterity. In *Oroonoko* the narrator's femininity is especially important because the similarities between the slave's and the woman's positions allow her her sympathetic insight into the hero's feelings at the same time as she creates a full sense of the difference of his race and culture. The limitations on women which Behn acknowledges, even exploits, within her narrative, do not apply to expression. As a character the narrator seems caught uneasily between admiration for her hero and allegiance to European civilization, but this means that she can present a picture of both sides. She ends with a flourish that implicitly asserts women's equal right to be recorders of events and interpreters of the world:

> Thus died this great Man, worthy of a better Fate, and a more sublime Wit than mine to write his Praise: Yet, I hope, the Reputation of my Pen is considerable enough to make his glorious Name to survive to all Ages, with that of the brave, the beautiful and the constant *Imoinda*.
>
> (V, 208)

The reputation of Aphra Behn's pen certainly was great at the time that *Oroonoko* was written, and she uses that reputation to present the female narrator as authoritative, disinterested and sympathetic, with as much authority as a male writer and also with special insights gained from her woman's position.

The marginality of the narrator's position is very important to Behn for another reason. It enables her to create her self-image as a writer, free from some of the restrictions on behaviour and feeling which operate on women as represented in the narrative. The contrast between the heroine, Imoinda, and the woman who writers her story is instructive. Imoinda is all that convention could desire of a noble hero's mate: beautiful, sensitive, ready to sacrifice all to preserve her chastity, capable of brave deeds in defence of her husband, and above all, devoted to him. Her qualities are best seen in her eagerness to die at his hands: when Oroonoko explains that he must kill her to preserve her honour, 'He found the heroick Wife faster pleading for Death, than he was to propose it' (V, 202). The narrator explains this attitude as part of exotic Coramantien custom: 'For Wives have a Respect for their Husbands equal to what any other People pay a Deity; and when a Man finds any Occasion to quit his Wife, if he love her, she dies by his Hand; if not, he sells her, or suffers some other to kill her' (V, 202). The killing of Imoinda shocks Oroonoko's European friends, but is presented as 'a Deed, (that however horrid it first appear'd to us all) when we had heard his Reasons, we thought it brave and just' (V, 201–2). Here an uneasy note creeps into the narrator's assessment of Coramantien, the place where natural honour and nobility are supposed to thrive. It has crept in before whenever women's position was considered. African polygamy is useful for the purposes of a satirical attack on European sexual hypocrisy, but Behn holds back from endorsing it as a real alternative by making Oroonoko vow to be true all his life to Imoinda alone; and the whole Coramantien episode shows that heroic society torn apart by the quarrel between Oroonoko and his grandfather the king over possession of the heroine. Writing *Oroonoko*, Behn was confronted with the problem of a woman's relation to the heroic ideal which she, along with other Restoration writers, endorsed. In some ways Behn identifies with her hero, but in the story of Oroonoko and his wife her position, as a woman, might be expected to be more analagous with Imoinda's, and that is an identification she does not want to make.

The female narrator Behn creates is important for *not* being the heroine. It is a pity that the autobiographical element of *Oroonoko* has caused so much criticism to centre on the truth or otherwise of the self-portrait within it, for Behn was deliberately not focusing on her own experience, and at a time when heroine and woman writer were coming to seem almost synonymous, she insisted on making a sharp distinction between them. If Imoinda, ideally lovely and noble, is Oroonoko's true mate, the narrator is his 'Great Mistress', sympathising with him, surviving him, recording his story, and assessing his significance. From the narrative stance Behn creates in this novel it is evident that for her being a writer was a way of escaping some of the limitations imposed on women.

Her prefaces claim a man's rights in writing, and her narratives claim something of a special authority as a woman, but without acknowledging any of the limitations on feminine expression that were later to come into force. Her double claim is well expressed in some lines she inserted into her translation of the sixth book of Cowley's Latin work, *Of Plants*. Here, unusually for her, she calls on the examples of Sappho and Orinda. The poet has been invoking Daphne, source of the poet's laurels, and then 'the Translatress in her own Person' addresses her:

I, by a double Right, thy Bounties claim,
Both from my Sex, and in *Apollo*'s Name:
Let me with *Sappho* and *Orinda* be,
Oh ever sacred Nymph, adorn'd by thee;
And give my verses Immortality.[19]

Behn's confidence in her own authority as a woman writer is not matched in the century following her death.

Notes

1. MARGARET CAVENDISH, 'A True Relation of the Birth, Breeding, and Life of Margaret Cavendish' (1656), in *The Lives of William Cavendishe, Duke of Newcastle, and of his wife, Margaret Duchess of Newcastle. Written by the Thrice Noble and Illustrious Princess, Margaret, Duchess of Newcastle*, ed. M.A. Lower (London: John Russell Smith, 1872), p. 309.

2. 'To the Authour, on her Voyage to the Island of Love', signed T.C., in *The Works of Aphra Behn*, ed. Montague Summers (London: William Heinemann, 1915), VI, p. 121. Maureen Duffy writes of Behn's friendship with Thomas Creech, and prints a letter of Behn's referring to her resentment of something he had done: Duffy suggests that Creech's concentration, in his poem, on the erotic side of Behn's writing had annoyed her. See Maureen Duffy, *The Passionate Shepherdess: Aphra Behn 1640–89* (London: Jonathan Cape, 1977), pp. 226–9.

3. Anonymous, 'To the Lovely Witty ASTRAEA, *on her Excellent Poems*', in *Works*, VI, p. 123.

4. CHARLES GILDON, 'Epistle Dedicatory, To Simon Scroop, Esq; of Danby, in Yorkshire', in *All the Histories and Novels Written by the Late Ingenious Mrs. Behn, Entire in One Volume*, 3rd edn, with Additions (London: S. Briscoe, 1698), sig. A4v.

5. Dedication to Henry Pain of *The Fair Jilt, Works*, V, p. 70.

6. Preface to *The Lucky Chance, Works*, III, p. 187.

7. Preface to *The Lucky Chance, Works*, III, p. 185.

8. KATHARINE M. ROGERS writes that '*The Rover* ... reveals a more masculine set of values than do the works of Etherege or Wycherley.... [Behn's plays] afford a striking example of the callous attitudes which later sentimentalists rightly rejected as antifeminist'. *Feminism in Eighteenth-Century England* (Urbana, Chicago, London: University of Illinois Press, 1982), pp. 98–9.

9. For a discussion of the treatment of arranged marriage in Behn's comedies, claiming that she gives the 'clearest articulation' of this problem before the 1690s, see Robert L. Root, 'Aphra Behn, Arranged Marriage and Restoration Comedy', *Women and Literature* 5 no. 1 (Spring, 1977), pp. 3–14.

10. *Love-Letters Between a Nobleman And his Sister, Part* I (London: J. Hindmarsh and J. Tonson, 1693), pp. 103, 104, 105.

11. *Love-Letters from a Nobleman to his Sister: Mixt with the History of their Adventures. The Second Part, by the same Hand* (London: Jacob Tonson and Joseph Hindmarsh, 1693), pp. 124–5.

12. *Love-Letters*, Part II, p. 210.

13. 'Advertisement to the Reader', *All the Histories and Novels*, 3rd edn, sig. [A5v].

14. *The Unfortunate Happy Lady, in Works*, V, p. 43. Except for the three parts of *Love-Letters*, not included in Summers' edition, all quotations from Behn's prose fiction are taken from Volume V of her *Works*, and further references to this are placed in brackets within the text.

15. A character named George Marteen is the hero of Behn's *Younger Brother*, posthumously produced in 1696. No Dangerfield appears in her plays, but it is possible she had intended to use the name. Montague Summers points out that the name Dangerfield appears in Sedley's *Bellamera*, and suggests that Behn 'gave' the name to Sedley: see *Works*, V, p. 523.

16. The truth or otherwise of Behn's narratives has been a source of controversy since Ernest Bernbaum claimed that she 'deliberately and circumstantially lied' in *Oroonoko*, and had never been to Surinam: see 'Mrs. Behn's Biography a Fiction', *PMLA* 28 (1913), p. 434. Her knowledge of the colony, however, is detailed, and not only Byam, but more obscure characters like Trefry had a real-life existence. A letter from Byam to Sir Robert Harley in March 1664 seems to refer to Behn's departure from the colony: see Duffy, pp. 38–40. Behn's use of Indian and African words is said to show authentic knowledge of both languages in B. Dhuicq, 'Further Evidence on Aphra Behn's Stay in Surinam', *Notes and Queries* 26 (1979), pp. 524–6. Behn also claimed to have brought back a feather-dress from Surinam, worn in a performance of Dryden's *The Indian Queen*; H.A. Hargreaves has investigated this and concludes that the statement is probably true. See 'New Evidence of the Realism of Mrs. Behn's *Oroonoko*', *Bulletin of the New York Public Library* 74 (1970), pp. 437–44. Behn's visit to Surinam is well established, then, but Oroonoko's existence is not. *The Fair Jilt* tells the story of Prince Tarquin's attempt, at his wife's instigation, to murder his sister-in-law, and of his narrow escape from the axe when his executioner fails to do his job properly. This story has usually been considered pure fiction, but Maureen Duffy has shown that a 'Prince Tarquino's' crime and the bungled execution were reported in newspapers of the day: see Duffy, pp. 72–3.

17. FRANZ K. STANZEL distinguishes this kind of 'teller-character', a 'narrative agent [which] dominated earlier novels', from the 'reflector-character' who is the focus of events in a narrative but does not comment on them. See 'Teller-Characters and Reflector-Characters in Narrative Theory', *Poetics Today*, 2 no. 2 (Winter, 1981), pp. 6–7.

18. This claim was made by Behn in the 'Epistle Dedicatory' of *Oroonoko* to Lord Maitland: see *Works*, V, p. 511.

19. 'Of Plants', in *The Works of Mr. Abraham Cowley*, 10th edn (London: Benjamin Motte, 1721), III, p. 440.

10 The Romance of Empire: *Oroonoko* and the Trade in Slaves*

LAURA BROWN

Although Laura Brown, like Jane Spencer, reads *Oroonoko* for signs of the conjunction of racial and gender oppression, her synchronic approach to feminist literary history locates textual meaning less in the author's gendered identity than in the unstable interplay of the novel's different discursive systems. Thus, women's central position in the text's two opposing discourses – aristocratic romance and bourgeois trade – not only reveals the similar roles accorded to the woman and the slave in colonialist ideology; it also produces the ideological contradiction which ultimately opens up the historical experience of slavery by establishing a surprising connection between the suffering of the African slave and the martyrdom of Charles I. Brown's is a feminist reading which draws on the concept of resistance central to Marxist and cultural materialist criticism: the internal contradictions of Behn's novel suggest that colonial literature, far from discursively containing the racial Other, generates sites of contestation and change.

Our victims know us by their scars and by their chains, and it is this that makes their evidence irrefutable. It is enough that they show us what we have made of them for us to realize what we have made of ourselves.

(JEAN-PAUL SARTRE, Preface to Frantz Fanon's
The Wretched of the Earth[1])

* Reprinted from *The New Eighteenth Century: Theory, Politics, English Literature*, ed. Felicity Nussbaum and Laura Brown (London and New York: Methuen, 1987), pp. 41–61.

Laura Brown would like to thank Walter Cohen, Judy Frank, Jeff Nunokawa, Felicity Nussbaum, and Mark Seltzer for their help with early versions of this article.

1

Aphra Behn's novella *Oroonoko: Or, the Royal Slave,* written and published in the summer of the year of the 1688 revolution in England,[2] no longer needs an extensive introduction for students of Restoration and eighteenth-century literature, or even for many critics in other fields. [. . .]

Feminist criticism has opened up *Oroonoko* to readers who twenty-five years ago would have stuck to Dryden, Rochester, or Congreve. But even though that feminist revision has been significant – especially for projects in political criticism like this one – the recovery of *Oroonoko* was quite unnecessary. In another tradition of cultural criticism apparently inaccessible to the feminist revisionists who 'recovered' Behn for students of literature, *Oroonoko* has long held a prominent place. The novella has been recognized as a seminal work in the tradition of antislavery writings from the time of its publication down to our own period. The story of Behn's 'royal slave' occupied the English stage for almost a century, in dramatic redactions by Thomas Southerne (*Oroonoko,* 1696) and John Hawkesworth (a revision of Southerne's play, 1759). And its sentimental authenticity was confirmed and augmented by the famous occasion in 1749 when an African 'prince' and his companion, previously sold into slavery but ransomed by the British government and received in state in London, attended a performance of Southerne's *Oroonoko*: affected 'with that generous grief which pure nature always feels, and which art had not yet taught them to suppress; the young prince was so far overcome, that he was obliged to retire at the end of the fourth act. His companion remained, but wept the whole time; a circumstance which affected the audience yet more than the play, and doubled the tears which were shed for *Oroonoko* and *Imoinda.*'[3] Historians of slavery have never neglected *Oroonoko*. In the two most important accounts of literary treatments of slavery that deal with eighteenth-century England, Wylie Sypher's *Guinea's Captive Kings* (1942) and David Brion Davis's *The Problem of Slavery in Western Culture* (1966), Oroonoko figures prominently as a significant and even prototypical character in 'a vast literature depicting noble African slaves' (Davis, 473), a crucial early text in the sentimental, antislavery tradition that grew steadily throughout the eighteenth century.[4]

Perhaps the feminist failure to attend to the primary concern of *Oroonoko* is partially due to the general neglect of race and slavery among critics of eighteenth-century literature. This is the period of the largest slave trade in history, when at least six million human beings were forcibly transported across an ocean, to produce a massive new work force on two continents and in the islands of the West Indies. England's economic participation in the slave trade, especially after the Peace of Utrecht in 1713 and the acquisition of the Asiento – the exclusive right to supply slaves to the West Indies – has been extensively documented.[5] For over forty years literary critics have had access to Sypher's exhaustive description of the pervasive references to slavery in the literature of the period, from William Dodd and Thomas Bellamy to Daniel Defoe and James Thomson. If critics in the field have been almost universally oblivious to race, feminists have only followed suit.

Thus, while *Oroonoko* is certainly a crucial text in the tradition of women's literature and in the development of the novel; while it supplies us with an interesting early example of the problematic stance of a self-consciously female narrator; and while it demonstrates almost programmatically the tensions that arise when romance is brought together with realism; it demands at this conjuncture a broader political reevaluation. *Oroonoko* can serve as a theoretical test case for the necessary connection of race and gender – a model for the mutual interaction of the positions of the oppressed in the literary discourse of its own age, and a mirror for modern criticism in which one political reading can be seen to reflect another, one revisionist school a plurality of revisions. Sartre's juxtaposition in the epigraph to this essay – 'what we have made of them' and 'what we have made of ourselves' – suggests the reciprocal movement necessary for such a political revisionism, both within the treatment of specific texts and in the discipline of literary studies at large. In Sartre's reading of Fanon, that reciprocity is the prerequisite for a relationship of mutual knowledge between the colonizer and the colonized. In this reading of *Oroonoko*, the figure of the woman in the imperialist narrative – a sign of 'what we have made of ourselves' – provides the point of contact through which the violence of colonial history – 'what we have made of them' – can be represented.

The conjunction of race and gender in the study of ideology and literary culture might seem almost automatic, since recent work on colonial and third-world literature has been so strongly dependent on the same analytical category that has underwritten much contemporary feminist theory: the notion of the 'other'. The staging of the relationship of alterity has taken many forms in contemporary theory. Beginning perhaps with the Hegelian scenario – and the paradigmatic play between master and slave – the 'other' can be internalized as a dimension of the psychological dynamic, or externalized as an account of social forms – producing, on the one hand, psychic models like that of the conscious and unconscious or the imaginary and symbolic, or sociological or anthropological paradigms like that of the in-group and the out-group or the cooked and the raw. Feminist critics have drawn widely from these interconnected dualisms to describe the position of women in patriarchal culture. More recently, third-world critics have consistently utilized the category of the 'other' in accounts of the relationship of colonizer and colonized, Occident and Orient, European and native, white and black. But with the exception of Gayatri Chakravorty Spivak, neither group has used the concurrence of terms as the occasion for a congruence of critiques. The force of Spivak's work, in this context, has been in her insistence on the distortions that occur when a feminist approach fails to take cognizance of colonialism and, reciprocally, in her reading of the literary culture of colonizer and colonized through the figure of the woman.[6] For most recent critics of colonial and neocolonial literature, however, gender enters not at all into the analysis of imperialist ideology. Such a striking irony is perhaps symptomatic of a constraint implicit in these dualisms – a binary logic that militates against the dialectical argument at which this essay aims.

In addition to forestalling the conjunction of critical accounts of race and gender, the category of the 'other' works to hold apart the historical categories of imperialist and native. This dualism is in part politically necessary: it enables Edward Said to detail the massive, diffuse spectrum of discursive power controlled by the colonizer, and gives Frantz Fanon a powerful terminology in which to advocate revolutionary struggle. For Said 'Orientalism' is a discourse of power, a 'distribution of geopolitical awareness' into various cultural forms – 'aesthetic, scholarly, economic, sociological, historical, and philological' – by which the Occident creates and concurrently intends to understand, 'control, manipulate, even to incorporate' the Oriental 'other'.[7] His study, then, documents and demystifies the discourse of the Occident from the perspective of the Third World, just as, from the same perspective but with the alternative strategy, Fanon's writings articulate the interests of the colonized – recounting, theorizing, and ultimately advocating a struggle to the death, through the absolute and violent conflict in the colonial world between the settler and the native.[8]

Following Fanon, Abdul JanMohamed provides perhaps the most schematic model for the role of the 'other' in the critique of colonialism. He argues that 'the dominant model of power- and interest-relations in all colonial societies is the manichean opposition between the putative superiority of the European and the supposed inferiority of the native'.[9] For JanMohamed, colonialist ideology and literary culture are constituted by a choice of identity with or difference from the 'other'. And Tzvetan Todorov, in his account of 'the conquest of America' – an account, in his words, of 'the discovery the *self* makes of the *other*'[10] – depends, perhaps more systematically than any other critic of colonialism, upon the argument from alterity. For Todorov, Columbus, like 'every colonist in his relations to the colonized', conceives of the native according to the 'two component parts' of alterity, absolute identity or absolute difference (42).

Said, Fanon, JanMohamed, and Todorov locate the 'other' in the historical struggle between the colonizer and the native. Homi Bhabha focuses instead upon an intrinsic otherness, the difference within the colonial subject, whether colonizer or colonized. When the dominant discourse of colonialism attempts the representation of the native, 'other "denied" knowledges enter upon the dominant discourse and estrange the basis of its authority'.[11] Thus although Bhabha argues directly against a 'power struggle between self and Other, or ... mother culture and alien cultures' (153), he does posit within the colonial subject a division that reproduces the dualism we have already observed. This position raises the problem of the status of opposition for some critics who adopt the perspective of alterity. Though Bhabha claims that 'the discursive conditions of dominance [turn] into the grounds of intervention' (154), his argument suggests that opposition is contained within the production of colonial power, that the only autonomy that remains for the native 'other' resides within the dominant colonial discourse. This notion of the pervasive, preemptive nature of power is often evoked by American Foucauldian critics and is defined by Stephen Greenblatt in a recent essay on Shakespeare's second *Henriad*. Discussing the 'alien voices', the 'alien interpretations' encountered by the first English settlers in Virginia, Greenblatt claims that 'subversiveness, as I have argued, was produced by the colonial power in its own interest'.[12] Here the category of the 'other' privileges the position of power while minimizing the possibility of resistance.

Productive and important as this binary opposition has proven, then, it seems nevertheless to have stymied a genuinely dialectical critique of colonial culture. It forecloses an approach that works through alterity to the interaction that may occur even in an oppressive relationship. And it sometimes also precludes finding a place for the struggles of the native in the complex edifices of power that seem to contain all resistance.[13] But the ideal of moving beyond absolute difference has been raised repeatedly by recent critics. Todorov ends with the hopeful assertion that 'self-knowledge develops through knowledge of the Other' (254). He seeks ultimately to locate a position beyond difference: 'We need not be confined within a sterile alternative: either to justify colonial wars ... or to reject all interaction with a foreign power ... Nonviolent communication exists, and we can defend it as a value' (182). JanMohamed too imagines a 'syncretic possibility', theoretically available through the dialectic upon which his manichean opposition is founded, but present in practice only as an unrealized negative example ('Economy', 65), symptomatic of the difficulty of transcending alterity. In the same way, Said turns to the 'human' at the end of *Orientalism*: 'I consider Orientalism's failure to have been a human as much as an intellectual one ... Orientalism failed to identify with human experience, failed also to see it as human experience.' 'Without "the Orient" there would be scholars, critics, intellectuals, human beings, for whom the racial, ethnic, and national distinctions were less important than the common enterprise of promoting human community' (328). 'Communication', 'syncretic possibility', 'human community' – however it is named, this gesture outside the 'other' is at best an adjunctive, utopian moment, attractive but obviously extraneous to the argument from alterity. It gives us a sentiment without a method; we can derive from these examples inspiration, but not critical practice.

My treatment of *Oroonoko* is extensively indebted to these critics, but it seeks to avoid what I see as the theoretical pitfalls of the 'other' and to substitute the dialectical notion of what Johannes Fabian, in a critique of modern anthropological writing, calls 'radical contemporaneity' (xi). Focusing on the discipline's constitutive use of time as a distancing mechanism, on temporalizations placing the native in the 'primitive' past or in a 'passage from savagery to civilization, from peasant to industrial society' (95), Fabian argues that this systematic 'denial of coevalness' (31) has operated in the ideological service of colonialism and neocolonialism by concealing the fact that 'anthropology's Other is, ultimately, other people who are our contemporaries' (143). Fabian proposes that anthropologists 'seek ways to meet the Other on the same ground, in the same Time' (164). His notion of radical contemporaneity is based on the Marxian theory of history as embodied in the formations of the present, on a view of 'the totality of historical forces, including their cotemporality at any given time' (158). Radical contemporaneity serves 'as the condition for truly dialectical confrontation between persons as well as societies. It militates against false conceptions of dialectics – all those watered-down binary abstractions which are passed off as oppositions: left vs. right, past vs. present, primitive vs. modern. . . . What are opposed, in conflict, in fact, locked in antagonistic struggle, are not the same societies at different stages of development, but different societies facing each other at the same Time' (155). For Fabian 'the anthropologist and his interlocutors only "know" when they meet each other in one and the same cotemporality' (164).

The critic of literary culture can rarely argue that either she or the colonialist author and her characters 'meet the Other on the same ground, in the same Time' (164). But from the perspective of radical contemporaneity, the texts of colonialism reveal signs of the dialectical confrontations embodied in the historical formations of the period. Though the colonialist and the native may never 'know' one another or their historical present, we can perhaps come to know something of both. The aim of this critical project, then, is to demonstrate the contemporaneity of issues of race and gender in a particular stage in the history of British capitalism associated broadly with commodity exchange and colonialist exploitation. Their conjunction in this particular text is sufficient to demonstrate the value of a pragmatic dialectical criticism, and indeed the political importance of refusing to posit any opposition as absolute.

2

As a test case for 'radical contemporaneity', *Oroonoko* may seem at first to provide a rather recalcitrant model: the novella lends itself with great readiness to the argument from alterity. Indeed, Behn's opening description of 'royal slave', Oroonoko, is a *locus classicus* of the trope of sentimental identification, by which the native 'other' is naturalized as a European aristocrat. In physical appearance, the narrator can barely distinguish her native prince from those of England:

> [Oroonoko] was pretty tall, but of a Shape the most exact that can be fancy'd: The most famous Statuary cou'd not form the Figure of a Man more admirably turn'd from head to foot . . . His Nose was rising and *Roman*, instead of *African* and flat. His mouth the finest shaped that could be seen; far from those great turn'd Lips, which are so natural to the rest of the Negroes. The whole Proportion and Air of his Face was so nobly and exactly form'd, that bating his Colour, there could be nothing in Nature more beautiful, agreeable and Handsome.
>
> (8)

If this account of Oroonoko's classical European beauty makes it possible to forget his face, the narrator's description of his character and accomplishments further elaborates the act of absolute identity through which he is initially represented:

> Nor did the Perfections of his Mind come short of those of his Person; and whoever had heard him speak, wou'd have been convinced of their Errors, that all fine Wit is confined to the white Men, especially to those of Christendom . . . 'twas amazing to imagine . . . where 'twas he got that real Greatness of Soul, those refined Notions of true Honour, that absolute Generosity, and that Softness that was capable of the highest Passions of Love and Gallantry . . . the most illustrious Courts could not have produced a braver Man, both for Greatness of Courage and Mind, a Judgment more solid, a Wit more quick, and a Conversation more sweet and diverting. He knew almost as much as

if he had read much: He had heard of and admired the *Romans*: He had heard of the late Civil Wars in *England*, and the deplorable Death of our great Monarch; and wou'd discourse of it with all the Sense and Abhorrence of the Injustice imaginable. He had an extreme good and graceful Mien, and all the Civility of a well-bred great Man. He had nothing of Barbarity in his Nature, but in all Points address'd himself as if his Education had been in some *European* Court.

(8, 7)

Oroonoko is thus not only a natural European and aristocrat, but a natural neoclassicist and Royalist as well, an absurdity generated by the desire for an intimate identification with the 'royal slave'. Like Columbus in Todorov's account, Behn's narrator seems to have only two choices: to imagine the 'other' either as absolutely different and hence inferior, or as identical and hence equal. The obvious mystification involved in Behn's depiction of Oroonoko as a European aristocrat in blackface does not necessarily damage the novella's emancipationist reputation: precisely this kind of sentimental identification was in fact the staple component of antislavery narratives for the next century and a half, in England and America. But the failure of Behn's novella to see beyond the mirror of its own culture here raises the question of Behn's relationship with the African slave.

For not only is the novella's protagonist an aristocratic hero, but his story is largely constructed in the tradition of heroic romance. Briefly, Oroonoko, a noble African prince, falls in love with Imoinda, the daughter of his aristocratic foster-father. The two are divided first by the intervention of the King, Oroonoko's grandfather, who covets Imoinda for himself, and then by their independent sale into slavery. Reunited in Suriname, the British colony in Guiana where Behn was a visitor, Oroonoko and Imoinda are at first promised their freedom, then lead a slave rebellion, and finally die – Imoinda at the hands of Oroonoko, Oroonoko (known, as a slave, by the name of Caesar) executed by the colonists. Oroonoko's exploits follow closely the pattern outlined by Eugene Waith for the 'Herculean hero', the superhuman epic protagonist who plays a major role in heroic form from the classical period through the Renaissance.[14] Oroonoko is invincible in battle, doing singlehandedly 'such things as will not be believed that Human Strength could perform' (30). He is also a man of wit and address, governed absolutely by his allegiance to the conventional aristocratic code of love and honor. When he declares his love to Imoinda, for instance, it is voiced entirely in the familiar terms of heroic romance: 'Most happily, some new, and, till then, unknown Power instructed his Heart and Tongue in the Language of Love . . . his Flame aim'd at nothing but Honour, if such a distinction may be made in Love' (10).

This formula is typical of the dramatic heroic romances by Davenant, Orrery, Dryden, and Lee that were prominent on the English stage especially from the Restoration through the 1670s. Behn made her own contribution to this genre in *Abdelazer*, a heroic tragedy produced and published in 1677. The main direct source of heroic convention in *Oroonoko*, then, is the aristocratic coterie theater of the Restoration. When Oroonoko swears his loyalty to 'his charming Imoinda' (71):

> they mutually protested, that even Fetters and Slavery were soft and easy, and would be supported with Joy and Pleasure, while they cou'd be so happy to possess each other, and to be able to make good their Vows. *Caesar* swore he disdained the Empire of the World, while he could behold his *Imoinda*.
>
> (44)

This abdication of empire for love is one of the most persistent motifs of late heroic drama, exemplified most prominently by Dryden's Anthony in *All for Love* (1677): 'Give to your boy, your Caesar,/This rattle of a globe to play withal, . . . I'll not be pleased with less than Cleopatra.'[15]

The hierarchical and rigid conventions of heroic romance made it particularly useful in the representation of the alien scenes of West Indian slavery. In a discussion of nineteenth-century travel writing, Mary Louise Pratt analyzes the strategy of 'reductive normalizing', through which the alien figure of the native is textualized and contained by the imperialist observer. She finds this textual device typical of writing about the imperial frontier, 'where Europeans confront not only unfamiliar Others but unfamiliar selves', and where 'they engage in not just the reproduction of the capitalist mode of production but its expansion through displacement of previously established modes'.[16] In Behn's text 'reductive normalizing' is carried out through literary convention, and specifically through that very convention most effectively able to fix and codify the experience of radical alterity, the arbitrary love and honor codes of heroic romance.

Emerging directly from this mystification is the persistent presence of the figure of the woman in *Oroonoko*. In heroic romance, of course, the desirable woman serves invariably as the motive and ultimate prize for male adventures. As this ideology evolved in the seventeenth-century French prose tradition, dominated by women writers like Madeleine de Scudéry and Madame de LaFayette, women became increasingly central to the romantic action. Behn's novellas, like other English prose works of the Restoration and early eighteenth century, draw extensively upon this French material, and the foregrounding of female authorship in *Oroonoko* through the explicit interventions of the female narrator signals the prevalent feminization of the genre.

This narrative must have women: it generates female figures at every turn. Not only is the protagonist represented as especially fond of the company of women (46), but female figures – either Imoinda or the narrator and her surrogates – appear as incentives or witnesses for almost all of Oroonoko's exploits. He fights a monstrous, purportedly immortal tiger for the romantic approval of his female admirers: *'What Trophies and Garlands, Ladies, will you make me, if I bring you home the Heart of this ravenous Beast* . . . We all promis'd he should be rewarded at all our hands' (51). He kills the first tiger in defense of a group of four women – who 'fled as fast as we could' (50) – and an unidentified, symptomatically faceless Englishman, who effaces himself further by following the ladies in their flight (50). On the trip to the Indian tribes over which Oroonoko presides as expedition leader, the female figure is again the center of attention. Along with the narrator and her 'Woman, a Maid of good Courage' (54), only one man agrees to accompany Oroonoko to the Indian town, and once there, the '*White* people', surrounded by the naked natives, stage a scene of cultural difference in which the fully clothed woman is the central spectacle:

> They were all naked; and we were dress'd . . . very glittering
> and rich; so that we appear'd extremely fine: my own Hair
> was cut short, and I had a taffety Cap, with black Feathers on my
> Head . . . from gazing upon us round, they touch'd us, laying their
> Hands upon all the Features of our Faces, feeling our Breasts and
> Arms, taking up one Petticoat, then wondering to see another;
> admiring our Shoes and Stockings, but more our Garters, which
> we gave 'em, and they ty'd about their Legs.
>
> (55)

Even at the scene of Oroonoko's death, the narrator informs us, though she herself was absent, 'my Mother and Sister were by him' (77).

The narrator herself makes it still more evident that the romantic hero is the production and expression of a female sensibility, of 'only a Female Pen' (40). The narrator's act of modest self-effacement here, and again on the last page of the novella, signals the special relevance she claims for the female figure, in contrast to the 'sublime' masculine wit that would have omitted the crucial naturalness and simplicity (1) of the tale for which the female pen has an innate affinity:

> Thus died this great Man, worthy of a better Fate, and a more
> sublime Wit than mine to write his Praise: Yet, I hope, the
> Reputation of my pen is considerable enough to make his glorious
> Name to survive to all Ages, with that of the brave, the beautiful, and
> the constant *Imoinda.*
>
> (78)

As the female narrator, along with the proliferative female characters who serve as her proxies, produces Oroonoko's heroic drama, so that they become in turn its consumers, Oroonoko also is represented as a consumer of the romantic form he enacts. He keeps company with the women in the colony, in preference to the men, and in their conversations he and Imoinda are 'entertained . . . with the Loves of the *Romans*' (46), a pastime that incidentally serves to forestall Oroonoko's complaints about his captivity. In the end, then, even Oroonoko himself is feminized, incorporated into the circular system by which the figure of the woman becomes both object and beneficiary of romantic form.

3

But the 'normalizing' model of heroic romance does not account for all the material in Behn's representation of West Indian slavery. In fact, neither the theme of slavery nor the romantic action would seem to explain the extended account of the Caribs, the native Americans of Guiana, with which Behn begins. This opening description deploys another set of discursive conventions than those of romance: the natives are the novella's noble savages. The notion of natural innocence, which civilization and laws can only destroy, is obviously incompatible with the hierarchical aristocratic ideology of heroic form; Oroonoko, educated by a Frenchman, is admirable for his connection with – not his distance from – European civilization. The account of the Indians belongs partly to the tradition of travel narrative, by Behn's period a popular mode describing voyages and colonial expeditions to the new world and including detailed reports of marvels ranging from accurate botanical and ethnographic records to pure invention.[17]

Behn's opening description of the Indians establishes her credibility in this context, but in its almost exclusive emphasis on trade with the natives, it also indicates the economic backdrop of the history of the 'royal slave':

> trading with them for their Fish, Venison, Buffalo's Skins, and little Rarities; as *Marmosets . . . Cousheries. . . .* Then for little *Paraketoes,* great *Parrots, Muckaws,* and a thousand other Birds and Beasts of wonderful and surprizing Forms and Colours. For Skins of prodigious Snakes . . . also some rare Flies, of amazing Forms and Colours . . . Then we trade for Feathers, which they order into all Shapes, make themselves little short Habits of 'em, and glorious Wreaths for their Heads, Necks, Arms and Legs, whose Tinctures are unconceivable. I had a Set of these presented to me, and I gave 'em

> to the King's Theatre, and it was the Dress of the *Indian Queen*,
> infinitely admired by Persons of Quality; and was unimitable.
> Besides these, a thousand little Knacks, and Rarities in Nature;
> and some of Art, as their Baskets, Weapons, Aprons.
>
> (2)

The marvels here are all movable objects, readily transportable to a
European setting, where they implicitly appear as exotic and desirable
acquisitions. Behn's enumeration of these goods is typical of the age's
economic and literary language, where the mere act of listing, the
evocation of brilliant colors, and the sense of an incalculable
numerousness express the period's fascination with imperialist
accumulation.[18] But the Indians' goods are at best a small factor in the
real economic connection between England and the West Indies; they
serve primarily as a synecdoche for imperialist exploitation.

This opening context is centered upon the feathered habit which the
narrator acquires, and which, she claims, became upon her return to
England the dress of the Indian Queen in Dryden's heroic play of the
same name (1664), an artifact of imperialism displayed in the most
spectacular manner possible – adorning the female figure of a
contemporary actress on the real stage of the Theatre Royal in Bridges
Street. The foregrounding of female dress parallels the scene of the
expedition to the Indian village, where the spectacle of the narrator's
clothing is similarly privileged. And in general, the items in the
opening account of imperialist trade reflect the acquisitive instincts
of a specifically female sensibility – dress, skins, and exotic pets. Pets,
indeed, in particular birds, were both sign and product of the expansion
and commercialization of English society in the eighteenth century.[19]
Even more important, the association of women with the products
of mercantile capitalism, and particularly the obsession with female
adornment, is a strong cultural motif in this period of England's first
major imperial expansion.[20] Addison's image of the woman fitted out in
the fruits of empire evokes the ideology to which Behn's account belongs:

> I consider woman as a beautiful, romantic animal, that may be
> adorned with furs and feathers, pearls and diamonds, ores and silks.
> The lynx shall cast its skin at her feet to make her a tippet; the
> peacock, parrot, and swan shall *pay contribution* to her muff; the
> sea shall be searched for shells, and the rocks for gems; and every
> part of nature furnish out its share towards the embellishment of a
> creature that is the most consummate work of it.[21]

Dressed in the products of imperialist accumulation, women are, by
metonymy identified not only with those products, but ultimately with
the whole fascinating enterprise of trade itself.

And of course the substantial trade and real profit was not in the Indians' buffalo skins, *Paraketoes,* or feathers, but in sugar and slaves. Behn's description of the slave trade, highly accurate in many of its details, is the shaping economic and historical context of *Oroonoko.* A letter written in 1663 to Sir Robert Harley – at whose house at St. John's Hill (49) the narrator claims to have resided – from one William Yearworth, his steward, may describe the arrival of the slave ship which Behn would have witnessed during her visit to the colony:[22]

> Theare is A genney man [a slave ship from the Guinea Coast] Ariued heare in This riuer of ye 24th of [January] This Instant att Sande poynt. Shee hase 130 nigroes one Borde; ye Comanders name [is] Joseph John Woode; shee has lost 54 negroes in ye viage. The Ladeyes that are heare liue att St Johnes hill.[23]

Behn recounts the participation of African tribal leaders in collecting and selling slaves to European traders, the prearranged agreements for lots in the colonies, the deliberate dispersal of members of the same tribe around the plantations, the situation of the Negro towns, the imminence of rebellion, and the aggressive character of the Koromantyn (in Behn, Coramantien) slaves – the name given to the Gold Coast tribes from which Oroonoko comes.[24]

Behn's account of the black uprising – an obvious consequence of the slave trade – has no specific historical confirmation, but the situation is typical. Revolts and runaways, or marronage, were commonplace in the West Indies and Guiana throughout this period. In Jamaica rebellions and guerrilla warfare, predominantly led by Koromantyn ex-slaves, were virtually continuous from 1665 to 1740.[25] Marronage was common in Guiana as well during the period when *Oroonoko* is set: while Behn was in Suriname a group of escaped slaves led by a Koromantyn known as Jermes has an established base in the region of Para, from which they attacked local plantations.[26] And Wylie Sypher has documented several cases like Oroonoko's, in which the offspring of African tribal leaders were betrayed into slavery, often on their way to obtain an education in England.[27]

The powerful act of 'reductive normalizing' performed by the romantic narrative is somewhat countered, then, by a similarly powerful historical contextualization in Behn's account of trade. Not that the representation of trade in *Oroonoko* is outside ideology; far from it. As we have seen, the position it assigns to women in imperialist accumulation helps rationalize the expansionist impulses of mercantile capitalism. We could also examine the novella's assumption – partly produced by the crossover from the code of romantic horror – that blacks captured in war make legitimate objects for the slave trade.

We cannot read Behn's colonialist history uncritically, any more than we can her heroic romance. But we can read them together, because they are oriented around the same governing point of reference – the figure of the woman. In the paradigm of heroic romance, women are the objects and arbiters of male adventurism, just as, in the ideology of imperialist accumulation, women are the emblems and proxies of the whole male enterprise of colonialism. The female narrator and her proliferative surrogates connect romance and trade in *Oroonoko*, motivating the hero's exploits, validating his romantic appeal, and witnessing his tragic fate. Simultaneously they dress themselves in the products of imperialist acquisition, enacting the colonialist paradigm of exploitation and consumption, not only of the Indians' feathers and skins, and the many marvels of the new world, but of slaves as well, and the adventure of the 'royal slave' himself.

These two paradigms intersect in Oroonoko's antislavery speech:

> *And why* (said he) *my dear Friends and Fellow-sufferers, should we be Slaves to an unknown People? Have they vanquished us nobly in Fight? Have they won us in Honourable Battle? And are we by the Chance of War become their Slaves? This wou'd not anger a noble Heart; this would not animate a Soldier's Soul: no, but we are bought and sold like Apes or Monkeys, to be the sport of Women, Fools and Cowards.*
>
> (61)

The attack on slavery is voiced in part through the codes of heroic romance: the trade in slaves is unjust only if and when slaves are not honorably conquered in battle. But these lines also allude to the other ideology of *Oroonoko*, the feminization of trade that we have associated primarily with the Indians. Oroonoko's resentment at being 'bought and sold like Apes or Monkeys . . . the sport of women' is plausible given the prominent opening description of the animals and birds traded by the Indians, in particular of the little 'Marmosets, a sort of Monkey, as big as a Rat or Weasel, but of a marvelous and delicate shape, having Face and Hands like a Human Creature' (2). In conjunction with the image of the pet monkey, Oroonoko's critique of slavery reveals the critique of colonialist ideology in one of its most powerful redactions – the representation of female consumption, of monkeys and men.

In grounding the parallel systems of romance and trade, the female figure in Behn's novella plays a role like that outlined by Myra Jehlen, the role of 'Archimedes' lever' – the famous paradoxical machine that could move the earth, if only it could have a place to stand.[28] Though they are marginal and subordinate to men, women have no extrinsic perspective, no objective status, in this narrative, either as the arbiters of romance or as the beneficiaries of colonialism. But though they have no independent place to stand, in their mediatory role between heroic romance and mercantile imperialism, they anchor the interaction of these two otherwise incompatible discourses. They make possible the superimposition of aristocratic and bourgeois systems – the ideological contradiction that dominates the novella. And in that contradiction we can locate a site beyond alterity, a point of critique and sympathy produced by the radical contemporaneity of issues of gender with those of romance and race.

4

On the face of it, the treatment of slavery in *Oroonoko* is neither coherent nor fully critical. The romance motifs, with their elitist focus on the fate of African 'princes', entail an ambiguous attack on the institution of slavery, and adumbrate the sentimental antislavery position of the eighteenth century. But the representation of trade and consumption, readily extended to the trade in slaves and the consumption of Oroonoko himself, and specifically imagined through a female sensibility, renders colonialism unambiguously attractive. This incoherence could be explored in further detail: in the narrative's confusion about the enslavement of Indians and the contradictory reasons given for their freedom; in the narrator's vacillation between friendship with and fear of the 'royal slave'; in the dubious role she plays in 'diverting' Oroonoko with romantic tales so as to maintain his belief that he will be returned to Africa, her collusion in the assignment of spies to attend him in his meetings with the other slaves, and the quite explicit threat she uses to keep him from fomenting rebellion; and even in the fascination with dismemberment that pervades the novella's relation with the native 'other' – both Indian and African – and that suggests a perverse connection between the female narrator and Oroonoko's brutal executioners.

A deeper critique of slavery emerges at the climactic moment in the ideological contradiction that dominates the novella. This insight originates in the hidden contemporary political referent of the narrative: the party quarrels in the West Indies and Guiana at the time of Behn's visit. Though the novella's account is sketchy, Behn names historical persons and evokes animosities traceable to the political tensions that emigrated to the colonies during the revolution and after the Restoration.[29] The relative political neutrality of the West Indies and Guiana attracted Royalists during the revolution and Parliamentarians and radicals after the Restoration. The rendering of the colonists' council (69), and the account of the contests for jurisdiction over

Oroonoko reflect the reigning atmosphere of political tension in
Suriname during the time of Behn's visit in 1663 and 1664, though
without assigning political labels to the disputants. In fact, the Lord
Governor of Suriname to whom the novella refers is Francis, Lord
Willoughby of Parham, intimate of the royal family and of Lord
Clarendon and constant conspirator against the Protectorate, who
had received his commission for settlements in Guiana and elsewhere
in the Caribbean from Charles II, at his court in exile. Willoughby is
absent during Behn's narrative, but the current governor of the colony,
William Byam, who orders Oroonoko's execution, was a key figure in
the Royalist struggle for control of Barbados in the previous decade,
and likewise in Suriname engaged in a continuous battle with the
contingent of Parliamentarians in the colony. In 1662, immediately
before Behn's arrival, Byam had accused a group of Independents, led
by Robert Sandford, of conspiracy, summarily trying and ejecting them
from the colony. Sandford was the owner of the plantation neighboring
Sir Robert Harley's, St. John's Hill, the narrator's residence. Harley
also was a Royalist and had been a friend of Willoughby, though a
quarrel between the two during Harley's chancellorship of Barbados
resulted in Willoughby's expulsion from that colony in 1664. There
were few firm friendships beyond the Line in this tumultuous period of
colonial adventurism. Indeed in 1665, shortly after Behn left Suriname,
Willoughby himself, in a visit to Guiana meant to restore orderly
government to the colony, was nearly assassinated by John Allen, who
resented his recent prosecution for blasphemy and duelling.

Behn herself may have been engaged with these volatile politics
through an alliance with a radical named William Scot, who went to the
colony to escape prosecution for high treason in England, and whose
father Thomas figured prominently on the Parliamentary side during
the revolution and Commonwealth.[30] The radical connection makes
some sense in that Byam, the notoriously ardent and high handed
Royalist, is clearly the villain of the piece, and Colonel George Martin,
Parliamentarian and brother to '*Harry Martin* the great *Oliverian*' (50),
deplores the inhumanity of Oroonoko's execution. But its relevance
need not be directly personal. The first substantial antislavery
statements were voiced by the radical Puritans in the 1660s;[31] there
was a Quaker colony in Suriname during this period; and George Fox
made a visit to the West Indies in 1671, where he urged the inclusion
of blacks at Friends' meetings.[32] Though as a group the Quakers in the
New World were ambivalent about slave ownership and often profited
from the slave trade themselves, individual Friends throughout this
period enlarged upon Fox's early example. William Edmundson spoke
against slavery in both the West Indies and New England.[33] Planters
in Barbados charged that Edmundson's practice of holding meetings

for blacks in Quaker homes raised threats of rebellion, and in 1676 the
colonial government passed a law to prevent 'Quakers from bringing
Negroes to their meetings' and allowing slaves to attend Quaker
schools.[34] Though modern readers often assume that the early attack
on slavery voiced in *Oroonoko* arose from a natural humanitarianism,
the Puritan precedent suggests that Behn's position had an historical
context. Such sentiments were 'natural' only to a specific group.

But there is no simple political allegory in Behn's novella. Though
the Royalist Byam is Oroonoko's enemy, Behn describes Trefry,
Oroonoko's friend, as Willoughby's overseer in Suriname; although he
has not been historically identified, Trefry must have been a Royalist.
His open struggle with Byam over Oroonoko's fate might allude to
divisions within the Royalist camp, divisions which were frequent and
intense in Barbados, for instance, when Willoughby came to power in
that colony. More important than direct political correspondences,
however, is the tenor of political experience in the West Indies and
Guiana in this period. For Behn and others, the colonies stage an
historical anachronism, the repetition of the English revolution, and
the political endpoint of Behn's narrative is the reenactment of the
most traumatic event of the revolution, the execution of Charles I.

From almost the instant of his beheading, the King's last days, and
the climactic drama of his death, were memorialized by Royalist writers
in a language that established the discourse of Charles's suffering as
heroic tragedy. *The Life of Charles I*, written just after the Restoration
and close to the year in which Oroonoko's story is set, suggests the
tenor of this discourse:

He entred this ignominious and gastly Theatre with the same mind
as He used to carry His Throne, shewing no fear of death . . . [Bloody
trophies from the execution were distributed among the King's
murderers at the execution and immediately thereafter] . . . some out
of a brutish malice would have them as spoiles and trophees of their
hatred to their Lawfull Sovereign . . . He that had nothing Common
in His Life and Fortune is almost profaned by a Vulgar pen. The
attempt, I confess, admits no Apology but this, That it was fit that
Posterity, when they read His Works . . . should also be told that
His Actions were as Heroick as His Writings . . . Which not being
undertaken by some Noble hand . . . I was by Importunity prevailed
upon to imitate those affectionate Slaves, who would gather up the
scattered limbs of some great Person that had been their Lord, yet fell
at the pleasure of his Enemies.[35]

Related images appear in a version published in 1681, shortly before the
writing of *Oroonoko*:

these Barbarous Regicides ... his Bloody Murtherers ... built a
Scaffold for his Murther, before the Great Gate at *White Hall*,
whereunto they fixed several Staples of Iron, and prepared Cords,
to tye him down to the Block, had he made any resistance to that
Cruel and Bloody stroke ... And then, most Christianly forgiving all,
praying for his Enemies, he meekly submitted to the stroke of the
Axe ... he suffered as an Heroick Champion ... by his patient
enduring the many insolent affronts of this subtile, false, cruel, and
most implacable Generation, in their Barbarous manner of conventing,
and Condemning him to Death; and to see his most bloodthirsty
Enemies then Triumph over him. ... they have made him *Glorious* in
his Memory, throughout the World, by a Great, Universal and most
durable Fame.[36]

Charles I was a powerful presence for Behn at the writing of *Oroonoko*,
even though the story was composed only shortly before its publication
in 1688, long after Charles's death, the Restoration, and even the
intervening death of Charles II – the monarch with whom Behn's
acquaintance was much more personal. Oroonoko's heroism is attached
to that of Charles I not just generically – in the affinity of 'Great Men'
of 'mighty Actions' and 'large Souls' (7, 47) – but directly. Behn's slave
name for Oroonoko – Caesar – is the same she repeatedly used for the
Stuart monarchs: Charles II is Caesar in her poem 'A Farewell to
Celladon on His Going Into Ireland' (1684), as is James II in her 'Poem
to Her Sacred Majesty Queen Mary' (1689).[37] Oroonoko, as we have
seen, is defined by his sympathy for Charles's 'deplorable Death' (7).
Sentenced, like Charles in these Royalist accounts, by the decree of
a Council of 'notorious Villains' (69) and irreverent swearers, and
murdered by Banister, a 'Fellow of absolute Barbarity, and fit to execute
any Villainy' (76), 'this great Man' (78), another royal martyr, endures
his death patiently, 'without a Groan, or a Reproach' (77). Even the
narrator's final apology – though it refers specifically to female
authorship – reproduces the conventional humble stance of the
chroniclers of the King's death: 'Thus died this great Man, worthy of a
better Fate, and a more sublime Wit than mine to write his Praise; Yet,
I hope, the Reputation of my pen is considerable enough to make his
glorious Name to survive to all Ages' (78). 'The Spectacle ... of a
mangled King' (77), at the close of the narrative,[38] when Oroonoko is
quartered and his remains distributed around the colony, evokes with
surprising vividness the tragic drama of Charles Stuart's violent death.
The sense of momentous loss generated on behalf of the 'royal slave' is
the product of the hidden figuration in Oroonoko's death of the
culminating moment of the English revolution.

214

But the tragedy is double in a larger sense. Abstractly speaking, both Charles I and Oroonoko are victims of the same historical phenomenon – those new forces in English society loosely associated with an antiabsolutist mercantile imperialism. The rapid rise of colonization and trade coincided with the defeat of absolutism in the seventeenth century. In a mediated sense the death of Charles I makes that of Oroonoko possible, and Oroonoko's death stands as a reminder of the massive historical shift that destroyed Charles Stuart and made England a modern imperialist power. Ironically, in this context, both King Charles and the African slave in the New World are victims of the same historical force.

We might imagine that the account of Oroonoko's death represents the moment of greatest mystification in the narrative, the proof of an absolute alterity in the confrontation between the colonialist and the native 'other'. What could be more divergent than the fate of Charles Stuart and that of an African slave? But the violent yoking of these two figures provides the occasion for the most brutally visceral contact that Behn's narrative makes with the historical experience of slavery in the West Indies and Guiana. Merely the information that Oroonoko is a Koromantyn (5) connects his story to eighteenth-century testimony on slavery and rebellion in the colonies. Bryan Edwards describes the character of slaves from this area:

> The circumstances which distinguish the Koromantyn, or Gold Coast, Negroes, from all others, are firmness both of body and mind; a ferociousness of disposition; but withal, activity, courage, and a stubbornness, or what an ancient Roman would have deemed an elevation, of soul, which prompts them to enterprizes of difficulty and danger; and enables them to meet death, in its most horrible shape, with fortitude or indifference.... It is not wonderful that such men should endeavour, even by means the most desperate, to regain the freedom of which they have been deprived; nor do I conceive that any further circumstances are necessary to prompt them to action, than that of being sold into captivity in a distant country.[39]

Edwards is obviously drawn to epic romanticization, but his historical account suggests the experience behind the romance in Behn's narrative. So common was rebellion among the Koromantyns, that Gold Coast slave imports were cut off by the late eighteenth century to reduce the risk of insurrection.

Edwards recounts one such rebellion in Jamaica in 1760, which 'arose at the instigation of a Koromantyn Negro of the name of Tacky, who had been a chief in Guiney' (II, 59–60). He details the execution of the rebel leaders, who were killed, like Oroonoko, to make 'an Example to all the Negroes, to fright 'em from daring to threaten their Betters' (*Oroonoko*, 70):

> The wretch that was burned was made to sit on the ground, and his body being chained to an iron stake, the fire was applied to his feet. He uttered not a groan, and saw his legs reduced to ashes with the utmost firmness and composure; after which one of his arms by some means getting loose, he snatched a brand from the fire that was consuming him, and flung it in the face of the executioner.
>
> (II, 61)

A correspondent from Jamaica to the *London Magazine* in 1767 provides a similar account:

> Such of them [rebel Negroes] as fell into our hands, were burnt alive on a slow fire, beginning at their feet, and burning upwards. It would have surprized you to see with what resolution and firmness they bore the torture, smiling with an air of disdain at their executioners, and those about them.[40]

And John Stedman, the period's most detailed reporter of the executions of rebel maroons, recounts the request of a man who had been broken on the rack: 'I imagined him dead, and felt happy; till the magistrates stirring to depart, he writhed himself from the cross . . . rested his head on part of the timber, and asked the by-standers for a pipe of tobacco.'[41]

In this context, Oroonoko's death takes on a significance entirely different from that conferred upon it through the paradigm of heroic romance or the figuration of Charles's death:

> [he] assur'd them, they need not tie him, for he would stand fix'd like a Rock, and endure Death so as should encourage them to die . . . He had learn'd to take Tobacco; and when he was assur'd he should die, he desir'd they should give him a Pipe in his Mouth, ready lighted; which they did: And the executioner came, and first cut off his Members, and threw them into the Fire; after that, with an ill-favour'd Knife, they cut off his Ears and his Nose, and burn'd them; he still smoak'd on, as if nothing had touch'd him; then they hack'd off one of his Arms, and still he bore up, and held his Pipe; but at the cutting off the other Arm, his Head sunk, and his Pipe dropt and he gave up the Ghost, without a Groan, or a Reproach.
>
> (77)

As far as this horrible fictional scene takes us from the image of Dryden's Antony or that of Charles Stuart, those radically irrelevant figures are the means by which this narrative finds its way to the historical experience of the Koromantyn slave – the means by which this passage offers not merely a fascination with the brutality depicted here and in the other historical materials I have cited, but a sympathetic memorialization of those human beings whose sufferings these words recall.

5

In *Oroonoko* the superimposition of two modes of mystification – romantic and imperialist – crucially conjoined by the figure of the woman, produces an historical insight and a critical sympathy that the argument from alterity cannot explain. This is not to say that Behn herself is any more unambivalent an emancipationist than we had originally suspected. But it does suggest that even though Behn can see colonialism only in the mirror of her own culture, that occluded vision has a critical dimension. As the 'normalizing' figure of alterity, the romantic hero, opens up the experience of the 'other', we can glimpse, in the contradictions of colonialist ideology, the workings of a radical contemporaneity.

I have tried to exemplify the notion of radical contemporaneity variously in this reading of Behn's novella. In Charles Stuart and Oroonoko we have seen two creatures who could never meet in this world joined as historical contemporaries through the contradictory logic of Behn's imperialist romance. We have used a feminist reading of colonialist ideology, which places women at the center of the structures of rationalization that justify mercantile expansion, to ground the account of the contradictions surrounding the representation of race in this work. And we have juxtaposed the figure of the woman – ideological implement of a colonialist culture – with the figure of the slave – economic implement of the same system. Though Behn never clearly sees herself in the place of the African slave, the mediation of the figure of the woman between the two contradictory paradigms upon which her narrative depends uncovers a mutuality beyond her conscious control.

These relationships of contemporaneity spring from the failures of discursive coherence in *Oroonoko*, from the interaction of the contradictory aristocratic and bourgeois paradigms that shape the novella. This interaction is the dialectical process that my reading of *Oroonoko* has aimed to define, the process by which we may 'meet the Other on the same ground, in the same Time'. By this means, we can position the African slave in Behn's novella not as a projection of colonialist discourse, contained or incorporated by a dominant power, but as an historical force in his own right and his own body. The notion of a relatively autonomous native position, of a site of resistance that is not produced and controlled by the ideological apparatuses of colonialist power, has crucial consequences for our conclusions about colonialist ideology, the critique of colonialism, and ideology critique in general. It suggests that we can read the literature of those in power not only for the massive and elaborate means by which power is exercised, but also as a source of leverage for those in opposition, that while sites of resistance may be produced within a dominant ideology, they are not produced by it, and they do not serve it. They are produced despite it, and they serve to locate opposition in a body and a language that even the people of the colonialist metropole can be made to understand.

Notes

1. JEAN-PAUL SARTRE, Preface to *The Wretched of the Earth*, by Frantz Fanon, trans. Constance Farrington (New York: Grove Press, 1968), p. 13.

2. For the date of composition, see George Guffey, 'Aphra Behn's *Oroonoko*: Occasion and Accomplishment', in *Two English Novelists: Aphra Behn and Anthony Trollope*, by Guffey and Andrew Wright (Los Angeles: William Andrews Clark Memorial Library, UCLA, 1975), pp. 15–16. Subsequent references to *Oroonoko* will be to *Oroonoko; or, the Royal Slave*, introduction by Lore Metzger (New York: Norton, 1973); page numbers are inserted parenthetically in the text.

3. *The Gentleman's Magazine* 19 (Thursday, 16 February 1749): 89–90. See also *The London Magazine* 18 (February 1749): 94. This event is described by David Brion Davis, *The Problem of Slavery in Western Culture* (Ithaca: Cornell University Press, 1966), p. 477; and Wylie Sypher, 'The African Prince in London', *Journal of the History of Ideas* 2 (1941), 242, among others. Page numbers for subsequent references to Davis's book and to Sypher's article are inserted parenthetically in the text.

4. WYLIE SYPHER, *Guinea's Captive Kings: British Anti-Slavery Literature of the XVIIIth Century* (Chapel Hill: University of North Carolina Press, 1942). Page numbers for subsequent references are inserted parenthetically in the text.

5. E.g. RICHARD B. SHERIDAN, *Sugar and Slavery: An Economic History of the British West Indies 1623–1775* (Baltimore: Johns Hopkins University Press, 1974), esp. pp. 249–53.

6. See GAYATRI CHAKRAVORTY SPIVAK, 'French Feminism in an International Frame', *Yale French Studies* 62 (1981): 73–87; '"Draupadi" by Mahasweta Devi', in *Writing and Sexual Difference*, ed. Elizabeth Abel (Chicago: University of Chicago Press, 1982); and 'Three Women's Texts and a Critique of Imperialism', *Critical Inquiry* 12 (1985): 243–61.

7. EDWARD W. SAID, *Orientalism* (New York: Random House, 1979), p. 13.

8. See FRANTZ FANON, *The Wretched of the Earth*, trans. Constance Farrington (New York: Grove Press, 1968).

9. ABDUL JANMOHAMED, *Manichean Aesthetics: The Politics of Literature in Colonial Africa* (Amherst: University of Massachusetts Press, 1983), and 'The Economy of Manichean Allegory: The Function of Racial Difference in Colonialist Literature', *Critical Inquiry* 12 (1985): 59–87; the quoted passage is on p. 63. Page numbers for subsequent references are inserted parenthetically in the text.

10. TZVETAN TODOROV, *The Conquest of America: The Question of the Other* (*La conquête de l'Amérique: La question de l'autre*, Seuil 1982), trans. Richard Howard (New York: Harper and Row, 1984), p. 4. Page numbers for subsequent references are inserted parenthetically in the text.

11. HOMI K. BHABHA, 'Signs Taken for Wonders: Questions of Ambivalence and Authority under a Tree Outside Delhi, May 1817', *Critical Inquiry* 12 (1985): 144–65; the quoted passage is on p. 156. Page numbers for subsequent citations are inserted parenthetically in the text. See also Bhabha's 'The Other Question – The Stereotype and Colonial Discourse', *Screen* 24 (1983): 18–36.

12. STEPHEN GREENBLATT, 'Invisible Bullets: Renaissance Authority and Its Subversion, *Henry IV* and *Henry V*', in *Political Shakespeare: New Essays in Cultural Materialism*, ed. Jonathan Dollimore and Alan Sinfield (Ithaca: Cornell University Press, 1985), pp. 18–47; the quoted passage is on p. 24.

13. JOHANNES FABIAN, *Time and the Other: How Anthropology Makes Its Object* (New York: Columbia University Press, 1983). Page numbers for subsequent references are inserted parenthetically in the text.

14. EUGENE M. Waith, *The Herculean Hero in Marlowe, Chapman, Shakespeare and Dryden* (New York: Columbia University Press, 1962).

15. JOHN DRYDEN, *All for Love*, ed. David Vieth (Lincoln: University of Nebraska Press, 1972), II.442–46.

16. MARY LOUISE PRATT, 'Scratches on the Face of the Country; or, What Mr. Barrow Saw in the Land of the Bushmen', *Critical Inquiry* 12 (1985): 119–43; the quoted passage is on p. 121. Page numbers for subsequent references are inserted parenthetically in the text.

17. In the earlier period, Richard Hakluyt's *Principall Navigations* (1589) and Samuel Purchas's *Purchas his Pilgrimes* (1625); in the later period Sir Hans Sloane, *A Voyage To the Islands Madera, Barbados, Nieves, S. Christophers and Jamaica . . .*, 2 vols. (London, 1707); Churchill's *A Collection of Voyages and Travels* (London, 1732).

18. See my *Alexander Pope* (Oxford: Basil Blackwell, 1985), Chapter 1.

19. J.H. PLUMB, 'The Acceptance of Modernity', in *The Birth of a Consumer Society: The Commercialization of Eighteenth-Century England*, ed. Neil McKendrick, John Brewer, and Plumb (Bloomington: Indiana University Press, 1982), pp. 316–34; the reference to exotic birds appears on pp. 321–22.

20. NEIL MCKENDRICK, 'The Commercialization of Fashion', in *The Birth of a Consumer Society*, pp. 34–99, esp. p. 51.

21. JOSEPH ADDISON, *Spectator* 69, 19 May 1711, in *The Spectator Papers*, ed. Donald F. Bond (Oxford: Oxford University Press, 1965), I. 295.

22. See ANGELINE GOREAU, *Reconstructing Aphra: A Social Biography of Aphra Behn* (New York: Dial Press, 1980), p. 56.

23. 'Letters to Sir Robert Harley from the Stewards of His Plantations in Surinam. (1663–4)', reprinted in *Colonising Expeditions to the West Indies and Guiana, 1623–1667*, ed. V.T. Harlow (London: Hakluyt Society, 1925), p. 90.

24. Koromantyn or Coromantijn is a name derived from the Dutch fort at Koromantyn on the Gold Coast; in Suriname it designated slaves from the Fanti, Ashanti, and other interior Gold Coast tribes. For background and statistics on the tribal origins of the Bush Negroes of Guiana, see Richard Price, *The Guiana Maroons: A Historical and Bibliographical Introduction* (Baltimore: Johns Hopkins University Press, 1976), pp. 12–16.

25. ORLANDO PATTERSON, 'Slavery and Slave Revolts: A Sociohistorical Analysis of the First Maroon War, 1665–1740', in *Maroon Societies: Rebel Slave Communities in the Americas*, ed. Richard Price, 1973; 2nd ed. (Baltimore: Johns Hopkins University Press, 1979), pp. 246–92, esp. pp. 256–70.

26. PRICE, *Guiana Maroons*, p. 23.

27. SYPHER, 'The African Prince in London', *Journal of the History of Ideas* 2 (1941): 237–47.

28. MYRA JEHLEN, 'Archimedes and the Paradox of Feminist Criticism', in *The 'Signs' Reader: Women, Gender and Scholarship*, ed. Elizabeth Abel and Emily K. Abel (Chicago: University of Chicago Press, 1983), pp. 69–95.

29. See the documents under 'Guiana' in the Hakluyt Society's *Colonizing Expeditions to the West Indies and Guiana, 1623–1667*, esp. 'The Discription of Guyana', 'To ye Right Honourable ye Lords of His Majesties most Honorable Privy Councel, The Case of ye Proscripts from Surinam wth all Humility is briefely but most truely stated. 1662', and 'Letters to Sir Robert Harley from the Stewards of his Plantations in Surinam. 1663–1664'; V.T. Harlow's detailed introduction to this reprint collection, esp. pp. xxvii–lv and lxvi–xcv; Goreau, *Reconstructing Aphra*, pp. 66–69; and Cyril Hamshere, *The British in the Caribbean* (Cambridge: Harvard University Press, 1972), pp. 64–65.

30. GOREAU, *Reconstructing Aphra*, pp. 66–69.

31. RICHARD BAXTER, *A Christian Directory, or, a Summ of Practical Theologie, and Cases of Conscience* (London, 1673), pp. 557–60. Cited in Thomas E. Drake, *Quakers and Slavery in America* (New Haven: Yale University Press, 1950), p. 3. Drake dates the section on slavery to 1664–65. Also sympathetic, though less explicitly antislavery, is George Fox, 'To Friends Beyond the Sea That Have Blacks and Indian Slaves' (1657), in *A Collection of Many Select and Christian Epistles, Letters and Testimonies* (London, 1698), Epistle No. 153; cited in Drake, *Quakers and Slavery*, p. 5. On Quakers see also Davis, *The Problem of Slavery*, pp. 304–26; Carl and Roberta Bridenbaugh, *No Peace Beyond the Line: The English in the Caribbean 1624–1690* (New York: Oxford University Press, 1972), pp. 357–59; and Herbert Aptheker, 'The Quakers and Negro Slavery', *Journal of Negro History* 26 (1940): 331–62. An even earlier, unambiguous antislavery statement from the radical Puritans appears in the Digger pamphlet *Tyranipocrit Discovered* (1649), quoted in

The World Turned Upside Down: Radical Ideas during the English Revolution, by Christopher Hill (Harmondsworth, Middlesex: Penguin, 1975), p. 337.

32. See DRAKE, *Quakers and Slavery,* p. 6 for an account of Fox's recorded sermons at this time. See also Bridenbaugh, *No Peace Beyond the Line,* p. 357.

33. Cited in DRAKE, *Quakers and Slavery,* pp. 9–10: copy of a letter of William Edmundson, dated at Newport, the 19th 7th Mo 1676, in Records of New England Yearly Meeting, vol. 400, a ms. volume entitled 'Antient Epistles, Minutes and Advices, or Discipline'. See Drake for other examples of early Quaker statements.

34. Cited in DRAKE, *Quakers and Slavery,* p. 8; see also Bridenbaugh, *No Peace Beyond the Line,* p. 358.

35. RICHARD PERRINCHIEFE, *The Life of Charles I* in *The Workes of King Charles The Martyr* (London, 1662), pp. 92–93, 118.

36. WILLIAM DUGDALE, *A Short View of the Late Troubles in England* (Oxford, 1681), pp. 371–75.

37. WILLIAM SPENGEMANN, 'The Earliest American Novel: Aphra Behn's *Oroonoko'*, *Nineteenth-Century Fiction* 38 (1984): 384–414; p. 401.

38. I am indebted to Adela Pinch (Department of English, Cornell University) for my reading of these lines.

39. BRYAN EDWARDS, *The History, Civil and Commercial, of the British Colonies in the West Indies,* 2 vols. (Dublin, 1793), rpt. (New York: Arno Press, 1972), II.59. Most of the detailed accounts of slavery in the West Indies and Guiana date from the later eighteenth century. But there is ample evidence of marronage, rebellion, and judicial torture throughout the West Indies and including Suriname from Behn's period on. Suriname passed out of British hands in 1667, and thus the fullest documentation of the treatment of rebel slaves in that country describes conditions under the Dutch. There is every reason to believe, however, in a continuity from British to Dutch practices historically in Suriname, just as there is every evidence of the same continuity throughout the West Indies and Guiana – British or Dutch – at any given moment in the long century and a half of active slave trade. For further documentation, in addition to the works cited in subsequent notes, see George Warren, *An Impartial Description of Surinam upon the Continent of Guiana in America* (London, 1667); *Historical Essay on the Colony of Surinam,* 1788, trans. Simon Cohen, ed. Jacob R. Marcus and Stanley F. Chyet (New York: Ktav Publishing House, 1974); Price, *Guiana Maroons*; Price, ed., *Maroon Societies.*

40. *London Magazine* 36 (May 1767): 94. Also cited in Davis, *The Problem of Slavery,* p. 477.

41. JOHN STEDMAN, *Narrative of a Five Years' Expedition Against the Revolted Negroes of Surinam* (1796; rpt. Amherst: University of Massachusetts Press, 1972), p. 382. Stedman's book contains the fullest account available in this period of the punishments for maroons in the West Indies and Guiana. Price finds Stedman's descriptions 'to have a solid grounding in fact', and he also shows that Suriname was the most brutal of the major plantation colonies of the New World (*Guiana Maroons,* pp. 25, 9).

ANNE FINCH, COUNTESS OF WINCHILSEA (1661–1720)

11 Anne Finch, Countess of Winchilsea: An Augustan Woman Poet*

KATHARINE ROGERS

Anglo-American gynocriticism, developed in the 1970s by feminist critics like Elaine Showalter, Sandra Gilbert and Susan Gubar, has given a central place in its critical agenda to the study of the specificity of women's writing. In identifying how and why women's literary texts differ from men's, gynocritics have on the whole foregrounded female experience, especially women's experience of subordination, rather than biology. Katharine Rogers's essay on Finch is characteristic of this gynocritical approach to women's writing. Rogers seeks to demonstrate that although Finch adopted Augustan genres, verse forms, and aesthetic and moral values, her experience as a woman is inscribed in her love lyrics, satires and nature poems and imparts a distinctly feminist edge to much of her work. While Rogers's comparative study broke new ground in attending to the impact of gender on Finch's poetry, the gynocritical analysis of female experience has since been criticized by feminists of materialist, poststructuralist and psychoanalytic persuasions for reproducing discredited humanist notions of the author as the origin of meaning.

Anne Finch, Countess of Winchilsea (1661–1720), is important not only as a gifted poet but as a unique example – a poet who was both a woman and an Augustan. In many ways a typical Augustan, she wrote in all the traditional genres, from flippant songs to ponderous Pindaric odes. Yet because she was a woman, her poems are subtly different from those of her male contemporaries. She shows a distinctive sincerity in her love poetry, a distinctive standard in her satire, a distinctive simplicity in her response to nature, and a distinctive freedom from the Augustan writer's obligation to make public statements.

---

* Reprinted from *Shakespeare's Sisters: Feminist Essays on Women Poets*, ed. Sandra M. Gilbert and Susan Gubar (Bloomington: Indiana University Press, 1979), pp. 32–46.

Generally speaking, this difference is not a matter of conscious outlook and aims. Winchilsea shared many characteristic Augustan attitudes, such as distrust for the mob and a sophisticated acceptance of human weaknesses coupled with suspicion of human grandiosity.[1] She consistently upheld reason – not only her satire on irrational deviations, but her devotion to her husband is rational, as well as her religion and her appreciation of nature. There is a reasonable basis for all her feelings, and none are expressed with sentimentality or 'enthusiasm'. Her love poems are restrained and her nature poems precise. She wrote in the usual Augustan verse forms, particularly heroic couplets, although she was less prone to smartly decisive antithesis than John Dryden or Alexander Pope.

As an Augustan writer who was also a woman, Winchilsea faced peculiar problems. Of course women authors have always written in a masculine tradition, but the Augustan period was especially male-oriented. For one thing, the poet saw himself as a public figure – celebrating national events, reprehending the vices of society, relating personal experience to universal moral principles. And women were confined, by their opportunities and experience and what was assumed to be their capacity, to private social life and the domestic sphere: they were not, supposedly, qualified to pronounce on the Use of Riches or the Reign of Dullness. For another, the poet was following in the footsteps of the Roman poets, who wrote from a conspicuously male point of view.

This is particularly evident in the genre of the love lyric. For the Roman erotic poets, love for a woman was a superficial feeling based on desire. It could be intensely pleasurable, though surprisingly often it was painful – but in any case it was classed with such sensual pleasures as drinking. Often love and drinking are balanced against the higher pleasure of friendship, which is always assumed to exist between men. Women appeared in this poetry only as more or less unworthy love objects, existing for the amusement of men.

Love poets of the Restoration and early eighteenth century followed this convention unquestioningly. Almost without exception, the love poems of John Wilmot, Earl of Rochester, Sir Charles Sedley, William Wycherley, and Matthew Prior (an almost exact contemporary of Winchilsea) are addressed to mistresses, not wives, and mistresses who are usually transient and never taken seriously. By definition they are beautiful (otherwise no one could love them); the only possible variations are that they may or may not be 'kind' (that is, willing to sleep with the poet without marriage),[2] and they may or may not be constant (until he is ready to move on). The woman appears always as a generalized sex object, never individualized enough to be identifiable. Wycherley even argues that an ex–mistress has no right to reproach him for leaving her, for it is she who has changed, not he: he has remained 'true to Love and Beauty' in leaving her for a younger woman.[3]

Because the Restoration poets wrote in reaction against the fatuous idealization of much Renaissance love poetry, their erotic verse is frequently hostile, showing the lover vilifying his mistress or relieving his frustrations by raping her.[4] The characteristic Restoration mood is total cynicism: honor and faithfulness are stupid, since women and men inevitably cheat each other. The fact that 'The Imperfect Enjoyment' (resulting from impotence) was a favorite theme in this poetry shows both the total physicality of the love involved and its chronically unsatisfactory nature.[5] The poet Rochester constantly associates love with negative feelings. Not pleasure, but pain is its sure proof – 'Kind jealous doubts, tormenting fears, / And anxious cares' provide the only reliable evidence. Even his relatively positive poems on love reveal a negative undertone. The love lyrics he exchanged with his wife led to the conclusion that she had better treat him with scorn and coldness lest she lose his love.[6]

Prior, writing some years later than the Restoration rakes, softened their attitude. But his affection for 'Chloe', his long-term mistress, is superficial and patronizing. 'On Beauty' would seem to flatter women by paying tribute to their power. However, this power is equated with beauty (as if that were a woman's only significance), and the triumph it produces is hardly complimentary: Chloe has shown her power by drawing him away from every important concern, from 'Ambition, Business, Friendship, News, / My useful Books, and serious Muse.' Her beauty has made him submit to sit with her and talk 'Of Idle Tales, and foolish Riddles.'[7]

Now how could a woman function in such a tradition? For one thing, unless she was prepared to cast off her reputation publicly like Aphra Behn, she was shut out by its licentiousness. Obviously, she could not write to her lovers as the men could write to their mistresses. Nor could she treat love as a trivial amusement, since it was not a pastime for her but a central focus of her life. The only man a respectable woman could write to was her husband, and in those days of mercenary arranged marriages she might well not find him a suitable inspiration. Winchilsea was fortunate in this respect – she and her husband loved each other deeply – so that she could write to him as passionately as the men did to their mistresses. More so, in fact, since the relationship she was celebrating was so much more significant.

In 'To Mr. F. Now Earl of W.' she cleverly makes use of the conventions to express her own deeper feelings. Her husband is away and has asked her to greet him on his return with a poem. In typical Augustan manner, she appeals to the Muses, who are ready to assist until they discover, to their amazement and shock, what she is asking them to do – to help her express love for her husband! No, they cannot lend their aid to such an outlandish enterprise. No beau in the coffee houses 'That wore his Cloaths with common Sense' (notice how the sly equation of reason with dressing suggests the beau's superficiality) could excuse 'mention of a *Spouse*'.

The Muses all send excuses, but Urania, the muse of heavenly love, tells the poet in confidence that heartfelt love can be expressed without the Muses' inspiration. So Winchilsea relies on her own feelings, realizing that to express tenderness for one you truly love requires no aid of Muse or convention. However, considering how unfashionable such endearments are, she decides to reserve them until her husband comes home and she can confide them to him privately – when they too can enjoy 'that Pleasure . . . Of stollen Secresy' which makes all the 'fancy'd Happiness' of illicit lovers.

Winchilsea did express her love openly in another poem to her husband, in which she dispensed entirely with classical convention. She opens with passionate simplicity: 'This to the Crown, and blessing of my life, / The much lov'd husband, of a happy wife.' Notice, first of all, the mutuality of their feeling: she loves him, and he has made her happy. Their love is of paramount importance, and it gives, as love should, perfect happiness. She expresses her appreciation for his 'constant passion', which conquered her initial resistance (perhaps she had resented the generally exploitative and superior attitude of contemporary men in love), and now flouts fashionable convention by combining the status of a husband with the attentive passion of a lover. For his sake she will even undertake 'What I in women censure' – presumably, conforming to the accepted female role of frivolity and fashionable accomplishments. What emerges here is a real relationship, based on deep love, involving mutual concessions (his efforts to win her 'stubborn, and ungratefull heart', her yielding to convention to please him), and irradiating both their lives equally.

Always preserving Augustan form and Augustan restraint in these poems to her husband, Winchilsea achieved an unusually personal, genuine tone simply by looking at their actual relationship directly. Her expression of uncomplicated wholehearted pleasure in the company of a loved spouse, free of pretentiousness in feeling or diction, is unique in her period. A good example is 'An Invitation to Dafnis', in which she urges him to leave his study and take a walk in the fields with her. Light Augustan wit precludes any air of sentimentality. Dafnis, immersed in military history, must not:

> . . . plead that you're immur'd, and cannot yield,
> That mighty Bastions keep you from the feild,
> Think not tho' lodg'd in Mons, or in Namur,
> You're from my dangerous attacks secure.

He must come with her into a natural field, where:

> The Cristall springs, shall murmure as we passe,
> But not like Courtiers, sinking to disgrace;
> . . . . .
> But all shall form a concert to delight,
> And all to peace, and all to love envite.[8]

Even when Winchilsea was writing on more modish themes, she introduced a refreshing feminine point of view. Considering men's constant complaints that marriage is a ball and chain, oppressive to the natural freedom of the male, it is nice to see a woman making exactly the same claim in 'The Unequal Fetters'. Accepting for the moment the Restoration attitude toward love, Winchilsea shows how unfair it is to women. To love would be worth our while, she opens – if we could stop time and preserve youth. But since we women must lose the beauty which has won your hearts, and since we know you will then seek it in new faces, to love is but to ruin ourselves – not through seduction, but through empty marriages. She, for her part, will remain as free as Nature made her, will not allow herself to be caught in matrimony, a male invention that restricts women far more than men.

> Mariage does but slightly tye Men
> 　Whil'st close Pris'ners we remain
> They the larger Slaves of Hymen
> 　Still are begging Love again
> At the full length of all their chain.

Happily, Winchilsea herself had escaped this dilemma by a marriage which, founded on a deeper feeling, did not turn into a galling yoke; but here she looked at marriage in general as it prevailed in her time. She claimed natural freedom as opposed to artificial institution just as the men did, but, considering contemporary marriage law, with much better reason. Like the typical Restoration wit, she saw how hypocritical and restrictive the institution was; unlike him, she saw and protested against its particular unfairness to women.

In her 'Epilogue to the Tragedy of Jane Shore', Winchilsea was inspired by the whore's progress of Jane to contrast the lifetime courses of women and men. A beautiful young woman dwindles to fine and well-dressed, then to 'well enough', and finally to merely good – which means she is no longer admired and has nothing to do but retire. A man, on the other hand, can pass from 'pretty fellow' to witty freethinker to politician, and 'Maintains some figure, while he keeps his breath.' While she makes no comment on this disproportion – it would be out of place in the flippancy of a neoclassical epilogue – the unfairness of valuing a woman in terms of her beauty alone is implicit.

Both these feminist protests are playful, but significant in that their subjects would never have occurred to a male writer.[9]

As a woman, Winchilsea could not treat love and marriage as flippantly as did men for whom they were a minor part of life; respectively, pastime or dull obligation. Because it was impossible for a woman to be comfortable in the convention, she could not follow it without question as they did. This inability proved to be fortunate, in view of its limitation and superficiality: the men's poems might be highly accomplished, but were rarely more. Generally the men were less interested in the women they claimed to love than in the cleverness with which they expressed their feelings. Almost never dealing with permanent or profound relationships, they had often to resort to obscenity or empty paradox in an attempt to give their songs liveliness and individuality. Isolated from this convention by her sex, Winchilsea was in a manner forced to be original. She looked directly at her feelings and described them sincerely, and thereby produced poems which were not only distinctively natural but refreshingly free of the superficiality and cynicism which tainted most love poetry in her time.

'Ardelia's Answer to Ephelia' likewise shows Winchilsea's personal adaptation of a popular Restoration form, derived ultimately from Horace (Book I, Satire ix) and more recently from Boileau (Third Satire). The poet meets a fool who aims at being socially pleasing, who takes possession of him or her for a long tedious time. A contrast with Rochester's 'Timon' will bring out the distinctive characteristics of Winchilsea's satire. Rochester's Timon, like Winchilsea's Ardelia, is taken in tow by a pretender to wit and fashion, who drags him home to dinner. First the forcible host reads poor Timon an insipid libel and insists Timon wrote it, in spite of his protest that he 'never rhymed but for my pintle's [penis's] sake'. The company at dinner consists of bullies who pretend to wit and, even worse, the host's wife, a faded beauty who retains nothing of youth but affectation and shows her stupidity by insisting on an idealistic view of romantic love. They praise a string of bad plays, commending them for the very qualities which any person of taste would recognize as faults. At length the discussion degenerates into a fight, and Timon escapes.

In contrast to Rochester's consistent detraction – there is nothing positive in his poem – Winchilsea judges the follies she satirizes against clear moral and rational ideals. She rejects the Town because she finds it uncongenial to friendship as well as to intellectual fulfillment. And she explicitly disavows detraction, the staple of Rochester's poem. She will not fit into fashionable society, she says, because she cannot supplement her wit with the ill nature necessary 'To passe a gen'rall censure on mankind,' to sneer at unsophisticated young people as foolish and at moral people as dull, to cheapen the genuine heroism of a soldier or the genuine inspiration of a poet. In contrast, most Restoration writers agreed with Rochester's assumption that wit has to be linked with cynicism, slashing universal criticism, and obscenity: whenever Rochester needed a simile, a phallic image leapt to his mind.

Almeria takes Ardelia in tow as Timon's host did him, but there is a significant difference between the two objects of satire. While both are fools, Timon's host is a fool because he aims at but cannot achieve true fashion; Almeria, on the other hand, is a fool because she conforms perfectly to the model of a sophisticated Restoration lady. Timon judges the fools as an insider, one who has mastered and consummately practices society's standards of wit and breeding. Ardelia prides herself on being an outsider from a society whose rules she considers immoral and irrational.[10]

Almeria is an accomplished lady of fashion, much like a female Timon. She has the same talent for seeing faults: 'she discerns all failings, but her own'. Yet to one's face she is effusively complimentary: she embraces Ardelia, protests she has pined hourly for her company, and insists she come to dine, though in fact she considers her an old-fashioned prude. Almeria never stops slandering the absent, but when the subject is present, she maintains ''tis want of witt, to discommend'. After dinner they ramble about in Almeria's coach to see the fashionable sights – or, actually, 'any thing, that might the time bestow'. Ardelia stops to enter a church, thus forcing Almeria to be, as she puts it, 'Porter to a Temple gate.' But Almeria does not waste her time: she 'Flys round the Coach' in order to display herself to the best advantage to any passing beau.

Almeria lists Ardelia's many faults to one of these fops, and thereby exposes herself, since she represents contemporary fashion in contrast to Ardelia's Right Reason. Ardelia not only 'Dispises Courtly Vice,' but insists 'That sence and Nature shou'd be found in Plays,' and therefore prefers the earlier Restoration masters, Dryden, Etherege, and Wycherley, to contemporary sentimental drama.[11] (Note that Winchilsea lists the good playwrights, while Rochester named only to pillory.) Moreover, Ardelia has no interest in Almeria's most absorbing concern – those trifles on which most women built their egos, as indeed convention encouraged them to. Almeria prides herself on judgment shown in such things as placing 'a patch, in some peculiar way, / That may an unmark'd smile, to sight betray, / And the vast genius of the Sex, display.' She is mortified that Ardelia drank tea without a single 'complement upon the cup', even though Almeria had braved a storm at sea in order to get her first choice of the china on an incoming ship. Instead of gratefully attending when Almeria advised her about clothing shops, Ardelia cut her off with 'I deal with one that does all these provide, / Having of other cares, enough beside.'

They rush from the church to Hyde Park, lest they should 'loose e're night, an hour of finding fault.' There Almeria points out an 'awk'ard creature', but when Ardelia looks for some monster she sees a lovely though undeveloped girl. Almeria proceeds to sneer at the gifted translator Piso (Lord Roscommon) – how can anyone consider him a wit when he makes no artful compliments on a lady's dress or new coach, never cries down a play for the fun of it, and refuses to praise every novelty? Almeria then greets her 'best of friends' in a voice that carries across the park; Ardelia agrees that this woman has a mind as beautiful as her person. But instead of being gratified, Almeria is clearly put out by this praise of her dear friend; and she immediately confides that the woman is disgracefully in love. Finally Almeria sees the most ridiculous creature of all – a poetess ('They say she writes, and 'tis a common jest'). Ardelia asks whether the poet is conceited or spiteful. Otherwise, what is wrong with a woman's writing? At length Ardelia manages to escape, to return to the country the next day.

Like any Augustan poet, Winchilsea satirized deviations from reason. But her enforced detachment from the fashionable world – attributable mostly to her sex – sharpened her ability to see where accepted social norms diverged from reason. As an outsider, she was better qualified to evaluate the ideals of the dominant group. Moreover, isolation from Restoration fashionable circles kept her free of the withering cynicism that made Rochester's satires (as well as his love poems) so negative. She had no patience with vice or folly, and she could appreciate the slashing satire of Wycherley (whom Almeria detested for his exposure of hypocritical women) – but she had clear standards of positive morality which included charity and kindness.[12]

Winchilsea could satirize women very sharply, but her satire is always modified by the fact that it comes from a right-minded woman rather than a male censor of the sex. Thus, she avoided patronizing generalizations and expected women to meet a universal human standard rather than a specifically 'feminine' one. She showed herself, as Ardelia in the 'Answer' or the speaker in 'On Myselfe', as one with sufficient rational morality to despise the frivolity charged to women, to value what is truly important, and, if necessary, to live on her own resources.[13] Moreover, she pointed out that society pressed women to be foolish: they are 'Education's, more then Nature's fools' ('The Introduction'). Small-minded Almeria conforms to conventional standards; it is Ardelia who is the social misfit. Finally, Winchilsea saw follies primarily as a waste of women's time and resources, rather than as an annoyance to men. Ardelia scorns shopping not because it is expensive or takes her away from home and family, but because she is more interested in intellectual pursuits.

Winchilsea was keenly aware of the niggling details that clog women's lives – necessary details that are piled on them, and the expansion and overemphasis on these details made by those who wish to distract women from more significant occupation.[14] Her 'Petition for an Absolute Retreat' is, like Andrew Marvell's 'The Garden' and John Pomfret's 'The Choice', a celebration of rational, virtuous retirement in nature, a common Augustan theme. But while Pomfret wants company, Winchilsea would exclude idle visitors, probably because women were obligated to entertain whoever came, while men could generally escape constant attendance (as Pomfret implies he would). Male authors of the period constantly twitted women for idle visiting; it took a woman to point out that it was a tiresome burden imposed by society's views of ladylike behavior. For the same reason, Winchilsea specifies that her table will not only be simply provided (as is usual in these poems), but 'spread without my Care'. Unlike male authors, women had to supervise their own housekeeping.

Pomfret would include female company in his ideal retreat – sometimes a man needs to relax in the sweet softness of women's conversation – but only in an incidental way. He specifies that he will not have a wife, but an obliging female neighbor who can provide occasional companionship without scandal. Winchilsea would have congenial friends of both sexes, primarily of course her husband:

> Give me there (since Heaven has shown
> It was not Good to be alone)
> A *Partner* suited to my Mind,
> Solitary, pleas'd and kind;
> Who, partially, may something see
> Preferr'd to all the World in me.

She proceeds to draw a blissful picture of a world in which a man and wife are all in all to each other.

This looks like a direct refutation of a passage in Marvell's 'The Garden', the prototype for both 'retreat' poems. Describing his idyllically peaceful garden and comparing it to Eden, Marvell rudely charged that in the original Eden 'man ... walked without a mate', until God made the mistake of adding a female help, as if a helpmate could be needed in a perfect place. That Marvell could put this piece of extreme and irrelevant misogyny into a pleasing philosophical poem, and that it could be accepted without question by generations of readers, dramatically demonstrates the need for a female voice in poetry.

Winchilsea's explicit feminism appears usually in connection with the plight of the woman poet. (The attitudes of her contemporaries are exemplified on the one hand by *Three Hours After Marriage*, by Pope, John Gay, and John Arbuthnot, in which a woman is pilloried for being a writer; and on the other by Prior's epilogue to a play of female authorship, in which he declares that a woman's writing must be praised because she belongs to the beautiful sex.[15]) More than any other eighteenth-century writer, Winchilsea adverted to the difficulties of the female author, from the petty details that distracted her to the widespread assumption that it was presumptuous for a woman to write poetry. She was unusually outspoken in maintaining that a creative woman has a right to express herself because it is wrong to force anyone to bury a talent. Far from apologizing for taking time to fulfill herself by writing, she roundly declared that the approved feminine occupations were unworthy of an intelligent person. Her description of the foolish pseudo-arts to which women were expected to devote themselves is withering: to

> ... in fading Silks compose
> Faintly, th'inimitable *Rose*,
> Fill up an ill-drawn *Bird*, or paint on Glass
> The *Sov'reign's* blurr'd and undistinguish'd Face,
> The threatening *Angel*, and the speaking *Ass*.

('The Spleen')

Her 'Introduction', written for a manuscript collection of her poems not published by her but wistfully left for publication, argues her right to be a poet. Starting with the common Augustan attack on various sorts of carping critics, she soon closes in on the charge all critics will find: her verses are 'by a Woman writt'. It is a general feeling that 'a woman that attempts the pen' is 'an intruder on the rights of men', that women should devote their minds to 'Good breeding, fassion, dancing, dressing, play.'

> To write, or read, or think, or to enquire
> Wou'd cloud our beauty, and exaust our time,
> And interrupt the Conquests of our prime;
> While the dull mannage, of a servile house
> Is held by some, our outmost art, and use.

In other words, men do not want women wasting their time and energy on anything that does not contribute to their usefulness to men, whether as sexual objects or household managers; nor do they want them to rise above trivia, lest they develop ideas of their own. She goes on to prove women's ability to write by some biblical examples, which may not appear very convincing today but seemed called for in an age when the Bible was constantly used to keep woman in her place. But Winchilsea's confidence falters when she considers the present state of women, and she comes to a depressing conclusion. Debarred from education, instead positively trained and expected to be dull, few women can rise above the mass. And if one is pressed by 'warmer fancy, and ambition' to try, she cannot help wavering: 'So strong, th'opposing faction still appears, / The hopes to thrive, can ne're outweigh the fears.' She concludes that she had best keep her Muse's wing 'contracted', keep her verses to herself and a few friends, not aspire to laurel groves but remain in her absolute retreat.

Such expressions of discouragement, and even more her occasional disparagement of her vocation as a feminine foible or disclaimers that her works would merit publication even if she were not a woman, show that Winchilsea was not completely at ease in her unconventional role.[16] Consistently, however, she insisted not only that she was a serious poet, but that poetry was the most important thing in her life. In 'Ardelia to Melancholy', she lists the various remedies for depression that she has vainly tried: first, social mirth; second, friendship; last, writing poetry. When that failed, she knew further struggles were useless. She was chronically plagued by depression, to which her difficulties and ambivalence as a woman poet may have contributed. Certainly it affected her most painfully by undermining her confidence as a poet. When depressed, she feared that her poetry was degenerating, and even that those who decried her writing as 'An useless Folly, or presumptuous Fault' might be right ('The Spleen').

Defending a woman poet against the unthinking sneers of Almeria, who follows fashion by viewing a female poet as a ridiculous object, Winchilsea asks: 'Why shou'd we from that pleasing art be ty'd, / Or like State Pris'ners, Pen and Ink deny'd?' (*Poems*, p. 45). Thus, she makes a bold equation between the legal restrictions on a prisoner (who is either guilty or imprisoned by what all would agree was a violation of traditional English liberty) and the customary restrictions on a woman, imposed simply because of her sex. Winchilsea was particularly concerned with liberty – not the public liberty so constantly cited in British literature, freedom from autocracy and oppressive laws; but rather the domestic liberty which was harder to establish, especially for a woman, freedom from the petty restrictions of convention and trivial obligations. Declining Ephelia's invitation to London, she suggests that the country be 'Our place of meeting, love, and liberty' (*Poems*, p. 39). They cannot express their thoughts and affection amid the fashionable conventions operating in London. In the 'Absolute Retreat' she petitions that 'the World may ne'er invade . . . My unshaken Liberty.' Liberty was not a feature of Marvell's or Pomfret's similar retreats.

Considering the importance of liberty to Winchilsea, one is tempted to read her tale 'The Bird and the Arras' as an allegory. A bird is caught in a room and mistakes the pictured scene on a tapestry for a real one, but, trying to alight on a tree, only beats herself against the flat surface. She rises to the pictured sky, seeing the pictured birds apparently flying there and glorying in her ability to rise above them. But then she strikes the ceiling and plummets to the ground. She flutters around 'in endlesse cercles of dismay' until a kind person directs her out the window 'to ample space the only Heav'n of Birds'. The bird imprisoned in a man-made room suggests a woman imprisoned in man-made conventions; the bird which makes doomed efforts to rise through the ceiling, the poet who 'wou'd Soar above the rest' of her sex, only to be 'dispis'd, aiming to be admir'd' ('The Introduction').

Limitation seems to have had a special meaning for Winchilsea: it was not the Augustans' decorous acceptance of human limits, but the Romantics' painful awareness of the discrepancy between human beings' aspirations and achievement. Her poem 'The Nightingale' anticipates Keats's 'Ode' and Shelley's 'To a Skylark' in its suggestion that the bird has a freedom and joy impossible to human self-consciousness. The poet aims to imitate the song of the nightingale, to compose a song as freely self-expressive as the bird's – for 'Poets, wild as thee, were born, / Pleasing best when unconfin'd, / When to Please is least design'd.' She aspires to unite the music of the bird with human awareness. But of course the attempt fails. The poem ends with a typical Augustan turn and moral, but the ideas of unfulfillable aims and of the loss when humans give up their natural freedom remain. It is the Romantic yearning to burst limits, perhaps occurring to Winchilsea because a woman was made particularly aware of the restrictions on human beings. An outsider by sex, as later pre-Romantics were outsiders by temperament, she anticipates the Romantic artist's yearning for something beyond the physical, social world in which she must live.

Winchilsea's 'Nocturnal Reverie' has been seen as a pre-Romantic work ever since Wordsworth singled it out for praise.[17] But actually the poem is Augustan in attitude and technique. It opens with the classical references that naturally sprang into educated eighteenth-century minds and proceeds to a series of beautifully exact bits of description characteristic of Augustan appreciation of nature. She describes the thin clouds that flit across the moon, the alteration in colors under moonlight – the foxglove is still recognizably red, though its hue is blanched – the greater clarity of odors and sounds at night, the swelling haystacks visible only as masses, the large approaching shape which frightens her until the sound of forage being chewed reassures her that it is only a horse. Winchilsea achieves her effects through precise detailing, not through suggestive appeals to passion or imagination; and her use of metaphor is subdued to the point that it is barely visible. Intense as her appreciation is, she perceives physical creatures as such, making no attempt to inflate them into some higher significance. The focus is consistently on her conscious reflecting mind – from her classical allusions in the first lines, through her moral observation on the glowworms ('trivial Beauties watch their Hour to shine'), to the direct description of her own mental state which ends the poem. She is stirred not to ecstasy, but to generalizing from her sensory impressions.

Description of the animals' activity at night leads her to delicate sympathy: 'Their shortliv'd Jubilee the Creatures keep, / Which but endures, whilst Tyrant-*Man* do's sleep.' She is not deprecating obvious cruelty (as Pope did in 'Windsor Forest'), nor even any specific oppression, but just the restrictions imposed on domestic and wild animals by man's dominion. The poet, too, enjoys an unaccustomed liberty in this peaceful solitary scene. In the subdued moonlight, she feels free from the distractions of day and able to respond to the spiritual influences which speak to her true nature; her 'free Soul' can feel at home even 'in th'inferiour World'. The soul's affinity and longing for Heaven is of course a traditional religious idea, but one thinks also of the imprisoned bird finally escaping into 'ample space'.

What is most distinctive in Winchilsea's poem is its personal quality. When the Augustans related physical nature to human concerns, they typically thought in terms of large moral or national issues. Pope's 'Windsor Forest' includes some lovingly precise nature description, but uses it as a springboard to celebrate the destiny of Great Britain. He starts his poem not with personal response but with an invocation followed by descriptive details neatly organized to support a generalization – 'order in variety we see' – and usually reinforced with a stock simile. He appreciates English oaks not because they are impressive in themselves but because they will be used to build the mighty British navy.[18] His description of reflections in a river,

> The watery landskip of the pendant woods,
> And absent trees that tremble in the floods;
> In the clear azure gleam the flocks are seen,
> And floating forests paint the waves with green,

is beautiful in its way; but it does not equal Winchilsea's simple, honest attempt to convey what such reflections actually look like: 'When in some River, overhung with Green, / The waving Moon and trembling Leaves are seen.'

Pope as well as Winchilsea finds observation of nature conducive to religious thoughts, but he seems to be expressing the state of Man in general rather than that of a particular person. Happy the man who retires to these shades to study or practice benevolence, who

> Bids his free soul expatiate in the skies,
> Amid her kindred stars familiar roam,
> Survey the region, and confess her home!

The distinction is subtle, since of course Winchilsea assumed that her feelings were representative; but her closing lines are unmistakably more personal: they grow out of her own feelings as accumulated in the poem, and are free of pompous diction and grandiloquent generalization.

James Thomson is closer to Winchilsea in his direct observation of natural detail and his study of nature for its own sake. But here again the public tone predominates. Thomson is not communicating his personal response to the Seasons, but the sensations and thoughts they inspire in everyman. His exhaustive descriptions aim at scientific completeness and are elevated by inflated diction and moralizing set pieces. They contrast strongly with the plain details of Winchilsea, who aims simply to convey her response to a beautiful setting as accurately as she can, not to rise to some imagined occasion but to say exactly what she sees and feels.

This distinctively personal tone in Winchilsea's poetry results in large part, I believe, from her being a woman – one who could not see herself as a public spokesman. Women would not feel it appropriate to voice institutional attitudes, because they were excluded from organized intellectual activity. Winchilsea certainly resented this exclusion: indignantly, as she claimed that a woman had a right to be a poet; wistfully, as she envisioned the easy comradeship of men exchanging witty conversation and knowledgeable criticism at a London tavern:

> Happy You three! happy the Race of Men!
> Born to inform or to correct the Pen
> To proffitts pleasures freedom and command
> Whilst we beside you but as Cyphers stand
> T'increase your Numbers and to swell th'account
> Of your delights which from our charms amount.

Her regrets for what she is missing lead her to open protest against the assumption that women are a mere peripheral part of the human race; it is little consolation to be men's occasional love objects, if that is all they can be ('A Poem, Occasion'd by the Sight of the 4th Epistle Lib. Epist: 1. of Horace').

But it is unlikely that such restrictions significantly cramped the development of her particular talent. Of course she was exceptionally fortunate: she was of sufficiently high social station to be safe at least from crude ridicule and to be free of Financial pressure and domestic drudgery; her leisure was increased by her childlessness and her enforced retirement from public life (when the Finches' patrons, King James and Queen Mary of Modena, were driven from the kingdom), which also gave her constant contact with nature, her primary source of inspiration. She had a loving and beloved husband, who not only permitted but encouraged her to write (and even publish), and she was surrounded by relatives and friends who did the same. Not only was she relatively free of inhibitions on her writing in general, but the circumstances of her life encouraged her to develop her particular gifts. It is probable that the personal lyrics and nature descriptions she did write are far better than the satires and philosophical poetry she might have written.

Always working within Augustan forms, Winchilsea adapted them as necessary to fit her distinctive talent and point of view, and in doing so she added a much-needed feminine voice to a masculine tradition. On the most basic level, the fact that her poems make a woman's consciousness the center of awareness distinguishes them in a literature where women generally appear only as an incidental part of life, as they do in Pomfret's 'The Choice' and most Augustan love poetry. In Winchilsea's love poems, woman appears not as an object to be idealized or fantasized about, but a human subject expressing her own feelings. In her poems on friendship, women are seen outside of sexual relationships, giving ardent affection or wise guidance to one another.[19] In her satire on women, the satirist is not a censor scolding or instructing an inferior class, but a right-minded person criticizing other human beings for degrading themselves below the standards which all should meet. Winchilsea's experience as a woman heightened her sensitivity to many things less evident to male contemporaries, especially the social restrictions upon human liberty. It is possible that she gained as much as she lost by her isolation from the masculine tradition, that this isolation, freeing her from conventional thought and feeling, helped her to develop her unique poetic voice.

Notes

1. See, for example, 'Song. Upon a Punch Bowl' and 'La Passion Vaincue'. All Winchilsea's poems will be quoted from *The Poems of Anne Countess of Winchilsea*, ed. Myra Reynolds (Chicago: University of Chicago Press, 1903).

2. Sedley's otherwise touching tribute to Celia says the whole female sex 'can but afford / The Handsome and the Kind'. Sir Charles Sedley, *The Poetical and Dramatic Works*, ed. V. De Sola Pinto (London: Constable and Co., 1928), I, 7.

3. WILLIAM WYCHERLEY, *The Complete Works*, ed. Montague Summers (New York: Russell & Russell, 1964), IV, 8.

4. See SEDLEY, I, 17–19; Wycherley, IV, 39–40.

5. See WYCHERLEY, IV, 249, and John Wilmot, Earl of Rochester, *The Complete Poems*, ed. David M. Vieth (New Haven: Yale University Press, 1968), pp. 37–40.

6. ROCHESTER, pp. 10–11, 81, 87–88. Compare Wycherley, III, 100; and Matthew Prior, *The Literary Works*, ed. H. Bunker Wright and Monroe K. Spears (Oxford: Clarendon Press, 1959), I, 705.

7. PRIOR, *Literary Works*, I, 441, 444–45, 707–708. Prior was decidedly unkind to Chloe in real life as well.

8. Her fondness for pastoral names for her husband, herself (Ardelia), and her friends is the most obvious concession to convention in her work.

9. The feminine point of view appears more seriously in her song 'The Nymph, in vain, bestows her pains', which counteracts the usual picture of joyous drinking by soberly describing what it is like to be married to an alcoholic.
    Some of Winchilsea's lyrics are, it is true, conventional for her period: for example, a complimentary poem to Prior (*Poems*, p. 102), 'The Bargain', 'A Song. Melinda to Alcander', 'Timely Advice to Dorinda', 'A Pastoral Dialogue: Between Two Shepherdesses'. But, despite the emphasis on female beauty in these songs, her more consistent attitude is represented by 'Clarinda's Indifference at Parting with Her Beauty', which puts in their place the joys of love as celebrated by male poets. What did beauty ever get her, Clarinda asks – certainly not 'a pleasing rule', meaning a satisfying influence over a man.

10. Interestingly, Rochester expressed values similar to Winchilsea's in his 'A Letter from Artemisia in the Town to Chloe in the Country', where he chose a woman for his mouthpiece.

11. See REYNOLDS' note to this poem, p. 420. Winchilsea added four lines on Wycherley to her poem, including specific mention of his satire on women.

12. WINCHILSEA's 'The Circuit of Apollo' likewise shows her distinctive adaptation of a popular Restoration form, in which a clear-sighted judge reviews contemporary poets. Her version differs from the usual both because the roster of poets is female and because – remarkably in a genre that consisted of wholesale detraction relieved only by a little grudging praise – she indulges in no acrimony against her contemporaries. She commends even Aphra Behn, though admitting that she wrote 'a little too loosly'. The only satire in the poem is directed against the conceited posturing of the male judge, Apollo, and his complacent assumption that he can easily cajole women. Contrast Rochester's 'An Allusion to Horace, the Tenth Satyr of the First Book', which finds nothing but faults in most contemporary poets, including Dryden.

13. In 'The Equipage', a translation from l'Abbé Reigner, she wishes for the qualities that will help her get through the vicissitudes of life; they are exactly what a virtuous man would wish for: justice, charity, independence, truth, health, and gaiety.

14. Compare JOHN STUART MILL's analysis of women's lack of time as an impediment to creative endeavor, in *The Subjection of Women, Essays on Sex Equality*, ed. Alice S. Rossi (Chicago: University of Chicago Press, 1970), pp. 209–211.

15. PRIOR, pp. 437–38. It used to be thought that Phoebe Clinket, the female author in *Three Hours*, was a satire on Winchilsea; but it is now agreed that their numerous disparities refute this theory. The identification does show the popular tendency to lump together all women authors, as if no distinctions among them could counterbalance the one anomaly they shared: being female and writers.

16. In the 'Preface' that follows her 'Introduction', Winchilsea declares that she cannot help writing and showing her works to friends, thus implying that a poet's talent cannot (and should not) be suppressed. But she goes on to suggest that her poems represent lapses from rational conduct and that she withholds them from publication not only to avoid abuse as a woman author, but because they are not worthy of publication.

17. *Literary Criticism of William Wordsworth*, ed. Paul Zall (Lincoln: University of Nebraska Press, 1966), p. 173.

18. Contrast Winchilsea's 'The Tree', where she appreciates the tree for itself – its beauty and shade – not for its utility as lumber.

19. See, for example, 'The Losse' (a lament for a woman friend who has died), 'Friendship Between Ephelia and Ardelia' (an Augustan version of 'How do I love thee'), 'Some Reflections. In a Dialogue Between Teresa and Ardelia' (Teresa's wise correction of Ardelia for a lapse in faith), and 'The Petition for an Absolute Retreat' (a section on how Arminda's love has helped her). She frequently compared the love between herself and a woman friend to that of David and Jonathan, there being no biblical or literary precedents for friendship between women. In 'An Epistle, From Ardelia to Mrs. Randolph' she even applies the biblical phrase that their love surpassed the love of women (meaning, of course, as in the Bible, that their love surpassed sexual love).

12 Anne Finch Placed and Displaced*

RUTH SALVAGGIO

French feminist theory, with its poststructuralist and psychoanalytic orientation, calls into question the political importance of reading women writers. Given that we perceive and understand the world through patriarchal discourse, there is no reason why a woman should write differently than a man; and given that gender difference is also linguistically produced, what chiefly matters in the struggle against patriarchy are not real, biological women, but the construct 'woman', patriarchy's repressed and marginalized Other. *Ecriture féminine*, which may or may not be written by a woman, disrupts the male symbolic order by staging the return of the repressed and excluded. Ruth Salvaggio's essay seeks to reconcile the French feminist interest in 'woman' with the Anglo-American concern for the historical predicament of actual women. She reads Finch's poetry both as the product of a woman writer displaced, as a woman, from Enlightenment culture and as a form of feminine writing – fluid, indeterminate – which subverts that culture's hierarchical discourses.

To be sure, we can only muse in the twilight byways of bad faith upon the positive reality of the Mystery; like certain marginal hallucinations, it dissolves under the attempt to view it fixedly.

(SIMONE DE BEAUVOIR)

Femininity . . . is not the opposite of masculinity but that which subverts the very opposition of masculinity and femininity.

(SHOSHANA FELMAN)

---

* Reprinted from Ruth Salvaggio, *Enlightened Absence: Neoclassical Configurations of the Feminine* (Urbana and Chicago: University of Illinois Press, 1988), pp. 105–26.

A Monarck he, and ruler of the day,
A fav'rite She, that in his beams does play.

(ANNE FINCH)

As a Woman

Anne Finch had a special fondness for shade. We might even say that
shady retreats were the landscape of her poetic imagination. Like
Alexander Pope's grotto and Isaac Newton's 'dark Chamber', these
partially illuminated areas became the spaces in which the creative
imagination generated its offspring. Nestling herself in these shady
areas, Finch would seem to partake in the same kind of birthing
process archetypally associated with the journeyer who seeks inspiration
in deep, dark spaces.[1] And yet I sense something different happening
with Finch, something distinct about the feminine retreat to shade. This
difference, it seems to me, requires an entirely 'other' reading of the
mythic descent into darkness and resurrection to light. For Newton
and Pope, I suggested that we use the terms of the dark-light as duality
to understand their inability to accommodate in their systems the
fusions and minglings of color. For Finch, however, I want to suggest
that we need to change the very terms of the dark-light myth. If the
feminine associations of darkness and the masculine associations of
light constitute a structure within which we can and have charted the
progress of man, we are going to have to dismantle this structure if we
want to begin to understand the *process* of woman.

I read Finch's desire for shade as both a shattering of light and
Enlightenment, and a disruption of structures long associated with
the systems of man. While Newton and Pope tried to force color to
conform to the definition of their universal systems, Finch, rejecting
the spaces of pure light and pure darkness, entered instead the
vaguely defined space of shade. If, as I will be suggesting, this space is
profoundly feminine, it does not simply oppose the light of man or the
darkness associated with woman. It splits that duality from within.
Shade is not the opposite of light. Instead, it is that which subverts
the opposition of light and darkness. Like Newton's 'Lady', Pope's
colorful women, and Swift's disruptive woman, the shade that Anne
Finch sought became a configuration of woman that could not be
accommodated within the structures of Enlightenment systems. And
in subverting the opposition of light and darkness, it also became, as
Shoshana Felman might say, a process that subverted the opposition
of the masculine and the feminine. For Finch, shade was not simply a

243

retreat, but the process of a radical displacement that was hers both as a 'woman' who wrote, and as a poet who wrote 'woman'.

The question of what it means to read and write 'as a woman' has recently generated a good deal of commentary and controversy.[2] And the problem seems to hinge on the word *woman*. From one perspective, that adopted by many feminist critics in the United States, *woman* refers particularly and explicitly to the female human being: to read or write 'as a woman' is to do so from the vantage point of a female whose biological and cultural identity shapes her responses as different from those of the male's. From another perspective, one more commonly associated with the French feminist writers, the term *woman* refers less to an individual person and more to a process, specifically those processes that disrupt the structures of male discourse and systems: to read or write 'as a woman' is to subvert those structures and open man's systems to the space of the 'other'. Both of these feminist perspectives have generated radical changes within academic disciplines by fostering entirely new and different visions of our cultural past and its bearing on the future. Yet within the feminist movement, there is some tension between those who see themselves involved in two apparently different projects – a concern with the historical predicament of actual 'women', and a concern with the disruptive and feminine processes of 'woman'.[3]

I write about Anne Finch in an attempt to capture the positive energies of that tension, and to seek in it the feminine potential for a writing that exceeds the dualistic oppositions fundamental to systematic thought, especially the opposition of 'women/woman'. In asking what it means for Finch to write 'as a woman', I have found that it means to write simultaneously in the historical predicament of an actual woman, and through the process of disruption that was suppressed in the discourse of Newton, Pope, and Swift. Anne Finch, it seems to me, is one of many woman writers who challenge us to explore the connections between the largely feminist concern with recovering the lost women of history, and the largely theoretical concern with figuring loss and absence as feminine. And she is particularly challenging because she writes 'as a woman' during that age that, as Alice Jardine explains, was bent on the consolidation and perfection of systems.[4] I try to read and write about Finch in response to that challenge – to speak at once about the concrete experience of a woman writer displaced among the major figures of the English Enlightenment, and about the process of displacement that is so alive in her poetry. Finch was a woman clearly displaced within and from her culture, but she was also a woman whose writing – in voicing and celebrating that displacement – became a feminine process that exceeded both Enlightenment systems and the larger classical structures that they epitomized.

The implications of this double displacement can tell us much both *about* and *beyond* the historical period we know as the English Enlightenment. Reading Finch within the context of England's classical age, for instance, makes it possible to understand her 'displacement' during this age in the same ways that we have conventionally understood the firmly 'placed' positions of Newton, Swift, and Pope. Just as I sought in these men the feminine configurations of absence that made their systems possible, I also seek in Finch the feminine identity and process that made her own absence from the Enlightenment world inevitable. But I also try to understand Finch's predicament in terms that exceed her historical context . . . To 'place' Anne Finch in the Enlightenment world is to add new material to a literary canon still dominated by Enlightenment men and their well-structured systems. To account for her 'displacement' within those systems, however, is to account for those very omissions of history that make 'man's story' possible. We cannot place Finch in a historical context when her womanly identity has already situated her among the material whose absence made that history possible. We cannot restore any woman to history when the system of history itself is constructed by and through the exclusion of woman – both the actual women of history, and the feminine configuration of otherness that she embodies.

And so my reading of Finch will take me beyond her historical place and displacement in the Enlightenment, and into many of our contemporary theoretical concerns with the process of reading and writing. That is to be expected, since Finch's virtual 'absence' from literary history is directly related to the gaps between history and theory, between the actual 'woman writer' and the process of 'feminine writing'. But I do not want to lose Finch to absence. In her descriptions of brightly colored tapestries, nocturnal reveries, and absolute retreats, I try to recover the discourse of the 'other' that was suppressed by Enlightenment men. In attempting this, I do not want to place Finch within systems from which she was excluded and whose values she was continually questioning. What she shared with the notable men of the Enlightenment was a fascination with the 'other' discourse which revealed itself in Newton's alchemy and optical fusions, in the problem that both Newton and Pope had with color, in Swift's fluid and disruptive writing. But what makes Finch different is that she did not suppress this discourse. Instead, she immersed herself in it – in much the same ways that Newton, Swift, and Pope celebrated systems of universal order. Occupying this seemingly impossible place of displacement, Finch is already outside the history to which we might return her. What's more, she has already questioned the terms of her return to that history. She has already made herself the subject of theories that seek to discover the material abandoned by history. She has moved into the shady realm where all the metaphoric associations of light and Enlightenment were eclipsed.

Wandering through shade

In a poem addressed to her husband, Finch invites him to leave his studies in mathematics and painting, and accompany her on a walk through the fields. The specific terms that she uses almost make the invitation seem as though it were an appeal to abandon the orderly world of Enlightenment systems, especially as she asks him to leave his 'busy compasses' that measure the ground, and the 'Rich colors' that he carefully applies to his painting.[5] In walking away from the controlled world of measurement and art, Finch 'strays', as she puts it, from two of the *'usual Employments'* of the age – two particular employments that we might easily associate with Newton's physics and Pope's controlled verse. She enters instead a natural world of 'disorder'd beauty', one that is 'Warm without Sun, and shady without rain' (1–5). Her preference for shade, or what we might more properly call her desire for shade, is directly related to her retreats *from* the masculine world that she associates with husband, science, and a poetry of men. It is also a desire that she expresses again and again throughout her verse. In the 'Introduction' to the manuscript collection of her poems, for instance, she concludes by acknowledging her 'fallen' abilities as a woman writer and accepts her position not in the light of men but in an obscure darkness: 'For groves of Lawrell, thou wert never meant; / Be dark enough thy shades, and be thou there content' (63–64). Her poem 'On Myselfe' concludes in a similar way, calling attention to her 'slight' abilities and to her 'retirement' from the 'Sun' where she will 'bless the shade'. Often these areas of shade are juxtaposed to those places where Finch prefers not to be, where her absence is her own choice. In 'Upon Ardelia's Return Home', Finch describes herself as having 'stray'd' far from home and into a 'secret shade' that she has difficulty leaving (24). When a friend invites her to the 'Town', she replies, in 'Ardelia's Answer to Ephelia' that she would prefer 'some shade' for her 'Pallace' (5). And in her 'Petition for an Absolute Retreat', a world of 'Windings' and 'Shade' becomes a place entirely other than the world of 'Crouds, and Noise' – a place where she wants to construct her own reality. [. . .]

Finch's shady world is, of course, the world of nature, and her continual excursions into this green world have prompted several critics to read her in terms of Wordsworth's belief that she was one of the first great nature poets.[6] No doubt Finch did distinguish herself from contemporary poets by writing a *kind* of nature poetry that differed from descriptions of manicured gardens and neatly designed landscapes. And yet there is much in her verse that is distinctly non-Romantic, qualities easy to understand when we keep in mind that Finch lived during the time when Restoration wits and Augustan writers were dominating the literary scene, and that she inevitably expressed many of their values and desires in her poetry.[7] Her longing for shade, however, was clearly not one of these Augustan values. Perhaps we could say, then, that Finch's displacement as a writer resulted from her different literary subjects – that in retreating to a shady, natural world, Finch simply deviated from the subjects that normally preoccupied her contemporaries.

Perhaps. There is, however, another subject to which Finch returns again and again in her poetry – the subject of her being a woman, of her being *different* because she is a woman. If her interest in nature has prompted some readers to place Finch among the nature poets, her concern about being a woman has more recently prompted others to place her within a tradition of women writers. Distinguishing Finch from the 'masculinist' writing of Wordsworth and Shelley, for instance, Sandra Gilbert and Susan Gubar have called attention to Finch as one of the first women writers to be painfully aware of her predicament as a woman. They recognize Finch as the woman who 'struggles to escape the male designs in which she feels herself enmeshed', who was 'imprisoned' by the very anxieties she felt about her ability to write at all.[8] And Katharine Rogers, who has put together the only edition of Finch's poems now readily available, distinguishes Finch in this same way, describing her as 'a woman imprisoned in man-made conventions'.[9] If Finch did feel trapped within man's world – the world not only of her contemporary writers but even of her husband and his 'Employments' with mathematics and painting – it would seem that her retreats into a shady natural world were directly related to her retreats *from* the domain of man and *into* the space of woman. It was not simply that she happened to write poetry about nature, but that her retreats to the shady, natural world were poetic ways of figuring her displacement, as a woman, in and from the Enlightenment world of men. Nature, shade, and woman all become linked in their associations with displacement.

Finch herself confirmed these linkages in her own configuration of woman, as she figured herself wandering through shady natural haunts. In 'The Appology', she explains her particular 'weaknesse' as that of the 'Woman' who must 'write tho' hopelesse to succeed', and reconciles herself to the fate of one who must 'follow through the Groves a wand'ring Muse'. This 'wand'ring Muse' seems especially descriptive of Finch herself, who typically 'strays' along 'winding' paths, and whose shady world seems to complement her own feminine deviations from the fixed world of pure light or darkness. The very process of 'wand'ring' and 'wav'ring' is one that Finch directly associated with both her retreats into nature and the very notion of woman. In her poem 'Adam Pos'd', she describes Eve as that elusive and perplexing 'New Element' in Adam's world. While his 'Skill' is that of fixing things in place, of assigning 'Just Appellations to Each several Kind', Eve's 'wav'ring Form' resists his attempts to give 'this Thing a Name'. This 'thing' that wanders and strays, that eludes man's attempt to fix it in place, that figures in his 'grand narrative' as Eve – could she be that fluid, continuous, diffusable 'woman-thing' about whom contemporary feminist theorists are speaking?[10] If I am correct in suggesting that Finch's configuration of woman involved both a portrayal of herself and the winding, shady spaces to which she retreated, then the 'woman-thing' in her poetry gives us a picture of both the 'woman writer' that Finch was, and the 'writing of woman' in which she engaged.

Two particular poems, I think, call attention to these concepts of woman that distinguish Finch not only as different from her contemporary male writers, but as herself a configuration of that which was necessarily absent from and displaced within their fixed systems. In her 'Petition for an Absolute Retreat', she longs for a place 'That the World may ne'er invade', a retreat through 'Windings' and 'Shade' (5–6). But what is especially interesting about this poem is its detailed vision of that other 'World'. She asks not for the 'Patriarch's Board', but a table containing 'Fruits' that 'did in *Eden* grow,' food that she describes as 'plain', yet that seems to exceed its own containment: 'Grapes, with Juice so crouded up, / As breaking thro' the native Cup; / Figs (yet growing) candy'd o'er, / By the Sun's attracting Pow'r' (30–47). For her garments, she wants something like the 'dazling white' robe of Solomon, though, as she is quick to add, 'not so Gay' – nor so stunningly light (64).[11] Instead of pure white, she would have color:

> Let me, when I must be fine,
> In such natural Colours shine;
> Wove, and painted by the Sun,
> Whose resplendent Rays to shun,
> When they do too fiercely beat,
> Let me find some close Retreat,
> Where they have no Passage made,
> Thro' those Windings, and that Shade.

(96–103)

Such notions of excess, figured in these descriptions of Edenic fruit and woven colors, seem to reflect a desire to transgress and blur fixed boundaries – a desire that Enlightenment men found both fascinating and threatening, and that they continually associated with woman. Finch's colors, however, are not the colors of Newton and Pope. Nor is the sun, which threatens to beat 'too fiercely', that source of light in which, as Newton put it, 'great and good men shine and illuminate others'.[12] Finch's retreat takes her away from the world of definition and light, and into a fluid time that she figures as 'some River' that 'slides away, / To encrease the boundless Sea' (130–31). What is perhaps most revealing of the feminine quality of her retreat is that she imagines transforming its shady space into a 'wond'rous Cave', not simply any cave, but like the particular one that Crassus escaped to when he fled the rage of Marius. Yet while Crassus, Finch tells us, was hardly 'content' with his cave, Finch would transform hers into a 'wond'rous' dwelling only partially illuminated, and filled with 'Rising Springs' that 'stray' over the ground (202–33).

This 'Absolute Retreat', this place of absence, was not simply some natural abode desired by the Romantic writer as he sought to discover his poetic voice in nature. Far from it, Finch's retreat took her away from man's poetic voice, absolutely away from his world, and into an other space that displays all the markings and configurations of woman. But I have suggested that it was not only Finch's descriptions of herself and her retreats that betrayed her 'writing as a woman'. It was also her very configuration of shade and wandering and wavering as feminine, as that elusive substance of a 'woman-thing'. In her poem 'Clarinda's Indifference at Parting with Her Beauty', Finch describes the very process of being woman in terms of wandering airs, fading colors, restless time, and spreading shades. The space of these movements and minglings is the very face of a woman parting with her beauty. Like Eve's 'wav'ring Form', Clarinda's cannot quite be captured and fixed by man. Finch configures this elusive quality in terms that might well remind us of Newton's inability to fix the minglings of light and color: her face is like 'Those morning beams, that strongly warm, and shine, / Which men that feel and see, can ne're define' (7–8). As woman is transformed through the processes of 'restless time', she leaves behind the light of morning for 'ev'ning shades' that begin 'to rise, and spread' (9–10).

What Finch describes as 'Clarinda's Indifference' to this process, to the loss of 'That youthfull air, that wanders ore the face' (5), is something we might well regard in terms of Finch's own acceptance of her process as woman – her identity as a 'woman writer' and as a poet who 'writes as a woman'. She accepts change and transformation, welcomes the 'shades' that take her away from man's world of light and into the process that is woman. Understanding Finch's longing for shade in terms of her own identity and writing as woman, we are perhaps in a better position to appreciate what shade meant to her, what her excursions into and figurations of shade tell us about a poet who wrote during a time when men were consumed with the 'Discourse of Light'. I would suggest that shade was the absent space in which Finch, as a woman writer, was displaced. At the same time it was also the feminine space that she desired. In both of these functions, it became a configuration of absence that was somewhere between the light that men desired and the darkness that they feared. It was in this displaced area between light and darkness that Anne Finch's shade became the undoing of the light-dark duality through which Enlightenment men figured their pursuits. In saying this, I am suggesting that shade for Finch was much like color for both Newton and Pope, and like fluidity for Swift. Just as color and fluidity exceeded the definition of system, so shade exceeded the very definition of light and dark, of liquid and solid. It seeps, as Catherine Clément might say, through the 'cracks in an overall system'.[13] And what it produces is not the enlightened world of man, but a world of fusion and process that is, in the case of Finch, the identity and writing of a woman.

But the comparison with Newton, Swift, and Pope ends here. When color and fluid infiltrated their systems, they reacted by imposing strict controls, by trying to force it to serve as part of the definition of man's systems. Anne Finch had little reason to defend these systems. She rejected the age's literary preoccupation with satire just as soundly as she walked away from the 'Employments' of her husband. 'I never suffer'd my small talent, to be that way employ'd,' she wrote when distinguishing her poetry from the 'abusive verses' of her contemporaries, verses that could be produced, as she said, by anyone 'who can but make two words rime....'[14] That she should describe her dislike for the dominant literary forms in terms of a 'facility' to 'make two words rime' is curious in itself. The closed couplet, after all, epitomized the rage for order and structure that revealed itself in eighteenth-century literary form, and though Finch relied on this general structure in most of her poems, she clearly wanted to avoid being considered any kind of 'Versifying Maid of Honour'.[15] We might well regard her disparaging view of the ability to 'make two words rime' as an indictment and rejection of the very compulsion to rally around structures, especially those structures in which she had no place and from which she desired to 'retreat'.

Her retreat into shade, then, was neither from light to dark nor from dark to light. It did not function within such a dualistic and 'coupled' economy. Shade was the configuration of Finch's attempt, as a woman, to come to terms with her displacement by mingling light and dark, by fusing and confusing its dualistic construction. I suggested earlier that if we are to understand what shade meant to Finch, we will have to dismantle the terms of the light-dark myth, the myth in which a man descends into darkness only to recover his own image and ultimately ascend to the world of light and himself. This dismantling, it seems to me, is figured not only in Finch's retreat to shade, but also in the processes of wandering, straying, and wavering – processes that take us away from the myth of light and dark, and bring us once again into the realm of color. What distinguishes these colors, however, is that they are woven together by women.

The weaving process

Finch approached her shady retreats through winding paths, by straying and wandering and, we might say, 'weaving' herself through her own poetic imagination. If this meandering approach constitutes a feminine deviation from the Enlightenment preoccupation with structure and hierarchy, how are we to recover the values associated with such deviation? How are we to recover, in Finch's poetry, the writing 'of a woman' and 'as a woman' that was suppressed in Enlightenment discourse? I suggest that we do this not simply by turning our attention away from the fixed categories and structures in which Enlightenment men contained phenomena, but by seeking 'other' metaphors of engagement with phenomena – metaphors that might allow us to recognize the values of both a 'woman' and a 'feminine writing' that strays and wanders.

And so I turn – with Finch herself, and with several feminist critics today – to the process of weaving and the myth of Arachne. This myth became for Finch a story about both herself as a writer and the more general plight of a woman 'writing as woman'. The story has also, perhaps not coincidentally, become the subject of recent commentary from literary critics who differ in their reading of Arachne's narrative – notably female critics interested in recovering the lost woman writer whom Arachne represents, and male theorists interested in using Arachne's feminine weaving as a kind of metaphor of textual 'indeterminacy'. I want to explore these different understandings of the Arachne story in terms of their bearing both on Finch herself and on the process of writing-as-weaving that becomes, through Finch, a feminine configuration of that which subverts classical systems.

Introducing a chapter in their study of *The Madwoman in the Attic*, Gilbert and Gubar cite these lines from Finch's poem 'A Description of One of the Pieces of Tapestry at Long-Leat' where Finch speaks about Arachne.

Thus *Tapestry* of old, the Walls adorn'd,
Ere noblest Dames the artful *Shuttle* scorn'd:
Arachne, then, with Pallas did contest,
And scarce th'Immortal Work was judg'd the Best.
Nor valorous Actions, then, in Books were fought;
But all the Fame, that from the Field was brought,
Employ'd the *Loom*, where the kind *Consort* wrought:
Whilst sharing in the Toil, she shar'd the Fame,
And with the *Heroes* mixt her interwoven Name.
No longer, *Females* to such Praise aspire,
And serfdom now We rightly do admire.
So much, All Arts are by the *Men* engross'd,
And Our few Talents unimprov'd or cross'd.[16]

Finch's particular account of Arachne's weaving, as Gilbert and Gubar point out, is 'closely associated with the female fall from authority'.[17] Arachne, though the loser in the weaving contest with Pallas, was at least able *through* her weaving to mix 'her interwoven Name' with that of heroes. For Finch, however, such a fate is 'No longer' possible. 'All Arts' are now dominated by '*Men*', she tells us, and the 'few Talents' of women remain 'unimprov'd or cross'd'. Figuring her own fallen lot as a woman writer by contrasting it with Arachne's, Finch associates her writing with the process of weaving. But it is a process that seems to take her nowhere – or to take her, perhaps, into that space of nowhere that I have been describing as displacement and absence. In her poem 'The Bird and the Arras', Finch relates a similar story. Mistaking a 'well wrought Arras for a shade', a bird hopes to rest there in order to avoid 'the scortchings of the sultry Noon'. Once inside the room in which this tapestry is hung, the bird, described by Finch as 'she', tries to fly into its skies – only to be 'dash'd' to the ground, unable to escape the room in which she is an 'imprison'd wretch' and left 'Flutt'ring in endless cercles of dismay.' The fall of the bird is perhaps akin to Finch's own fallen predicament as a woman writer, and as one whose weaving fails even to attain the recognition given to Arachne.

Yet in weaving a poetry that will go unrecognized, as caught within the very process of weaving itself – Finch would seem not so much to differ from Arachne, as she would seem to be exactly in her predicament. Her art, like Arachne's weaving, has found a place in the myths of man only to be eclipsed by a poetry that relates the exploits and victories of the gods. Pallas, the victor, weaves the story of those victories, while Arachne spins depictions of women who were their victims. Arachne loses the contest in the same way that Finch must necessarily lose: in writing and weaving about women, they are pitted against the very forces whose prominence and splendor have already been inscribed in our mythic and poetic consciousness. Not only fallen *from* authority, but also fallen *within* the very process of her weaving, the woman writer is doomed, like Arachne, to take on the shape of an insignificant creature who ceaselessly spins webs.

If she is afraid that her writing will not be able to compete in the poetic contests of men, Finch nonetheless continues to weave – to wander and stray through her shady retreats. She chooses, in other words, to write a poetry figured through weaving even though she knows that her fate as such a writer is not even as promising as Arachne's. To understand why Finch does this, and what compels her to reject fixed systems and structures in favor of weaving, we need to probe deeper into the associations between woman and weaving. We need to inquire into the nature of the process itself, and discover its peculiar feminine qualities. Gilbert and Gubar, who seek these associations in the work of several women writers, call attention to the myths of both Arachne and Ariadne – mythic women who weave their way through their own prisons, and who serve as the prototypes of women writers who must spin their way through the 'problematic' nature of their narratives.[18] More recently, Nancy K. Miller has used the term *Arachnologies* to describe both 'a figuration of woman's relation of production to the dominant culture' and 'a possible parable . . . of a feminist poetics'. If we are to recover women's writing, Miller argues, we need to 'reappropriate' the story of Arachne – read it not in terms of a 'web of indifferentiation' but as the construction of 'a new object of reading, women's writing'.[19]

As much as I agree that we need to 'reappropriate' the story of Arachne for the woman writer, I wonder if we should not be just as concerned with the dangers of appropriation, an act that Hélène Cixous associates with the male's attempt to reach out and claim woman only so that he can finally 'return to himself'.[20] Nancy Miller, for instance, wants very much to distinguish between the poststructural appropriation of mythic stories about women weaving, and the feminist reappropriation of the woman artist. What she particularly has in mind are the 'deconstructive' readings of Arachne and Ariadne by Geoffrey Hartman and J. Hillis Miller who, instead of recognizing the victimized women in these mythic stories, find in woman and her associations with textual weaving a metaphor of language.[21] Although I sense the urgency of Nancy Miller's caution that we 'preserve women from the fate of woman' (p. 283), I also sense the urgency of recovering the indeterminate and subversive processes that have long been associated with woman, so that we can tap their energies in transforming a world that has been all too exclusively structured and hierarchized. The question is not so much whether we can 'preserve women from the fate of woman', but why we should want to recover women writers at all if we cannot locate in their writing a profound critique of exclusive systems. If we are to seek in women's writing a poetics that is truly other than and different from that associated with masculine writing, and especially if we are discovering that difference in the process of weaving, it seems to me that we should acknowledge and celebrate the feminine process of textual indeterminacy that undoes the 'grand narratives' of man, narratives largely responsible for the suppression of both women writers and a writing of the feminine. We need to be open to a reading of woman's texts not only as narrative tapestries different from those of men, but as processes of weaving that dismantle the structure of his narratives.

An important part of this effort is to read the story of Arachne as Nancy Miller reads Finch's description of her tapestry, in the 'tradition of recognition that Gilbert and Gubar have described, in a gesture meant to restore woman to her text . . .' (p. 287). We need to acknowledge, in this way, the very different values attached to a literature that is spun by women – webs that, as Virginia Woolf said, '"are the work of suffering human beings, and are attached to grossly material things, like health and the houses we live in"'.[22] Following the urgings of such feminist critics as Gilbert, Gubar, and Miller, we can come to discover in Finch the actual woman who wrote, the female person who found her poetic voice through the process of weaving her way through shady retreats, wandering and straying within and away from the systems of her male contemporaries. Yet at the same time we also need to recognize in this weaving the process of subversion that undoes the 'grand narratives', the process of 'writing as a woman' that has already inscribed Finch as displaced within Enlightenment systems just as it had inscribed Arachne's woven narrative as 'other' to Pallas's account of the conquests of the classical gods.

If Finch's retreats into shade, as I suggested earlier, do not simply oppose the light of Enlightenment, but shatter and subvert the very opposition of light and dark, I would suggest that her engagement with the process of weaving not only opposes the fixed systems of Enlightenment thought, but instead subverts the very construction of those systems. In her poem 'The Prodigy', Finch cautions women not to be moved by men who proclaim their love for them: 'Assert your pow'r in early days begun, / Born to undo, be not yourselves undone' (51–52). We might read her caution in terms of the myth of Arachne who also wove the story of women victimized by love. While Pallas weaves her depiction of the grand exploits of the gods, Arachne weaves a very different picture – of women who were loved and then betrayed by the gods. In one sense, Arachne constructs a definite narrative, a narrative about women. In another sense, however, her weaving undoes Pallas's account, questioning the magnitude of the gods' conquests by removing them from their grandiose context, and setting them next to portrayals of their abuse and betrayal of women. To weave as Arachne weaves, we might say, is both to construct and dismantle – to deconstruct the narratives of man through the agency of woman.

If Finch does desire to enjoy the fate of Arachne, her desire is not only to construct a poetry as respectable as that of her contemporary male writers, but to dismantle the assumptions that have been used to designate their subjects as primary and important, and hers as secondary and inferior. She would not, I believe, reverse this hierarchy, but rather dissolve it. Like Swift, she preferred the disorder of the waters to the definition of the land, though unlike Swift, she had no qualms about saying so. In one of her songs, 'The Nymph, in vain, bestows her pains', Finch describes a nymph who tries to thrive in Bacchus's kingdom, but who ultimately finds herself drowned in 'his torrent' of 'Immages'. Finding him 'inaccessible, and cold', she says that he 'makes an Island, of the heart'. The very paradoxical idea of drowning on an island shows, I believe, Finch's own predicament as a weaver. She would weave a poetry that might be comparable to that of men – just as she herself would merge into the pleasures of Bacchus's kingdom. And yet she is overcome by the very pleasures she seeks – just as her identity and process as a woman makes that pleasure inaccessible, makes her heart into the 'Island' that she would shun.

Yet though she felt overcome by the very waters she sought – the fluid, wandering processes so different from the fixed islands and systems of the Enlightenment – Finch was nonetheless able to celebrate the fluid world with all its mixings and mergings. In 'The Bargain', she has Bacchus and Cupid engage in a dialog, debating whether Bacchus's reign over the 'mighty punch bowl' or Cupid's reign over 'hearts' and 'tears' is absolute. In the end, Cupid suggests that the two 'joyn' their realms, 'To mix my waters, with thy wine.' And in her Song 'For my Br. Les: Finch. Upon a Punch Bowl', she imagines 'the whole Universe floating' in a punch bowl that invites us to forget the 'Titles' and 'Places' of 'History'. All this is not to mention the flowing rivers and streams that figure in much of Finch's descriptions of nature, or the fluid and fusing colors of the natural world that mingle in her landscapes. These fusions blur the systematic distinctions that Enlightenment writers sought, just as shade shattered the light of pure emanation. No wonder Finch described poetry, in the final lines of 'Enquiry After Peace', as 'the feav'rish Fit, / Th' overflowing of unbounded Wit.' It overflows and exceeds boundaries just as the juices of her Edenic fruits described in the 'Petition for an Absolute Retreat' seem almost to burst their own forms, or as the river 'slides away' to 'the boundless sea'.

The 'woman-thing' described by Luce Irigaray as 'fluid', as 'continuous, compressible, dilatable, viscous, conductable, diffusable',[23] has much in common with the poststructural configuration of 'woman' as indeterminate and therefore subversive of enclosed structures. Yet this 'thing' is also intimately connected to the writing *of* woman and *as* woman that defines both feminine identity and process. For Cixous, such writing is also intimately connected with the body, with inexhaustible processes that exceed the systems and stratagems of the head, and that 'articulate the proliferation of meanings that runs through it in every direction'.[24] If we can envision the mind as producing the clarity and definition of illumination, we might envision the body as a kind of prism, generating the 'proliferation' of color. These colorful minglings and proliferations are also connected to the process of weaving, once again through the story of Arachne. Ovid describes the weaving contest as strikingly colorful. But what is perhaps more curious about his account is the way he describes the *fusions* of color. He speaks about those vague spaces where green becomes blue and blue becomes violet, the spaces between distinctions . that Newton was so determined to define. The dyed threads woven by Pallas and Arachne are as richly fused as Newton's colors – like a rainbow, Ovid says, that casts a thousand different colors that merge into each other and remain dazzlingly indistinguishable.[25]

That Finch herself was far more enamored with the weaving of colors than the fixity of light is something we can sense in the distance she perceives between her own work and that of the sun god. In her poem 'The Consolation', she describes Phoebus as a 'Monark' who is 'ruler of the day', and the 'soaring Lark' as 'A fav'rite She, that in his beams does play.' Associating herself with what we might regard as the feminine play of light and color rather than the godlike control of the sun, her consolation – though she ostensibly identifies it with the coming of morning – may well be that as a woman she does not need to defend the light of the gods or, I might add, the systems of man. Nor does she rely on the service of Apollo and light. In her 'Upon Ardelia's Return Home', she petitions Apollo for his 'Chariot', only to be refused and assigned instead to a 'water cart' that is transformed, through her own imaginative powers, into a 'tryumphant Charret' (88–89). This cart, a far cry from Apollo's chariot of the sun, rested in a 'Beeche's secret shade' (24) – the place to which Finch, as Ardelia, has 'stray'd', and from which she will be transported, like water, to her home.

Weaving herself through the reflections of light, through its shadows and colors, Finch also wove a poetry that was remarkably different from the poems of men we now recognize as the 'masters' of the age. Her different subjects made her, in a sense, opposite to them. But the process of her weaving was also a feminine subversion of the very structures – light and dark, solid and liquid, male and female – that they relied on to construct their 'grand narratives'. Finch reminds us that Arachne's story, told again and again throughout the centuries, is one that we must recover for the woman writer. But she also reminds us that the subversive force of Arachne's weaving is what makes her story worth recovering.

Nature, science, and caves

All along I have been describing Finch's displacement as a literary displacement that was 'en-gendered' by her identity 'as a woman' writer and her process of writing 'as a woman'. Reading Finch in terms of her historical, literary context only shows how she did not fit in that context – how her feminine wanderings and strayings into shady, natural retreats marked her difference from the very contemporary writers among whom she wanted a place. [. . .]

But what would happen if we were to read Finch's preoccupation for nature and straying and wandering in a scientific context, in terms of what I have been sketching out as the larger cultural context of Enlightenment systems that shaped both the classical structure of Augustan literature and the development of modern science? I pose this question because it seems to me that if we are to recover 'woman' as both identity and process, or as Irigaray would put it, if we are to '(re)discover a possible space for the feminine imaginary',[26] we need to envision her displacement within the larger spaces of the masculine world. It is not enough to say that Finch wrote nature poetry at a time when the vogue for nature poetry was not the literary fashion, or that she described herself as wandering away from fixed places and into shady retreats when her contemporary writers were seeking structure and illumination. Her *literary* preoccupations marked both her literary displacement and a profound *cultural* displacement through which she wrote as a woman. We need to remember that Finch wrote about wandering and wavering at a time when science was fixing the universe in place. We need to remember that she wrote about nature at a time when science had set out to dominate the natural world, which it had rendered again and again as feminine. [. . .]

Francis Bacon, we should recall, encouraged the scientist 'to follow and as it were hound nature in her wanderings', so that 'you will be able when you like to lead and drive her afterward to the same place again'.[27] He would seek, as Carolyn Merchant explained, to claim nature, and in so doing, to reclaim the dominion over nature that man lost through Eve in the garden.[28] In this scientific quest, Bacon was at one with a group of poets who reclaimed and celebrated the garden, and who made its neat design and perfect symmetry into a metaphor of their own sense of order. Pope's *Windsor-Fores* . . . not only epitomized a nature reflective of the designs of men, but one that provided a model of universal and imperial order – a world that England could clearly 'lead and drive', and master.

It is hard to imagine Anne Finch leading or driving nature anywhere. It is hard to imagine her own immersion in natural retreats as reflective of such attempts to control and master. But what is most important to realize about Finch's wandering through nature is not simply that she views nature differently, but that in her wanderings and absolute retreats she actually embodies the very material of the scientific conquest. If her excursions through nature took her into a place other than that which was the object of scientific and literary mastery, this other place, I would suggest, *was* the displacement of her identity and process as woman.

When science figures nature as woman, the woman who wanders through and writes about nature becomes a configuration of that which science seeks to dominate. Woman is already part of a sexual economy in which she functions as the desired object of man's appropriation. I have discussed, especially in the first two chapters of this book, the ways in which the feminist critiques of science are questioning its implicit androcentric and masculine bias. And I have tried to show, through my readings of Newton, Swift, and Pope, that the new science was hardly alone in its desire to differentiate itself from and appropriate phenomena that it variously regarded as feminine – that it was in league with a classical literature that was bent on the same desire to consolidate its systems. The connections between literature and science, in other words, are not only implicated in matters of gender, but reflect hierarchies that have been socially constructed and ingrained in our minds – hierarchies that privilege culture over nature, system and definition over disorder and fusion, male over female.[29] For if Enlightenment literature and science not only shared in the effort to consolidate systems but actually figured all that was displaced from these systems in terms of 'woman', it is impossible to view the exclusion of women from these systems as either a purely literary or distinctly scientific phenomenon. Woman's displacement – and we can see this all too directly in Finch's immersions in nature – was a necessary part of man's classical pursuits. A literary woman who wrote about nature, and who wrote about woman, figured as forcefully in the scientific quest for dominion as if she herself had been the metaphoric Lady whom Newton figured as the disturbing and problematic side of his otherwise fixed mathematical calculations.

When we hear Bacon speak of the scientist 'entering and penetrating into those holes and corners when the inquisition of truth is his whole object',[30] we might pause to think how profoundly the quest for truth has been figured in terms of the penetration of dark, isolated, and mysterious spaces. Alice Jardine even suggests that the exploration of such spaces is 'the very essence of philosophy', something we can understand more clearly when we consider 'the "exemplary images" used by philosophers since antiquity to define the world: for example, Plato's "cavern", Descartes' "closed room", Kant's "island", or, in another register, Kierkegaard's "finger in the mud"'.[31] If the philosophical purpose of this penetration is to fill the void, to think it into some shape and meaning, its sexual connotations are all too obvious. Jardine cites Michèle Montrelay's description of this philosophical quest in terms of a male fantasy: '"First",' Montrelay writes, '"a central tube which cannot be the closed and satisfying container of an interior. . . . Intestine, pipe, image of cavern, of dark, deep, inner spaces, all that exists, but submitted to forces of suction that empty them in the most painful fashion. Or else, the void is already established . . . Or else, the fullness is such a tremendous threat that it must be parried at all costs"' (p. 70). We have already seen in Pope the threatening fullness of the feminine cave, and the cost of his suppressing this fullness – the cost to woman. Belinda's 'Cave of Spleen' in his *Rape of the Lock*, the caves of Poetry and Truth in the *Dunciad*, Pope's own underground grotto – these are all feminine spaces in which he figured the void of thoughtlessness, whose fluid fullness so threatened him that he would have it suctioned out and replaced with the substance of thought, the material of the enlightened mind. His fantasy – like Bacon's, like that of philosophers since antiquity – is to penetrate the hole, claim dominion over the feminine cave, that darkest and deepest recess of nature.

And yet what of the woman in that cave? What of the woman who is the cave? In order to recover this woman and her subversive energies, we need to question not only the masculine assumptions inherent in any quest to 'penetrate' nature – inherent in the act of thrusting, intruding, and dominating – but also the unacknowledged assumption that these spaces are feminine and therefore an appropriate object of the male quest. We need to deconstruct, in other words, the philosophical system – the entire metaphysic – whose meaning and closure are dependent on the 'penetration' of cavelike spaces. Such a metaphysic is bent on a kind of excavation, a removal from the cave of that void which troubles the philosophical mind, so that it can claim dominion over the woman who occupies this space. Thus we find Orpheus making his way back to the world of light while Eurydice is abandoned to the caves of the underworld.[32] Then there is Echo, whose punishment – for falling in love with a man who was consumed with himself, and for warning vulnerable maidens of gods who would assault them – was to be imprisoned in caverns where her utterances would echo throughout the forests and hills. And there is the tradition of the gothic, particularly the gothic novel in the hands of many eighteenth-century women writers, where women encounter the horrors of their own sexuality by being sequestered in dark interior spaces, secret chambers, dungeons, locked staircases, and attics.[33]

Anne Finch also occupied caves, such as the one she described in her 'Petition for an Absolute Retreat', one that she would transform from a 'lonely' to a 'wond'rous' space. This 'wond'rous' cave that she seeks, I believe, is exactly that place of fullness not yet suctioned into thought, not yet conquered by the enlightened mind. It is, as she describes it, a 'commodious ample Cave', with 'Beds of Moss', 'Rising Springs', and 'Canopy'd with Ivy' (209–23). We might compare Finch's underground retreat with Pope's grotto, set with bits of mirror, where he enjoyed visual pleasures that he denied himself in the world of light. Or we might compare it to Newton's 'dark Chamber', where he, too, indulged in a space of reflected light. Yet while Pope and Newton organized their dark retreats into artificial structures that ultimately reflected and refracted the light of Enlightenment – places where their systems of thought were at once the subject of analysis and definition, Finch's retreat is steeped in the material of nature – moss, ivy, water – material that conceals the demarcations that the Enlightenment mind so desperately wanted to uncover.

But Finch's caves were not always so comforting to the woman who was seeking this 'Absolute Retreat', this space of 'Peace and Rest' – '(Peace and Rest are under Ground)' she says (233). Just as Pope's Belinda was plagued by her 'Cave of Spleen' with all its inversions, hallucinations, and distortions, so Anne Finch was plagued by 'Spleen' – her own cave, the cave in which she figured her tormented femininity. Finch's poem, 'The Spleen', perhaps her most famous,[34] shows not only the personal cost to the woman who writes, but the cost of writing 'as a woman' during an age that often figured woman in terms of disease. The Enlightenment, as we have seen, was fascinated with hysteria and hypochondria, a fascination that shows the intricate connections that the age forged linking disease, madness, and woman.[35] It can hardly be coincidental that Anne Finch, the female poet how achieving recognition in the Augustan literary canon, should describe herself as infected with the hysteria that the age figured through woman. For as I have already suggested, she herself – as a woman – was the substance of that which science excluded from its systems and attempted to appropriate. With Newton, Swift, and Pope, we can watch the male dynamics of this appropriation in action: as the man seeks to establish his orderly system, he purges it of disorderly elements that he renders as woman. With Finch, however, we witness some very different dynamics in action. Hysteria begins to speak. But it is not an uncontrolled hysteria, not complete madness or otherness. It is the voice of a woman who wants to be able to speak in this world of men, and who finds herself imprisoned in a world that allows no space for the feminine.

In our own time, Luce Irigaray describes the world in terms of 'masculine parameters' in which woman has always been defined, confined, and silenced. 'And yet that woman-thing speaks,' she tells us.[36] I have heard her speaking in the repressed utterances of Enlightenment men, where her voice truly sounds hysterical because it has been repressed. But I also hear her in the voice of a woman who wanted something other than that repression, who wanted herself to be something other than the voice of hysteria. Finch was confused by her gender, deeply perplexed by what it meant to be a woman during a time when the feminine was itself the substance of a dis-ease that plagued systems of order. 'Spleen' becomes for her, I believe, the very perplexing substance of her femininity, toward which she felt simultaneously repulsed and drawn.

The subject of her poem is, of course, the ailment of woman, whose 'secret' and 'mysterious ways' only 'baffle' the 'Physicians' who try to control it (138–41). That Finch herself was tormented by this ailment, not simply as a woman, but as a woman writer, is all too obvious from her own admission: 'O'er me alas! thou dost too much prevail: / I feel thy Force, whilst I against thee rail; / I feel my Verse decay, and my crampt Numbers fail' (74–76). In their reading of these lines, Gilbert and Gubar pose the question: 'Is it crazy, neurotic, splenetic, to want to be a writer?' Their own feeling is that Finch, like so many women writers, fears that it is – and that she in particular is driven 'into a Cave of Spleen in her own mind'.[37] They are surely correct in suggesting that Finch is caught in the dis-ease of being a woman writer, the illness that dooms her to possess all the characteristics and desires of woman and yet to strive to write like a man. That disease, it seems to me, is the spleen that repulses her. Yet at the same time, Finch is also caught in the dis-ease of writing the feminine, the poetic expression of desires very different from those of her contemporary male writers – and that disease, I would suggest, is the spleen toward which she is implicitly drawn.

No doubt that Finch derogates her illness, portraying herself as victim to its powers. And yet the terms she uses to describe both spleen and its effects are remarkably similar to those that she uses elsewhere to describe her own poetic endeavor. She finds spleen, for instance, '*Proteus*' in form, something that she cannot 'fix' into 'one continued Shape' – like the calm of a 'Dead Sea', or the rage of a 'Storm', or like 'Shadows' that intrude on 'Sleep' (1–12). Its 'varying' and 'perplexing Form' seems very much like that 'wav'ring Form' embodied in Eve, the woman who perplexed Adam with her 'various Fashions, and more

261

various Faces', the 'New Element' that he was unable to fix in place by assigning it a 'Name'. ('Adam Pos'd') Eve, of course, enjoys Finch's poetic admiration, while spleen is the object of her fears. Yet both the woman and the disease are figured through the same metaphors. Something similar happens when we consider Finch's figurations of spleen as fluid – as both sea and storm, and when we consider her associations of spleen with shadows and sleep. We need to remember that water and fluid motions also expressed for Finch the unfixed and wandering quality of her own poetry. In her 'Absolute Retreat', for instance, she compares her own 'Windings' through nature and her progress toward 'Eternity' to a 'River' that 'slides away, / To encrease the boundless Sea' (130–31). And the cave that she transforms into a 'wond'rous' place is filled with 'Rising Springs' that 'stray'd' over the ground (222–23). If, in her poem 'The Spleen', she feels her verse 'decay', then we should consider the possibility that the idea of decay may only have been a disparaging reference to what Finch considered characteristic of her poetry all along – its *process* of moving away from the fixed forms of expression that we associate with Augustan verse, and that she herself associated with the poetry of those 'who can but make two words rime'.

Her associations of spleen with shadows and sleep are perhaps most revealing of the ways in which Finch was drawn to the very disease of woman that plagued her as a writer. Just at the moment when she speaks of those who are 'to thy Shades inclin'd' (73), she proceeds with the description of her own illness as a poet who feels her verse decaying. The two images – of being inclined to shade and feeling unable to resist the decomposition of her verse – must have been at least as closely associated in Finch's mind as they are in these lines from her poem. The comfort that Finch experiences in the shades of nature, and the torment she experienced in the shades of spleen, may well be different versions of her fate as a woman writer. When she becomes the poet who writes through a certain metaphor – as that of shadow and shade – the metaphor becomes a poetic expression, the subject of her writing. Yet if we can envision shade, as I suggested at the beginning of this chapter, as a subversion of the dualities of light and dark through which the Enlightenment defined itself, Finch's poetic metaphor can also become much more than the subject of her poetic expression. It can become the very feminine thing that the Enlightenment mind feared – the absence of distinction between light and dark, the fluid annihilation of boundaries. It was this feminine shade, I believe, that became for Finch the disease of spleen. It was this feminine shade that was not the comforting subject of her nature poetry, but the tormenting substance of her own process of writing as a woman, writing the feminine, writing dis-ease.

In her poem 'An Invocation to Sleep', Finch imagines herself 'seal'd' in a space of 'Silence' and 'darknesse'. She desires this space, and wonders how she may best 'wooe' the 'gentle rest' that will bring her this calm (1–14). In a different poem, 'A Nocturnal Reverie', she imagines something similar – a '*Night*' when she can see the 'waving Moon and trembling Leaves' in 'some River, overhung with Green', when '*Glowworms*' illuminate a fine 'Twilight', when 'darken'd Groves their softest Shadows wear, / And falling Waters we distinctly hear' (9–24). All nature is covered with shadow, and she imagines the creatures of the wood enjoying 'Their shortliv'd Jubilee' while 'Tyrant-*Man* do's sleep,' and where there is 'no fierce Light' to 'disturb' the 'Content' (37–40). Almost as if inverting the desires of Enlightenment man, she writes: 'In such a *Night* let Me abroad remain, / Till Morning breaks, and All's confus'd again' (47–48).

Anne Finch's nocturnal reverie is like a dream, the space of a feminine imaginary that Enlightenment man figured as darkness, as the space within woman and of woman, as cave and spleen, womb and hysteria – the dis-ease that his systems could not tolerate. He wanted, as Francis Bacon had, to 'penetrate' this space – excavate its fullness and establish there the definition of structure, system, and thought, the light of Enlightenment. But Anne Finch lived in this space. She wanted its fullness, because it was an excess that she could feel in her own femininity – a femininity that was not the opposite of enlightened masculine systems, but that became the substance of wandering, fluid processes that subverted the structure of those systems. In these processes, we find the feminine substance of Enlightened Absence. And it is this femininity that belongs to Finch as a woman who wrote, and as a poet who wrote woman.

Notes

Epigraphs: Simone de Beauvoir, *The Second Sex*, trans. H.M. Parshely (1952; rpt. New York: Vintage Books, 1974), p. 293; Shoshana Felman, 'Rereading Femininity', *Yale French Studies* 62 (1981): 42; Anne Finch, 'The Consolation', *Selected Poems of Anne Finch, Countess of Winchilsea*, ed. Katharine M. Rogers (New York: Fredrick Ungar, 1979), ll. 7–8.

1. See my discussion of this archetype and its gender implications in 'The Journey to Light', in *Enlightened Absence* (Urbana and Chicago: University of Illinois Press, 1988).

2. See, for instance, Peggy Kamuf, 'Writing Like a Woman' in *Women and Language in Literature and Society*, ed. S. McConnell-Ginet et al. (New York: Praeger, 1980), pp. 284–99; Jonathan Culler, 'Reading As a Woman', *On Deconstruction: Theory and Criticism After Structuralism* (Ithaca: Cornell

University Press, 1982), pp. 43–64; and *Gender and Reading: Essays on Readers, Texts, and Contexts,* ed. Elizabeth A. Flynn and Patrocinio P. Schweickart (Baltimore: Johns Hopkins University Press, 1986).

3. For a fruitful discussion of these differences between the Anglo-American and French perspectives, see *New French Feminisms,* ed. Elaine Marks and Isabelle de Courtivron (New York: Schocken Books, 1981); Toril Moi, *Sexual/Textual Politics: Feminist Literary Theory* (London: Methuen, 1985); and Alice Jardine, *Gynesis: Configurations of Woman and Modernity* (Ithaca: Cornell University Press, 1985).

4. Jardine, *Gynesis,* pp. 84–85.

5. 'An Invitation to Dafnis', *Selected Poems of Anne Finch, Countess of Winchilsea,* ed. Katharine M. Rogers (New York: Fredrick Ungar, 1979), ll. 15, 17. All references to Finch's poetry are to this edition; for lengthy poems, I will note parenthetically in the text references to line numbers.

6. See Katharine Rogers's discussion of this matter in her introductory comments to *Selected Poems of Anne Finch,* p. xvi.

7. See Reuben A. Brower, 'Lady Winchilsea and the Poetic Tradition of the Seventeenth Century', *Studies in Philology* 42 (1945: 61–80, and Rogers's introductory comments to *Selected Poems of Anne Finch,* pp. xvii, xxiii–xxiv.

8. Sandra Gilbert and Susan Gubar, *The Madwoman in the Attic: The Woman Writer and the Nineteenth-Century Literary Imagination* (New Haven: Yale University Press, 1979), pp. 13, 17, 211.

9. See Rogers's introductory comments to *Selected Poetry of Anne Finch,* p. xv. Also see Rogers's essay on Finch in *Shakespeare's Sisters: Feminist Essays on Women Poets,* ed. Sandra Gilbert and Susan Gubar (Bloomington: Indiana University Press, 1979), pp. 32–46.

10. Celeste M. Schenck suggests as much when she discusses Finch in the context of women elegiac poets who 'refuse or rework the central symbolisms and procedures of elegy' by deconstructing 'the genre's valorization of separation' and by reconstructing 'alternative elegiac scenarios that arise from a distinctly feminine psycho-sexual experience'. 'Feminism and Deconstruction: Re-Constructing the Elegy', *Tulsa Studies in Women's Literature* 5 (Spring 1986), pp. 13, 18. For Luce Irigaray's description of a 'woman-thing', see *This Sex Which Is Not One,* trans. Catherine Porter (Ithaca: Cornell University Press, 1985), p. 111.

11. For Finch's reference to the 'dazling white' robe of Solomon, see her own note to these lines, in Rogers's edition, p. 163, n. 26.

12. See Newton's *Observations Upon the Prophecies of Daniel, and the Apocalypse of St. John* (London: J. Darby and T. Browne, 1733), p. 17.

13. Catherine Clément, 'The Guilty One', *The Newly Born Woman,* trans. Betsy Wing, Theory and History of Literature, vol. 24 (Minneapolis: University of Minnesota Press, 1986), p. 7.

14. 'The Preface' in *Selected Poems of Anne Finch,* p. 12.

15. Ibid., p. 9.

16. This poem is not included in Rogers's *Selected Poems of Anne Finch.* See Gilbert and Gubar, *Madwoman in the Attic,* p. 478. Their source is the now

out-of-print edition of Finch's verse, *The Poems of Anne Countess of Winchilsea*, ed. Myra Reynolds (Chicago: University of Chicago Press, 1903), ll. 1–13.

17. GILBERT and GUBAR, *Madwoman in the Attic*, p. 525.

18. Ibid., p. 526.

19. NANCY K. MILLER, 'Arachnologies: The Woman, the Text, and the Critic', *The Poetics of Gender*, ed. Nancy K. Miller (New York: Columbia University Press, 1986), pp. 272–74.

20. HÉLÈNE CIXOUS, 'Sorties', *The Newly Born Woman*, p. 80.

21. See, for instance, J. Hillis Miller, 'Ariadne's Thread: Repetition and the Narrative Line', *Critical Inquiry* 3 (1976): 57–78, and 'Ariachne's Brooken Woof', *Georgia Review* 31 (Spring 1977): 36–48.

22. Cited in NANCY MILLER, 'Arachnologies', p. 275.

23. IRIGARAY, *This Sex Which Is Not One*, p. 111.

24. CIXOUS, 'Sorties', p. 94.

25. See Ovid's description of this colorful weaving in Book VI of the *Metamorphoses*, vol. 1, trans. Frank Justus Miller, Loeb Classical Library (Cambridge, Mass.: Harvard University Press, 1966), p. 293.

26. IRIGARAY, *This Sex Which Is Not One*, p. 164.

27. Cited in SANDRA HARDING, *The Science Question in Feminism* (Ithaca: Cornell University Press, 1986), p. 237.

28. CAROLYN MERCHANT, *The Death of Nature: Woman, Ecology, and the Scientific Revolution* (New York: Harper & Row, 1980), p. 174.

29. See, for instance, Sherry Ortner, 'Is Female to Male as Nature Is to Culture?' in *Women, Culture and Society*, ed. M.Z. Rosaldo and L. Lamphere (Stanford: Stanford University Press, 1974).

30. Cited in HARDING, *The Science Question*, p. 237.

31. JARDINE, *Gynesis*, pp. 70–71.

32. See GILBERT and GUBAR's discussion of this matter, *Madwoman in the Attic*, p. 99. Also see Maurice Blanchot's reading of the Orpheus and Eurydice myth as the story of the artist's desire to gaze on feminine darkness, a desire that we might understand as yet another 'appropriation' of feminine space. *The Space of Literature*, trans. Ann Amock (Lincoln: University of Nebraska Press, 1982), pp. 171–72.

33. See MARGARET A. DOODY, 'Deserts, Ruins and Troubled Waters: Female Dreams in Fiction and the Development of the Gothic Novel', *Genre* 10 (Winter 1977): 529–72.

34. See GILBERT and GUBAR on this poem, *Madwoman in the Attic*, pp. 60–63.

35. See my exploration of these matters in Chapter One of *Enlightened Absence*.

36. IRIGARAY, *This Sex Which Is Not One*, p. 111.

37. Gilbert and GUBAR, *Madwoman in the Attic*, p. 61.

Glossary of Terms

AGENCY The capacity of men and women to shape history by resisting the normative models of conduct produced by the ruling culture in its own interests. Agency is an important concept in the study of early women's texts, the very existence of which would appear to undermine any claim for the omnipotence of ruling culture.

APPROPRIATION A key concept in materialist–feminist and cultural materialist criticism, appropriation refers to the creative transformation of dominant discourses by oppressed and marginal social groups. Appropriation is thus an instance of social *agency*.

BINARY OPPOSITION A fixed pairing of two opposed terms (culture/nature, reason/passion), the binary opposition is always hierarchical, presupposing the superiority of one term over the other. Drawing on the work of Jacques Derrida, the French theorist Hélène Cixous argues that all binary oppositions are coded versions of the fundamental opposition male/female.

BIOLOGICAL ESSENTIALISM/BIOLOGISM The belief that men and women have distinct 'essences' or natures which are biologically given. Biological essentialism conflates *gender* with sex.

CANON The hierarchy of great works of literature considered worthy of study within the university, the canon has of late come under attack for reproducing the values and prejudices of white, middle-class European men and suppressing the voices and literary achievements of women and other marginalized groups. Feminist critics have proposed three opposing strategies to deal with this problem: the enlargement of the traditional canon, the creation of an alternative canon and the rejection of all canons as inherently hierarchical and oppressive.

CULTURAL MATERIALISM More Marxist than the predominantly American *new historicism*, British cultural materialism combines a diachronic with a synchronic historical perspective, arguing for a dialectical view of culture as the locus of both discursive power and contested meanings. Culture, then, is seen as a material practice in its own right, and not merely as an offshoot of the economic base, as in earlier versions of Marxist theory.

DISCOURSE For Foucault, discourses are modes of speaking and writing developed within specific social institutions and practices which wield enormous prescriptive power, producing the categories of social inclusion and exclusion and determining the subject positions which prevail during particular historical periods.

ÉCRITURE FÉMININE (feminine writing) 'Feminine' here refers not to the author's sex (which may well be female, although it need not be), but to that which is excluded from and denied articulation in the male *Symbolic Order*. In French feminist theory, *écriture féminine* is writing which gives expression to the repressed feminine and so disrupts the dominant culture's oppressive discourses.

ESSENTIALIST HUMANISM The belief, which had its tentative beginnings in the Renaissance, that human beings are possessed of a universal and transhistorical nature. Feminist criticism has on the whole joined in the general theoretical critique of essentialist humanism, arguing that identity, not least *gender* identity, is socially and historically constructed rather than natural.

FETISHIZATION As used by Laura Mulvey, this is a key psychoanalytic concept in feminist critiques of the objectification of women in Western art. In a *Symbolic Order* sustained by and through the Oedipal crisis and its threat of castration, the female image symbolizes the lack of the penis and hence arouses castration anxieties which the male unconscious may disavow through the strategy of fetishism: by turning the represented woman into a highly eroticized object of desire, as in the cult of the female star.

GENDER The distinction between 'sex', the purely biological differences between men and women, and 'gender', the culturally constructed notions of femininity and masculinity, has traditionally been thought fundamental to feminism's struggle against the *patriarchal* strategy of representing femininity as natural.

GYNOCRITICS The term coined by Elaine Showalter to designate the branch of feminist literary studies focused exclusively on women writers. Concerned to explore the specificity of women's writing, women's culture and the female literary tradition, gynocriticism tends to identify women's experience of patriarchy as the root cause of the difference between male- and female-authored texts.

HUMANISM Constructed in the course of the seventeenth century, humanism has since become the dominant *ideology* of the West. At its centre stands man the individual: a sovereign *subject* with an integrated, interior identity, the maker of his own meaning. Under the influence of various poststructuralist approaches, all of which assume that meaning is produced by language rather than anterior to it, feminist criticism has increasingly distanced itself from the early Anglo-American tendency to portray the woman writer in humanist terms as the autonomous and self-determining origin of meaning.

IDEOLOGY A Marxist concept revised by Althusser, ideology has many definitions but refers here to the largely unconscious and unexamined assumptions of a culture, the cluster of social practices and representational systems through which a social order perpetuates itself by naturalizing particular constructions of reality.

MARGINALITY The subordinate position of women within *patriarchal* culture. While Anglo-American feminism tends to advocate strategies to rectify women's exclusion from the centre, French feminist thought frequently stresses and celebrates the subversive potential of women's occupation of the margins.

MATERIALIST FEMINISM The branch of feminism characterized by its anti-humanist, materialist analysis of patriarchal structures and women's oppression, materialist feminism is also concerned with such issues as the workings of ideology and the relationship between gender, class and race.

NEW HISTORICISM Usually thought of as the mainly American wing of the new historical criticism, in contrast to the British *cultural materialism*, new historicism is heavily influenced by Foucault and tends to view cultures as synchronic systems, distinct in their separateness from the present, whose signifying practices actively produce subjection to power.

267

Early Women Writers

PATRIARCHY Literally, 'the rule of the fathers', the term has been widely employed in feminist criticism to denote any social system that guarantees the dominance of men over women. Seventeenth-century English society was more precisely patriarchal, its concepts of social order based on an analogy between the power of the king and that of the father.

PHALLOCENTRISM Literally, 'centred on the phallus', phallocentrism is a term coined by Lacan and denotes a system which makes the phallus the primary symbol of power. The phallus, then, is not the penis, but its symbolic connotations of social privilege and psychic wholeness.

RESISTANCE An important term in much feminist and *cultural materialist* criticism, both of which tend to reject the *new historicist* view of ruling culture as absolutely powerful and to stress instead the capacity of the oppressed to resist, contest and alter the meanings which ruling culture attempts to impose upon them.

SEMIOTIC Julia Kristeva's version of the Lacanian Imaginary: the pre–Oedipal period, linked to the mother's body, in which there is no sexual difference. Repressed upon the child's entry into the *Symbolic Order*, the semiotic can re-emerge in language which evokes its tonal and rhythmic qualities.

SEXUAL POLITICS In her groundbreaking book *Sexual Politics*, Kate Millett attacked the traditional distinction between the personal and the political. Because politics is about the exercise of power, relations between the sexes, based on an inequality of power, are necessarily political as well as social and personal.

SUBJECT/SUBJECTIVITY The *humanist* notion of the self which emerged in the course of the seventeenth century and attributed to the (male) individual an autonomous and coherent identity. This historical process has been of interest to feminists because it was so clearly *gendered*: the male *humanist* subject was constructed by virtue of his difference from the female who, Renaissance texts show us, found ways of resisting her subjection. In psychoanalytic and poststructuralist theory, the term 'subject' is often used in an anti-humanist sense to denote the instability and social construction of human identity, to represent a position in discourse rather than an autonomous self.

SUBVERSION/CONTAINMENT *New historicism* and *cultural materialism* differ over the relationship between culture and social *agency*: while *new historicism* is inclined to invest culture with a power so pervasive that it produces subversion in order to contain it, *cultural materialism* prefers to see history in dialectical terms, as the interplay of culture and social struggle – a view which makes subversion rather more than the tool of the ruling elite. Feminist criticism often shares with cultural materialism a view of literary texts, especially female-authored ones, as sites of contestation.

SYMBOLIC ORDER In Lacanian theory, the Imaginary – the pre-Oedipal phase of childhood characterized by an imaginary unity between the child and its mother – comes to an end with the Oedipal crisis and the acquisition of language, when the child enters the Symbolic Order of social and cultural life, ruled by the Law of the Father. The repression of desire for the mother produces the unconscious, which in French feminist theory becomes an ungendered, pre-Symbolic space capable of challenging the dominance of the Symbolic Order.

WOMAN; WOMEN While French feminist theory focuses on 'woman', the product of *patriarchal* discourse's imposition of gender on an ungendered libido, Anglo-American feminism focuses on real biological 'women' whose oppression at the hands of *patriarchy* it aims to challenge.

Further Reading

(1) Introductions

The readers, surveys and collections of essays listed below provide useful introductions to the theoretical debates within feminist literary studies, to materialist feminism, to French feminist theory and to new historical criticism.

Feminist theory and criticism

CATHERINE BELSEY and JANE MOORE (eds), *The Feminist Reader: Essays in Gender and the Politics of Literary Criticism* (Basingstoke and London: Macmillan Education, 1989).

MARY EAGLETON (ed.), *Feminist Literary Criticism. Longman Critical Readers* (London and New York: Longman, 1991).
—— (ed.), *Feminist Literary Theory: A Reader* (Oxford: Basil Blackwell, 1986).

GAYLE GREENE and COPPÉLIA KAHN (eds), *Making a Difference: Feminist Literary Criticism* (London and New York: Methuen, 1985).

MARIANNE HIRSCH and EVELYN FOX KELLER (eds), *Conflicts in Feminism* (New York and London: Routledge, 1990).

MARY JACOBUS (ed.), *Women Writing and Writing About Women* (London and Sydney: Croom Helm, 1979).

DONNA LANDRY and GERALD MACLEAN, *Materialist Feminisms* (Oxford and Cambridge, Mass.: Basil Blackwell, 1993).

TORIL MOI, *Sexual/Textual Politics: Feminist Literary Theory* (London and New York: Methuen, 1985).

JUDITH NEWTON and DEBORAH ROSENFELT (eds), *Feminist Criticism and Social Change: Sex, Class and Race in Literature and Culture* (New York and London: Methuen, 1985).

ELAINE SHOWALTER (ed.), *The New Feminist Criticism: Essays on Women, Literature and Theory* (New York: Pantheon Books, 1985; London: Virago, 1986).

JANET TODD, *Feminist Literary History: A Defence* (Cambridge: Polity Press, 1988).

French Feminisms

HÉLÈNE CIXOUS and CATHERINE CLÉMENT, *The Newly Born Woman* (Paris: Union Générale d'Editions, 1975; Manchester: University of Manchester Press, 1986).

LUCE IRIGARAY, *This Sex Which Is Not One*, tr. Catherine Porter (Ithaca: Cornell University Press, 1985).

ELAINE MARKS and ISABELLE DE COURTIVRON (eds), *New French Feminisms: An Anthology* (Brighton: Harvester Press, 1981).

TORIL MOI (ed.), *The Kristeva Reader* (Oxford: Basil Blackwell, 1986).
—— (ed.), *French Feminist Thought: A Reader* (Oxford: Basil Blackwell, 1987).

New historicism/cultural materialism

JONATHAN DOLLIMORE and ALAN SINFIELD (eds), *Political Shakespeare: New Essays in Cultural Materialism* (Manchester: Manchester University Press, 1985).

ARTHUR F. KINNEY and DAN S. COLLINS (eds), *Renaissance Historicism: Selections from English Literary Renaissance* (Amherst: The University of Massachusetts Press, 1987).

H. ARAM VEESER (ed.), *New Historicism* (London: Routledge, 1989).

RICHARD WILSON and RICHARD DUTTON (eds), *New Historicism and Renaissance Drama. Longman Critical Readers* (London and New York: Longman, 1992).

(2) Early women's writing: primary texts

This list makes no claim to be exhaustive, referring only to some of the most recent and readily available editions.

Mary Wroth

JOSEPHINE A. ROBERTS (ed.), *The Poems of Lady Mary Wroth* (Baton Rouge, La.: Louisiana State University Press, 1983).

LADY MARY WROTH, *The First Part of the Countess of Montgomery's Urania*, ed. Josephine A. Roberts (Binghamton, N.Y.: Center for Medieval and Early Renaissance Studies, State University of New York at Binghamton, 1995).

Katherine Philips

PATRICK THOMAS (ed.), *The Collected Poems of Katherine Philips: The Matchless Orinda*, 2 vols. (Essex: Stump Cross Books, 1990, 1992).

KATHERINE PHILIPS, *Poems*, ed. Travis Du Priest (Delmar, N.Y.: Scholars' Facsimiles and Reprints, 1992).

Margaret Cavendish

JAMES FITZMAURICE (ed.), *Margaret Cavendish: The Sociable Letters* (New York: Garland Publishing, 1997).

KATE LILLEY (ed.), *The Blazing World and Other Writings: Margaret Cavendish. Women's Classics Series* (New York: New York University Press, 1992; London: Pickering Chatto and Windus, 1993).

Aphra Behn

APHRA BEHN, *Five Plays*, ed. Maureen Duffy (London: Methuen, 1990). Includes *The Lucky Chance, The Rover, Part One, The Widow Ranter, The False Count* and *Abdelazar*.
——, *The Rover and Other Plays*, ed. Jane Spencer (Oxford and New York: Oxford University Press, 1995). Also includes *The Lucky Chance, The Feigned Courtesans* and *The Emperor of the Moon*.
——, *Oroonoko, The Rover and Other Works*, ed. Janet Todd (London and New York: Penguin Books, 1992).

JANET TODD (ed.), *The Poems of Aphra Behn: A Selection* (New York: New York University Press, 1994).
—— (ed.), *The Works of Aphra Behn*, 7 vols. (Columbus, Ohio: Ohio State University Press, 1992–96).

Anne Finch

MYRA REYNOLDS (ed.), *The Poems of Anne, Countess of Winchilsea* (Chicago: University of Chicago Press, 1903; New York: AMS Press, 1974).

KATHARINE M. ROGERS (ed.), *Selected Poems of Anne Finch, Countess of Winchilsea* (New York: Fredrick Ungar, 1979).

DENYS THOMPSON (ed.), *Anne Finch, Countess of Winchilsea: Selected Poems* (Manchester: Carcanet Press, 1987).

General

MOIRA FERGUSON (ed.), *First Feminists: British Women Writers, 1578–1799* (Bloomington: Indiana University Press, 1985).

ELSPETH GRAHAM et al. (eds), *Her Own Life: Autobiographical Writings by Seventeenth-Century Englishwomen* (London and New York: Routledge, 1989).

GERMAINE GREER et al. (eds), *Kissing the Rod: An Anthology of Seventeenth-Century Women's Verse* (London: Virago, 1988).

KATHERINE USHER HENDERSON and BARBARA F. MCMANUS (eds), *Half Humankind: Contexts and Texts of the Controversy about Women in England 1540–1640* (Urbana and Chicago: University of Illinois Press, 1985).

VIVIEN JONES (ed.), *Women in the Eighteenth Century: Constructions of Femininity* (London and New York: Routledge, 1990).

ROGER LONSDALE (ed.), *Eighteenth-Century Women Poets: An Oxford Anthology* (Oxford and New York: Oxford University Press, 1990).

N.H. KEEBLE (ed.), *The Cultural Identity of Seventeenth-Century Woman: A Reader* (London and New York: Routledge, 1994).

(3) Early women's writing: secondary texts

ELAINE V. BEILIN, *Redeeming Eve: Women Writers of the English Renaissance* (Princeton: Princeton University Press, 1987). A study of a broad range of

271

Tudor and Stuart women authors and translators which seeks to identify and define an early modern tradition of women's writing.

CLARE BRANT and DIANE PURKISS (eds), *Women, Texts and Histories, 1575–1760* (London and New York: Routledge, 1992). A volume of essays which attempts to return women to the history of the early modern period. The essays deal with a diversity of genres, exploring the changes and contradictions in early modern discourses of sexual difference as well as the range of women's responses to those discourses.

MARGARET W. FERGUSON, MAUREEN QUILLIGAN and NANCY J. VICKERS (eds), *Rewriting the Renaissance: The Discourses of Sexual Difference in Early Modern Europe* (Chicago and London: Chicago University Press, 1986). A valuable collection of essays examining discursive power by way of the discourses of gender and sexual difference prevailing during the Renaissance.

CATHERINE GALLAGHER, *Nobody's Story: The Vanishing Acts of Women Writers in the Marketplace, 1670–1820* (Berkeley and Los Angeles: University of California Press, 1994). Not a polemic on women's exclusion from literary history, but an analysis of the way the categories of woman, author, marketplace and fiction, as kindred signifiers of nothingness and disembodiment, define each other in the fiction of Behn, Manley, Lennox, Burney and Edgeworth.

ISOBEL GRUNDY and SUSAN WISEMAN (eds), *Women, Writing, History 1640–1740.* (Athens, Georgia: The University of Georgia Press, 1992). This collection of essays brings together different critical and theoretical perspectives on the questions of female identity during the early modern period, women's interventions in writing practices, and the role of history in literary and cultural analysis.

MARGARET PATTERSON HANNAY (ed.), *Silent But For the Word: Tudor Women as Patrons, Translators, and Writers of Religious Works* (Kent, Ohio: Kent State University Press, 1985). This collection examines the way that the restriction of Tudor women to religious translation and writing stimulated the dissemination of Protestant thought and led to their appropriation of religious discourse for personal and political ends.

ANNE M. HASELKORN and BETTY S. TRAVITSKY (eds), *The Renaissance Englishwoman in Print: Counterbalancing the Canon* (Amherst: The University of Massachusetts Press, 1990). This volume of essays proposes to open up the Renaissance canon by counterbalancing representations of women in male-authored texts of the period with recently recovered writings by Renaissance women.

MARGO HENDRICKS and PATRICIA PARKER (eds), *Women, 'Race', and Writing in the Early Modern Period* (London and New York: Routledge, 1994). This is an important interdisciplinary collection of essays dealing with early modern discourses of gender, class and race. The essays stress the instability of the term 'race' in early modern Europe and foreground the concern of feminists of colour that feminist theory and criticism have been dominated by a white bourgeois feminist agenda which has reproduced Eurocentric assumptions and ignored or misrepresented the lives and struggles of women of colour.

CHARLES H. HINNANT, *The Poetry of Anne Finch: An Essay in Interpretation* (Newark: University of Delaware Press; London and Toronto: Associated University Presses, 1994). A study of Finch's poetry which seeks to broaden our understanding of her relationship to her culture by locating her work within a tradition of Tory feminism. Hinnant's readings are also alert to the tensions between Finch's politics and her sexual politics.

ELAINE HOBBY, *Virtue of Necessity: English Women's Writing 1649–88* (London: Virago, 1988). Hobby's study of women's writing from the end of the Civil Wars to the Glorious Revolution examines the wide variety of genres which women adopted and rewrote in their struggle to 'make a virtue of necessity': to negotiate small spaces of self-determination within the limits of their male-dominated world.

HEIDI HUTNER (ed.), *Rereading Aphra Behn: History, Theory, and Criticism* (Charlottesville and London: University Press of Virginia, 1993). The essays in this collection deploy a variety of interpretative strategies – historical, theoretical and critical – in an effort to illuminate the ideological and discursive complexities of Behn's writing and of the Restoration culture she inhabited.

ANN ROSALIND JONES, *The Currency of Eros: Women's Love Lyric in Europe 1540–1620* (Bloomington and Indianapolis: Indiana University Press, 1990). A stimulating analysis of the complex and diverse modes of negotiation with which Renaissance women (mainly continental, though Mary Wroth is included) inserted themselves into and transformed the lyric discourses of early modern Europe.

TINA KRONTIRIS, *Oppositional Voices: Women as Writers and Translators of Literature in the English Renaissance* (London and New York: Routledge, 1992). In a study of six Renaissance women writers and translators (including Margaret Tyler, Elizabeth Cary and Mary Wroth), Krontiris offers a feminist/cultural materialist analysis of the strategies (albeit limited) which they adopted as a means of opposing dominant ideologies, especially those of gender.

BARBARA KIEFER LEWALSKI, *Writing Women in Jacobean England* (Cambridge, Mass. and London: Harvard University Press, 1993). Lewalski deals with three major women writers of the Jacobean period (Elizabeth Cary, Aemilia Lanyer and Mary Wroth), with women of the royal family and with women whose lives and writings agitated for equal rights with men. She situates her subjects within their repressive Jacobean milieu and examines the different modes of resistance inscribed in their writings.

NAOMI J. MILLER and GARY WALLER (eds), *Reading Mary Wroth: Representing Alternatives in Early Modern England* (Knoxville: University of Tennessee Press, 1991). A collection of essays which seeks to evaluate Wroth's literary achievements and her relationship to the culture she inhabited. The essays explore the implications of her illustrious family heritage, her rewriting of generic conventions, and the construction in her work of female subjectivity.

JACQUELINE PEARSON, *The Prostituted Muse: Images of Women and Women Dramatists, 1642–1737* (New York: St. Martin's Press, 1988). A wide-ranging study of women in the Restoration and eighteenth-century theatre which examines women as theatre managers and spectators, images of women in male-authored plays of the period, and the work of early modern female dramatists.

MARY PRIOR (ed.), *Women in English Society, 1500–1800* (London and New York: Methuen, 1985). This collection of historical studies of early modern women eschews the traditional economic focus of women's history, choosing to explore other aspects of women's lives. Experiences of childbearing, the lives of Catholic women and of widows, and the increasing prevalence of women's writing are some of the subjects examined.

KATHARINE M. ROGERS, *Feminism in Eighteenth-Century England* (Urbana, Chicago and London: University of Illinois Press, 1982). Employing a broad definition of feminism as concern for the problems women face in a male-dominated society, Rogers finds feminist feeling in a wide range of eighteenth-century women writers, and examines the liberating effects for women of rationalism and sentimentalism.

MARY BETH ROSE (ed.), *Women in the Middle Ages and the Renaissance: Literary and Historical Perspectives* (Syracuse, N.Y.: Syracuse University Press, 1986). Dealing with a wide range of topics, including women's role in education, the economy and the Church, Shakespeare's representations of women and women's contributions as literary patrons, translators and writers, this collection aims to help recover the 'lost past' of medieval and Renaissance women.

MARY ANNE SCHOFIELD and CECILIA MACHESKI (eds), *Curtain Calls: British and American Women and the Theater, 1660–1820* (Athens, Ohio: Ohio University Press, 1991). This collection of essays, which includes studies of Margaret Cavendish, Katherine Philips and Aphra Behn, aims to revise eighteenth-century theatre history by recovering the important and diverse roles which women played in it.

—— (eds), *Fetter'd or Free? British Women Novelists, 1670–1815* (Athens, Ohio: Ohio University Press, 1986). Dealing mainly with eighteenth-century women novelists (although there is material on Behn and Delarivière Manley), this collection of essays seeks to increase our familiarity with previously neglected female authors, examining their work in relation to such issues as gender and genre, feminine iconography and literary strategies.

HILDA L. SMITH, *Reason's Disciples: Seventeenth-Century English Feminists* (Urbana, Chicago, London: University of Illinois Press, 1982). Smith argues for a distinct tradition of seventeenth-century feminist thought, which perceived women as a separate sociological group, appropriated rationalism to argue for women's equality with men, and challenged patriarchal ideology by contending that sex roles were culturally constructed rather than natural. According to Smith, this form of feminism declined with the growth of sentimentalism in the eighteenth century.

JANE SPENCER, *The Rise of the Woman Novelist: From Aphra Behn to Jane Austen* (Oxford: Basil Blackwell, 1986). Spencer's important book seeks to uncover both the central role played by women writers in the early history of the novel and the influence of women's literary traditions on the novel's development. One of Spencer's key concerns is to explore the complex implications for feminism of the rise of the woman novelist during the eighteenth century.

JANET TODD, *The Sign of Angellica: Women, Writing and Fiction, 1660–1800* (New York: Columbia University Press, 1989). Todd's feminist history of the woman's novel traces its development from the sexual frankness of Behn and Manley through the cult of sensibility to the achievement of respectability and literary authority by the close of the eighteenth century.

MARILYN L. WILLIAMSON, *Raising their Voices: British Women Writers, 1650–1750* (Detroit: Wayne State University Press, 1990). Williamson's book is framed by two central arguments: first, that there were two distinct traditions of women's writing during this period, one modelled on the chaste and feminine

Katherine Philips, the other on the libertine Aphra Behn; second, that there is an unbroken history of feminist thought stretching from the early seventeenth century to the present.

KATHARINA M. WILSON (ed.), *Women Writers of the Renaissance and Reformation* (Athens, Georgia: The University of Georgia Press, 1987). Combining primary and secondary material, this book explores the lives and works of a broad range of fifteenth- and sixteenth-century women writers, both continental and English.

VIRGINIA WOOLF, *A Room of One's Own* (London: Hogarth Press, 1929; London: Grafton Books, 1987). Woolf's analysis of the material conditions and ideological pressures which have inhibited women's literary production takes in Margaret Cavendish, Dorothy Osborne, Aphra Behn and Anne Finch.

Index

Early Women Writers